EASTERN BENGAL BALLADS

Eastern Bengal Ballads

(Ramtanu Lahiri Research Fellowship Lectures for 1929-31, in Two Parts)

Vol. IV : Part I

Compiled and Edited by
Dineshchandra Sen, Rai Bahadur, B.A. D.Litt. (Hons.)

GYAN PUBLISHING HOUSE
NEW DELHI-110002

Eastern Bengal Ballads

ISBN: 81-212-0906-4 (Set)
ISBN: 81-212-0910-2 (Vol. IV)

Published in 2006 in India by
Gyan Publishing House,
5, Ansari Road, Daryaganj, New Delhi-110002
E-mail: books@gyanbooks.com

Laser Typesetting at: Vinayak Printers, Delhi
Printed at: Salasar Imaging System, Delhi

CONTENTS

GENERAL INTRODUCTION.

1. Bengali—A Form of Prakrit.

The Bengali writers of old knew our language to be a form of Prakrit. The name ' Banga-bhasa ' (Bengali Language) by which we call it now was unknown in this country a century ago. The old writers called it 'Prakrit.' I have given numerous examples of this from old Bengali poems in my work Bangabhasa-O-Sahitya (p. 28, 5th edition). Such instances may be easily multiplied.

Latterly Bengali was greatly Sanskritised, and this refined Bengali was called by some writers of the 19th century 'Gaudiya Sadhu Bhasha.' It is a dignified name which the literate people gave to their language in order to show that they had Sanskritised it. But this epithet was not accepted by the masses.

With the advent of the English the language of Bengal began to be called ' Banga Bhasa ' or the Bengali language, —an appellation which has now been universally adopted.

From the 15th to the 18th century there was a regular craze among the classical writers of Bengal for effecting a Sanskritisation of our dialect. There was, however, no fixed standard of Bengali orthography up to the 18th century. Even the Sanskrit Pandits, who so scrupulously observed the rules of spelling of Sanskrit words while writing Sanskrit, did not consider it worth their while to follow any such canon when they wrote Bengali. While copying a Bengali book even scholarly writers were not at all particular about spelling. The same word was spelt in different ways by a writer in the pages of a manuscript copied by him. No discrimination was observed in the use of শ, ষ, স, জ, য, and র, ড়. The Sanskrit words were in course of time so largely imported into Bengali that some of the metrical verses in different Sanskritic metres written in Bengali by our poets, if only written in Devanagri characters, might be easily taken for Sanskrit verses, by the Pandits of Poona or Kashmir unacquainted with Bengali.[1] But the spelling continued to be corrupt in written literature for a long time.

From the beginning of the 18th century the Bengali writers began to observe the incongruity of their action and tried to remove such freaks and caprices in the spelling of words. The correction of Bengali words on the lines of Sanskrit commenced from that period. Grammar began to be written in our language on the model of Sanskrit grammar in which the rules of Mugdhabodh and Panini were laid down for the guidance of Bengali writers. The genius of the two languages, however, are as divergent as two poles. So all attempts to saddle our language by Sanskritic canons proved futile. Bharatchandra in the 18th century introduced Sanskrit words and metres in Bengali more than any other Bengali poet and succeeded in giving to Bengali a form almost as dignified and stately as Sanskrit, so that even in the eyes of the purists Bengali ceased to be a contemptible patois that it had been prior to the advent of that gifted poet.

There was a time when the orthodox Christian writers had tried by all their hair-splitting and subtle ingenuity to prove that all the languages of the world were derived from Hebrew in which God had delivered His message in the

1 For instance read the following Bengali hymn to Siva by Bharatchandra :—

"जय शिवेश शङ्कर वृषध्वजेश्वर मृगाङ्कशेखर दिगम्बर। जय श्मशाननाटक, विषाणवादक हुताशभालक महेश्वर।"

Bible. Equally vain was the attempt of the Sanskrit Pandits of the age following that of a Bharatchandra to prove that Bengali was derived from Sanskrit. When the black paint is washed off from the face of an English player of Othello on the stage, his real colour is revealed which is sometimes as white as that of Desdemona. Even so if the mask of artificial orthography and too many Sanskrit words, borrowed to embellish our languages in the comparatively modern age, are thrown off, our language will appear in its natural colour and show itself to be not a whit more dignified than any of the various loose Prakrits of Eastern India.

The ballads have, beyond all shadow of doubt, clearly shown that Bengali is a form of Prakrit, as the Bengali writers themselves designated this dialect three or four centuries ago. Whether its origin is to be traced to Ardha Magadhi, to Paisachi or, as late Dr. Anderson held, to Tibeto-Burman, is a controversial point of which this is not the proper place to attempt a solution. But wash off the Sanskritic paint from its orthography and pronounce each word as the rural people do in the countryside, it will then be apparent that Bengali is not at all a daughter of Sanskrit as Pandits Ramgati Nyayaratna and Loharam Siroratna had supposed—a view recently shared by Mr. Srinath Sen, Pandit Sarat Chandra Sastri and other representatives of the old school.

Curiously though we have adopted now the Sanskrit orthography in all forms of written Bengali, the spoken dialect still adheres to Prakrit. I shall presently give a list of some of the words from the Eastern Bengal Ballads taken down from the lips of the singers at random which will show the words of our language in their unassumingly natural Prakrit form.

The purist may purse his brows and sneer at our language when presented in this nude shape but still this is the real form of Bengali current in the country, and though the decent people may take objection, I for myself do not feel any hesitancy whatever in declaring that I prefer this rural form of our language to the artificial Sanskritic shape in which we find our written literature at the present day. I am not ashamed to avow my liking for the spoken form of Bengali, though it is so remote from its written diction, for the simple reason that I find in it the very words which I heard in my childhood from my parents, kith and kin and which still possess their great appeal—as I hear them all around—when I return to my village home.

The Ballads bring to me a lively message from my dear motherland and howsoever greatly I may admire Sanskrit and its wonderful lexicon, the Bengali classics pervaded with Sanskritic importations can by no means be so near and dear to my heart as this direct gift from our rural home.

The list given below is by no means exhaustive or complete but it is surely an index to the sort of language that has contributed to the characteristic simplicity and charm of the Ballads. We are, however, so greatly accustomed to the artificial form in our written literature that the natural form may strike some of the readers with a feeling of surprise even verging on disgust, but I need not be apologetic for this reason.

List of words found in the ballads and their Śanskritic forms.

প্রাকৃত	সংস্কৃত ও অপভ্রংশ	প্রাকৃত	সংস্কৃত ও অপভ্রংশ
ইন্দু	হিন্দু	আছরা	আশ্রয়
কাইনি	কাহিনী	মুখচন্দিকে	মুখচন্দ্রিকা
বির্দ্দ	বৃদ্ধ	পরতিবাসী	প্রতিবেশী
শুকুর	শুক্র	গেরাম	গ্রাম
বৈদেশ	বিদেশ	বরমা	ব্রহ্মা

প্রাকৃত	সংস্কৃত ও অপভ্রংশ	প্রাকৃত	সংস্কৃত ও অপভ্রংশ
মুরতেক	মুহূর্ত্তেক	শাউড়ী	শাশুড়ী
হেজা	সজারু	পকেলা	পাকা
কুইল	কোকিল	জিগায়	জিজ্ঞাসা করে
চান	চাঁদ	ব্যাভার	ব্যবহার
পরবেশ	প্রবেশ	যুদি	যদি
কৈতর	কবুতর	পঙ্খি	পাখি
কাঙ্খে	কক্ষে	অন্ত্রিম কাল	অন্তিম কাল
যইবন	যৌবন	অইতে	হইতে
সুদর	সহোদর	তিরুডি	ত্রুটি
সুতের	স্রোতের	কাড়ালি	কাণ্ডারী
সন্দে	সন্দেহ	বিছরাম	বিশ্রাম
তিরভুবন	ত্রিভুবণ	আশ্রা	আশ্রয়
গরাস	গ্রাস	অসরমানি	অসম্মান
পন্নম	প্রণাম	ভগমান	ভাগ্যমান
বছর	বৎসর	ভরমন	ভ্রমণ
ভমর	ভ্রমর	হাপনার	আপনার
অকরসাৎ	অকস্মাৎ	ডাইল	ডাল
আগন	অগ্রহায়ণ	নইক্ষত্র	নক্ষত্র
পূব	পূর্ব্ব	দ্যাসে	দেশে
রাইত	রাত্রি	ধম্ম	ধর্ম্ম
বাণ্ডি	বাণ্ড	চক্কে	চক্ষে
সাউধ	সাধু	ঐষ্টক্ষণ	অষ্টক্ষণ
উবাস	উপবাস	সিঙ্গাসনে	সিংহাসনে
দোয়ারে	দ্বারে	জোয়াফুল	জবাফুল
মৈলান	মলিন	লাডি	লাঠি
বর্ত্ত	ব্রত	পিড্	পিঠ
পরাচিত্ত	প্রায়শ্চিত্য	হাপ	সাপ
পরখিয়া	পরীক্ষা করিয়া		

প্রাকৃত	সংস্কৃত ও অপভ্রংশ	প্রাকৃত	সংস্কৃত ও অপভ্রংশ
হাউড়ি	শাশুড়ি	বুগর	বুকের
ভাও	ভাব	ছিসা	সিসা
দই	দধি	কেল্লেশ	ক্লেশ
কিরপা	কৃপা	আত্তি	হাতি
চান্দমা	চন্দ্রমা	ছিরি	শ্রী
সিনান	স্নান	বিরথা	বৃথা
ধুমা	ধূম	মিডা	মিঠা
পরদিম	প্রদীপ	বস্‌সা	বর্ষা
ইরামতি	হীরামতি	ভিডা	ভিটা
বিরক্ষ	বৃক্ষ	ছাওয়া	ছায়া
বামুন	ব্রাহ্মণ	অরষিত	হরষিত
পরতি	প্রতি	পশছাৎ	পশ্চাৎ
উরদেশ	উদ্দেশ্য	ভমরা	ভ্রমর
চৈতমাস	চৈত্রমাস	এন	হেন
পরবুধ	প্রবোধ	বেরোধ	বৃদ্ধ
পরখাই	পরীক্ষা	পরতয়	প্রত্যয়
বরমান	ব্রাহ্মণ	সাঁইজ	সন্ধ্যা
খিদা	ক্ষুধা	জর্ম্মের	জন্মের
আইশানা	আশ্বিন মাসের	চাদ্দর	চাদর
মাজনে	মহাজনে	রোইদ	রোদ
শায়ন	শ্রাবণ	দ্যবতা	দেবতা
পুখুর	পুষ্করিণী	পুষ্যের	পুরুষের
গিরে	গৃহে	ব্যালা	বেলা
পিরথিমি	পৃথিবী	মাডি	মাটি
মুইট	মুষ্ঠি	কাডি	কাঠি
বৈমুখ	বিমুখ	পেড	পেট
মশইর	মশারী	তুয়ান	তুফান
পরতিজ্ঞা	প্রতিজ্ঞা	ঠাডা	বজ্র

প্রাকৃত	সংস্কৃত ও অপভ্রংশ	প্রাকৃত	সংস্কৃত ও অপভ্রংশ
ছিরাম	শ্রীরাম	কাখে	কক্ষে
দৈমত	দ্বিমত, দ্বিধা	উয়র	উপর
সোয়াদ	সাধ	স্তিরি	স্ত্রী
পাণি	পানীয়	আউন	আগুন
গিরধিনী	গৃধিনী	কোরধ	ক্রোধ
ধরম	ধর্ম্ম	হাচ্ছুরিয়া	সাঁতারিয়া
পদুম	পদম	হেঁদু	হিন্দু
পরবাসে	প্রবাসে	কন্ন	কর্ণ

2. The New Hinduism.

It is well known that we owe this Sanskritisation of our language to the Brahmins of Kanauj who brought with them the earliest message of new Hinduism to Bengal, hitherto ridden by Buddhistic religion which disseminated its culture amongst the masses mainly in Pali and Prakrit in Eastern India. The Sen Rajas were the great champions of the Brahmanic Renaissance so in those places where the Sen Dynasty had established their firm rule the priestly religion known as Brahmanism became firmly planted.

This Brahmanism was quite different from the earlier form of Hinduism which had flourished in the country in the palmy days of Hindu power.

The Hindus and the Buddhists of ancient times were great navigators. Their naval activities throughout the world in ancient days are facts admitted, and eulogised, unanimously by scholars. Side by side with the glories of the Boro Bodro temples of Java showing Buddhistic activities shine the splendid relics of the temples and of the Hindu colony in Prahmbanam in Bali. But the priestly religion which sprang up on the grave of old Hinduism forbade sea-voyage. The old Hindu customs favoured ' Svayambara ' or election of bridegrooms by the girls themselves, but the new Brahmanism enacted that the girls should have no voice in matrimony but be absolutely guided by the will of guardians. In ancient days Sabitri was ordered by her father to take an excursion in his royal chariot all round the neighbouring countries to find out a proper mate for her, and Damayanti, Sakuntala and Rukmini wrote letters conveying to the bridegrooms they had elected, the messages of their devoted love. Such courses were forbidden in the new Hindu community.

The age of marriageable girls was not limited in the palmy days of ancient Hinduism. Even Gauri of Kalidas who passed through penances and austerities wishing Siva to be her lord was already a grown-up lady on whose lips, beautiful as the ' Bimba fruit,' Siva cast his gaze and lost for a moment all control over himself. This account of Kalidas gives lie to the traditional belief that the custom of child-marriage owes its origin to the union of Siva and Durga. The word ' *Gauri-dan* ' therefore is meaningless in the face of Kalidas's account of Gauri—a lady in the full bloom of youth. The new Hinduism solemnly laid it down that the proper age of a girl's marriage is seven. In the eighth year also her marriage is held propitious and at her ninth and tenth years it may be admissible with an apology, but if the girl passes her tenth year and the parents have failed to give her in marriage, all her ancestors up to the 14th generation, according to the Jurisprudence of the Brahmanic revivalists, would be doomed to hell.

It is also well-known that in ancient times there was no stringency of caste-rules in marriage. There are innumerable instances of intermarriage between different castes. The custom of 'Svayamvara' and the conditions required to be fulfilled by the suitor of a girl's hands in certain cases did not impose any restriction from the view-point of caste. There was a general invitation to all people to try in the field of competition on such occasions.

There are many such important points which show a striking difference between the ancient Hinduism and the modern. One would wonder how the Hindus who glory in their Vedic religion, which is characterised by a broadness of sympathy for all—and particularly for the fair sex, could become so narrow and apathetic to human misery as they have grown now, and still maintain that they are the followers of the creed of the ancient Rishis.

The distinguishing feature of modern Hinduism is the monopoly of all power by the Brahmins. The Purans, or more correctly a great part of their later interpolations, have the distinct mission of promulgating the indisputable Brahmanic authority. The general belief is that the Brahmin's benedictions produce all earthly good fortunes and his curses cause all imaginable mischiefs. Why was the disc of moon blemished with dark spots? It is due to a Brahmin's curse. Why is the water of oceans saline? The reply again is Brahmin's curse. What mark is there on the breast of the great God Vishnu? That of footprints of a kick by an angry Brahmin. Why was the great dynasty of Rakshasas killed in Lanka? Why was the heaven of Indra deprived of the grace of the Goddess of Fortune? Why was the great clan of Jadus extirpated from the earth? The answer of all these is Brahmanic curse. In fact in the Pauranic works and in the Bengali classics permeated by Brahmanic influence everything that is good is declared to be the result of Brahmanic blessing and all misfortunes ascribed to Brahmanic irc, to which gods and men stand equally exposed. One would come across an encyclopædic mass of legends and tales invented to glorify the Brahmins in the Bengali Mahabharata compiled by Kasidas.

In fact when the political domination of the Hindus of Bengal passed away to the hands of the Turks, the Brahmins reorganised Hindu society by spreading all incredible tales and legends amongst the masses indicative of their divine commission to rule and guide the society. They were called Bhudev—gods on the earth; and the vast Hindu community stood as one man paying their tribute of worship to the Brahmin. No political or autocratic power could have such sovereignty over the populace as the Brahmins in Hindu India. People shook in all their limbs if they offended a Brahmin fearing lest they would be overtaken by Brahmanic curse.

But what the new Brahminism taught was not all evil. This Brahmanic rule has a bright and redeeming side which justly deserves praise, but this would lead to a topic with which our ballad literature is not at all concerned.

I have said that the new Brahminism penetrated into the interior of Bengal with the spread of the power of the Sen Dynasty—the great patrons of the Brahmins. Those countries which lay beyond the pale of the political jurisdiction of the Sens retained their belief in ancient Hinduism which in a previous age had been considerably influenced by Buddhistic ideas.

3. *The Ballads.*

The ballads are chiefly found in those districts of Bengal which the Sen dynasty could not conquer,—in Sylhet, Chittagong and mainly in Mymensingh.

There are undoubted proofs that at one time the whole of Bengal was flooded over by ballads. The chief burden of the songs were the enterprising adventures of great princes and the devotion of lovers. New Hinduism, however, ordained that no secular thing should be the subject of writing. Men's deeds should not be extolled, however great these men might be. Sexual romance was forbidden in society and literature. The literature of Bengali Hindus under the sway of Brahminism mainly consisted of translations from Purans and Epics. In our Calcutta University Library out of about ten thousand old manuscripts, at least six thousand are translations with additions of some indigenous stories or something of Brahminic propaganda. The poets did not stress action, but emphatically praised devotion. Vaishnavism, it must be said, was the revolting child of this Brahminic revival. It upset the social foundation of the Hindus by rejecting caste and disseminating culture amongst the masses. But inspite of this refractory character of Vaishnavism it developed that devotion to God which was the gift of the Brahminic Renaissance and in many respects held its view in common with new Brahminism. But for Vaishnavism the spirit of Renaissance would never have entered deep into the lower stratum of the society ; the Brahmins positively disliked that their spiritual message should be conveyed to the lower castes. They have composed several Sanskrit verses, condemning the work of Bengali translations of the Epics and Purans.

In the Brahminic districts of Bengal the ballads, as they deal with human action and sexual love, were ousted and in their place we have a galaxy of Kirtan songs, and of Kathakatas and dissemination of the texts of Purans mainly promulgated by the efforts of the Vaishnavas. But one who would make a scrutinising search in these districts also, might yet find scraps of ancient ballads here and there, showing that at one time the ballads had flourished there as in other parts of Bengal. There are many references in copper-plate inscriptions of the Sens and Pals which prove the existence at one time of an extensive literature of ballads throughout Bengal. The ballad-literature was systematically discouraged even by Vaishnavas.[1] It essentially belonged to the masses and dealt with secular topics as we have already said. Not to say of the Renaissance-Brahmins, even the Vaishnavas had laid it down that all culture should be spiritual. What are after all these topics of human deeds worth? The glory achieved by the mightiest had not in their eyes the value of a particle of dust of the feet of a devotee. What is the worth of all this literature of sexual romance? This so-called love is only an infatuation and is a mere vanity and illusion. It gives exaggerated value to the hankerings of our mortal body of dust and clay. Spiritual love is the only thing to be sought.

These views of the Renaissance-Brahmins shared also by the Vaishnavas came as a great scourge on the old popular culture, and ballad-singing stood condemned and gradually dwindled into insignificance—making way for those songs which extolled devotion, praised devotees like Prahlad or Dhruva or deified mortals like Ram and Krishna and the great heroes of the epics claiming their descent from Gods. In those parts of Bengal which became the stronghold of these ideas the ballad-literature became gradually extinct, so we do not expect any striking discovery from Western Bengal in this field.

The Sens could not penetrate into the back-woods of Eastern Bengal where the Hinduism of the old school flourished for a long time. These places adhered to the old custom of giving education by folklore and ballads. Mymensingh—especially the eastern part of the district—successfully combated the Imperial march of the Sens. Ballal Sen's enemies found shelter in that hilly region.[2] The Hajangs,

1 There is an ungracious reference to the Bengali Ballads in the Chaitanya Bhagabat, by Brindaban Das, a devout Vaishnava writer of the 16th century.

2 There are numerous evidences to prove this point. See General Introduction to E. B. Ballads, Vol. I, Part I.

the Kirats, the Rajbansis and the Chakmas established their power after the fall of the great Gupta Empire in good many localities near the Garo hills, and held sovereignty for a long time, successfully resisting the Sens by guerilla warfare.

The banks of the Kansa, the Bhairab, the Dhanu, the Someswari and the Brahmaputra were the places where the Aryanised hill-tribes had adopted the essence of Shaiva religion influenced by Buddhist creed and attained a high level of culture to which the ballads and folklore prevalent in that country will supply a strong testimony. The political supremacy of these lands passed direct from the hands of the hill-tribes to those of the Turks, so that the new Brahminism favoured by the Sen Rajas could not lay its hold upon them. The jurisprudence of Raghunandan had no voice in the lands of Hajangs and Garos.

In regions domineered by new Brahminism the Chattopadhyayas, the Bandyopadhyayas, the Mukhopadhyayas and the Gangopadhyayas became the *kulins* amongst the Brahmins. They had obliterated their old family surnames of Dhar, Kar, Das, etc., in order to show that their origin was divine and that they had nothing to do with the people of other castes. The titles which they created became their absolute monopoly which no other caste was privileged to adopt. These titles, I need hardly say, are more or less of recent origin, being taken from the names of special localities. The Gangulys were the descendants of those Kanouj-Brahmins who had settled on the banks of the river Gangur. The Mukhutis and the Chattatis were elevated to Mukhopadhyayas and Chattopadhyayas and Bandaghatis to Bandyopadhyayas.

In the Eastern districts of Mymensingh the Chakrabartys are still the *kulins* amongst Brahmins. The Ghoshes, Basus, Guhas and Mitras, the modern nobility among the Kayasthas, were not heard of there until recently, and the

Dattas occupied the highest status in society. Thus it will be seen that in those remote eastern parts the old order still prevailed though at the present day the western influence is gradually penetrating into these woody lands.

The Pathans and other people obtained the possession of these places, as I have said, not from the Sens but from the hill-tribes direct. Someswar Singh, a Brahmin general of upcountry, ousted one Vaisya Garo from Durgapur and occupied the place in 1280 A. D. Near Sherpur there was an independent chief named Dilip Samanta. He had a fort near by called Gar Jaripa. (The word Jarip being an incorrect form of Dilip.) Majlis Humayun, a general of Feroj Sha, killed this Dilip Samanta in 1491 and occupied his kingdom. Dilip Samanta was a Koch, and the Koch tribe had spread up to Savar, in the north of Dacca where Dhimanta Sen, son of Bhim Sen, a relation of Ballal, defeated them in the 12th century. Isha Khan, one of the twelve sub-lords of Bengal, occupied Jangalbari in Kishoregunj (Mymensingh) by a sudden attack on Lakshman Hazra of the Rajbansi tribe in 1580. In the same way Bokainagore, Madanpur, Kaliajuri, and other places of the district where the Aryanised hill-men reigned as independent chiefs passed to the hands of the Pathans in the 13th and 14th centuries.

It is for this reason that the rich ballad-literature published by the University has been mainly found from these remote eastern localities. The message they bear is unique—distinct from the culture of the Brahmanic Renaissance. The western districts of Bengal, as I have said, totally drove the ballads away. They have been for long centuries safe in these eastern strongholds, and this mode of popular education by folk-literature has continued in these eastern stronghold—remote from the influence of the new Brahmins.

The female characters of the ballad-literature bear a striking affinity with those of the standard Sanskrit works of the Gupta period. Some of the heroines of the ballads are like so many Sakuntalas and Urbasis. They choose their own lords without waiting for the permission of the parents. The pre-nuptial love is romantic in each case, the fair ones breathing an air of perfect freedom in the matter of the election of their bridegrooms. It is strange that even the illiterate poets of these rural districts are found quite familiar with the spirit of the word '*swayambara,*' which in their local districts they name '*Ichcha bar.*' The time had of course long gone by when a Hindu king would proclaim the *swayambara* of his daughter inviting the princes of the surrounding countries to come and participate in the competition. Such a course in those days when the Hindu had lost their political supremacy would be more or less fraught with danger. Portuguese and Magh pirates and sometimes young members of Mahomedan aristocracy would get an opportunity to come and forcibly seize the beautiful girls, but still, so far as it was consistent with safety, a free scope was given to the girls for choosing their mates and the society had not shut its portals against sexual romance.

Women often showed a devoted love even when their parents and guardians opposed them. A country poet sings that there are a hundred and one sweet things in the world, but nothing is so sweet to a woman as when she gets for her husband one whom she loves. The uncle of Sonai, Bhatukram, had arranged her marriage with a Mahomedan autocrat, but the girl wrote a letter to her lover asking him to carry her off. Bhelua when she came to know that her father was not inclined to give her in marriage to her lover, on the ground of his inferior social status, left her father's palace, and fled away with the lover. Such instances may be easily multiplied. Old Bengali literature breathing the air of priestly renaissance is a rigid field in which we seldom come across such love-romances. The ballads reveal an astonishing freedom in our women to which the modern Hindus are not accustomed.

The age-restriction is nowhere in this romantic literature. Since all the heroines first fall in love and then marry, it is natural to suppose that all of them should have passed that stage where the present society would commit them to the absolute care of their guardians in matrimonial matters, rendering them into the veiled toys of the inner apartments when mere children. Sometimes we find a girl attaining her 21st year before her marriage and still there is no hurry about her felt by her guardians. In one ballad a very sober and simple Brahmin girl of orthodox community offers her heart to a lover in private. This man plays perfidiously with her. The father is shocked at the conduct of the young man and asks his daughter to make a choice from amongst her numerous other suitors, but the girl refuses to marry and prefers a life of celibacy. Such conduct in a Brahmin girl could not be permitted in the present Hindu society. The society described in these ballads is free as sky, where the lovers sing their love-songs like larks. Bhelua,—the daughter of a rich merchant—absconds with her lover but is forcibly parted from him by a tyrant who takes a fancy for her. She remains in the harem of the wicked Abu Raja for days and months much like Sita in the Asoka Garden. Thence she flees to the palace of a friend of her mate, but this friend proves a traitor and conspires to kill him. For nearly a year during which she passed her days in the utmost anguish of heart, she is carried off and on from place to place like a prize or a precious booty, paying the inevitable penalty of beauty. But it is curious that after all these vicissitudes of her fortune she is not only cordially admitted to her father's home, but even the father of her lover agrees to accept her as his daughter-in-law. The couple is married with great *eclat* on the sea. Instances of such toleration and forgiveness we seldom find in Hindu literature of the Renaissance. It may be the case that this ballad was to a certain extent tainted by Tibeto-Burman influence, for in the Hindu society of remote Eastern parts of Bengal there is surely a Mongolian element of female freedom in the air. The conduct of Bhelua, it must be said, is all through unexceptionable and without blemish, though not quite consistent with the ideal of Brahmanic purity.

The caste seldom proves a bar to the union of lovers. In some ballads a king gives a general permission to the prince—his son, to marry any woman whatever might be her status in society (*vide* Mukut Roy, p. 93). I believe before the rigorous priestly element was introduced, there had been many cases of '*Pratilom*' marriage, now condemned by the Hindu society. In some parts of Hindusthan even now a Hindu Raja may take a Moslem wife allocating a separate harem for her where she may follow her own religious practices. The sloka 'স্ত্রীরত্নম্ দুষ্কুলাদপি' was at one time no dead letter, but actually the stalwarts of society were privileged to marry from any caste. From all these evidences we conclude without any hesitancy that throughout this vast literature of ballads in Bengal there is absolutely no preponderance of the modern Brahmanic ideas. Everything described is fresh, lively and vivifying.

The new jurisprudence of the Hindus forbidding sea-voyage had no hold on the people of Mymensingh and Chittagong for a long time. Beautiful and interesting are the accounts of the ships sailing towards distant countries and of their return home laden with cargo. When a merchant came back to his native shore with rich merchandise, it was the ladies who had to accord him welcome first of all at the landing ghat. They adorned the prows of the ships with vermilion, and made offering of tufts of grass and grain,—observing other religious rites before the cargo was landed ashore. In this matter the accounts given in our ballad-poetry offers a striking contrast with those of sea-voyages described by Kabi-Kankan, Bijaygupta, Kshemananda, Ketakadas and other Renaissance-poets. They have given incredible legends about the ancient sea-voyages with a free play of their unrestrained imagination, which sometimes read like Arabian Nights tales. Kabi Kankan while describing the perilous condition of the sailors in a stormy sea directs his ill-seasoned humour at the East Bengal pilots. Such passages may be praised as powerful satire but they do not give us any idea of life in the sea. In the ballads we have many animated descriptions of storms in vast waters. The horrors of the sea in commotion when the large waves rise like hill-tops rending the very bosom of the vast waters and touching the sky,—the sails and the ropes being snapped off by violent gusts of wind, and the crew appearing helpless and small like pygmies in that dreadful commotion of nature,— the bewildered pilot disabled from steering the course of the ship or controlling the helm and the great whirlpools below looking like dreadful monsters with gaping mouths—all these are portrayed in such a life-like colour that we seem to be in the midst of the sea participating in the general panic and desperate struggle of the voyagers.

Such descriptions are very vivid in the ballads recovered from Chittagong sea-side. In the ballad of Nasar Malum the figures of the Harmads—the Portuguese and Burmese pirates—have been presented with their picturesque dress, bent on attacking merchant-vessels and plundering the booty. They were men of short stature with coats of scarlet colour, hats and stripped turbans, and their leader had always a telescope in his hand. They committed inhuman atrocities on the captives whom they killed, mutilated or sold in the southern countries. The duties of a Malum or captain are clearly defined. He was generally an expert not only in navigation but in drawing charts of the sea. He kept with him birds of a particular species which possessed an instinctive knowledge of the sea ; where waters were shallow these birds would indicate the danger-zone by their shrieks. I do not know if this part of the account is a mere legend. The Malum knew from observation of the sky the varying conditions of the weather and could take precaution when he anticipated danger. Tamasa Gazi's account of his voyage is very interesting. He finds women in a populous city doing marketing, ploughing and many such functions, while men perform the duties of kitchen. This evidently refers to Burmese women. The shores he describes are occasionally enlivened with small hilly ranges where the deer and buffalo graze freely and drink from small fountains and narrow water-courses. The merchant is unfamiliar with cocoanut trees, so he wonders at the tall trees bearing cups of water at the top. In the Bay they generally traded in dry fish. Many are the descriptions where the sea water entering the ship in storm drenched the dry fishes producing a bad odour, which invited the vultures and other birds of prey hovering in the sky to swoop down and carry them off. In the ballad of Bhelua the march of a naval expedition is graphically described. The war-fleet consisted of fourteen ships. The contents of each of them are mentioned. The front ship was laden with Korans and scriptures, as if to ensure divine sanction for war in a righteous cause. The meeting of several fleets from four directions, when Bhelua's marriage was to be celebrated on a turbulent sea, presented a superb and majestic spectacle, and the poet shows considerable power in delineating the grand ceremony in which Abu Raja was made the victim of a secret conspiracy of the wronged heroine. We know from these ballads that it was the custom in some of the merchant families of Bengal to perform the wedding of a betrothed couple in the deep. One merchant says—"Sea is my home" (Vol. II, Part I, p. 146). All this shows the extent of commercial activities conducted on the sea by the people of this ancient land where in the14th century or a little earlier sea-voyage was forbidden. Occasionally the scenes described in the sea are picturesque. The sandy isles where there is scarcely to be seen any human habitation, desert-like without any sign of vegitation—where the crocodiles stretch their body lazily, half in water and half in the sandy shore, hatching their eggs—are presented with the vividness of a scene enacted before one's eyes. Sometimes the sailors see hundreds of cocoanut fruits carried on the foams of the waves, no one knowing from what island they came floating in such superabundance.

4. *The Hindus and Mahomedans.*

We have up to now published 54 ballads. Of these at least 15 were composed by Mahomedans. In many cases though a ballad was composed by a Hindu it used to be sung by Mahomedan minstrels. As the purists of Brahminic Renaissance gradually imposed more and more stringent rules in regard to social morals, some of the finest of ballads breathing a refreshing air of freedom were condemned as unholy, and Mahua, Kamala, Kajal Rekha, Bhelua and many other ballads of great poetical beauty and charm bore the ban of Brahminic canons and were expelled from Hindu homes. We owe their existence to Mahomedan 'Gayans' who did not set a pin's fee at the angry look of the Brahmins. The poet Jamatulla, whose another name was probably Amir, wrote the most excellent ballad of Maniktara. We have been able to recover only a part of this interesting ballad. Its realistic scenes give us actual visions of life with all the light and shade of a rural atmosphere. Jamat-ulla is a perfect master of the poetic style. His description of the village-quack Tinkari, of the young friends who gradually became confirmed dacoits, of Vasu's love-romance and the rich repast served in his father-in-law's house are graphic and enlivened by sparkling humour. The wonderful Maniktara—the heroine of the tale,—is a great figure. We have no space here for analysing the unique and complex character of this woman. She was trained for domestic as well as for martial life, and her stratagems revealed in the incomplete ballad are worthy of a Machiavelli. Jamat-ulla's close knowledge of Hindu society does him great credit. In this he is not a whit inferior to Alwal, the author of Padmabati (*vide* Bangavasa O Sahitya, 5th ed., pp. 478-86). He occasionally cuts a joke at his Hindu friends but that is well merited and there is no sting about it. The poet Mansur Bayati, author of Dewan Madina, is a prince of rustic poets and the devoted Madina, the best of his creations, has justly drawn admiration from Romain Rolland. The ballads of Nasar Malum, Nurunneha and Manjur Ma composed by Mahomedan poets display remarkable literary powers. Some of the Moslem poets whom I have named here rise far above the shoulders of the average Hindu poets of old Bengali literature. If our Moslem brethren still contend that the old Bengali literature is essentially Hindu in its character they will be very greatly mistaken. The Bengali Moslems have as much ground to take pride in their mother-tongue as the Hindus themselves, and if a true estimate of merit is made by impartial critics, I am not sure whether the palm would be carried by Hindus or Mahomedans. It is due to Moslem patronage that the Bengali literature first obtained a footing and recognition in the society of the learned in Bengal. In the countryside where the Fakirs and

Moslem singers still spread their culture by Bengali songs and aphorisms, they command an audience far larger than the so-called cultured writers do in our modern literature. The literature of ballads,—of the Manasa cult and of folk-lore generally—are almost entirely in the hands of Mahomedans in Eastern Bengal.

But though most of these authors are devout followers of Islam yet their heart is not debased by any narrow or ill-bred sentiments of racial prejudice. The poet of Manjur Ma puts it in the mouth of his hero that his wife was a fairy of Bhest, a veritable flag of heaven, sacred as a Tulasi leaf and beautiful as Dasabhuja. The Màhomedan poet of the ballad Nuranneha pays his salute to the Pirs and Saints as well as to the local Hindu deities—Buramai and Srimai in his prologue. Another Mahomedan poet says, "The Moslem and the Hindu are like ropes from the same bundle. One calls Him, Alla Rashul and the other Hari." Such preliminary verses breathing good will and appreciation are very common in these ballad-literature. I quote another verse from a Mahomedan poet which has the same catholic idea. "Ram and Rahim, Bismilla and Vishnu are the different names of the same Being." The Mahomedan writer of the ballad of Nizam Dacoit says, "I pay my humble tribute of respect to Nur Nabi and to Koran—the word of God.......I next salute the shrine of Vrindaban with all its associations of Radha and Krishna, and to the memory of Sita—the jewel of chaste womanhood and to Ram—the prince of the dynasty of Raghu." The Moslems in the ballads are generally most loud in their profession of such magnanimous feelings, and the Hindus are not slow in giving a fitting response to them. In the ballad of Kanka and Lila we find how the cult of Satyapir was promulgated by a Mahomedan Fakir with the help of a young Hindu poet. The poet Kabi Kanka was a well-known writer of the sixteenth century—a contemporary of Chaitanya. He was a devoted disciple of a Mahomedan Pir and had such respectful love for him that he ate the refuse from his Master's plate without any scruple. The Mahomedan and the Hindu poets have described love-tales in which the lovers belonged to the two different communities. In one case a Mahomedan princess falls in love with a Kshatriya youth and in another there is a most devoted love verging on martyrdom between a Brahmin girl and a Mahomedan youth. In yet another instance we find a Hindu widow of high status in society running away with her Mahomedan lover. All of these three ballads are written by Mahomedans. In the ballad of Chandravati composed by the poet Nayanchand we find Jaychandra, a Brahmin youth, marrying a Mahomedan girl. Such accounts never created any racial bitterness. They did not originate from communal prejudices but were products of guileless hearts which believed that the blind deity was indifferent to all social and communal considerations. The Hindus and the Mahomedans enjoyed these ballads alike. A Moslem poet who never cared for the exclusive interests or prejudices of his community writes the following verse : "Do not trust my brethren on a cow which is allowed to graze in the pastures near a hill (any moment it may be killed by a tiger). Trust not, my brethren, on a house that stands on the banks of a river (such houses are generally washed away in Eastern Bengal by the Padma, the Brahmaputra and other big rivers every year). Trust not, my brethern, on the wife of a Mahomedan and on the beard of a Hindu (the author means to say that the Mahomedans allow their women the right of divorce and of taking another mate. So the security of a Hindu husband cannot be theirs. The Mahomedan keeps the beard as a matter of religious compulsion whereas the Hindu keeps it to-day and shaves it off to-morrow at his will). The Mahomedan poet of the ballad Maniktara passes many jokes at some of the incongruous customs of the Hindus, but the tone is one of good will and friendliness so that no Hindu could take any offence.

That a large section of the Buddhists, maltreated by the Hindus after the downfall of Buddhism in Bengal, eventually accepted Islam will be seen from the supplementary portion of the Sunya Puran by Ramai Pandit, in which it is written that the prophets and the angels of the Mahomedans incarnated themselves in Bengal and Orissa in order to punish the Brahmins. I have got a copy of an old Bengali poem of the Nath Cult with me in which a long account of the relationship that existed between the followers of the Natha cult and of Islam is given. It is clear from this book that a large section professing the Natha cult had a pro-Moslem tendency which no doubt ultimately developed in many of them turning Mahomedan converts. One of the apostles of the Natha cult sings in this strain: "The Moslem Pirs, prophets and Saiyads are but the manifestations of thee, oh lord!" He philosophically interprets the 'Roja' ceremony of the Mahomedans and pays his respects to some of the distinguished 'Sheks' and Dervishes. When we find this spirit in a scripture of the Natha cult preserved in a Dharma temple we are naturally reminded of the Sanskrit work Sekh Subhodaya attributed to Halayudha,—written in honour of a Mahomedan saint.

There are many evidences to prove that in the earlier days of Mahomedan conquest, the Hindus tried to assimilate the best elements of Islam in their religion. Some of the Mahomedan Pirs and Fakirs, especially a band of Aulias who came from Arabia, lent their powerful support in bringing about this happy union in the 15th and 16th centuries. Out of this feeling came into existence the cults of Satya Pir and Manik Pir which were broadbased on a sympathetic appreciation of all that is good in the two communities. The Mahomedan ballad-makers have clearly indicated how they made the atmosphere of Bengal congenial for their habitation in the nighbourhood of the Hindus in terms of perfect amity, goodwill and peace. When we come across the present state of communal trouble what a contrast do we find? It is not surely due to any bitterness inherent in the Hindu or the Mahomedan ; the seed has come flying in the air from some unknown region.

After a careful study of this ballad-literature I find that there are some points in which the Mahomedan poets have easily surpassed the Hindus. It is impossible for a Hindu poet, however broad his views may be, living in an environment of orthodox ideas as he does, to depict a character like Manjur Ma, in the true spirit of sympathy as the Mahomedan poet has done. Such sympathy for the fallen girl is impossible to be shown by a Hindu poet whose heart would naturally revolt against a false wife in spite of all things that might be said in her defence. The old Bengali literature abounds with Baramasis. But no Baramasi I think matches the wealth of domestic love and pathos which we find in the Baramasi of Dewan Madina. Kabi Kankan no doubt gives a very powerful Baramasi in his Chandi Kabya, but Fullara's misfortunes, though they possess great pathos, cannot be a match for the exquisite touches of the realistic account associated with the field-work of a rustic pair during the twelve months of the year that we find in Madina. The love of Madina and Dulal in fact gives a picture of the ideal nuptial in the cottage of peasants. The love of the pair which began romantically gradually developed into an adamantine bond by daily co-operation in household work. The very nature of their duties drew them to one another till one was indispensable for the other. They were literally the flesh of flesh and the blood of blood of each other. No poet has done so much to show the sacred tie which bound a peasant with his wife as the poet Mansur has done by portraying the fidelity, purity and child-like trust and dependence of a peasant wife. The repentant Dulal, fearing a catastrophe, comes in slow paces to his deserted home beholding sights which confirm his presentiments. He sees the favourite cow of the house reduced to a skeleton, evidently with no one to give it grass or water, straying away from its shed,—the pet bird of his wife loosened from its beautiful cage and crying piteously from the roof of the house, —the favourite cat mewing in despair near the kitchen which is evidently deserted by the mistress. The mango-plant which had been reared up by the couple with so much care he found eaten up by a goat or cow, and the hedge raised for its protection broken in places. These situations the poet does not huddle together in an inartistic fashion, but they are given after pauses and intervals gradually accentuating the effect of the coming tragedy.

Another Moslem poet—the author of Nasar Malum—is almost an equal of Mansur Baiti in giving domestic touches. We have no space here to review the poetry of this wonderful ballad which the reader will find in the present volume. We wonder how the heart of these Moslem poets, untrammelled by social orthodoxy (and who probably inherited the spiritual culture of a more catholic religion than the modern Hinduism) was a veritable store-house of such fine poetical ideas. The ballad of Nuranneha evinces remarkable poetical powers. Even such a prosaic ballad as the Hati Kheda or Elephant-capture has been redeemed by lively touches of true poetry which we scarcely expected in such a dry subject. The Mahomedan peasantry of East Bengal living in the Gangetic valley, which abounds with rich landscapes enlivened by large rivers, have got from their picturesque country not only a fresh and warm heart pulsating with domestic tenderness —but also a subtle power to analyse the psychology of human heart, under the spell of emotional pain and joy—dwelling in the infinite calm of their rural atmosphere.

5. *Ballads and Vaishnava Padas.*

I should ask my readers to study carefully the four ballads: Mahua, Sham Ray, Andha Bandhu and Maishal Bandhu. They sparkle like gems of the same brilliance and quality. But their chief interest lies with me in their giving us in an unmistakable way the very sentiments of our great poet Chandidas with all the rhythm and wealth of emotional thought rendered so familiar to us by him. These ballads bring a message, which we find spiritualised by Chandidas, of highest martyrdom in the cause of love. The heroes and heroines of these ballads care not for caste or for any social canon. They trample upon every form of ordinance imposed on women in Hindu society. The heroine often runs through great sacrifices for love, but she is not cast in a stereotyped form and has a stamp of individuality which is peculiarly her own. The linguistic forms used in the ballads at times verge on the very words of Chandidas. The situations described by Chandidas in lyrical songs find their counterpart in actual dramatic incidents described in the ballads. Read how the prince in the song of Dhoparpat exposes himself to rain in a dark night waiting for the washer-maiden and it will appear that the well-known poem of Chandidas 'এ ঘোর রজনী মেঘের ঘটা,' etc., has been pictorially illustrated in the ballad. The Andha Bandhu's flute and its wonderful effect remind one of many charming passages of Chandidas dealing with Krishna's divine flute. The very language seems to be similar in some places. The exuberance of lyrical ideas in the Maishal Bandhu in all their flowering beauty discloses the exquisite touches and poetry which inspired the poet of Nannur. Sham Ray and Maishal Bandhu are more dramatic but still both of them possess a superabundance of emotion investing the drama of love with a truly lyrical charm. What we greatly regret in the modern versions of Chandidas's poems is a lack of order in the arrangement of songs. The editors have often times, in the craze of conforming to the rules of poetics, failed to grasp the original order of the songs. In the modern editions occasionally a song comes to us like an unconnected piece. Reading between the lines one would see that these songs were not only sung but there were probably intervening prose narrations which are missing now. The players with their artistic gestures and motions also supplied gaps explaining the situations, and these links are now missing. Both in the ballads and in Chandidas's lyrics there is an unmistakable element of dramatic skill. The former being composed in the form of a narrative have often left no blanks to be supplied by acting on the stage. In Chandidas's poems, however, many omissions are to be supplied by the imagination of the reader. Take for instance, the song referred to above.

এ ঘোর রজনী মেঘের ঘটা কেমনে আইলে বাটে।
আঙ্গিনার মাঝে বঁধুয়া ভিজিছে দেখিয়া পরাণ ফাটে॥
ঘরে গুরুজন ননদী দারুণ, বিলম্বে বাহির হনু।
আহা মরিমরি সঙ্কেত করিয়া কতনা যাতনা দিনু॥
বঁধুর পিরীতি আরতি দেখিয়া মোর মনে হেন করে।
কলঙ্কের ডালি মাথায় করিয়া অনল ভেজাই ঘরে॥
আপনার দুঃখ সুখ করি মানে আমার দুখের দুখী।
কহে চণ্ডীদাস কানুর পিরীতি শুনিয়া জগৎ সুখী॥

In this poem the first line is evidently addressed to the lover, of the rest some appear to be said in confidence to Radha's maiden-friends and others are a soliloquy addressed to herself. All these gaps which originally used to be filled by prose explanations and artistic gestures are now to be supplied by the reader's imagination only.

It is a curious thing to find that of all the Vaishnava poets of Bengal, it is Chandidas alone who has a marvellous affinity and close resemblance with our early ballad-makers. In the three out of the four ballads mentioned by me the heroine is of low birth,—a fact which cannot fail to remind us of the inspiration which Chandidas derived from Rami. Even in Andha Bandhu, though the social status of the blind lover is not mentioned, love between the pair is between two unequal characters. Another thing to be noticed in this ballad is that both the hero and heroine stand on the same level of purity and devotion. In most of the other ballads the heroes cannot retain the integrity of their original impulse but betray the fair ones, turning treacherous. Here, however, the man and the woman are almost equally conspicuous in their devotion and sacrifice. In this ballad the man does an extraordinary act of renunciation by committing suicide. She whom his heart has all along yearned to meet, with all the thirst of a warm passion has offered herself to his arms without his seeking, but he rejects the great opportunity and triumphantly rises above the situation, from a superior sense of duty. All these figures have giant's strength. Love has given them a heart of steel to bear the worst shafts of ill fortune,—it has fortified them against every thought of worldly pleasure and endowed their soul with a true spirit of martyrdom. We forget that they were transgressors of social laws,—that they often gave great pain to their parents,—that they were no better than social outlaws. Yet, these figures rise far above those of the ordinary mortals of this mundane world of ours. Here do we see the true character of a divine emotion revealed in all its beauty. We instinctively feel that all the flowers of the forest bloom as tributes to this godly feeling in man and that heaven itself, with its myriads of stars, comes every night to look with wonder upon these angels of devotion who carry with them the very air of heaven. We find in the ballad-literature many instances of martyrdom in love, besides an emotional phraseology developed in course of long centuries which has made our language so sweet. This dear land of Bengal of ours was once a spacious field of martyrdom where frail women and green youths proved their giant strength by heroic sacrifices. The secular side of sweet emotion is shown in the ballads and the spiritual side we find developed in Vaishnava literature. The heaven to which the Vaishnavas had risen became accessible because here in this country there was a great culture of tender feelings, to which our rural literature bears an undoubted testimony. The atmosphere was prepared for the advent of one whom his loving countrymen has called "নবদ্বীপ-চন্দ্র" or the Moon of Navadwip.

From a reference to Andha Bandhu we find that it was composed sometime after Chandidas, but from the mannerisms, the style, the spirit of the tale and other points, we are led to suppose that the poet of this ballad did not live in a distant age,—the ballad-maker might have been even his contemporary. None of these ballads show any spirit of imitation or copying. The similarities show that the poet lived in the same age and were imbued with the same spirit. The language of the four ballads and of Chandidas's lyrics seems to be of a particular epoch and not the result of imitation.

The ballads unmistakably prove as to why the religion of Chaitanya had such a strong hold on popular imagination. The emotional poems sprang up as an indigenous plant in this soil leading to renunciation of a high order and Chaitanyaism is a fruit of that plant. Bengal is the chosen soil of the emotional creed in a sense in which no other place can lay an equal claim to the spiritual message of

Chaitanya. The ballads prove the development of the history of Vaishnavism in Bengal.

Chronological considerations should not lead us to wrong conclusions. The earliest of these ballads may be traced to the 10th or 11th century, though their language has undergone considerable changes in course of their recitations through several centuries. The four ballads I have named appear to belong to 14th-16th centuries; but the majority of the love-ballads are productions of post-Chaitanya age. The tradition of their poetry and also its phraseology, however, have come down from a remote age. In a ballad of Mahipal the origin of which may be traced to the 10th century there is a passage which bears a close resemblance with a song in Maishal Bandhu and another in Bhelua, composed many centuries after. It is this old poetic tradition of the earlier ballads that serves to illustrate the history of the growth of Bengali Vaishnavism.

The practice of *Sati* is now out of date and held to be a barbarous rite founded on superstition and compulsion. Many Europeans, however, have borne testimony to the devotion and uncompromisingly heroic attitude of some of the *Satis*. No one will stand to defend this rite now-a-days but let us not—the descendants of *Satis*—decry them in the spirit of the missionaries. The *Satis* and these women of our ballads are sisters prompted by the same divine feeling of sacrifice. They prove that the Bengali nation after great sacrifices and acts of renunciation of ages had become ready to receive a message from heaven. This message came through Chaitanya.

Stories like Kajal-Rekha, Kanchanmala and Malanchamala are some of the oldest in our folk-lore. Inspite of the supernatural element that we find in them the women of these tales are figures of pure and unalloyed gold—unsurpassed by any character in literature outside our province. In the subsequent folk-lore also, the women have risen far above the level of ordinary heroines. What nation could produce a woman of the type of the princess who loved the blind youth? She craves permission of her husband to join her lover. There is no morbid sentimentalism in her. She smoothly slips away from her golden bed in the palace with her husband's consent to the companionship of a poor blind man. Any other writer would have disfigured her by an abnormal colour. But the Bengali rustic has preserved her immaculate purity—white as ice and transparent as crystal. She abandons a loving husband who is fondly devoted to her—and demands that he should give her to the blind beggar. This piece of atrocity has been rendered so graceful and easy that we find in her conduct the white heat of virtue only—the element of extraordinary devotion which challenges our admiration. The poet has unravelled a most complex knot in human psychology and made the whole thing simple and easy. The trial by which the Sannyasi in the story of Kanchanmala tested the strength of her devotion is harder than what we find in the 7th book of the Ramayan. The poet's study of human nature is wonderful—he hits at the weak point in a woman's character with an unerring aim. Let us not disparage these great gifts because they come from rustic hands. The diamonds and rubies lose nothing of their value, though picked up and delivered to the jewellers by the Garos of the Aracan jungle. I do not consider our peasants uncultured, though they may be unlettered,—the civilizing influence of the Vedic religion, of Buddhism and of the Jain creed has come down to them as heritage, and if one mixes with them he will find in a short time that they possess all the elements of a great culture transmitted through many long centuries, though they may not possess even a bare knowledge of letters.

This part of the 4th volume does not contain translations of Malayar Baramasi, Jiralani, Laments of Pari

Banu (Begum of Shaha Suja), and Sona Rai-Chand Ray. The original texts of these ballads will be found in Part II, Vol. IV. Want of space did not allow me to give the translations here of the above ballads. Malayar Baramasi is important as it comes from the pen of the celebrated poet Kanka. The ballad of Pari Banu throws further light on the last days of the unfortunate prince Suja.

DINESHCHANDRA SEN

BEHALA,
October 20, 1931.

THE BALLAD OF RAJA RAGHU

PREFACE TO RAJA RAGHU

The ballad is based on an historical episode which occurred in the sixteenth century in the district of Mymensingh. There are many ballads describing this anecdote, one of which, composed by the poet Adhar Chandra, has already been published in Vol. II. The present ballad gives an account of the supplementary portion of the story to be found in the published ballad.

The historical event is well-known to the people of East Bengal. Both the ballads have clothed a simple historical story in a poetic and legendary garb; but the historical element in both of them preponderates, and the legends only lend a charm to the story by a play of rural imaginativeness.

We have referred to the historical facts described in the two ballads in the preface to the song of 'Rani Kamala' (in Parts I and II, Vol. II). The death of the pious Queen Kamala who sacrificed her life at the altar of a popular superstition is a fact, and instances of such sacrifices are not at all rare in our country.

Raja Raghunath, the baby-prince of this song, has been mentioned in the other ballad as well,—and the first part of this song tallies with that ballad in its main features, differing only in some of its details. The affection of the mother for the child forms one of the attractive elements in both the ballads. The Raja surely died of a broken heart. Up to now the popular belief in Susang is that he lost his wits by losing his beloved queen—a fact corroborated by the evidence in the two songs.

The Raghu Khali is still seen in the vicinity of Jangal Bari. At the time of its excavation, it was made to join the ditch round Jangal Bari with the river Dhaniar Thala, but in course of time it silted up in places and now its course may be traced off and on in the locality.

That the infant prince was carried off from the prison of Isha Khan by this canal is evident from its name, for, what other reason could be there to name the canal after Raghunath in such close neighbourhood of Jangal Bari, the capital of his enemy, the sturdy chieftain Isha Khan?

I have given a brief history of Susang Rajas, so far as it is relevant to the story of the ballads, in the preface alluded to and there is no need of repeating it here. The first part of this ballad, which gives an account of the good King Janakinath's sorrows over the loss of his queen, and an account of his anxious solicitude for the little child, has a melody of sound and a fine touch of pathos, which it is not possible to preserve in translation. The story is told in the form of a legend and will remind one of Tennyson's Morte D'Arthur and Sir Galahead. When history is mixed with legends the poetry becomes very attractive in rural ballads but there is some limitation to it. In para. 3 (lines 168-189), where the rural poet speaks of the powers of Isha Khan to be so great that he regarded the Delhi-Emperor as a worm, or in para. 5 (lines 189-201) where the baby-prince is described as groaning under a stone, 22 maunds in weight, the crudeness of rustic exaggeration gives a shock to all sentiments of poetry.

The loyalty of the citizens of Susang to their king, specially of the Garo subjects, is very vividly described. The whole ballad is composed in animated and lively verse,—the beginning creates an atmosphere of mild pathos and poetic tenderness, while the end upholds the dignity of a martial expedition in brisk and rapid measure.

The ballad of Raja Raghu was sent to me last year by Babu Nagendra Chandra Dey. No doubt it was composed about the time of the occurrence of the historical event, though like all old ballads it has undergone some-change in course of its recitation by the ballad-singers of subsequent periods.

There are many historical ballads of this type lying strewn over Bengal, and these, if fully recovered, will supply historical materials of considerable value.

DINESH CHANDRA SEN.

Raja Raghu

(1)

The good king had gone to his outer-bungalow for taking rest. But the recollection of his beloved queen gave him no rest. A deep anguish was rending his heart all the while.

" O my dear queen Kamala," said he, " whither hast thou gone deserting me? As a blind man seeks a lost thing with his hands but in vain, so do I seek thee, but to no purpose."

Separated from the beloved one he had lost half his weight; and his colour, once dazzling bright, had lost its usual lustre.

" More dead am I than alive, O my darling!" he moaned, "grieving over thee, night and day. The baby withers away without thy suckling; how can I save it, poor thing, from death?"

He thought in this strain till his brain reeled and the world looked dark and dismal to him. He knew no rest till his distracted mind found a balm in sleep.

In dream he saw his queen once more before him. It seemed to him that she rose slowly from her watery grave. He saw her stand before him in that outer-bungalow and heard her soft whispering words, which ran thus : " On the eastern side of yonder tank which bears my name, O King, order a house to be built for the baby. Let it be there in the night all alone, and I will come there and nurse it every night. Suckled by its mother, the child will grow doubly strong."

After this the vision of the queen faded away and the king rose from his sleep—startled and agitated—and pondered over what he had seen in his dream.

"No dream it is," he thought. "All this is real, for her words seem still to ring in my ears, and the touch of her soft hands I feel still on me. A dead sleep, unlucky as I am, seized me and I lost unheedingly the treasure that had come to me. Incoherent are many things that I had heard in the dream,—but her touch was real, for I feel it still on my body, and the words that she spoke were real, for the soft whisper still rings in my ears. No doubt the queen had come herself for the sake of her dear son."

He believed the words that he had heard, and had a house built forthwith, with gates towards the east on the bank of the tank. The house was furnished with a bed suiting the baby-prince. In the evening the servants carried the child on their arms for a ramble outside the compound. But when night came it was brought into the new house and placed in that milk-white bed.

There in the depth of night when all became still, the queen rose from the tank and softly entered the house. She laid herself by the side of the baby and suckled it every night.

What a baby ordinarily gains in strength in six months, the prince gained in a single night,—fed by the milk of a mother, now a dweller of heaven.

The king trusted and doubted, but still hoped that the words he had heard were actual and not a fantasy of his brain.

He filled a betel-box with betels and spices, and placed it in a corner of the bed, hoping that the queen might be pleased to take one or two of them.

But she never touched the betels nor the spices. No longer was she a being of this earth. She felt unconcerned about worldly things, for how could an immortal fall into the trap of affection laid by a mortal ? She came only for the baby, caring for the preservation of the royal line. If she did not protect the baby, the glorious line of the kings would come to an end, as there was no other issue.

"It is not for a personal object, nor even for affection, nor for a weak hankering of heart that I come here! Why, O dear, why dost thou tempt me with a betel or a betel-nut, when I have given up all my earthly ties?" That was her mild and silent censure on one who was once the lord of her heart. (Ll. 1-52.)

(2)

Thus did every night the queen Kamala come and go and no one knew of it. She came to suckle the child and, her purpose done, she passed out of the house unperceived by others.

The strange growth of the child—its ruddy health,—confirmed the belief in the king that the queen surely came to the house by night, and though he watched and watched every time—he could not know by which way she came and went.

Near the outer-bungalow was the king's own parlour—a big hall where he used to take his rest. There the king sat night and day and brooded over the queen's mysterious course—as to how and by what passage the beloved one came and went every time.

"To-night I will not shut my eyes for a moment," he resolved, "but keep my gaze fixed on the path to find her out."

With eyes fixed, the king remained staring at the house,—and often stealthily glanced at the tank. "This night I must find out the truth at any risk," he thought, "and will not give up my pursuit till I have ascertained the fact."

He laid himself down in his bed but with eyes wide open, and pondered thus:—"If it is from the Kamala-tank that my Kamala should rise, I must watch the tank all the night."

The first quarter of the night passed away,—it was noisy and full of confused voice of men and women,—the second quarter passed too,—though not so loud, yet noisy still,—two quarters and a half passed and there came a dead lull over the sweet face of the earth. Then there was no sound, no noise, everything lay still under the spell of a death-like sleep. The sky was over-cast with clouds and it was dark. At such an hour of night—lo! what was that mysterious sight which confronted the good king's eyes!

All on a sudden a strange light burst forth from the centre of the tank, illuminating its water. So clear and bright it was that even the bottom of the tank lay bare before the king's eyes.

From the deep water of the tank the amazed king saw a figure rise slowly, decked in gay costumes, bright like the image of the goddess Lakshmi.

On all sides was a halo of light—soft and beautiful, and the king astonished and maddened by the sight gazed in wonder over the lustrous halo that strangely spread itself on the tank. Oh! how glorious did the light look at that midnight hour!

Like the bright image of the goddess Lakshmi—she rose up from the waters—surrounded by a halo of light and it took no time for the good king to discover that it was his own dearly loved queen Kamala.

As he saw her, his soul seemed to leap out in joy from the body.

"To-night shall I confine her to my embrace and never let her go again from me."

Thinking thus, the king walked stealthily towards the tank. The queen in the meanwhile rising from her watery bed, slowly advanced towards the new house. And with the nectar-like milk of her breast she suckled the beloved child of her heart and then gently lulled it to sleep.

She then stepped out of the house and came to the tank casting her glances on its blue water in an unconcerned way.

The king had hidden himself in a place near by. As the queen was walking out of the house in slow steps he came up, stretched out his hands and held the edge of her '*sāḍi.*'

Not a word did she utter, but tried to free herself from his tight hold. The king entreatingly said, "By all that is sacred, I pray you dear, do not give me up. I request you with bended knees, O dearest, do not forsake me thus. When you have been pleased to come to me once again, do not forsake me thus; save me, dear queen—save me from my unbearable pangs. Should you leave me again now, I will not survive the desertion but die of grief. For I can no more bear the pangs of separation. For your sake, queen, I observe fast and vigil, and I do not relish food or drink. Though living, I am more like dead. Just feel my heart and see how rapidly it beats.

"Be gracious unto me and promise to me that you will no more come near this evil-starred tank again. I have caught you this time and know it surely that I will not give you up. Wherever you will go, thither will I follow you."

He caught tight the edge of the flowing *sāḍi* of the queen, but the queen forcibly tried to extricate herself from him. They both struggled hard, the fugitive and the pursuer, till the queen dragged herself to the tank and fell into it.

In the Kamala-tank, she melted away from sight like an aerial being, and he sought in vain for her, swimming and struggling through its deep waters in all directions.

Like one that had lost his precious treasure, he sought with his hands every creek and corner of the tank, weeping all the while. In his struggle, profuse water entered his mouth and he almost lost his senses. But all this came to no purpose. Fatigued and jaded, he could not still find the dear one and came once more to the bank and there cried like a child.

He had been living on scanty meals—but this time he gave up food altogether—nor drank a drop of water inspite of intense thirst.

Thus did the good king pass away from this earth, unable to bear life separated from his dear queen. (Ll. 52-110.)

(3)

The child was called Raghunath. He was born, when his royal parents were both advanced in years and now the great mishap took place and he was left an orphan when yet a baby.

One year passed—then two years--and thus did time roll on. The courtiers installed him on the throne, when the prince was five years old.

The viziers and other officers with utmost care nourished the prince and they ruled the state with prudence and deep affection for the prince who would take its reins in hand in the fulness of time.

The rayats were happy under the rule, though their king was as yet so only in name.

Meanwhile Isha Khan heard of the death of the good king of Susang. He had fought many a hard battle, when he lived. None had yielded to his enemy and both of them were on par in the field.

Isha Khan was a strongly built man, brave and skilled in arms, and he reigned from Jangal Bari, the capital that he had founded years ago. The tale of his giant-strength sounds like a myth. In the world there was none who might be called his peer. He held an elephant tight by his proboscis and moved him to and fro dragging the huge animal with his arms. The earth and heaven trembled in fear of Isha Khan, the great hero, and he looked like a moving mountain, when he walked. The bank of a river would crumble into its water while he would pass by, and his voice sounded like the roar of distant clouds.

He challenged mighty heroes to war and his people believed that there was none in the world to cope with his might. He dreaded not even the Great Moghul—whom he regarded as an ant or a petty worm.

Our good king of Susang Janakinath, was his equal—the only man who fought all his life with Isha but did not yield.

Now when Isha Khan heard the report of the king's death, he proceeded in all haste towards Susang.

He surrounded the fort of Susang with a large army, but the people there said, "Lo, a jackal has come to the lion's den!"

For three months there was hard fight and the town of Susang was under siege of mighty Isha. After three months, by manœuvre and craft, the Khan succeeded in catching hold of the infant Prince. He was arrested and brought to Jangal Bari.

A great agitation and alarm spread over the State. The whole town of Susang was in mourning. All said, "The saintly king has gone to his place of eternal rest, leaving a baby, his only son. The only lamp of this great house is the baby-prince. Isha Khan has bound him hand and foot and carried the child off as a captive."

The bereaved subjects prostrated themselves to the ground grieving for their infant king. Many of them wandered like mad men distracted by the dire calamity, lamenting thus:—"It is due to our ill luck that the State has gone to rack and ruin."

The whole State assumed an air of menacing silence,

which presaged a storm. From the upper hills descended the sturdy Garoes—like a torrent—in a formidable body. They came one and all, and their number was legion. They looked like mad men, fierce and desperate in grief and they said, "Foolhardy is that chief of Jangal Bari, who could dare take away our infant prince. We can know no rest until we have cut off the head of Isha Khan and thrown it into the stream of the Dhaniar Thala. Till we have done so, there will be no end to our shame. We must destroy the town of Jangal Bari and break it piece-meal. Sufficient must be our retaliation for this act of atrocious meanness."

Alas, the royal throne is vacant. The kingdom loses all its charm and attraction without the king. For that baby-king, their grief was great and they walked here and there like mad men. Some proceeded towards Jangal Bari.

They took, in their hands, spears and tridents; some were equipped with long swords called *Rām Kātāri*. "Seize and kill" was the cry they raised on all sides.

They formed an army, thirty thousand strong. They danced in wild fury as they marched, and the earth trembled under their feet.

The thirty thousand Garoes marched, indignant and desperate; the villages and open fields were flooded by them. They came to the town of Jangal Bari at once without halting at any place. (Ll. 110-168.)

(4)

Dewan Isha Khan of Jangal Bari was as clever as he was ferocious. He had dug a deep and wide ditch round his town which lay well-protected by it. Who would dare cross it ?

At midnight the Garoes approached the ditch—it was so vast that when they came near it, their courage seemed to fail them for a time. No means could they devise to cross the ditch. Each had his plan and all of them thought over the matter but the task seemed impossible. Unable to settle their course of action, they hid themselves for the night in a neighbouring jungle. There the leaders assembled to discuss the course to be adopted. Many suggestions were offered and rejected, but at last the advice of an old Garo was accepted by all.

Six miles off, there was a river called the Dhaniar Thala. If a canal could be dug, joining the ditch with that river, their object might be fulfilled.

They all approved of this advice. During the next day they hid themselves in the deep shades of the great forest, and when evening came, bringing in its train an impenetrable darkness, they all came out, and each of the thirty thousand, with a spade in hand, began to dig the canal which was to join the ditch with the river. Thirty thousand spades rose and fell, working incessantly over the ground of that forest-land, and the canal was dug in the space of four hours.

Each of the Garoes dug out a small well to have a little water for washing his spade and thus the tank now known as the Kudal Dhowa (spade-washing) tank was constructed. (Ll. 168-189.)

(5)

The whole town of Jangal Bari was enjoying great festivities as the infant prince of Susang was caught and brought thither. For three days they made themselves merry, forgetful of everything else. They could not, in the height of their festive joy, know that the big Bhowlia boats of Isha Khan which had lain anchored on the river-bank, were seized by the Garoes, who came to Jangal Bari, all armed, on the very boats of Isha Khan!

They broke open the prison house and found the young prince lying under a heavy stone—they removed the stone and carried off the prince to the boats, which, rowed by the thirty thousand Garoes, flew like an arrow, arriving at Susang in three hours,—the path ordinarily took three days to travel. So suddenly was this flight managed by the Garoes, that even the ever-vigilant Isha Khan could not have any inkling of what transpired in the heart of his own town at the time. (Ll. 189-201.)

NURANNEHA AND THE GRAVE

PREFACE TO NURANNEHA AND THE GRAVE

This ballad was collected by Babu Ashutosh Chaudhury in the beginning of August, 1928. It is complete in 632 lines. Ashu Babu heard the ballad sung by an old minstrel named Haibat Ali, more popularly known by the name "Kadirar Bap" (father of Kadira). Chaudhury first came to know of this song from Mr. Sher Ali Khan—the well-known Zamindar of "Bara Uthan," a village lying at the foot of the Dewang Hills. Though the major part of the ballad was obtained from Kadirar Bap, yet the compiler had an opportunity of comparing the texts and adding to them by consulting several other versions which were recited to him by other singers. Of these he mentions the names of the following persons, all of them inhabitants of the district of Chittagong :—

(1) Hakim Khan—a Mahomedan peasant and a native of Char Chaktai (Police station—Katwali).

(2) Gunna Mia—a native of the village of Popdia (Police station—Boal Khali).

(3) Paithan Chandra Dey—a farmer of the village Noa Para (Police station—Rouzan).

The minstrel Haibat Ali is a strange sort of man. He is now advanced in years but has retained his exquisitely sweet voice. Chaudhury had to take a good deal of trouble to find the man out. He has no fixed residence and the Bay may be more aptly called his real home. After a wearied quest the man was found at a village named Peshkarer Hāt. Ashu Babu hired the *champan* belonging to Haibat Ali for a trip to Chittagong Port. The boat wended its course through a small river. Haibat Ali stood erect at the prow. He wore on his head a large hat made of cane. It protected him from the sun and rain. While he sang, he drooped a little to the front and kept time by striking the waves with his oar. Omar Miah and a few others, his colleagues, sang in chorus. The voice of the old man rose higher and higher till the farmers on both the banks of the small river left their ploughs and assembled to hear the song. The occasional wayfarers stopped in the midst of their journey and stood listening to it in wonder; for the voice of the old man was sweet and it trembled when he touched a woeful topic, creating pathos that melted the heart of the audience. Chaudhury writes in a warm strain that he would never forget the memorable day when the ballad was thus sung to him continuously for eight hours. Haibat Ali, at the end, pointed to the small river through which they were travelling, and said, "This river is very dear to me ; it has been my favourite place for singing this song for many long years!" The villagers bore testimony to this statement declaring that the people of the neighbouring villages always heard the song recited in the still hours of the night and in the early dawn, and they had often woke up from their sleep at the melody of the voice, sweet as the warble of birds.

I am afraid I have taken a rather long space in describing the minstrel. It is due to the warm appreciation of Ashu Babu who in an inspired language related to me the story of the old man.

The ballad bristles with interesting facts regarding the local geographical and historical aspects of the period when it was composed.

We find in it references to the following villages :—

(1) Rangdiar Char—There is no island in the Bay of this name now. But close to the village Anwara at the foot of the Dewang Hills, there is now a village called

Rangdia which in all probability was an island at that early period and which latterly has become a part and parcel of the mainland.

(2) Deogaon—This village was one of the nine important *Chaklas* when the survey and settlement of Chittagong first took place in 1764 A.D. It is at the foot of the Dewang Hills. It has lost some of its importance in modern times but is still a flourishing village.

(3) Panch Gaira—Or the "Five Waves" are still to be observed in the north-west of Cox's Bazar in Chittagong. Down here in the Bay there is a terrible spot, where one by one five big-sized waves rise, and gradually approaching the mainland dash against the shore and melt away. After one has counted five, there is a dead lull in the sea and then again one by one the five waves rise again and beat against the shore as before. These five waves rise with a foam on their crest and perform the same function continuously. The spot in the Bay is called the "Five Waves" or "Panch Gaira." No one has been yet able to ascertain the cause of this curious physical phenomenon.

(4) Kala Pani—Gradually receding to the south of the Bay, one comes to view a vast space where the blue sea becomes one great sheet of dark-coloured water. This dark-blue space is called the Kala Pani.

Ujan Tek—There is a Steamar station of this name on the way to Cox's Bazar from Chittagong. This is the Ujan Tek of the story. Formerly it was a resort of the Harmads (Burmese and Portuguese pirates).

(6) Laldia and Sonadia—These two small islands are the great centres of fish-trade. They have been recently included within the jurisdiction of Chittagong district.

(7) Dhan Chibanya and Andar Char—These islands are also two chief centres of fish-trade, and are now within the jurisdiction of the district of Backergunj.

The ballad graphically describes the oppression which

the Portuguese pirates committed throughout the country. "Harmad" is a word derived from the Portuguese word 'Armada' denoting ships. The Portuguese have left indelible marks on the Bengali language, and at one time when the Moghul power was on the wane, the Portuguese played an important part in the political sphere of this province. In the competitive struggle which followed in the beginning of the 18th century, the Portuguese lost their power and gradually beat a retreat, unable to withstand the aggressive march of the English. They are now satisfied with the small possession of Goa in a corner of the Indian continent. At one time they were a great power in Bengal, and the Bengali language, as I have already stated, has a great intermixture of Portuguese words in it.

The "Phiringis" or a mixed race which sprang up by inter-marriage between the Portuguese and the Indians, and who now claim to be called Anglo-Indians, are still to be seen in profuse numbers in the Chittagong side. They now dwell in the following, among other villages of the district—Madar Bari, Bandel, Jamal Khan, Deang, Shahamirpur, Alkaran, Gomdandi, Gujra, Baklia and Changaon.

Perhaps the earliest reference to the words—Phiringi and Harmad—occurs in the celebrated poem of Mukunda Ram, written in the year 1577.

The Harmads or the Portuguese pirates became a terror in the Bay and its coasts, and innumerable references to their oppressions are to be found in the classical old literature of Bengal. Mukunda Ram himself says of the Harmads as a dangerous people dreaded by the native population. In his description of Dhanapati Sadagar's sea-voyage there is a couplet which, in a short compass, bears a testimony to the general panic created in the country by the depredations of these marauders :

"ফিরিঙ্গির দেশখান বাহি কর্ণধারে।
রাত্রিদিন বাহি যায় হার্ম্মাদের ডরে॥"

(The captain left the country of the Phiringis and steered the ship day and night for fear of the Harmads.)

In the poem of Padmavati, written by Alwal in 1658, the poet in his preliminary autobiographical notice describes how in his journey from Fatehabad to Aracan, his ship was attacked by the Harmads. In the hard skirmish that followed, his father Samsher was killed fighting valiantly with the Portuguese. Many are the references to the atrocities committed by the Harmads on innocent persons, particularly on women, and I have spoken of these in detail in my introductory notes to the previous volumes of the Eastern Bengal Ballads. Further details on this point are to be found in Sir Jadunath Sarkar's articles in the Asiatic Society's Journal and in the 'Prabashi,' published quite recently.

In some of the genealogical works of Chittagong, the authors have given short accounts of the Harmads and their atrocious plunders. Chaudhury quotes the following couplet from one of these books :—

"ডাকু হার্ম্মাদের ডরে হেনকালে দেশে।
গোলাম ধোপা নাউ বসাইল আশে পাশে॥"

The rich, the poor, the young and the aged were often indiscriminately murdered or taken as captives by them to the southern ports of India to be sold as slaves to the French and other European traders. In the song of "Lament of Shah Suja's Daughter" a reference is found to the Harmads. But the most graphic account of their oppressions is to be found in this ballad itself. The Portuguese pirates often joined hands with the Burmese robbers, and the word Harmad, originally applied to the Portuguese pirates alone, latterly denoted the Burmese robbers also. They had no mercy for any particular sect or community, and Hindus and the Mahomedans equally dreaded them. They made men, women and boys captives and made holes in their palms through which they passed cords to bind them. When rendered perfectly disabled in this way, they were kept confined under the deck of their small boats and carried to distant countries for being sold as slaves. The expressions, 'Harmad's Müllück' or 'Mager Müllück' were in extensive use and were applied to anarchical countries. The Harmads lived in the country thus dreaded by all, and in their manners and customs were more like the Mahomedans than the Hindus.

The upper classes of the Hindu and Mahomedan population often combined and presented a bold front against the Harmads. For this purpose they indented army from the up-country and formed strong alliances among themselves. When going on sea-voyage their ships made a procession and went united under the leadership of a veteran fighter. Such processions were called *Bahars* and the leader was called the *Bahardar*.[1] The Harmads were often massacred by the retaliating people of the sea-shore; but they were completely reckless and were prepared as much to take lives as to lay down their own. In the present ballad we find some of them cruelly avenged by valiant fishermen whose boats had been plundered by them.

The ballad has not only an historical interest but contains fine touches of intrinsic poetry. The domestic sketches are so faithful that we come across vivid pictures of life in the hut. The provincialisms may be uncongenial to the refined sense of our modern readers, but there is nothing erotic or gross in the humour of the poem. The crude words of Eastern Bengal, in the remote back-woods of the province, may fail to please the ears of those readers who

[1] See E. B. Ballads, Vol. IV, Part I, Introduction.

care too much for refinement in language. But in the linguistic field, the standard of refinement is a fleeting one, and words which seem elegant in a particular age become crude after half a century. Even Raja Rammohan's prose, which was held as a model of composition in the nineteenth century, is not appreciated now. Apart from the question of elegance of style, the crudeness of provincial dialect in this ballad, instead of diminishing the interest of the poem, adds force to the descriptions. The words are so apt and expressive that no amount of lexicographical knowledge would enable our learned readers to substitute more appropriate forms of expression for them. This provincialism pleases my ears, for the poet, evidently free from all restriction of cultural refinement, speaks of things as he saw and heard, untrammelled by any artificiality, in the language which his mother had taught him—than which there is no truer or more forcible vehicle for conveying one's ideas.

The descriptions of love-making of the young couple, that of famine and of oppressions of the Harmads, the account of fish-traders in the sea, of the experience of sea-voyages and of naval fights,—all have contributed to the creation of a background for this rural love-episode which is full of vivifying poetry and of intense interest to the students of history. The measured course of the rhythm, sometimes brisk and sometimes languid and slow, suiting the needs of the narrative, shows the high poetical powers of the rustic poet. The *Śāri* song of the boatmen particularly moves in measured steps, keeping pace, as it were, with the sound of oars, and presenting the picture of merry boatmen and their trip over the deep in a charming metre, swift as the sea-breeze and abrupt as the rise and fall of the waves.

I have more than once referred to the instinctive control which the rustic poets evince in dealing with love-narratives. Though omitting no details in the descriptions of love between young couple, they are always on the guard, and in this ballad there is not a word or line to which objection may be taken by the most fastidious critic. It is strange that the illiterate rustic poet shows such a masterly sense of æsthetics which is rare in the works of classical poets. Even the great Milton has passages which cannot be read aloud and which the attempts of the poet to raise them to a classical dignity by a manipulation of high-sounding words, have been rendered ridiculous rather than dignified. Instances of indecency are rare in the ballads of Bengal, and in this one particularly the poet's caution, which is natural and not a result of conscious effort, is to be highly praised. This song is one of the gems of this ballad-literature and I am sure there are many more of "purest ray serene" in obscure villages which for want of small financial help may be lost to us. Unless our *Alma Mater,* which bears the motto of Advancement of Learning, is more generously disposed towards this treasure, it is destined a few years after, to pass into the region of oblivion, beyond any chance of recovery.

One word more about characterisation. The ballad contains a narrative which touches us by its pathos, especially towards the tragic end. It is full of romance, and the voice which speaks from the grave at the end, gives to the tale a legendary charm. The characters however do not strike us by any solemn renunciation or spirit of sacrifice which raises some of the Bengali ballads to ethical sublimity. It is a romantic tale full of interesting scenes which will be enjoyed by the reader, but Nurenneha, though in the point of suffering, she yields to none among the Bengali heroines, has not the grand appeal of reliant Madina or patient Kajal Rekha, nor the silent majesty of Kamala the queen, or the capacity of endurance displayed by Kamala—the merchant's daughter. She is not a towering figure like Malua, nor is she resourceful like Mahua, or dignified and self-controlled as Chandravati. The spirit of self-sacrificing love shown by Kanchan of Dhoparpat belongs to a higher sphere. Yet in this garden of full-blown roses, she is a small *jessamine* or *belā*, sweet and fragrant, and we shall never be able to forget her tragic death caused by crushing sorrows. Like Juliet, she is all sweetness and fell a victim to conventional and domestic circumstances over which no one had control.

The poet has given us the highest message of love by the legend of a "voice from the grave," which declares the immortality of love. The sinews and nerves, the flesh and blood may go, as they are bound to do by the inevitable decree to which all mortals are doomed, but love never goes. In this fleeting world, love lasts for ever—its ever-wakeful eyes remain broad open over the darkness that enshrouds the region of death, like stars watching the earth when it is in the stupor of midnight sleep. The rustic poet says all these things quite naturally. There is no pedantry, no ostentation in his sayings. It is not in this ballad alone that we find this great philosophy of love. There are many others already published in which the readers will find such elevated sentiments in the peasants' own language.

I also refer the readers of this ballad to its preliminary hymn. The poet salutes not only the Creator but also his creation. He pays his homage to his native land, to all the great shrines within his own direct knowledge bearing associations of saints and prophets. He is cosmopolitan and pantheistic. In everything of this world he perceives divinity and the holy spirit of the Deity. He is absolutely beyond all superstitions and communal narrowness. To the Hindu goddess 'Srimai' he makes his obeisance and says in a bold language that there is one god whom the Hindus, the Buddhists and the Mahomedans all worship under different names of Vishnu, Phara and

Allah. This catholicity of views is born of the atmosphere of Bengal and pervades its royal mansions as well as its huts of straw. The great saints and the humblest farmers owe this liberal spirit to the atmosphere of the country, which, for ages, has been permeated with Vedantic philosophy and the higher truths of the Upanishads—propagated by a hundred institutions, such as the Kirtan, Kathakata, Baul songs, Panchali, Jari-gan, Murshida-gan, Jag-gan, and Sari-gan.

DINESH CHANDRA SEN.

Nuranneha and the Grave

(1)

Hymn.

With a feeling of veneration do I behold all created objects around me. Bearing thus a feeling of deep respect for all, have I attained a state of undisturbed composure. All the eighty thousand *pirs* (saints) and nine lacs of prophets of whom I have heard, are holy to me and I bow down to them with due respect.

This port of Chittagong possesses a special sanctity in my eyes as it is my dear native land. The dust of Nashirabad rendered sacred by Saha Sultan, the great saint, where people of all description assemble to pay their homage —is thrice holy, and I bow to it with due humility.

Next to these, my obeisance goes to Shek Farid, whose famous disciple Nizam Aulia deserves the high esteem of all. The villages and ports at the mouth of the river Kaincha are associated with many sacred things and they are all like a shrine to me. In the village of Bat-tali is the grave of Mohsin, the great *pir*, and I bow to the holy place. Briefly do I speak of the famous villages on the banks of the Dulu and Sutanali. The lake Thamthami, the rivers Chunti and Pakli, the village Haita, all are in my eyes like holy shrines and I pay my respects to all of them.

In the village of Chaskhola, the goddess Burama Srimai is established. In Ragnai the presiding deity of the river Ishamati is held in high regard. All of them are to be respected.

The Hindus and Musalmans, brethren, are ropes from the same bundle—some call Him Allah and Rasul, others know him as Hari.

Bismillah and Vishnu are the different names of the same deity, and the different sects under the names of Ram and Rahim worship Him who is Almighty and Indivisible. (Ll. 1-18.)

(2)

The Laments of the Hero.

" The breeze of April and the note of the cuckoo are sweet in this season. Why do you, and in quest of whom, do you, O dear pilgrim, tread this path at this pleasant time? An ornamental ring adorns your nose; as you walk gaily—it swings from side to side, adding grace to your face. Why are you alone in this public road and who is that fortunate man for whose sake you tread this way. May I ask you, O dear one, if I still occupy a little space in your heart."

Chorus—" Oh my mad soul ! "

" I have no control over my mad heart—I try in vain to keep it in the right way. In the depth of night, I cannot have a wink of sleep. My thoughts run in a wild strain and there is no end of them !

" No hunger and no thirst do I feel, no passion, no feeling moves me. It is the thought of your sweet self that keeps me occupied day and night.

" I find no pleasure in food or drink—there is no sleep in my eyes—the costly blankets and shawls give no warmth. How lucky am I that in this condition of mine I have met you here to-day and all alone !

" Gaily does the flowing end of your *sāḍi* move to and fro. As I look at you, it seems as if the very ribs of my heart would break.

" How joyous were the days when we two played under the bamboo groves—sweet to me is the memory of the sports that we played as children. How could you render your heart into stone to forget those tender associations of the past ?"

The girl gracefully drew her veil over her head and looked back and glanced at him. Then did she address him thus, soft and tender were her words :—"Not a day passes, dear, that I too do not remember you. In your own heart you may feel a reflection of mine.

"Do not obstruct my path in this manner. Yonder is my hut, half-hid under the banana groves. Come hither, my young friend, as a guest and I will myself prepare chicken curry and thickened milk to entertain you. I will do my best to please you and I assure you, you will have hospitable reception there, and if my parents give their consent, there will be no difficulty in arranging the union you desire."

O my audience, eager you must have become by this time to learn who this girl is and where is her home. You perhaps feel also a curiosity to learn who this young man is, who accosted the girl thus on her way and all alone!

I will relate to you the story. (Ll. 1-30.)

(3)

Nuranneha.

Behind the hill of Dewang is the Bay—and there sprang up an isle which they called by the name of Rangadia.

It was a small island newly formed, the habitation of men was new, the plants were new and in the bushes and jungles of the sea-coast, lay hidden hundreds of Leta [1] and Rishya fishes.

The new soil yielded bumper crops. But hard was the task of the cultivators to protect their fertile fields from the

[1] Ophiocophalus Leta.

onrush of saline water. They built embankments to keep the brine off.

The bulls, the cows and buffaloes there looked stout and they were so healthy that one would suppose them to be besmeared with grease. But if the flood or plague appeared there, they died by hundreds.

In this island of Rangadia, near the sea-coast the fishes often appeared of such giant size that they could swallow men. Plenty were the sharks and crocodiles which sported in the mid-stream.

The waters near were a home of all kinds of fish. The Leta, the Rishya, the Tailya, the Faishya, the Koral, the Boal, the Chandra, the Churi, the lobster, the Sheal fish (Boali) and various other fishes were plentiful there.

The new island sent, as it were, a silent invitation to the fishermen far and near. And the Aracanese, and the Mahomedans came in large numbers and settled in the fertile plains.

The land there was so fertile that an acre yielded crops hundred times more than what could be generally expected.

From the Eastern country came down a well-to-do peasant named Azgar, and settled at Rangadia. He built a number of huts covering the roofs with straws of the fine *Ulu* species. He excavated a small tank near his house—the water was as sweet as the milk of cocoanut. Many were the fields that he ploughed, and the fertile land gave high promise ; a passerby would often hear him uttering meaningless words, such as " Hera," " Thi," " Thi " and the like, while driving the bullocks over his fields.

The farmer Azgar had an only daughter, who like the moon illuminated his house with her bright smile and they called her Nuranneha.

Her wrists were adorned with bracelets and she looked so beautiful with them that the neighbours, the good matrons and dames, cast admiring looks upon her.

They all said, "How beautiful is this little daughter of Azgar!" The swings of her golden nose-ornament lent such a charm to her face that it was sufficient to win one's heart at a single glance!

The daughter of the old farmer was conscious of her growing youth and with an over-joyous heart did she work in the fields of her father !

When the west-wind blew and the sea roared with joy the girl felt an overflowing emotion at the advent of her youth,—she cast frequent wondering looks at her blooming features!

At this stage of life, she met her old friend—the companion of her childhood.

Oh, the attachment of early youth! It bears through life and is sticky like the gum of the jack-fruit! However hard one may try, one can not get rid of it.

The attachment of early years is verily like the note of the cuckoo. Though there be a temporary lull, it repeats itself sending a thrill into the heart.

The attachment of early youth is like the cocoanut oil. During the winter night it freezes and becomes hard but the touch of the sun's rays melts it, and it becomes its own self again.

The attachment of early youth is like the Bhang or the Ganja drug—one who has been a prey to it can never get off, his senses reel and he knows not how he acts.

Here shall I relate the story of an attachment formed in early years and which bore through life making the pair tenderly attached to each other with a devotion which has hardly a parallel. (Ll. 1-44.)

(4)

The Early Life of Malek.

The name of our hero is Malek. Deogaon is his native village. A fine beard adorns his face. He is a full-grown young man. Fastened to one of his arms with a silk-thread, is a charmed locket of silver. Though he was far above the age when young men are married in the countryside, Malek had not yet taken a wife.

His father was a rich farmer—the headman of the village, and owned extensive lands in the village of Deogaon.

Naju Mia—the father of our hero—was a good-natured and straight-forward man. He said his *namaj* every day in strict accordance with the scriptures and observed fast (*roja*) for thirty days in the year.

In his heart, the holy words of the Koran were engraved, and when he sat in judgment over others he showed impartiality and a great power of discernment.

His granaries were filled with paddy, and his ponds with a great variety of fishes. Behind his house was a big orchard with fruit-trees yielding their unfailing treasures in due seasons.

He stored his ships with *Bālām* rice and undertook his voyages for trade against the tide often in the streams of Kaincha, visiting the towns and villages on her banks.

But luck, fickle luck, left him. The thunder of divine wrath fell on him, and people never saw again the smile of that ever-smiling face.

It was the month of April when the strong rays of the sun heated the water of the Kaincha, making it a bed of fire. Violent blasts blew over it; Naju Mia with his ship-load of paddy was crossing the river. It was a great risk to cross the stream, and Naju cautiously advanced taking shelter in the turns and nooks of its banks. But he could not help crossing the river at a certain stage. So he came up to the midstream. There the breakers caught the ship, which began to whirl round and round like a spinning wheel.

Naju had taken his seat near the captain, and he watched the course of the ship ; the helm could no longer control it; the wind was so high that the sail was torn to pieces; the ropes and the cords became torn shreds, and the ship reeled like a drunken man. The hind part of the ship sank down, the prow rose high up ; the great store of a thousand *aris* of paddy went to the bottom of the river ; but this was not all—Naju himself was drowned in the dreaded water of the Kaincha.

The mother was dead long ago, and now that his father departed, the child Malek had none left in the wide world save an old grandmother ! She was eighty years old and yet had to cook meals for herself and for the child, twice every day. Thus was the old lady occupied with her daily work and she brought up the child with all tenderness. When the tide came and the water of the Kaincha rose high, she could not control her surging grief. It would rend one's heart to hear her wailings. A strange sound of wail would burst forth from her throat. Like those deep-mouthed crocodiles of the Bay, she too cried " hoot," " hoot ! "[1]

" Oh my son, you never returned home either in the flow-tide or in the ebb-tide ! Oh ill-luck, what crocodile, what shark has swallowed my darling ! " Thus lamented the old mother while she held her grandson tightly in her breast. " O my son, " she cried, " you did not live to get a bride for this young pet of mine."

The whole locality resounded with the loud lamentations of this half-mad old woman, but there is an end to

[1] " Hoot " a corruption of ' poot '—a son.

everything, and she died of broken heart grieving over her dear son lost in the river. (Ll. 1-40.)

(5)

Nuranneha and Malek.

Now shall I relate to you what happened next. When Naju Mia lived in Deogaon, there was a man named Azgar who was his close neighbour. They were not well-disposed towards each other—though their houses stood facing one another and were separated only by a cornfield!

Naju and Azgar could not agree on any point. Why their feelings were strained, I will describe in proper time. The story is interesting and strange, and love is the main thing of our topic to-day.

When the grandmother died, the child lived all alone in the house, and Nur, sweet Nur, often came there and cooked meals for the boy.

It was indeed a heart-rending sight to see the poor child Malek in this utterly forlorn condition, and Azgar felt deeply for him.

The old enmity was forgotten. The tale of quarrel between Azgar and Naju was a thing bygone, forgotten by the survivors. The little girl's simple heart melted at the sight of Malek's sorrows. She felt a deep sympathy for him. She cleaned his house with care and brought a pitcher full of cool water for him every day, and did other household work. But if he looked at her, she would draw her veil over her face.

Oh flower, how changeful art thou! It was only yesterday that I found thee to be a bud and to-day thou art a full-blown flower,—bees are humming around thee, attracted by the honey!

She was all day cooking meals for Malek and doing other household work like a little housewife!

But underlying all these there was something else. Each act she did, added to the strength of that sweet attraction which silently grew between them.

Now and then she cast a glance at him,—a glance which sent a thrill of joy into his heart,—a glance which can only be compared to a streak of lightning that comes to brighten everything for a moment, and then hides itself in the bosom of the clouds.

But when Malek glanced at her, she lost all power of control and became transfixed to the spot as if struck by thunder.

Love had come and conquered their hearts and melted them! Oh, what a pain does this love's first dart bring!

Malek began to grow emaciated and thin day by day!

Nur's bodice half-covered the growing breasts, the black paint adorned her eyes, Malek became love-sick and crazed.

Oh, the attraction of first love! It takes one by surprise,—the heart palpitates and the head grows giddy—one becomes insensible to feelings of shame or danger. There is nothing like love in the world. In the heart of a woman, it is God's highest gift and blessing.

The house looks splendid if a garden of flowers or an orchard is attached to it.

The home of a man is joyous if there is a housewife to grace it.

The youngman's face looks splendid with new beard.

The green leaves adorn a tree, and the flower adorns the green leaves; the forehead of a woman looks bright when she wears the red vermilion, her sign of luck—when her ears are adorned by pendants of pearls and her nose by nose-ornament. But all these things that embellish and adorn are nothing as compared with the joy and beauty of the first meeting of lovers.

First love is like sweet drink to thirsty souls. It is like a dream in life—a struggle between fantasy and reality. The eyes catch a strange gleam and the heart is subdued by a strange emotion. Oh, how long can the embankments of sand resist the force of tide? It is a thing not to be hidden or to pass unobserved.

The mother of Nuranneha treated Malek with great affection. She often brought him to her house and entertained him with water-melon and cucumber. She offered him thickened milk of buffalo and delicious cakes sweetened with the juice of sugar-canes.

When the farmer Azgar went to the field, Malek used to accompany him. He would follow Azgar with the '*hukā*' and fire preserved in straw-bundles. Fine rice of the *girning* species and the curry of lobster he carried to the field in banana-leaves, and Azgar and Malek would sit together, like father and son, on the ridge of the corn fields and have a hearty repast.

Youth seemed to burst forth through her thin *sāḍi* and when with a pitcher under her arm she went to the river-ghat, she often eyed Malek on the wayside. Near the landing ghat of the river was a tamarind tree. Its crooked fruits hang down in numbers from the boughs. Under this tree they often met in the evenings, on the way to the river-side.

In the compound of Azgar's house was a place reserved for husking rice. The corn was brought there and bullocks, yoked to a post, had to go round it for threshing the corn—and Nur watched the bullocks going aright. While she was thus engaged, Malek would take his seat on the bank of a pond and play on his flute.

Malek, in the still hours of the noon, often enjoyed a pleasant nap in his house, all alone. Nur would silently creep into the room, and with a *pānkhā* in her hand fan the sleeping youth. She would often prepare fine betels with cloves and cardamoms and gently rouse him from his sleep in order to offer her presents.

The beauty of a woman at the dawn of youth is like sun's rays, it floats playfully all around and Malek was deeply merged in its sweet stream. (Ll. 1-66.)

(6)

The Flood.

That year, by the cruel dispensation of Providence, a great storm overtook the land. The sea rushed froth, overflowing the banks, and hundreds of houses were carried away. The farmer lost his crop of paddy, and the rich harvest, almost ready for the reaper's scythe, was all destroyed by the flood.

The raging waves advanced and swept away men and beasts—no one could swim across the vast waters as no bank or landmark could be seen anywhere in it.

The cornfields, with all species of fine rice—*fenabati, bijmali, balam, thinnal, girning, binni* and others of various names and quality—too many to be mentioned here—were devoured by the flood.

Famine overtook the country. The survivors could hardly get means for sustenence. Alas the terrible flood! It spread far and wide and was a scourge to the country. Land and water became, as it were, one clear silvery sheet. What a terrible roar burst forth in the sky, rent by lightning which showed itself like a sharp sword! The boatmen themselves were drowned in the rushing waters. The Moulavi lost his dearly prized Koran and the dealer in betels lost all his goods! Some ascended the roofs of their houses, but no safety even there—water rose higher and higher and overtook them. The cows, the buffaloes, the sheep and other domestic animals died by hundreds. The prices of paddy rose to 5 *āris* ($1\frac{1}{2}$ mds.) per rupee. The householders sold their wives, sons and daughters. Many died of cholera for they lived upon the leaves of trees.

Azgar fell into extreme distress. He had not even rice-dust to live upon; starvation stared him at the face.

The house had lost all its posts and the roof was gone. All the goods he had were carried away by the flood. Malek had gone away and nobody knew where. Azgar sorely grieved his loss.

The fields lay uncultivated, no one was there to plough them. In the river and in the swamps, corpses floated by hundreds. The bullocks that drove the plough were all dead. The reserved seed-rice, the yoke, the plough were all gone.

For a while Azgar meditated as to what course he should take, and then went to Rangadia. It was a newly formed isle and the lands were distributed there without rent for the first few years. Azgar got a *drone* of land (20 bighas) rent-free. He was not required to pay any *nazar* to the Zemindar for it, and was besides provided with cows and paddy-seeds of the species of *banbari*.

It was a highly fertile land; if any one threw paddy-seeds carelessly on the ground there, he was sure to have a rich harvest. Azgar made Rangadia his home and lived there with his wife and daughter. His was a changing lot, and he spent his days there, partly in happiness and partly in sorrow.

Malek in the meantime had searched Nuranneha all over the country for days and months, and at last come to Rangadia. He passed his days in great unhappiness, not being able to find Nur. When he recollected his own homestead where no lamp burnt now in the evenings—the dear place now in a state of complete desertion, he felt a sharp pain in his heart. He came to Rangadia, a solitary wayfarer, seeking the shelter of hospitable people for a temporary lodge. (Ll. 1-44.)

(7)

The Re-union.

I have now told you briefly the early history of the pair, and now I am going to relate to you the interesting episode of what they suffered for love.

Nuranneha herself was always thinking of Malek with deep affection. After one full year she now found her lover. In the western sea, the waves played with wind, Nur was fully sportive that day, entering the house and coming out of it a hundred times without reason. She lighted the evening lamp in the house, but knew no rest. With her mother she prepared curries of different kinds for entertaining the dear guest of the evening.

Her parents were engaged in conversation with Malek, and Nur, peeped out and saw what was going on, through the crevices of the thatched wall.

There were talks on all conceivable topics, but neither the mother nor the father of Nur, gave Malek the least hint about his marriage with Nur—which the former had expected with all the warmth of his nature. Malek bent his head down and began to reflect sorely on this.

His heart burnt in anguish. He himself thought of introducing the topic and at one time the word almost came to his lips, but a feeling of shame stopped him from referring to the delicate point. In deep disappointment tears came to his eyes and he was struggling hard in his mind over this problem. Last of all Azgar said, "Malek, my son, it is a late hour now, let us take our meals and go to rest. You have fasted the whole day and you are apparently hungry. Come, dear boy, wash your eyes with cool water and finish the supper."

Both of them sat to eat, face to face, and Nuranneha came up with the plates to serve them. The rice was fine and it was warm. Smoke issued out of the warm plates. But all unmindful of the food, Malek glanced at Nur again and again.

Nur chose small Rishya fish full of grease and eggs. She dropped a score of them on Malek's plates. Eggs fried in oil were rendered delicious with onions and pepper. There was besides an excellent curry of Lata fish. The fowl-curry was of exceedingly good taste. All these were highly relished by Malek. The food was varied and rich. Last of all came the cakes named Semai, and Malek left the plate after finishing his meal. Nur came up next with a *hukā* in her hand and Malek leisurely enjoyed the pipe. After many days Malek had the good fortune of again taking betels prepared by Nur.

In the outer-house a fine mat was spread and Malek went to sleep. It was a long wintry night, and we need not dwell upon what anguish of heart and doubts, the youth passed through—reflecting on his present and future.

In the inner apartment Nur too lay on her bed, but midnight passed and there was no wink of sleep in her eyes. Her heart trembled and she felt uneasy. As when the cover is put on the rice placed on fire, the grains try to come out of the pot, so the more she attempted to suppress her emotions, they seemed to burst forth the more.

The southern breeze was pleasant, and sweet was the note of the cuckoo, and she murmurred to herself, "Perfumed with cocoanut oil have I done my hair with care, will you not, my friend, come to see me once? Just come and see the pomegranate tree bent under its load of fruits. Our past days are full of pleasant memories. In childhood, we contracted affection. Oh my friend, do not tear that tie of childhood and wound my heart. Natures differ. How for the sake of shame could you suppress this sacred fire of the heart."

Thinking on in this strain the good girl lost all

control over her feelings. Her parents were sleeping in another room and the sound of their snoring, indicating deep sleep, was heard. She gently opened the door of her own room and came out. She advanced a step and then retraced it, full of hesitancy. It seemed that her delicate frame quaked in pain and restlessness.

It was a deep hour of night. The whole house was still and quiet. Malek himself was sleepless, all on a sudden he rose up startled, and came out of the house. He saw Nur standing in the courtyard. The southern wind was blowing and some stars were glittering in the sky. (Ll. 1-58.)

(8)

The Harmads.

On the west of Rangadia was the illimitable sea. The small island which was brought under the plough quite recently, was gradually increasing in size. Down the sea, when the flow-tide came, the breakers roared and dashed against one another. Many were the Godhu and Balam boats, loaded with rice, which marched through the Bay—their name was legion. The dreaded Portuguese pirates, the Harmads, were constantly watching the movements of these boats, stealthily following them through the nooks of the coast. They plundered the boats and assassinated their crew, and the boatmen and captains of the sea-side trembled in fear of the Harmads.

There is a spot not far from the coast called the Panch Garia[1] (the five waves) beyond which is the terrible Bay—the *Kālāpāni* (*lit.* black waters). The waves there are high as mountain-summits and they fiercely played with the wind. The boats and ships were raised to a great

[1] It is a channel lying between Cox's Bazar and Mahishkhali.

height to be thrown down to the lowest pit alternately. When rough gales blew there, all of a sudden the waves of the Panch Garia roared and touched the very heaven in their fierce dance. These waves of the Black Waters are dreadful. Ships with sails puffed up by winds, struggled hard to preserve themselves, and the crew were dismayed when crossing this portion of the deep; and some pledged a thousand rupees to be offered to the great saints if they could go back to the land with safety. The Hindus prayed to Kali and the Mughs (the Burmese) offered prayers to *Phara*, and all cried, "Oh Lord, save us from this crisis."

When the fierce Kālāpāni has been crossed, the sea becomes a pleasant sight; it is calm and the new islands look beautiful in the East. These islets have no trees or plants but yet they look fresh and delightful.

But now let us resume the story of the Harmads.

In the up-stream of the Bay, there are many turns by the side of the coast; the pirates conceal themselves in these nooks watching the boats. The boats come from foreign countries, earning large profits by trade—their flags are raised high fluttering in the wind. Swift are the small boats of the pirates which pass over the Bay like birds over the sky. The Harmads do not at all care for their lives; they are a set of desperate people and in naval fights they show unflinching courage and tact.

They used to plunder the goods and sink the boats in the depth of the sea. They would sometimes take the boatmen of the ships they plundered captives—bound in chains.

Now, at the time of which we are speaking, Nur and Malek had fallen head-long in love and were enjoying themselves when the Harmads visited the island of Rangadia.

They attacked the house of Azgar, opened the big chest and seized all its contents. Nothing of value was left in the house. Azgar cried like a helpless child and Nur struck her head with her hands. But the tragedy did not end there. The pirates bound both Nur and Malek with ropes and carried them away.

Did they mean to celebrate the marriage of the betrothed pair?

The old peasant, quite helpless, began to cry and his wife joined in his laments. The greatest grief they felt was for their daughter. How tenderly had they cherished the hope of seeing her happy in marriage. (Ll. 1-50.)

(9)

Encounter.

Playful are these boats of the pirates, They marched, keeping time as it were, with the motion of the waves! Like the vultures that hovered over the sea, they marched flapping their wings of sail. In one of these, lay poor Nur fastened to a cabin. There was no cloth on her person, how could she preserve her decency ? The wind had a share in the oppression of the poor girl, for it opened the rich treasure of her hair which fluttered dishevelled on all sides.

The hands of Malek were bound behind his back so tightly that the pain was excruciating and unbearable.

The leader of the gang was charmed with the beauty of Nur. He approached Malek and said, " What is this girl to you? Who is her father, and who her father-in-law? "

Malek stared at the face of the leader but gave no answer. At this the leader took a sharp dagger in his hand. Nur gave a shrill cry, when all on a sudden a violent gale blew, tearing the ropes of the sails to pieces. Losing the sail the boat fell into one of the dreaded whirlpools which made it reel round and round, till it was carried desperately into a sandy shoal. The red orb was sinking in the western horizon. There was no plant, no tree in that land far or near;—sand on all sides, and nothing else. A few fishermen were catching fish in the Bay. The whole gang of robbers forcibly entered the boat of these fishermen. Some of them had just kindled fire in the hearth for boiling rice and others were dressing fish, when this great mishap befell them. (Ll. 1-24.)

(10)

Retaliation.

All the fishermen of the locality in the meantime had gathered there. Some of them were armed with swords, some with ropes of sail and long bamboo poles. Some carried oars and helms and they attacked the robbers in a body. A great skirmish took place in that sandy shore. Many were killed outright and many had their skulls broken.

There was one aged fisherman who came up at this stage with a large quantity of powdered pepper. He threw handfuls of these into the eyes of the robbers. They staggered at this unexpected blow and could not keep standing. They fell down upon the sand. The robbers were disarmed by the fishermen and were bound, hand and foot. Liberally were they served with blows, slaps and kicks.

Having thus made the Harmads captives, the fishermen proceeded to judge the criminals. Some of them set up a great uproar, demanding the indiscriminate massacre of these wicked men ; they cried, " With our sharp daggers let us at once cut off their heads ; " but the more merciful ones said, " No brethren, tie heavy stones with their necks and throw them into the middle of the illimitable sea in that condition."

When the fishermen were clamourously talking in this manner, Malek overheard their angry speeches,—bound as he was in the dock of the boat of the robbers. Then Malek cried aloud rending the very sky with his lamentations. Some fishermen heard his voice and with torches in their hands came up for enquiry. They took pity on Malek and set him free and heard every thing from his lips from the beginning to the end. Next they went to rescue poor Nur, who had fainted. They raised her up, but her head could not be kept erect. As often as they tried to raise it, it bent down. Malek had her eyes gently opened, but they seemed to be bereft of sight and did not twinkle. There was no sound in her heart, and her pulse did not beat. Her hands and feet had grown cool as ice—she lay thoroughly prostrate and her teeth were clenched.

They brought her to the boat of the fishermen. Some of them poured water on her head and some fanned her ; and disconsolate Malek cried all the while like a child at her pitiable condition and lamented wildly. "Look at me, dear sister, get up and let us once more go to our house at Rangadia,—rise up, oh my full-moon, diffusing light and life ! Alas, who will now prepare betels for me? Who will offer me tobacco? In the dry season, who will refresh me by offering cool drink? Rise up, oh lamp of my house ! Who will spread a nice mat on the floor for my repose ! Rise up dear one, let us go back and you will once more prepare sweet curd for me and store it in new earthen vessels. Then at night we will watch the fowls hatching their eggs in the hut. Wake up from this sleep and let us go back quickly to our deserted home."

Thus did Malek cry, sitting near the girl, and did not find consolation any way. The old fisherman brought from a little box a pill which he mixed with cool water and made the girl take it. He also sprinkled water all over her face and eyes.

Malek raised her up and placed her in his lap and began to fan her. He said that he perceived a little breath in her nostrils. There, the beams of the moon fell on her beautiful face and the southern wind brought a freshness as it blew over her. A little after the girl opened her eyes.

She sat on her bed and said a word or two. They gave her a handful of rice to eat after having washed it with water. She enquired about her father and mother. Slowly, after a time, did Malek acquaint her with all that had happened.

One of the robbers, kept bound under the deck, had, in the meantime, broken his chain and helped others to do the same. They then silently made their escape, unnoticed by the careless fishermen. (Ll. 1-58.)

(11)

They meet again.

In the Bay, which had no limit, no end, the young couple lived in the cottage of a fisherman on the sands, made of straw and leaves. They were pressed with anxiety and could not sleep in night or in day. In the night when everything was still, they saw the play of the waves from afar.

Their happiness was like that of a fish, which dragged upon the land, makes its escape and gets into water again—or like that of a stream which after a long circuitous course gains its utmost goal, the sea; or like the creepers *Jhinga* or long gourd when they find a refuge on a bamboo-platform, or like a poverty-stricken man when he comes all on a sudden in possession of untold gold, or like that of Eusof when he met Jelukha.

The next day, the fishermen stirred themselves up and drew a programme of their work. They decorated their boats with flags and proceeded to cross the Bay,—the large boats, the *Gadhu*, with enormous sails had their decks filled with dry fish and other goods. Then they marched through the deep in a row. The boatmen made themselves merry in various ways. Some played on reed-flutes, some sounded the horns—the Gadhu danced on the waves, keeping time with this wild music. It was the boundless sea that inspired them with wild ecstacy. Some of the boatmen sang *sāri* songs, others joined their voice in chorus.

The song of the Boatmen.

"Cold is January, the chill wind blows! Merrily did we throw our *tengha* net on the stream of the Karan-khali in the south.

"We dragged the net and came up to Bosai—lo! we found *baila*, *boṛal* and *bōāl* entangled in the threads of the net.

Chorus—"Cold is January, etc.

"We threw the *bain* net,—in the night late we came, as much time was taken in dining. We reached Dhan Chibaniā and Andar Char—the pet homes of fishes.

"From our net some leapt out, some escaped through crevices, and some remained entangled in the net.

Chorus—"Cold is January, etc.

"We have rowed our boats up stream and down.

"We have travelled too by the deep red shores of Haldia and by the newly-settled Nayachar—where it is a terror to behold the waves stirred up by wind.

"There, oh brethren, the coast abounds with fishes.

"Strangers are we, friends; we have come from distant lands!

Chorus—" Cold is January, etc.

" Near the turn of Sonadia the ' gold island,' to the north—fishes of all kinds are seen floating on the surface of the bay—the *taila,* the *risha* and large-sized *churi*—the sea-fish. These struggle hard in the nets and often tear them off. (Ll. 1-32.)

Chorus—" Cold is Jauuary, etc."

(12)

The boatmen spent these days merrily, singing and playing on their flutes as they rowed. After three days they came down to Rangadia, and Malek and Nur met bereaved Azgar on reaching the place.

The old man burst into tears as he embraced the youth. Nur's mother in ecstacy of joy kissed the girl over and over, pressing her lips tenderly on hers. Happy were they, as when one about to be drowned in a river at last reaches its bank, or a blind man who lost his stick suddenly gets it back while searching it with his hands.

The butter melts near the fire, a woman cannot control her feelings long if love has grown in her mind. However carefully may you try to purify saline water through a cloth, the salty taste will continue. Love, dear friend, cannot be got rid off, howsoever may you try to free yourself from its control. Love's nature is growth. You cannot prune or suppress this ever-growing gift of God. Its impression like a thing engraved on stone cannot be effaced away. You may try to conceal it with all your might but you cannot help exposure. Azgar and his wife both understood that Malek and Nur had fallen in love.

One day when the sun was setting on the sea, Azgar took Malek with him for a ramble on the shore.

Affectionately did the old man thus address Malek :

" Oh, my dear youth, know it for certain that I have loved you as my own son. But I must caution you against one thing. You must not marry my daughter Nuranneha.

" You do not know the past tale. Your father Nazu considered me to be his enemy. I remember the day when your father married. I recollect how pompously the function was celebrated. But some one spread a scandal, and when you were born, dear boy, the quarrel between your parents rose to a high pitch—the result was that your father divorced his wife.

" She cried bitterly over her lot, and when she came to my house praying for help in her distress, I forthwith married her.

" Deogaon, my native town, became since a hot bed for me, I could find no rest in my house. The memory of those cruel days still rends my heart like a shaft. The people of the town became hostile to me; my grannery became empty of its store and not a *cowri* was left in my box. I cannot describe to you how bitterly I suffered at the time. Your mother was to me then like a fountain of cool water in an environment of fire. This world is full of knaves. Your father, shortly after, departed from this world of woes, and I was left to suffer my portion. Now I eagerly look for permanent rest in the grave, which is to be my bed of repose after the weary days that may yet be in store for me.

" This Nuranneha is handsome as a statue of purest gold. She is the heart of my heart, dear as a rib of my chest. She is your sister. Do not think that you are any way distant from me. You are my nearest kin and not a whit less than a son. But how can you think of marrying Nur, your own sister, born of the same mother? Our scriptures prohibit such an unholy match." (Ll. 1-46.)

(13)

Malek could not keep standing after this. He sat on the ground like one who had received the hardest blow. The sky seemed to break down and fall on his head and the world trembled before his eyes.

His eyes moved not and his face became dark. He felt the weight of a heavy stone on his breast.

Darkness prevailed on the earth and the Bay roared—the boats were swiftly coming to the shore with their thin sails puffed up by southern wind.

Azgar said, "It is late hour, Malek, let us return home."

Malek replied, "Do you better go home, I will follow a little after."

The simple old man could not read the mind of Malek and went away, saying "Do not tarry, Malek, come home quickly."

Nur in the meantime had prepared the meals. But why did she feel a sudden throb in her heart? The father took his meal and the mother also finished hers, but Malek did not return.

"Has the spirit of the Sea possessed him?" thought Nur.

The curry of *funda* fish and the *sali* rice, warm on the hearth, gradually grew cold. Nur's head reeled, she sat and rose up again and again,—often did her eyes close in sleep—midnight passed in this way. Azgar asked his daughter if Malek had come. "He has not come—where has he gone then?" They asked each other. Azgar thought "Like the parrot which cuts the rods of the cage with its beak, has the lad cut off all the ties of affection with which we tried to bind him to us and fled away!"

With a torch in his hand, Azgar searched every road, every turn of the sea-shore, calling Malek aloud by name. The old man visited every locality and every house of Rangadia, seeking him in vain.

Malek that evening came to the landing ghat and sat there with head bent down, thinking and reflecting within himself. At this time a *balam* boat loaded with goods arrived at the place. Without any plan for the future Malek went on board the ship.

When Nur was weeping for him with plates full of delicious food ready near her, Malek had already enlisted himself as one of the oarsmen and as the flow-tide had set in, it made the waves swell up and the boat rushed towards the North displaying its sail. (Ll. 1-34.)

(14)

God had created the girl but alas! where was the match for her ? The flower faded away, its own bee did not turn up. Oh this mystery of creator! How unsteady are all things! The world and its affairs are as unsteady as a drop of water on a lotus-leaf!

Nur had fallen ill. Alas, who was there to assuage the pain of her head with a soft touch ? Who was there to make hourly enquires about her condition, prepare her bed and give her medicine ? None was there to offer her a drop of water. For, two days ago the father and the mother had both died of small-pox. What can men do if Providence is against them ? Nur also had got the fatal disease and death seemed to be in sight. At this hour she thought of her own Malek. "Alas, my hopes have remained unfulfilled for ever. I shall not see him again," she murmured in painful despair. And then the bird flew away leaving its cage.

Five years later Malek visited Rangadia again. He was now a rich merchant. How splendid did his boat look, rowed by sixteen oarsmen! It was loaded with all sorts of valuable merchandise !

The first thing Malek did on arriving at the place, was to pay a visit to Azgar's house. There was no trace of that home of theirs. The old man was not there, nor the beautiful Nuranneha, nor her mother. He heard from the neighbours that by the cruel dispensation of Providence they had all fallen victim to small-pox. First of all died the father, then the mother, and then Nuranneha—last of all. That home of theirs had thus become a void. Malek's eyes dropped incessant tears. His heart writhed in agony and the world looked dismal and dark before his eyes.

He made further inquiries and at last found three graves on the sea-shore. He fell prostrate on one of them and stretched his limbs and lay there unconscious of everything else in the world. The day closed and the night came in—he lay insensible all the while. Towards the latter part of the night he saw an amazing sight! The grave trembled and he heard the voice of Nuranneha clearly saying "Come, dear brother, and take your seat on the side where my head lies. Do not grieve for me. I no longer possess the body of flesh and blood, my sinews and nerves are all gone. I am a spirit now. But still my heart bleeds for you. I have not been able to forget you. The tie of earthly affection is too strong, and I confess that though a spirit now—my earthly attachment still continues with unabated fervour. My heart weeps for you day and night."

When Malek heard that dear voice he became maddened and was convinced that death sets no seal on true love. Four days passed and Malek lay there without food or drink. He did not feel the stings of hunger or thirst. He moved not from the spot nor slept for a moment. The captain of his boat, the oarsmen and servants all came there and tried to raise him from the grave ; but no request, no solicitude or even compulsion could break his vow of fast. Alas where lay his *Balam* boat rowed by sixteen oarsmen or the ensigna and flag of variegated colour—and where lay all his goods and wealth ? Malek did not even once cast his glance on these things, nor cared to know who took away his vast wealth, nor showed any liking for his life of luxury !

In the western sea, many a boat loaded with rich merchandise passed by, and the boatmen sang *sāri* songs as they rowed the oars. From afar Malek who was now a mad man, looked towards those boats listening for a moment to the boatmen's songs and then made his usual rounds by the grave of the dear one.

A strange thought seemed to agitate him, but he uttered not a word. He wore a torn cloth, a torn coat and had no cap on his head. (Ll. 1-60.)

SHILA DEVI

PREFACE TO SHILA DEVI

The ballad of the Princess Shila Devi was collected by Babu Chandrakumar De about the middle of September, 1927. It was sent to me in the first week of October (4th Aswin, 1335 B. S.). It was obtained from two men—Kalu Sekh of Adam Guzi and Nandalal Das, a boatman of Kadamsri ; both these places are in Mymensingh.

This ballad was once popular in the district of Mymensingh. I cannot say that the present version is genuine from the beginning to the end—the ballad seems to be based on an historical event, and Shila Devi's name is widely known in the district. There are places near Nava Brindaban which are associated with the incidents of her tragic end.

A gentleman named Gopal Chandra Biswas of Gopalasram in Mymensingh had, some years ago, collected another version of this ballad, a summary of which was published in the 'Ārati,' a local magazine of the district. Gopal Babu is now 70 years old. He informed Babu Chandrakumar De that the ballad which he had collected was missing. Gopal Babu's version of the tale differs materially from the present one in some important points, and I am inclined to believe that the lost version was the more genuine of the two.

The earlier portions of both the texts are analogous and present different readings only occasionally. The Moonda comes to the Brahmin Rajah as a supplicant for help falling in great distress, and the Rajah receives him with compassion and gives him an appointment. He lives in comfort for many years and then makes the astounding demand for the Princess's hands in place of his remuneration which was due He is thrown into prison in chains, but possessed of superhuman strength as he was, he breaks the chain at night and flies to a distant forest. There he collects a force of wild Moondas and attacks the palace of the Brahmin Rajah all unawares in the depth of night. The soldiers of the king are dismayed and many are killed encountering poisoned arrows shot by the Moondas.

The Moondas looted the treasury and marched to the inner apartments with a view to secure the Princess. But the Rajah in the meantime had fled with his daughter and other members of the family by a private door, and the Moondas could not get any trace of them. They occupied the palace and established a reign of terror there.

Up to this point both the versions are in perfect agreement. But there is much difference in the subsequent development of the story as related in the two texts. The present version says that the Brahmin Rajah took shelter in the palace of a Hindu king of a neighbouring province. His name is not given nor the name of the prince. This seems to me rather unusual. It at first suggested to me the possibility of this version having been composed long after the historical event had happened, so that the ballad-maker relied upon some materials supplied by rural people who had only a dim recollection of an earlier ballad on the subject. But the summary of the ballad supplied by Babu Gopal Chandra makes this point very clear. It says that the Brahmin Rajah fallen in great distress seeks the help of one of the Gajis—Mohamedan rulers who were very powerful in Bengal in the 13th and 14th centuries. The Gaji built a new palace for his illustrious guest where the Brahmin Rajah lived with his family for some time in peace. But the young son of the Gaji took a fancy for the Princess Shila, and the Rajah felt his position there to be very insecure and precarious. He fled in all haste one night and went to the Rajah of Tipperah to seek his help.

The Rajah of Tipperah offered him all help, and when

he heard of his distress promised to send an army against the Moonda Chief, provided the Rajah agreed to give his daughter in marriage to his young son. The Rajah agreed to do so, and the King of Tipperah sent the prince, his son, on the promised expedition.

The young prince and Shila Devi were already in love, and when the prince went at the head of the army Shila Devi followed him disguised as a young general.

The Moondas, aware of the grave danger that was imminent, threw away the embankment of a neighbouring river, and the flood that overtook the country carried away the Tipperah army, and the young prince and Shila Devi, when engaged in fighting with the foe, were both plunged in the waters and met a tragic watery grave. Eventually it was not difficult on the part of such a mighty king as the Tipperah Raja to conquer the untrained Moondas. A second army of the Rajah of Tipperah succeeded in entrapping the whole troop of the Moondas by a net of strong ropes. They were all made captives, and three cannons discharged one after another in a place called the *Kakrar chara* blew the wild people off, reducing them to ashes.

It is evident that a second recensionist altered this story in certain points, with some omissions, and this is not to be attributed to the vague recollection of the people who had supplied him with the material, as I had first supposed, but the recensionist did so deliberately in order to eliminate the Moslem element in the narrative. The attempt of a Moslem prince to court the hands of a Brahmin princess was not certainly to the taste of the people, and the author of the second version struck off the portion altogether.

The Tipperah Rajahs in the age gone by were very eager to form alliances with the higher classes of the Hindu community and it is not unnatural that the king here would enter into an agreement with the Brahmin Rajah to recover his kingdom from the hands of the usurper and restore it to him on condition that the beautiful Brahmin princess would be given in marriage to his son.

As the older version has not been obtained I make my surmises from the summary of it given in the Ārati—sent to me by Babu Chandrakanta De.

It is clear from the language of the texts that an old ballad was recast and handed to us in the present form, but the composition of this ballad, even as it stands, could not have been later than the sixteenth century. If it were so, many more figures of speech and over-drawn metaphorical expressions following the depraved classic taste of the later centuries would have been in evidence in the present text. While offering some apparent signs of interpolations and changes the ballad has retained to a great extent its primitive simplicity.

The character of the Moonda—his towering and giant figure, his savagery and the audacity of his insulting proposal, his great physical strength and dogged vindictiveness have been very vividly described. The ballad gives some glimpses of the sort of life the Moondas led in the forests.

Love is the main theme of these ballads. The earlier ones give the finest specimens of love-anecdotes ; there, the lovers pursue a course of patient devotion to each other, undaunted by any circumstance, however untoward, or by any adventure however risky and hard. But as we come down to later ballads, this lofty emotion receives a colouring from the imagination of the people imbued with the somewhat corrupt taste of classical pedants. This element of classic taste is very prominent in some of the latest ballads where we find artificiality, vagueness and exaggeration in the place of rural simplicity, relevancy and the attractive style of the village peasants. The earlier ballads are brief yet fully expressive of the noble ideas they want to promulgate, covering a galaxy of dramatic events, all relevantly strung together with a true artistic cleverness.

In the stories of a later period we come across exaggerated images and too much of abnormal colouring which distort true poetry. In the present ballad the laments of the princess verge on extravagance though there is a restraint which has saved it from being atrociously so. We have liked the ballad for the elements of primitive simplicity preserved in it and for supplying certain facts of administrative history of the century gleaned from its accounts. The country used to be run over by the raids of nomadic jungly people and from these even a Rajah was not safe in his palace. The women even belonging to the higher society were often counted as property to be plundered with jewels by the hooligans.

The well-known maxim 'none but the brave deserves the fair' is illustrated in many of these ballads. Brides were not won by the pedantry and learning of youngmen as we find in the days of Vidyasundar, but by real valour and manliness which form the characteristic feature of many of the heroes of the ballad-literature, while a spirit of courage, devotion and patient suffering distinguish the heroines and make their striking personalities objects of our true admiration and regard.

DINESH CHANDRA SEN.

Shila Devi

(1)

The Moonda and the King.

"A poor Moonda am I. Hut or hovel have I none in this wide world to call my own. An wanderer am I, travelling from land to land."

It is Providence that has brought this poor pitiable Moonda to the realms of the Brahmin Rajah.

No recollections of parents has he. He wanders for alms from house to house. Sheer Providence has brought this forester, this wretched Moonda, to the realm of the Brahmin Rajah.

Born was he in the forest. Wild from birth the Moonda comes to the king's Audience Hall and stands before His Majesty with folded hands.

"Thou art the Lord of this vast realm. Oh King! I am a beggar," says the Moonda, "no roof I own but live under the shade of trees, oh Brahmin King."

He stops a moment and then says sobbing, "I have no brother, nor do I remember my parents. Like a straw floating in the stream I am drifted from shore to shore, helpless and miserable.

"Some one surely sold me in the market-place for a few *cowries* when I was a mere child but I do not remember who he was. I suffered greatly as a serf and absconded from my master's house, unable to bear his oppression.

"From that day I have turned a vagabond. When rain comes pouring on my body or the rays of the sun becomes intense, I hardly find shelter under a tree in dreary waste-lands through which I pass. My luck, alas! is against me, whom shall I accuse?"

The King.

" I am sorry for you, poor Moonda. Live in this capital of mine and I pledge my word you will have everything here that you may need for maintenance. I will give you a house to live in and a garden for growing vegetables. You will have wages besides, for I appoint you as Kotwal of this town from to-day."

The Moonda.

" I do not want any land or house. I will thank God if you, oh great king, grant me a place at your lotus feet.

" When I sit by a stream, my eyes shed tears which overflow its banks. For ten years have I lived a wanderer's life visiting regions untold. Take me for a slave of thy feet, oh Monarch! I will guard the palace—no robber, no thief will dare enter the house. Inured to forest-life from my childhood I fear neither a buffalo nor a tiger,—with my two arms stretched out I stop the course of wild elephants. The forest is my home and I do not hold the ferocious beasts in awe. Look at my arms strong as iron bars and my breast, oh King, is hard as a slab of stone."

The king looked at him and saw his vigorous iron-frame. He felt a shudder but hiding his feeling said in a tone of apparent mercy.

" Look at the dark pond there at the precincts of the palace. Thither go and make your station on its banks. You will get rice and other necessaries of life from the royal store. Cook your meals in the kitchen, and in the big hall with a spacious verandah attached to it you will live in comfort. I have a police force twelve hundred strong, and you will be the head of them all."

When the Moonda heard the word of the king he bowed to him a hundred times as a mark of his gratitude and deep regard. (Ll. 1-66.)

(2)

The King's daughter—Ten years old.

A ten years old girl was she—the only daughter of the king. Her handsome features dazzled all eyes like gold. With her five maid-attendants she played in the palace. Beautiful was she as a *champa* flower—her hair fell behind her back in many a luxuriant curl and they touched her knees She looked through her thick dishevelled hair as does the lustre of the moon through dark clouds.

Her teeth were beautiful like the pomegranate seeds and when she smiled it seemed as if a *champa* had bloomed. Her eyes were soft and beaming like the morning star—and her rosy colour spread a charm which one, who would see it once, could never forget.

Even the enemies of the king became charmed, and those who were nobody to princess Shila, yearned for her friendship. She grew in years, and the good king became anxious for getting a suitable groom for her.

"This little bud of *kadamba* flower will be a blooming thing ere long. To whom shall I offer her?"—thought the king.

Even from that time he began to send messengers for seeking a bride-groom. With flowers and betels in hand the match-makers visited the countries far and near. (Ll. 66-90.)

(3)

The dawn of youth.

Her childhood was spent in plays and sports—the five maiden friends were her constant attendants ministering to her wishes in all matters.

Now came youth like a dashing stream on her person. When and how the tide set in—nobody knew nor could foretell.

" Your days of sports and plays are over, dear Princess—the time has come when you will have to leave your old home for one completely new—to which you are as yet a stranger.

" Nobody had told you, dear Princess, that a great change would be coming over your life; yet all unnoticed the change has come. Nobody had told you, oh Princess, that your play-house was going to break for ever—yet the course of life has come to take a new turn. In the garden the flower has bloomed. The short life of the bud is now a mere recollection and a dream.

" Like a bird you will now flap your wings for a flight in the open sky; this home of childhood like a nest will then be all uncared for, and your five maidens, who are dear to you as life, will be nobody to you."

* * *

The Princess.

" Oh! my maidens—tell me how is it that the voice of the cuckoo brings a new message to my ears which startles my senses. When in the cage the bird, Suka, and its mate sing a song—it awakens in my heart an emotion I cannot define. I cannot say what has become of me, but my heart feels a strange desire which oppresses me forsooth both with pain and joy. Verily does my mind like a cuckoo sing a song that has a strange burden, and lo! my attire seems scarcely enough to cover my person. Tell them, oh! maidens, that new costumes should be ordered for me—the old ones do not suit me now.

" I forget to do my hair in time. I have grown forgetful of every thing.

"Remind me of the hour when I shall attend to my toilet. If I sleep late in the morning awaken me in time. The flowers delight me not, nor the moon either, which I once so heartily enjoyed. It seems to me that the whole world is covered with darkness. I forget the hours of meal and sleep. What will my parents say if they know all this.

" What Providence has changed the old world to my eyes I know not. Alas! the charm and spell of sweet home are broken for ever—the old joys have been snatched away from me by Providence. No longer do I feel any appetite or a desire to sleep."

Her maid.

" Oh, my soft bud do not bloom. The bee will attack you and destroy all your sweetness.

" Do not weep, oh Princess, your mind is yearning for love—some one will be coming to you. You do not yet know him yet, for him your mind is disconsolate by mere presentiment.

" He will give a new attire to add grace to your youth and your charm will appear through it as does the lustre of the moon through the clouds. The old way of doing hair he will change and himself make a chignon to his choice—the black paint of your eyes he will wash away and with his own hands paint your eyes charmingly. These jewels which adorn your ears now he will throw away and decorate them with blooming flowers from his garden. Your jewelled nose-ring he will reject and put a nice flower-ring in its stead.

" Love is like a touchstone, which as it touches a clod of earth, it turns into gold—so does a lover's touch brings on a change in a maiden's mind." (Ll. 90-171.)

(4)

The Moonda again.

Slowly do the years roll on—one, two, three and in this way five years are gone. The Moonda has again come to the Audience Hall.

He pays his respects to the king and says, "Here am I with a prayer, oh King. Give me now the remuneration due to me. I have not drawn any pay for these five years that I have been here. On getting my outstanding dues I will leave your palace and go to Tipperah."

The King.

"Go to the treasury and take from it whatever your remuneration may be. I give you full liberty to draw your pay."

The Moonda.

"Little do I care, oh great King, for money. I will tell you something now which I venture to hope your Majesty will hear patiently. No wealth I want, but at this hour of leaving your Majesty's city I will ask of you one thing which I value more than all riches. All the wealth in your treasury are as filth and dust compared to what I am going to ask of you. Now you have a daughter, oh great King, who is in her full youth and you have not yet given her in marriage. For God's sake, fulfil this humble prayer of mine and give me this daughter of yours. Save my life, oh, great King! for I am hopelessly in love. No money, no gold or pearl do I want. For full five years I have served your Majesty with all my power and all for this one reward. I beseech you, oh Monarch, give me this fair daughter of yours and I will consider all my labour as richly rewarded." (Ll. 171-195.)

(5)

Again to Forest.

The King was all ablaze with wrath at this insulting proposal. All the Kotwals, who were present in the court, bound the Moonda hand and foot—some inflicted blows on him with their fists, others beat him with clubs—some suggested that the wretch should be put to fire and be burnt alive. The executioner rolled his sword over his head and said, "Come here wretch, if you would marry the Princess."

The Moonda cared not for life, he was not frightened by all these threats. In the depth of night he broke the fetters, that bound him in prison, and a forester, as he was, he fled to the forest once more. (Ll. 195-205.)

(6)

The victorious robber.

Three years passed. The Moonda organised a party of foresters in a wild woodland. One day he invited the party and cooked meals for them. After they had finished their repast the Moonda said, " Oh Brethren, let us to-day go to the Brahmin king's capital. His riches are unlimited. If we succeed in looting his treasury, by one day's labour we shall be masters of provision for life."

These forest people generally pass their days on poor morsels and are half-starved. When they heard of such immense wealth, they became maddened by a desire to loot.

Each carried in his hand a Dao and a scythe and disguised himself as a day-labourer or coolie. But in the huge bundle they carried over their shoulders, they concealed poisoned arrows, bows and other weapons. No one suspected that the bundles contained these implements of war. So they easily passed from village to village as ordinary labourers. The residents of the villages called them as they passed by their doors and wanted to give them work.

The Moonda.

" It is not at all to our profit to work in this country of yours. We have often found that after having got their workdone by us, the people do not pay us wages. We must leave this place and go to the city of the Brahmin king."

It took them three months to go to the city of the Brahmin king. The wicked Moonda hid himself in the day-time and sent his men to the city to seek work as day-labourers.

In the deep hours of the night the Moonda attacked the palace with his men. Like a hundred bees coming out all on a sudden from the honey-comb, the men swarmed under the lead of the Moonda at the palace-gate. The guards and other soldiers were now broad-awake and they hastened to the room where weapons were kept.

The Moonda's followers shot poisoned arrows at them so that before the king's men could equip themselves well, they fell dead on the door way. The Moonda had in the meantime set fire to the palace, and as the guards hastened to quench the fire, the wicked men looted the treasury and valiantly approached the gate of the inner apartments. But when they entered, they found the rooms empty. The Rajah had fled with the members of his family to the city of a neighbouring king. (Ll. 205-246.)

(7)

The Rajah as a guest.

The Brahmin Rajah there addressed his friend, the king, and said,—" Ill luck has brought me to your doors as a beggar, oh King. All unexpected, the robbers seized my palace and have now conquered it. A youthful daughter have I with me and finding no place of refuge I have come to seek shelter in your city. All on a sudden this mishap has fallen upon us like a thunder-bolt. Placed in a critical position, as I am, where else could we go now with this young daughter of mine!"

The king as he heard this sad tale immediately ordered a new house to be built near his palace for accommodating his friend in distress and said :

" Stay with me for sometime, oh King, until I arrest the vile Moonda and restore you to your kingdom."

Thus did the good Brahmin king stay as a guest in the city of his friend and full six months passed. I will now relate to you the developments that took place in the meantime. (Ll. 246-250.)

(8)

The Prince—a Suitor.

The Rajah of this new city had a son, a sprightly lad who had just stepped into youth. Handsome was he as an angel with eyes beautiful as those of an antelope. His manly figure gladdened all eyes and he lorded over his father's kingdom—respected everywhere and beloved of all.

The Rajah was thinking of marrying him and had sent match-makers far and near in quest of a bride.

In the new garden attached to the guest-house the princess Shila went one day to pluck flowers as usual with a cane-basket under her arm. The soft breeze was blowing and she felt a pleasing sensation.

An event occurred now changing the course of her life. " Why do you O cuckoo " she said, " sing a song of such tender appeal? Who is it that has given pain to your heart?"

The Prince.

" Will you tell me, Oh Princess, why you pluck flowers every morning? What God do you worship with these? You are yet unmarried. For what object do you worship Him daily ?

"To tell you my mind, I have been maddened by your beauty. You daily weave a garland with some of these flowers. May I ask who is the lucky person whose neck you would adorn with it? You are a princess. Have you got a suitable youth to whom you would like to offer yourself? If you would not reject me, fair princess, may I be permitted to ask your father's permission to marry you?"

Princess Shila.

"Ill becomes you, oh stranger, to touch the flowing end of my *sari* in that way. You have addressed me as a princess. True it is that I was once so, but to-day we are beggars at your palace for maintenance. Driven from home we are here seeking lodging and food, depending on your charity. My father has not known a wink of sleep in the nights these long six months. He spends his nights in shedding incessant tears. You are the master of this large kingdom. Why should you wish to marry the daughter of a Brahmin beggar?"

The Prince.

"Do not, oh dear girl, give pain to my heart by talking in this strain. People say that men are hard-hearted but I see that women are so. The *ketaki, karabi* and many other flowers have bloomed around, but none of them is so beautiful as you are—a rude touch may hurt you,—so soft you seem!

"Many a time have I come and gone away but never dared to approach you lest I give offence or pain. I have long suppressed my feelings but could not do so to-day. Excuse me; do not be annoyed with me, oh princess. I have come to your garden without permission. From the day you have come to our city I have become an admirer of your beauty. The sight of your beauty opens as it were the portals of heaven to my eyes. May I expect that you would condescend to come to my apartments to-night? There shall I open my whole heart to you in confidence. I will not touch you nor approach you too closely—I will enjoy a sight of your sweet face from a distance."

Shila.

"Excuse me, prince. Have control on your mind. Your parents will get a handsome girl for you suited to your rank."

The Prince.

"Mind seeks its own object of choice, oh princess. Hundreds of fine things would not give a person satisfaction ; until he finds the thing of his own heart he remains a beggar. Riches and power I want not, they are as dust of your feet. Here am I at your door an humble beggar. If you give me your hands that I seek, the precious gift I will accept bowing down my head. Even if I have to lose my kingdom I should like to spend my life happily in a dreary forest but without you nothing remains in the world to attract or please my mind."

Shila.

"You do not know, prince, the vow taken by my father. It is a very hard one and I myself worship the gods with the same object. To-day I find that I have not been able to make myself ready for worship. It has already been a late hour for it. My father has taken the vow that he who will be able to bind the Moonda hand and foot and bring him here in that condition, to him will he offer me as bride and to none else.

"He will not care whether the person be a *hāḍi*, a pariah or a *chāṇḍāl*—a man of the lowest castes, but he will fufil this pledge by giving me to the conqueror of our foe."

The Prince.

"Oh my princess, ready am I for this adventure. To-morrow will I go to fetch the wicked Moonda up here bound in chains. Whether I die or live in the battle is no concern to me. To-morrow I will with my father's permission march on this errand. To-day go to your own compartments, dear princess. Know it for certain that to-morrow I go to wage war against the vile Moonda."

Shila.

(*Soliloquy.*)

"Alas! what have I done! Why have I mentioned the condition of this pledge to the prince? I do not want the kingdom nor power nor wealth. Alas! why have I endangered the precious life of the prince? My kingdom seems like a trinket lost in the sea. Why should his valuable life be at stake for picking it up from the bottom of the unfathomable deep?

The Moonda is a tough fighter: the result of war is uncertain. How shall I be able to live in peace when he will have gone to fight with the Moonda?" (*She weeps.*)

The Prince.

"Do not weep, oh princess. Do not fear. He is a savage of the forest. I will conquer him easily and return victorious here. I will bring the wicked fellow bound in chains here. I give you my word."

The princess took heart at this assurance and patiently waited in her compartments. (Ll. 260-356.)

(9)

He returns a Victor.

In the morning the prince sought permission from his father to go to war. He also sought the permission of his mother and of the Brahmin Raja. He could not approach the compartment of the princess Shila Devi. From a distance he looked towards her room and tears glistened in his eyes. "Rest in peace, sweet soul," he said within himself, "till I return with the Moonda, as a prisoner. When I shall return victorious, I will build a summer-house in the midst of our tank. There the servants will make a bed of flowers for us."

The prince marched with his army. 'Cut down, kill and attack,' these were the sounds that arose everywhere—the archers went by thousands and the cavalry marched onwards. The sound of the horses' hoofs rose to the sky. The dust beaten by the hoofs rose high up in the air. The army crossed many a channel, many a river in their way.

It was a journey of three months but so rapid was the march of the army that in three days the prince arrived at the capital of the Brahmin king. He broke through the vanguard of the Moondas. The untrained foresters could not stand the disciplined attack of the prince's army. The vile Moonda made a last attempt, coming like a tornado sweeping with sheer force on the ranks of his enemies but the latter soon overpowered him. Fallen in a critical position the Moonda receded and fled with all the speed of his feet.

After conquering the foe the prince returned in triumph. The sound of drums filled the capital. Princess Shila, lying on the bare floor in deep anguish of heart, rose up like a mad soul struggling between hope and despair. (Ll. 356-390.)

Soliloquy.

I have seen him for one day only but that golden day is never to be forgotten.

Dearer to me are you than the black paint of my eyes. Fain would I paint them with your image. It is in that garden of flowers where the bee meets the flower of its choice, that we both met first. For a few moments did I see him and lost him also so soon! Fain would I keep you, oh my pet bird, confined to the cage of my heart. Had you been, my love, one of the *champak* flowers that bloom in the garden I would have decorated you with gold and worn you on my ears like an ear-ring. Were you a dark-blue *sari* I would never for a moment leave you but would have felt your touch on me day and night. Were you, oh dear, the long hair of my head I would do a braid with it and decorate it with flower-wreaths. You are the soul of my body. How could you leave me and go away? Oh cruel God! why did you not make one figure of us two? This cruel separation would not arise in that case. Oh Soul! I shudder at the thought of the coming battle. I do not wish my kingdom back nor my riches. If you do not return, all will be wormwood to me. (Ll. 390-418.)

The Dream.

Oh friend, I have dreamt of you in the night. I am a weak woman and have not the power to speak out my mind. The tears abundantly fell over my pillow and silently I suffered for you.

A meeting with you, oh prince, was to me valued like a sandal-tree yielding flowers—an unexpected and rare fortune. But suddenly the cruel Providence set fire to the garden reducing the flowers and flower-trees to ashes and spoiling the fragrance which had spread in the air. (Ll. 418-429.)

The Marriage.

Prose.

[After the victory, the Brahmin Raja with the consent of his friend returned to his own capital with the princess Shila. The marriage of the prince and Shila was settled. On the day of the marriage the Moondas again came to the city of the Brahmin Raja to attack it, disguised as drummers and musicians.]

The maidens wore garlands of *malati*, *champak* and other flowers. They all began to sing festive songs on the occasion. The palace was filled with the merry voice of women sounding '*ulu ulu*.'

The princess was helped in her toilet by her maidens. They washed her body with myrobalan and perfumed it with scents. Water secured from twelve holy shrines was poured on her for holy bath. The queen's eyes glistened with joy as she lifted up the princess's face beautiful as the moon and saw it with a thirsty soul. She put the lucky sign of red on her forehead. The princess wore gold bracelets and other ornaments on her arms. The dark-coloured *megha-doombur sari* she wore and her eyes were painted with *kajal*. She wore in her ears golden flowerets and her feet were decorated with the red paint *mehdi*. The *sari* was fastened with an waist-belt with golden pendants which made a jingling sound as she walked. Experts were engaged to help in her toilet. Banana plants were placed at the gate-way with lamps fed by butter on their tops. (Ll. 429-445.)

The False Musician.

Then came the musicians from the neighbouring countries. From the north came a band with flutes, drums and tabors. The musicians who came from the south carried big drums and red flutes. The band who came from the east played on cymbals and beat drums to indicate a victorious march.

From the west came a band who are not known. The leader of them declared that he was expert in various styles of music. He had a large number of followers. The leader paid his respects to the king and said, "I have come to your Majesty to prove our skill on this occasion."

When it was midnight this man began to beat a drum. The sound was so loud that the whole city came to the palace. But at this moment the evil-minded Moonda who had disguised himself as a musician threw away his false dress and took a huge bow in his hand.

The arrows which were poisoned fell on the troop of the Brahmin Raja in incessant showers. The prince left his bridal costume and riding his war-horse came out to meet the foe. He came on the Moondas,—his men like a deluge sweeping them all before their victorious march. (Ll. 445-466.)

Lament of the Princess.

Alas! for whom, oh my maidens, have you woven these arlands of flowers? The crown of flowers on my head is yet fresh, not a petal has faded! Oh musicians! stop. Play no more on the flute. This is not the bridal night. Know ye not that Providence has set fire to my luck reducing all my joys to ashes? The moon was rising on the horizon but the dark clouds have covered her. The rain is overflowing the rivers in July but it is owing to my ill-luck that the river of my hope has dried up in this full rainy season. All that I wanted to tell him have remained untold. Alas! cruel Providence has blasted my hopes for ever. Your breast was soft; its touch was like that of a flower to me. The evil Moonda pierced it with his poisoned arrow and the arrow went through it. The wicked Moonda has ruined me by destroying your life. All my hopes of wedded life—

my long-cherished hopes are blasted for ever. Oh ye birds and beasts, will you have patience to listen to my tale of grief—it is an endless tale!

Oh, cruel poison, why not take me also from this world and lead me where my husband has gone? My golden couch and the bed of flowers should be removed from the room! I bid adieu, oh my parents, to you. I will no longer live in this city of yours. I shall henceforth forego the joys of your company. I will not have the heart any more to meet again our good citizens who have been so kind and good to me.

The lamp of the house has been put out for ever. The city is covered with clouds. No streak of the rays of the moon or of the stars is to be seen. I do not like to stay in this world polluted by the vile presence of the Moonda. Oh poison, you are ambrosia to me; end my life so that I may be his companion. (Ll. 466-502.)

The Cannonade.

The Brahmin king was disconsolate and as the wicked Moonda gathered an army and would not yield easily he asked the help of the Raja of Tipperah. The latter sent a large army of archers and gun-men who hastened to the city of the Brahmin king. They packed up their weapons in their large bags which they carried on their backs and rode horses whose speed was like that of the wind. The distance a traveller would take three days to travel they travelled in a day. The wicked Moonda as he came to know the approach of the army was filled with dismay. With much hesitancy, yet seeing no other way, he advanced to meet the Tipperah force. These Moondas were foresters. They knew the tactics of guerilla warfare but had no training in the art of open war. They were dispersed all over the rural country, but their course was stopped so that none of them could escape. Being thus made captives they were led to the city of Tipperah. By the order of the king they were made to stand in rows on a plain outside the city. Three cannons were discharged and the whole army of Moondas instantly disappeared in a cloud of smoke. (Ll. 502-520.)

MUKUT ROY

PREFACE TO MUKUT ROY

The story related in this song, strictly speaking, is more of the nature of a *rupa-katha* than that of a ballad. It presents a type which is to be found in Kajalrekha (Vol. I) and Kanchanmala (Vol. II) in my collections. The origin of the *rupa-kathas*, however changed they may be in form and spirit in course of their recitation during long generations, is to be traced originally to a remote period ranging from 10th to 13th century. They have some special characteristics which distinguish them from ordinary ballads, most of which have a historical origin. The *rupa-kathas* have, on the other hand, generally speaking, a mythical basis. During the period which I have ascribed to the *rupa-kathas*, Bengal was permeated by the teachings of Buddhist 'Tantriks.' Charms, magic and incantations were more or less the noteworthy factors of popular theology of the Buddhist Tantriks in Bengal, and in the *rupa-kathas* we find an abundance of these elements. The supernatural dominated over the religious creeds, and those saints and mystics were most praised who could, like the Druids of Gaelic legends, cry "Flesh unto flesh and bone unto bone" and by incantations make a decomposed corpse whole again. In the Gaelic legend, the mystics often changed their shapes or laid a whole town or city under the spell of sleep by magic. These features are so frequently to be met with in the anecdotes of the 'Tantric' Buddhists in India, that the orientalists trace such elements in European legends to the spirit of the Tantras, which according to them, travelled from East to West and invaded the Western mythology. I have discussed this point at some length in my "Folk Literature of Bengal" and shown the analogous features of the Western myths and Indian Tantric tales by illustrations.

In the Bengali folk-tales we frequently come across the magical feats of the "Siddhas." This we find in an extraordinarily exaggerated form in the Maynamati songs. Bengal seems to have been the cradle of Tantric supernaturalism, as a hundred stories are prevalent here describing the wonderful achievements of the "Siddhas," not only in her *rupa-kathas* and folk-tales but also in the vernacular recensions of the Ramayana and the Mahabharata and in the Dharmamangala poems. The story of Mahi Ravana, which is chiefly based on mystic charms and magic, was a later indigenous conception engrafted on the Ramayana. The episode describing Hanuman's adventure in the inner apartments of Ravana to steal the charmed arrow to kill him, also bears the stamp of Tantric influence. In the Mahabharata, Chinta changed her shape in order to avert a critical situation. This is also a purely indigenous episode annexed to the main epic. A similar story is found in the account of Inda, the magician, described in the Dharmamangal poems.

The story of Malanchamala is by far the best of these *rupa-kathas*. Life and romance have been so cleverly interwoven with each other in this tale that it seems to be one of the most remarkable folk-stories ever composed. Mr. Gourlay, who wrote a foreword for my book, had first taken my warm appreciation to be a mere effusion of patriotism. Curiously however, he joined his voice with mine later, on and praised the story as warmly as I had done, saying that every word that fell from me was true.

Another element that I find in these *rupa-kathas*, is the strikingly sublime conception of female virtues. The heroine, Malanchamala, is simply peerless. Kanchanmala and Kajalrekha are also very superb figures. In the present *rupa-katha* the character of the forest-woman, originally a princess, reaches a towering height. But of her we will speak more fully in due course.

The story had evidently a Hindu or Buddhist origin and there is little doubt that in the shape in which we find it now, it has been remodelled and recast by some Mahomedan propagandists. There is however no atrocious element of attack on paganism in the story. But enough evidence is there to show that a Mahomedan propagandist latterly took up an old Hindu story with the object of singing the glory of Islam. The feats generally attributed to the 'Siddhas' and 'Munis' in local stories of this class have been metamorphosed into '*keramats*' or supernatural deeds of Pirs and Paygambars. Towards the end, the writer clearly declares his mission of propagation of the Muslim creed, which, he says, inspired him to take up the task in hand.

The character of the forest-girl, as I have said, is a striking one. One may not be wrong in comparing her with Miranda or Kapal Kundala, but there is some striking difference in the background of their respective situations. When she first comes to our view, dressed in bark, with a bow in one hand and arrows in another, her look fixed on a dying bird, she not only looks beautiful as a nymph of that woodland but also majestic as a Diana. She had been a princess but unfortunately her lot was cast with that of wild hunters. This preliminary account she does not give us herself. She is verily like the statue of a Greek goddess, mute and glorious,—suddenly moved to strange thrills produced by first love. Never was a more wild bird caged and domesticated, and never was a woman subjected to more cruel freaks of fate. The writers of this folk-literature are generally more often suggestive than explicit and plain. We find in the beginning of the poem the prince rejecting paragons of beauty, one after another; this conduct seems irritating, though it was absurd that his imperious father should pass on him the sentence of death for this fault. But we learn latterly that Prince Mukut had dreamt a strange dream in which the forest-girl had appeared before him and fully conquered his mind. This little incident is incidentally referred to in a later canto. It makes the whole case clear and explains why he had rejected the beautiful women whose pictures the match-makers had shown him. Our modern writers would not have omitted an important point like this in the early part of their narrative. The writers of folk-tales, however, with a keener dramatic sense, reserve many things for future, waiting for the opportune moment to introduce a reference. The simple line in which the prince refers to his dream, in the second canto, has a dramatic effect in explaining the earlier incidents of the story.

Behula is the typical female character in the ranks of the noble heroines of our ballads. She is now inseparably associated with the Manasa-cult, but we find the type in many old ballads,—in Malua, and in this ballad particularly. In what remote age a chaste woman travelled over the vast rivers of this country with the corpse of her husband killed by snake-bite, and eventually succeeded in restoring his life through the skill of a physician, is not known to anyone. But surely there once lived a woman of this type in this snake-infested Gangetic valley, full of swamps and *hāōrs*, who had undergone unheard-of sacrifices and hardships and succeeded in bringing her husband to the land of living from the oblivious region of death, where he was supposed to have passed ; and that memorable incident of remote antiquity became the basis of a myth which has since inspired the rustic imagination of this country from age to age. Thus we find the incidents repeated in many a tale. The story of Behula became the most prominent in this class, having been treated by so many gifted poets and also having been so closely associated with a popular religious festivity. The other heroines to whom similar feats have been ascribed by rural people have been cast into a comparative shade and Behula now stands almost alone in the field.

The end of this story is like the sequel of many other folk-tales of Bengal. It will remind one of the story of Nala and Damayanti. In many *rupa-kathas* the same manœuvre is played for bringing in a re-union of the married couple.

Though it is a folk-tale it does not lack in some materials of history. The state of administration shows tyranny and aristocratic procedures. Though the voice of councillors is sometimes recognised as a potent factor in the decision arrived at by a monarch, so absolute is his power that generally speaking his ministers when called upon to submit their opinion in respect of a particular case, are found to play the sycophant and endorse the view taken by the monarch. This was the defect of the administrative constitution. It was for this that the poor forest-girl was doomed to a cruel sentence when the prince was found dead. The councillors were consulted in the case and they unanimously approved of the verdict. But another view may also be taken. In those times witchcraft was a matter of popular belief and the sentence the king passed was *bonafide*. The facts which could not be accounted for were attributed to witchcraft. The people could not make out how the prince was killed and the forest-girl who had been picked up from a wild home, was naturally looked upon with suspicion by people. They easily believed her to be a monster who lived upon human flesh. So the councillors might have acted up to their conviction when advising the king to inflict a cruel punishment on her. Poor Kanchanmala in the *Rupa-katha* named after her was charged with witch-craft and banished for a similar cause. The councillors' judgment, however, was not always clouded or influenced by sycophancy.

When the king committed the prince to the public executioner, it was the intercession of the ministers which brought about his release and made the king pass a more humane order.

It appears from the last line of this ballad (p. 106, l. 31) that it once formed part of a big poem containing adventures of several princes in the field of love-making. Each of these fables composed in the form of a ballad or a *rupakatha* had for its sequel, the triumph of Islam. Though the ballads were originally Hindu, they were latterly transformed into songs of Moslem victory. The present ballad gives us the account of a southern prince; the other parts have not yet been recovered.

DINESH CHANDRA SEN.

Mukut Roy

(1)

In the southern part of this vast country ruled a mighty king named Raja Shilla. His army was vast and his retainers, horses and elephants countless.

Glorified with his earthly possessions, happily did Raja Shilla rule his vast empire. And Providence, last of all, to fill the cup of his joys, granted him a son.

Oh my chorus, raise your voice to keep pace with mine.

The young prince was so beautiful that he was a delight to the eyes. In the cities of south scarcely could his peer be found among the sons of princes and noble men.

They thought that he hailed from the fairy land. Resplendent did he look like a living flame.

Verily was he like the moon-god dropped on earth, and so attractive were his looks that if he smiled and glanced at a person, ill could he withstand the charm, but stretched his arms to embrace the lovely young baby.

He gradually grew in years and attained the age of twenty. How wonderfully handsome was he! The king, his father, justly prided in him and thought of finding a suitable bride for his darling.

He called the viziers and ministers to the court and said, " The prince has now come to the age when we must seriously think of his marriage. Do you now all try your best to get a girl worthy of him? Call for the painters who have collections of pictures of handsome princesses and make a selection. The prince Mukut is a paragon of beauty and his wife should be his match in every respect and not a whit less." (Ll. 1-26.)

(2)

The north is famous for its garden of roses and thither did the king send his messengers in quest of a bride. He sent messengers to the east, to the west and also to the south, in quest of handsome-looking girls.

From the north the men returned and informed His Majesty that the king of that region had a daughter of exceeding beauty. She might be compared with the evening star. So profuse was her long curling hair that her maids had to hold it up when she walked, lest it trailed on the earth. Her colour was like that of the *champak* and the flush of youth on her person was like the new flood that fills the earth with verdure in early August. The picture of this girl was shown to Prince Mukut, but he sighed and said, "No."

Then came the messengers from the south with their rich collection. One of the princesses looked wonderfully handsome with her two starlike eyes and with her flowing hair that fell to the ground. But Mukut, the young prince, pursed his brows and threw it aside.

The princess of the east, on whom they had counted, was handsome beyond words. The painter had drawn her seated with a parrot in her hand on a golden couch. The spot where she sat seemed to be illuminated by the glow of her presence and the mild effulgence of her person seemed to brighten the dark water of the tank near by.

She sat on a golden *palanka* in a room which was adorned with profuse paintings in gold. Her image lent a grace to the whole house—far greater than anything else. Even this perfection in female form, Prince Mukut unceremoniously rejected.

The messengers returned from the western region. The princess of that land had no match in the world. Her flowing hair, her noble demeanour and attire were unexceptionable in every way, and her eyes sparkled with heavenly fire. On a couch she slept and on another her profuse hair was laid by. In her face was the bloom of a hundred *champa* flowers. Her waist seemed too slender for her fully developed form, and as she walked, a hundred maids were always in attendance, like the stars waiting on the moon. But even this lady did not impress the inexorable Prince Mukut who threw away her picture with apparent disgust.

The king when he heard of his son's conduct, became wrath. In great rage did His Majesty commit the prince to the public executioner and order that his head should be cut off. "Thou vile son," he said, "thou hast insulted me in this way by rejecting my choice over again ; thou deservest this sentence, ungrateful wretch."

The ministers and courtiers assembled in a body and interceded on behalf of the prince. The Raja's wrath abated and he passed a favourable order, addressing the prince thus : "Look here, oh son, I give you entire freedom of choice. Take from my stall a hundred of my finest steeds, another hundred of the best elephants and select from the royal army any number of my picked men and with these travel all the world round. On whomsoever will your choice fall amongst the princesses of the world, I will get you married to that lady. But if you do not find a woman to your choice from the noble rank, I give you freedom to marry any one from the lowest castes. From the ranks of the washermen, the barbers and the shaving attendants who wait on the gentry, whomsoever you may choose, you will marry and there is my clear permission for it."

Hearing this mandate of the great king, Prince Mukut marched in quest of a bride, with a large army. The younger brother of the prince and his mother shed bitter tears at the parting, and the subjects thought that with the prince the shining rays of the sun were being taken away from that smiling region. (Ll. 1-60.)

(3)

Seven big oceans the prince crossed and thirteen rivers. The big swamps he passed through and then came to a city called Neoga. From Neoga he travelled eastward and taking advantage of a favourable tide he came to the south, to the border of an impenetrable forest.

This forest comprised 400 miles. The big reptiles of this wilderness were of enormous size. They swallowed living goats, tigers and buffaloes, and were the lords of this forest. Here the prince called his escorts, companions and soldiers and addressing them said, " Return from here ; go back to our city and if my mother asks about me, tell her that I have been devoured by wild tigers of the forest and that before I died, I had asked you to convey my salutes to her.

" If my father asks any news about me, convey to him my respects and tell him that I have been eaten up by a large reptile and that I shall never more return to our dear city."

He stopped here to wipe away a drop of tear that had sprung to his eye and then he rode on his favourite race-horse. The colour of the animal was deep crimson like that of the red *karancha* fruit. Its mouth was a deeper scarlet and looked like vermilion. Swift as a bird was this prince of animals, its two ears stood erect as it marched and its tongue was like a living flame. Its hoofs were of golden colour.

When he rode this noble animal, it flew like an arrow, the wild plants broke under its feet and the army of the prince lay far behind. In the evening he arrived at a village dotted by huts of wood-cutters. He called at the hut of one of these woodmen and said, "Will you, my friend, allow me to sleep in a corner of your house?" There the prince passed the night in that humble house—pleased with the poor man's hospitality. He was there for seven days, taking rest all the while. On the eighth he rode his horse and started for hunting. (Ll. 1-40.)

(4)

On his back hung a quiver full of arrows and in his right hand he held a bow. In the steep jungly path, the horse found obstruction at every step. So the rider alighted and walked on foot. A little time after he saw a beautiful parrot seated on the bough of a tree. On its brow was a yellow mark of the colour of gold and its wings were also of light gold colour. It was of the *Hiraman* species and a peerless bird. The prince thought that it would be a prize if only he could seize it alive, but the bird flew in the air. He followed it with eyes fixed upwards at it and was very fatigued with his walk in the steep jungly path.

Walking in this way for some time, he saw a beautiful damsel before him. She wore a bark dress adorned with leaves and flowers. Her features were faultless and regular, as if finished with a chisel and her colour was of the bright *champak* flower. Her long and dishevelled hair fell behind her back in wild curls decked with flowers, and in one of her hands she held a bow and in another a shaft. The girl too was walking swiftly with her gaze fixed upwards. The prince now followed her with eager steps.

After a little while the prince saw the girl kneel down on the ground. Her right hand was placed on the string of the bow and her left held an arrow. At this stage Prince Mukut saw the parrot quietly seated on the bough of a *Daruk* tree near by. It was half hid behind the new leaves of the tree. Quickly did the prince take the bow in hand, shoot an arrow, which forthwith killed the bird. It fell down on the ground from the bough where it sat. The girl saw the bird in that condition and glanced behind to see who had done this cruel deed.

The Prince.

"Hear me, dear maiden, it is I who have killed your bird. If you are bent on retaliation, kill me, I shall offer no resistance."

She glanced at him and her eyes were fixed. 'Strange! how could this stranger come to this lonely forest of ours?' she thought. She then opened her lips and said, "To this impenetrable forest, how could you come alone and for what purpose? Who are your parents and brothers? What a handsome figure do you possess! I could not even dream of one so beautiful! For myself I know that I am a poor forest-girl living with my parents in this wilderness. My avocation is hunting. I hunt birds and animals and eke out my living in that way. I am an unlucky woman, the daughter of a poor hunter. Why did you kill my pet bird, will you say?"

The prince said, "I am the son of the king of southern countries. In my spacious room called the *Jor-Mandir*, I slept at midnight and saw one night your moon-like face in my dream. It enchanted me and I have been wandering all over the world in quest of you. The pictures of many a princesses have I seen. Paragons of beauty are they. Some of them have the handsome figures of fairies and look jolly like heavenly birds. But they had no attraction for me. So I travelled on, till after having wandered over many a place I have come to this wild forest of yours. I have at last found my dream realised ; the figure I had seen in my sleep, stands before me in flesh and blood.''

The damsel when she heard him, shed tears and said weeping, "Madly hast thou acted, oh handsome prince, by coming to this place. You may lose your life and may not again see your father and mother. Alas, you are not perhaps destined to inherit the kingdom of your father. You are not aware of the wild dwellers of this forest. They are uncultured hunters and kill everyone whom they happen to meet here. They are a set of heartless people. When they meet a man in the way, they aim their sharp arrow which pierces the breast of strangers. They have no heart and are dead to feelings of kindness or sympathy. They are to be dreaded more than the ferocious beasts. Alas, dear prince, my flowing hair is not long or thick enough to hide or cover you within its folds! Had you been my life-blood, fain would I lodge you in my heart of hearts. I would have hid you within me, if you were my life. If you were the balls of my eyes I would have concealed you within my eyelids. You are to me far greater than all these. Life of my life you are. What may I not sacrifice to find a place at those beautiful feet of thine to cover and conceal you from the sight of others!''

She wept and threw away the bow, its string and the arrows. How intense was the love that this wild girl of the forest felt at the first sight. It was not a month, nor even a day; only a few minutes, and the rustic damsel was over head and ears in love, quite overcome with her emotion. She felt like a poor man who suddenly comes to possess a diamond worth the riches of seven kings. She reflected within herself what device she would take recourse to, in order to save the life of the stranger. (Ll. 1-82.)

(5)

For one whole night she kept him concealed under the dense leaves of a *Daruk* tree. The next day she had him hidden in the cavity of a large tree and yet another day she kept him covered with leaves, tendrils and branches of wild plants and the fourth day she kept him behind her hut unseen by others.

Thus did the forest-girl keep him concealed from the hunters who usually came home late at night and left in the early dawn. From this time forth she did not wander a-hunting in the forest. If anyone questioned her about her staying day and night at home, she made the pretext that she was suffering from a severe headache.

She wanted to get away from these ferocious men but could devise no means for it.

But when the prince one day asked her to leave the forest and go to his city, then was she taken by a rapturous joy at this suggestion and resolved to fly away.

One day an opportunity presented itself ; the wild people had gone away far into the very heart of the wilderness when she easily absconded with her lover. (Ll. 1-14.)

(6)

In the southern province there were joy and tumult everywhere. The report went that the prince had returned home taking a forest-woman for his wife. The father was glad and had a nice little pleasure-house built in the midst of a pond where the prince passed day and night with his consort. The house was neat and commodious, and there were golden couches and cushions in it. The attending maids fanned he little queen with mica fans when the weather was hot, and many were the valuable ornaments which the prince had presented her. Her feet were adorned with golden anklets and on her breast she wore á precious garland studded with jewels. On her head there was a crown which shone like stars with a hundred diamonds and she wore a rich *sari* of up-to-date pattern. Hard it will be for me to name all the various ornaments which were given to her. The forest-girl no more looked wild, but with her gay costumes and ornaments appeared as the very nymph of heaven.

The bee is drunken with honey in the spring and giddily did the prince pass April and May in the first intoxication of love. The beauty of the forest-girl did not abate a bit in course of time but increased day by day, and the prince drunken with ever-increasing joy enioyed the company of his wife—unmindful of everything else in the world.

But stop. You will now hear what a tragedy was enacted by the intrigues of the foul enemy.

Now, chorus, dance well, keeping time with my voice by striking your feet against the ground. You will have to sing a song quite different from what you have sung up to now. (Ll. 1-20.)

(7)

One day it was a pleasant time, the wife was serving betels to the prince, and he in the height of love was beside himself with joy, enjoying her company and both seemed happy like a pair of pigeons. Their cup of pleasure, however, was full to the brim.

Be not too much elated over your good fortune, friend, —the fate is behind you at every step and follows you with its inevitable decree. The joy of to-day is but an index to the sorrow of to-morrow. Laugh to-day, as hoarse as you can, to-morrow it may be a different lot, and you may have to weep the whole livelong day.

To-day you are humming a sweet tune, to-morow the song may go and tears may flow.

They will put you in a coffin under the earth. They will dig the earth with their spade and hide you from this world in the oblivious grave. There, no father, no mother will go to visit you and alas! your love for your wife will be a forgotten tale—worms will enter into your body and make a feast of it.

But, my chorus, let us leave this philosophical topic now, and with the permission of the learned audience turn to the topic of the song.

One day, I was relating to you, is it not ?, as to how the pair were enjoying themselves. They were gaily talking in the pleasure-house—the breeze was playing soft over the pond and the evening was slowly passing away—when lo! a poisoned arrow shot by an unknown cruel forester struck the breast of the prince.

His head reeled and instantly he fell unconscious on the floor, vomiting blood. The arrow pierced the breast right through and showed itself from the other end. She took him up in her arms and lamented saying, "Alas! alas! how has he been hit from this unknown enemy! Raise your eyes dear ; is it right that you should go away leaving me here alone ? I have no parents, no brother, none here to call me their own. I was like a wild bird living in forest. You trained me to the ways of domestic life. I was caged in this beautiful palace, and woe to me that my dream of happiness is all over so soon. Friend, allow me to depart from this world instead! Pray you live long and may I at the hour of my death see you happy."

She placed her lips on his and kissed him again and again. Her tears flew without ceasing and covered his face.

"A stranger here am I," she said, "and I know not the temper of your people yet. I was just going to learn your ways and manners. When to-morrow morning your mother will question me about you, what reply shall I give to her enquiries? What consolation shall I offer to her?

"The people of this vast kingdom will put the same question and what reply am I to make to them? The citizens will abuse me—they will openly call me a witch, a murderess of husband."

She lamented thus and in the pleasure-house passed the night in bitter agony.

In the morning, everyone came to learn the bitter truth. Round the corpse of the son gathered his father, mother and relations. Crying and lamenting, the maids and male attendants lamented wildly rolling on the ground. The ministers, the courtiers, and all were struck with grief and charged Providence with cruelty.

The king sat in judgment and said to the forest-girl, "How did my son die?" Her words were not believed by him. The courtiers suggested that she should be put in chains. They said that she was a monster who lived on human flesh. She had killed the prince with a view to eat his dead body.

The Raja discussed the case fully with his ministers. By the order of the king a large wooden chest was constructed. The corpse of the prince was laid in it and along with it the girl, bound hand and foot, was placed by his side.

The chest was locked up. It was thrown into the river and away it went floating.

Two fishermen had cast a net and the chest was caught in it. They drew it to the land and when they opened it they found a dead body and a living person inside! They were frightened with the sight of this strange love between the living and the dead, and fled away in all haste, struck with fear.

The girl came out of the coffin, taking the corpse with her. She lifted him up and placed him on her shoulders. In this state she wandered like a mad woman in the shades of the deep forest. She cried and lamented, saying :—

" Awake, my dear! Open these beautiful eyes once again! I had no father, no mother, and no brother—unlucky forest-people that we are, cruel is our destiny and I regret it not. It seems that I got a kingdom in a dream and have become a begger in another! Yea, my whole life seems to me to be a strange dream! But little do I care for the kingdom I have lost. I will embrace the forest-life again and be once more happy—if I can get you back. Oh Lord! oh God! where art Thou ? Take mercy on this poor forlorn daughter of yours and accept my humble salute." (Ll. 1-90.)

(8)

Above seven regions from this earth there is the golden palace of God. He was seated on His throne in His absolute Majesty. The laments of the unhappy girl reached His throne and it shook.

God called unto him thirty of His recognised saints. He addressed the Prophet and said, "The princess of Neoga is in deep distress losing her husband. Go thither and save her life by restoring life to the dead prince."

The worms that had swarmed on the corpse slowly ate it up. With her own hands she threw them away. The flesh gradually left the bones. Yet she cried, "Oh husband, oh my life of life!" There came to her thirty prophets sent by God at this stage. They said to the girl, "Your father, dear girl, is the king of Neoga, you have suffered a great deal in your wild career in the forest. By the will of the Creator, we will restore your husband to life. Go to thy father's city at Neoga. Leave us alone. You should not see the process of restoration. Human eyes should not behold that sight. The saints can give life and they can also take it. But the process is mysterious and if witnessed by human eyes, the work may fail and life may not come to the dead body. We will restore life to your husband in the very depth of this jungle-land and not even a bird will know of it."

The girl fell on the ground at these words of the saints, saying, "How shall I know that my husband has got life ?"

Meantime the Prophet Rasul gathered the bones and restored them to their right place. Then they all uttered incantations and bone joined to bone and flesh grew upon the skeleton.

Then did the saints again utter incantations and the body was covered with skin.

At this stage the saints said, "Now you have seen enough of our feats, and we believe you can now place faith on our action. You may now leave the forest. Go straight to the city of Neoga. We will now give life to your husband."

Then did the prophets call the Fairy-lord Navi, who came thither instantly and carried away the girl through the air to the city of Neoga. (Ll. 1-41.)

(9)

The dead prince is restored to life. Who can expect a fortune like this? Raja Shilla is now happy beyond measure.

The prince hastened to his pleasure-house in the pond to meet his dear wife. But there he did not find her. He enquired of his father and others. He examined and cross-examined all the relatives and servants of the palace. But no one said anything. He felt sure that she was killed. But who was it that did such a foul act? Like life she was to him—who was it that had deprived him of his best treasure on the earth. He gave up food and drink and turned stark mad. Again the palace turned sorrowful. Dark cloud covered sun's rays. Full moon's light was now extinct from the sky.

The royal drum beat in public places announcing the gift of half the kingdom to one who would be able to cure the prince of his insanity.

The drum beat north and south, it beat east and west.—The messengers were sent to the countries far and near. (Ll. 1-16.)

(10)

In the meantime, a word about the Raja of Neoga. The princess who was lost had returned. The city was smiling with joy, so handsome looked the princess that wherever she went, she carried light and joy with her, she was fully grown up and the king, her father sought a suitable bridegroom for her. With her portrait did he send many a match-maker to countries far and near.

At this time the drummers sent from Raja Shilla, came to Neoga, announcing the reward for the cure of the prince. The Pir was there. He appeared in the market-place and touched the drum. He was brought to the Raja Shilla. When questioned, he said that he would assuredly cure the prince. The remedy he suggested was that Prince Mukut would at once be married to the princess of Neoga. This done, he would regain his senses at once.

Messengers were forthwith sent and the portrait of the princess of Neoga was secured. He who was looking aghast and abstract-minded, fixed his eyes on the picture and was all attention for some time. And then he placed it on his breast and began to shed unceasing tears.

He lamented, saying, "This is the portrait of the dear one. Alas, who has killed her! My father and mother have turned my enemies. Who is there in this world whom I may call my friend? None. They have thrown my life of life, my bone of bone into the river. Alas! alas! I shall leave this unholy palace of Shilla Raja."

Thus the prince lamented, beating his forehead with his hand. Here also a scene similar to this was enacted at Neoga. The princess had turned mad. She had also left food and drink and with her teeth tore off her valuable *saris*. She dressed herself scantily and did not make her hair. "Oh my husband, oh my heart of hearts" was the cry that incessantly came from her lips.

The king of Neoga was sad. He also ordered a drum to be beaten announcing the reward of his kingdom to the person who would cure the princess. The sound of the drum went far and near, in the jungles and in the cities and the same Pir touched the drum promising the cure of the princess.

The princess of Neoga was thus brought again to Prince Mukut.

Their happiness now was beyond measure. The *Hiraman* had now found its own *Shari*. The snake had found its crest-jewel. The blind man, all on a sudden, had got back his sight! (Ll. 1-54.)

(11)

Then Raja Shilla fell at the feet of the Pir and said, "I have got my son through your kindness. Say, what part of my kingdom, what riches shall I offer you as reward?" The Pir said, "I am a *Fakir*, what shall I do with riches?"

The Raja came to know the wonderful powers of the Pir. He at once read the Kalma and turned a Mahomedan convert. The king of Neoga also did the same. They accepted Islam with all their citizens. Thus did the *Kafers* find the true light.

Oh my brethren take the name of Allah and believe in the Prophet. Read the sacred scriptures. You will sin if you do not do so. You are taking pride in your youth—but know that God and His Prophet are true, all the rest are vanity. To-day I see a smile on your lips ; wait till the noontide of to-morrow, the gloom of sorrow will darken your face. To-day you are enjoying a short hour of pleasure in fickle things but to-morrow the world will present a dark picture to your eyes. They will dig a grave for you with a spade ; when you will be put therein, they will cover you with earth. Then in that dismal hour you will see none near you, neither your father, nor your mother! Your body will be eaten up by worms. Alas, where will all these pleasures of the fleeting world go?

Oh my learned brethren, take the name of Allah and sing His glory. He alone is true in this vast world. The smiles and tears are all for a day only. Alas, who is your friend? For whom do you weep and regret? This relationship with all its joys and sorrows is unreal. There is yet time, brethren. Throw yourself upon the mercy of your Preceptor. There is yet time, brethren. Resign yourself to the will of God.

We have now finished the story of the southern country. I will now relate to you one of the east, the country of the *Kafers*. (Ll. 1-31.)

THE BALLAD OF NASAR MALUM

PREFACE TO THE BALLAD OF NASAR MALUM

Nasar Malum is a ballad which like Nuranneha has been collected by Babu Ashutosh Chowdhury from Chittagong sea-side. He first collected a portion of it from one Nur Hassan Bhaia of the village Kathal Bhanga under the Police Station Raujan in Chittagong. 'Bhaia' or Bhabuk (*lit.* thoughtful, but it may also be a corruption of the word *Bhrātā,* brother) is the title of the members of a family of minstrels of which Nur Hassan is a scion. Nur Hassan's father Korban Ali and grandfather Haidar Ali were distinguished minstrels whose vocation was to sing ballads in the country-side. Nasar Malum was the most favourite ballad of these minstrels and Haidar specially achieved a high reputation as a singer of this pathetic song. Many a night a large crowd of peasantry sat around this remarkable minstrel, spell-bound by the pathos of the ballad. Nur Hassan also sings this ballad, but though he follows the vocation of his ancestors he is no expert. Besides, he remembers only scraps which he anyhow patches up and completes the tale by adding episodes of his own inferior composition. The chief quality of his song is his musical voice.

Ashu Babu got little help from him beyond noting down the small original scraps. But he got a summary of the tale from this minstrel and then tried other sources to complete it. He went to the village of Maishamura where he got a further clue. Maishamura is a village very adjacent to Kathal Bhanga. There a man named Gura Mia who was known to be a *hāri gāin* (a singer of *sāri* songs) supplied him with some further stanzas of the ballad of 'Nasar Malum.' Chowdhury journeyed over a large tract on the sea-coast and at the junction of the river Karnafuli with the Bay he happened to meet Rahaman Ali, the captain of a *shampan*. This man knew the whole ballad. With his help he revised the collection he had already made and completed the ballad. I got it from him in its present shape in May, 1929.

It is so difficult to reproduce the pathos and the exquisite poetry of an old Bengali ballad in English that the translator is always conscious of his limitations. I have highly enjoyed it in the original and as I am revising the translation I am sorry to find a considerable part of the charm of this old-world song lost. The pathos created by the distress of Nasar Malum and the navigators' troubles over a ruffled sea,—the scenes of storm sweeping over the vast waters and the condition of a small boat trembling over its high-swollen waves like an aspen leaf—all this is presented with the vividness of a picturesque natural phenomenon disclosed all on a sudden by a flash of lightning. The *harmads* attired in short-coats and equipped with scabbards, guns and telescopes are brought before our eyes in living colours in the original ballad which is so concise and epigrammatic that it hardly contains a passage which requires a pruning. The writer undoubtedly had a first-hand knowledge of the subject he treated to be able to make his descriptions so vivid and life-like.

Though it is a realistic poem it reaches an idealistic level in its last part. The meeting of the lovers after years of separation, both reduced to the extreme point of misery, is so full of pathos that it will be difficult for the reader to restrain his tears. The lover who, yielding to a youthful impulse, turned treacherous for a while and forgot a love which was ever true and pure, comes later on to know the value of his loyal wife's constancy after passing through bitter experiences—the high price by which he acquired this wisdom; and the last two lines of the ballad show by a gesture that he had now learned the value of his own great treasure never to make a mistake in life again. Great credit is due to the poet for the artistic finish of the tale. No amount of description, however poetic, could suggest the happy end as powerfully as these two short lines do.

The incidental accounts of various places, peoples, articles of trade and other things, specially of the cruel atrocities committed by the *harmads* with which the ballad abounds are full of interest and give us a clue to many historical facts some of which I am going to mention below.

The *harmads* (a word derived from Armada—the Portuguese term for their great naval fleets) originally signified in Bengali the Portuguese robbers who carried on depredations on the Bay and its adjacent lands. The Portuguese robbers in course of time became an ally of the Arakanese. So latterly more often the word *harmads* denoted the Arakanese robbers who became dreaded in the country for their tyranny early in the 17th century. The word was thus used in a more comprehensive sense implying both the Portuguese and the Arakanese pirates. They are described as wearing black trousers, red coats and turbans on their head. They kept scabbards bound to their waist-belts and had guns in their hands. Some of them carried telescopes by which they surveyed the merchant-ships in the Bay from a distance.

This ballad belongs to a period well-known in the history of Chittagong. It relates to incidents occurring during the reign of Shaista Khan (brother of Nurjehan) who collected a fleet of boats and an army of 13,000 men (India Records, Vol. III, Bd. 1664) for conquering Chittagong. The fleet marched from Dacca and after storming the forts of Ingdia and Alumgir-nagore took possession of Sandwip which had been held by the Arakanese for a number of years.

The Portuguese were in the employ of the Arakanese king Sudharma. Some of them were bribed by Shaista Khan and induced to join him. The Moghul army proceeded to the city of Chittagong which was conquered by Shaista Khan and its name was changed to Islamabad. The king of Arakan had a powerful navy consisting of 200 galleys with a large number of small boats. "It is a most surprising thing," says Tavernier, "to see with what speed these galleys are propelled by oars. Some of them are so long that they have up to 50 oars on each side but there are not more than two men to each oar. You see some which are much decorated—where the gold and azure have not been spared."

In spite of a large array of the pirates, the Arakan army could not hold its own against the skill and superior mode of warfare of the Moghul army. The precipitous haste with which the Arakanese fled from the aggressive Moghul army is a celebrated episode in the history of Chittagong and is called Magh Dhauni (*lit.* the retreat of the Maghs). We have some description of the Magh Dhauni in this ballad. It is well-known that the Maghs while fleeing towards the south buried their great wealth in particular places of which they kept records in mysterious signs known to themselves alone. Long after peace had been restored in the country they came back in parties in quest of the treasure and sometimes dug up the wealth from underground.

There is mention of one such case in this ballad. In recent years many bronze and bell-metal statues have been discovered from underground near Deogaon—evidently buried there during the course of this flight of the Maghs. They were found huddled up together in a place and no part of these statues was broken. Most of these are statues of the Buddha. In a few cases other images such as that of Ganesh were also found. The terrible account of the sufferings of the Maghs during this Magh Dhauni is still fresh in the memory of many old men of the country who heard it from their ancestors having first-hand knowledge of them.

The Arakanese kings, whose army of robbers and sea-pirates was a terror to the country, despite these oppressions, patronised religion and did other good works. Their friendship with the Portuguese is well-known. I subjoin below a letter which will show that a king of Arakan built at Chittagong at his own cost a Catholic church and allotted a yearly endowment towards its maintenance for the benefit of Portuguese Christians who enjoyed great favour in his court.

BISHOP'S HOUSE,
RAMNA, DACCA.

Dated 16th August, 1929.

FROM

RT. REVEREND J. LEGRAND, C.S.C.,
BISHOP of DACCA,

To

REVEREND MOTHER AMBROSE PROVINCIAL,
THE CONVENT, CHITTAGONG.

DEAR REVEREND MOTHER,

Relative to the title of the Mission to the grounds on which stand the St. Schelastica's Convent School, Chittagong, I beg to say that the Mission is in possession of these grounds as also the site of the church, the cemetery and the St. Placid's School from time immemorial, at least two hundred years. The whole area of Bandel on which the Mission stands and of which St. Schelastica's grounds form a part was donated to the Mission by the King of Arakan in return for services rendered him by the Christian community of Chittagong.

The British Government when it took over the administration of Arakan also honoured the commitment of the former native administration. Hence the Chittagong Government treasury to this day pays the Roman Catholic Chaplain of Chittagong the amount granted to the Chaplain by the King of Arakan.

When the residence of the Bishop was burnt down in Chittagong, the Mission archives were destroyed. This explains the regrettable loss of all the old documents. The Bishop's residence itself occupied the very site which you desire to make over to Government. The title of the possession of the Mission property has never been called in question and the fact that Government has accepted the liability of the Arakan Ruler in the matter of salary to the Roman Catholic Chaplain of Chittagong may be taken as proof that the Government of the day equally honoured the gift of land made by the Arakan King.

I do not know if documentary evidence is available, but surely a prescriptive title of over two hundred years' quiet possession suffices to establish the right of the Roman Catholic Mission to the grounds in question.

I remain, Dear Revd. Mother,
Yours sincerely,
J. LEGRAND, C.S.C.,
Bishop of Dacca.

Portuguese pirates—the Harmads—had occupied the Sandwip under their leader Gonzales about 1638 and he carried on depredations on such an extensive scale that the merchant-vessels for a long time ceased to carry on trade in that part of the Bay. It was during this time that one Mukut Roy, a Magh chief, was the master of Chittagong and an ally of the Arakanese King.

Some notes are necessary for geographical references found in this ballad. The place named 'Dianger Pari' (দিয়াঙ্গের পাড়ি) is evidently that part of the Bay which is adjacent to the celebrated port 'Deung' (দেয়াঙ্গ). In the records left by the Portuguese we have often found mention of the Port Dyanga (ডায়াঙ্গ).

The islet Gobadhya (গোবধ্যা) mentioned in the ballad stands near the junction of the Karnafuli with the Bay. It is often submerged under water when there is an overflow of the river. But it reappears as a shoal soon after and in consequence cannot give a sense of security to settlers, but it serves the purpose of a convenient resort of the gangs of pirates wandering in the Bay. These pirates after the defeat of the Arakanese king lost possession of all their centres of activities and carried on their depredations on a smaller scale lying hid in shoals and corners near the sea-coast.

Pari Dia or Shaha Pari Dia (Dwip) as it is now called, is an island lying about 150 miles to the south of Chittagong. Formerly it was an important centre of trade. Its trade of *Laukha* fish was once very flourishing. The town of Angi seems to be a port of Burma.

DINESH CHANDRA SEN

The Ballad of Nasar Malum

(1)

Prayer and Benediction.

First of all do I bow down to the Great Allah ; next do I pay obeisance to the Prophet—the giver of light.

No space in this vast world have I to call my home. From place to place do I wander without any fixed abode. I am not trained in music—its modes, measures and tunes are unknown to me. When my master sang I fortunately got a seat near him in order to keep chorus. I can reproduce from memory some songs that I heard from him. I have adopted singing of ballads in the houses of rich folk as my calling, and thanks to the blessing of you all, I am able to eke out a living by this means. (Ll. 1-8.)

(2)

The Heroine's Laments.

Chorus—" The separation from love in the rainy season."

The honey stored in your house is enjoyed by strangers, while you, oh fool, wander in foreign countries like a vagabond.

The storm has arisen and there is drizzling rain all around. Merrily do the *koi* fish lift their head over the surface of the stream. In this season who will be my companion of the night ? The cold comes creeping into my very bones which tremble by its force. I cover myself with a cotton *kantha* to warm myself. But what medicine is there to remove the pain of my heart (caused by parting from you) ?

The thunder rolls above and the sky seems to break and fall down on me. How can I in this season live all alone in my hut ? The water overflows the banks of the pond near my house, unable to contain itself, but to whom am I to tell the tale of my grief when it overflows my heart?

The plants grow plentiful where the land is high, but the plants of my hope nourished in childhood are all destroyed by the stream of my ill-luck.

The fish drinks the drops that fall from heaven (when water is scarce below). Alas ! there is none above to give me sweet drops of hope or consolation in this lonely hour !

The *jhinga* plant affords shelter to the sparrow and its mate. They fly here and there in daytime in quest of food but they long for union and rest in the hours of night.

When he went away he gave a hope of return in two months. Two years, alas ! have passed. Cruel separation like tiger is gnawing my heart but if a real tiger comes, fain would I offer myself to be killed by it !

The youth of a woman is like flow-tide in a river; for a time it swells up overflowing the banks, but when it subsides there is an end of all attraction that the river boasts of.

The sword unused gets rusty. The uncultivated soil is overgrown with wild plants. Eat rice when it is warm ; there is no joy in taking it when it is cold.

If my youth fades what good will ensue by your return? My bodice of *satin* once fitted my body tightly—now it is getting loose. Look, the lustre of my youth is waning by degrees.

The bracelets of my wrists are loose as I am getting thinner. Anxieties and pain of separation are, as it were, drinking my life-blood.

The neighbours are quick in spreading all sorts of scandal and they are whispering many a tale to my parents who seem inclined to get a divorce for me from my husband.

There is no lack of bees to hum their tales of love to the flower which is your own and of none else. Alas to what distant shores have you gone? For whom are you earning money? Fie on your desire for wealth. The thieves are watching for opportunity to loot your store. For what purpose have you gone to foreign lands? Tell me, my darling! If I die now, you will be responsible to God for my death. I am not your mistress, nor was I married under the *Shanga* system. Alas! being your true and legitimate wife why am I doomed to all these cruel freaks of luck? (Ll. 1-44.)

(3)

Their Early Life.

Amina Khatun is the only daugher of her father. For six long years she has been separated from her husband. Alas what should she do now!

Their home lies in the village Majergaon. Haider is her father's name. He is a poor man living from hand to mouth as a day-labourer. He owns no land, nor has he any plough or bullock of his own. He builds straw-sheds for other people and thus gets a living; many a day does he fast for lack of food. He got a son-in-law but, as already stated, for six long years the young man has gone away from home and no clue have they got yet as to his whereabouts.

The name of this son-in-law is Nasar. He is the son of Haider's sister. This young man is the cause of poor Amina's sorrows. I shall relate here the story as to how the nephew became the son-in-law.

When Nasar was still in the womb of his mother, his father died. The mother passed through all conçeivable worry and trouble to bring him up.

To add to his ill-luck the boy lost his mother when only five years old and from that time was brought up in his uncle's home.

Nasar was older than Amina by two years ; and Amina even as a little girl loved him with all her heart. The poor income they had was scarcely sufficient but still the pair were cheerful and happy in each other's company.

Nasar made toy-boats with banana leaves and floated them in the pond. Thus the two played when mere children, and they talked, walked and ate together. Like the dove and its mate they remained together and could not bear separation.

The girl became now a maiden of sixteen. Youth with all its charm appeared in her person. The rose bloomed and the bee's mind was drunk with its honied fragrance. The young plant grows in the corner of the ground,-from where it draws its life-giving juice is not unknown to the roots. The serpent knows its own jewel on the hood and the frog knows when the rain will come. When one's heart feels the first attraction of love it does not take a long time for others to discover it.

The lad looked plump and sprightly and was in his full youthful vigour. Amina's mother at this time made him her son-in-law. They had no son, no lands—nothing to call their own. The daughter was now the only prop of the family. (Ll. 1-38.)

(4)

Esak pursues Amina.

Howsoever tenderly the young one of a cuckoo might be brought up in the nest of a crow it forgets its debt to the latter. It was sheer ill-luck that led Nasar to leave this house of his father-in-law which had given him shelter when he had none.

The parents felt sharp pangs of despair when they thought of their daughter Amina. Alas who will give her a shelter hereafter? "For six years," they thought, "Nasar has gone away. Alas! when we shall be no more, to whom would Amina go seeking help?"

The birds *maina* and *salik* discover paddy-seeds from the ground and pick them up. In the depth of the pond the fishes find out a hole for dwelling. The lover follows the course of his own mind in the same way. The bee is drawn by the flower when it blooms and unperceived by others, yearns for it with all its heart.

The young man Esak secretly feels the pangs of love and often does he come to the house of Haider on some pretext or other.

Amina's father has gone away from home to attend his daily-work and the mother is also out to the river-ghat. Amina is all alone in the house.

The moment is opportune. Esak comes with a bottle of scented cocoanut oil and a bundle of betels. He knocks at the door and asks Amina to open it. He makes gestures to her with his eyes but Amina seems not to understand what he hints at. With head bent low under a veil she comes with a pipe and betel and offers these to Esak. As a fisherman throws a net at a distance and makes the near water muddy in order to drive the fish towards the net, even so does Esak take recourse to many a wily manœuvre to win the girl's heart. But howsoever hard you may try, oil will not mix with water, nor sugar with salt. Esak and Amina were made likewise of opposite metals. They were not meant to be one. (Ll. 1-28.)

(5)

His Offers.

Esak's home stood in the middle of the village. He belonged to a house with high traditions. They were opulent and influential. In the spacious compound of his house a big bed-room stood with four slanting roofs. Round the homestead was a large ditch protecting the house from outside. There was a beautiful room with eight slanting roofs made of *ulu* grass facing the tank near the inner apartments, which was 15 feet deep. Esak was already a married man ; his wife Mamazam was as beautiful as the full moon. She was born of a high family but, despite all, Esak did not find pleasure in her company. No one can tell the secret course of love—the origin and growth of love is a mystery. Some find joy in drinking milk and others wine.

Ever since Esak saw Amina Khatun he fell in desperate love. It pierced his heart like a spear. The pangs are not to be healed or suppressed—the more one tries to do so, the greater is the hurt one causes to oneself.

Esak could not bear the anguish of his heart any longer. He approached Haider one day and opened his mind to him. " My heart," he said, " breaks at the thought of Amina's sorrows. If she agrees to marry me I will take the charge of maintenance of her parents on myself for life. On the fertile banks of the Sankha I will give you eight *kanis* of land. The ears and the nose of Amina will glitter with gold-flowerets weighing a tola each. She will have a gold crown with jewelled pendants for her head and valuable bracelets for her hands. You have become old and it does not become you to labour hard. Ill can you in the present condition bear the weight of anxieties for Amina. I will make you completely free from all anxieties for the sake of yourself and of Amina.

Haider bent down his head for a little time and thought over the matter. He then said, " Will you treat Amina as a slave?"

Esak said, " This can never be. If she is to be treated as a slave what will people say of the high prestige of our family at such a treatment of one who is to be my lawful wife? I will present you with eight *kanis* of land, and cover her head, arms and ears with jewels and gold."

Haider said, " All right. Inclined am I to favour your proposal. The final word of consent I will give you on knowing the mind of my people."

The mother came and spoke to Amina all about this proposal.

Amina sat bending her head downwards. She lifted not her head, nor said a word. But so afflicted was she by the offer that for four days she did not take her usual meals, nor slept at night. (Ll. 1-40.)

(6)

The Magician and His Art.

In that village there was a man named Budha—an expert magician was he. He performed hideous rites, and it is said, by exorcisms, mantras, and incantations could do marvels. A woman suffering from delivery pain was easily cured if she took a little from the betel-leaf made potent by his magic touch. He sold lockets of wonderful power, which if a woman wore, she forgot her home and hearth, and a man who wore it gained his wishes in no time. His locket had such high efficacy that one wishing to win the heart of a perfect stranger could easily do so by its power. Its charm, if he so desired, would create ill-feelings between two linked together by the warmest affection and they would fall out with one another in no time. If it was new moon on a certain Saturday or Tuesday, Budha would go hunting after some roots of plants. He gathered curling hair from a woman's head and a portion from the crown she wore on the night of marriage, nails cut off from one's fingers, and a few threads from a woman's *sari*—all these he packed together in a bundle and imparted power to the ingredients and thus made an infallible remedy for which night and day people thronged at the house of Budha the magician and healer.

Some one came with a cup of vegetable oil, others with betels for being turned efficacious by the touch of this man and they presented him with baskets full of brinjals and other edibles. They offered him fine rice, esculent roots and sundries in profuse quantities, and Budha was right glad in accepting these gifts from people, with outstretched hands. (Ll. 1-18.)

Esak and Budha.

So it turned very well for Budha's trade all these long years. He took excellent rice and curry of fish in the day time, he drank cupful of buffalo's milk and in the night he was served with curd and butter. His granaries were full of rice and his chest full of gold and silver. By the trade of a magician Budha had become a man of great power and riches. His fame had spread far and near, and attracted by his name Esak one day approached him.

In his heart there was fire, and his face blushed with shame. Half by gestures and half by words and partly by movements of his head Esak tried to explain his mission to the magician, for he lacked expression to speak out his mind.

Budha.

"Well master, what it is that has brought you to me! I understand that some lady is at the root of all your trouble. Will you tell me who she is?"

Esak.

"It is Haider's daughter. You know, sir, that this man is my close neighbour—his house stands to the north of the path leading to the market-place. I must at any cost get his daughter Amina. Save me, oh Prophet, from the pangs of death which I am suffering. Tell me the means of winning her. I can tell you, sir, in confidence, since this flame of love has grown in my breast I have lost all taste for food, and when I go to sleep it is her thought that occupies me and upsets all my attempts to close my eyes.

"Ten *drons* of land, twenty buffaloes with adequate implements of cultivation will I give you and rest assured, sir, that whatever money you may reasonably expect from me you will get in full—not a whit less than your expectations. The rats are destroying the rice stored in my granaries. Alas! I have no heart to watch them and do other duties of the field; Amina is the sole object of my thought and my mind is full of bitter sorrow for her."

Budha.

"Early in the morning to-morrow, go to the house of Nasir, when he will set his bullocks for extracting oil. Watch the process. You are to fetch from there the first seven drops of oil that will come out of his grinding machine.

"On next Saturday bring these seven drops in a phial to me—I will apply my magic to these and then I will see how the beautiful Amina would resist the power of my charm."

Esak lost all patience. Like a bird feeling a desire to fly, his mind became restless and found no joy in home-life.

Like the flood during the rains rushing onwards without knowing which way it will flow, his mind was unsettled and wanted to break a new path for seeking happiness, not knowing which turn it should take.

His mind was void of pleasure and he scarcely spoke; but like a sly cat seeking the hole of rats, his mind was in quest of some secret means to find its goal.

He now frequently called on Budha and opened his mind freely to him and discussed ways and means to win Amina Bibi. (Ll. 1-34.)

(7)

The Manœuvres of Parents and Amina's Flight.

In the meantime the parents of Amina one day said to her, "Wait in the house ; we will go to pay a visit to a relation of ours. Our stay, dear daughter, will be short and we will return by evening at the utmost."

Clad in a striped *lungi* and with a black coat on, Esak looked at a mirror while putting his cap in the right place on his head. He rubbed the magic oil given by Budha on his face. Dressed in a decent attire Esak came out of his house.

The sun had just set and darkness was slowly covering the earth. In the horizon the thin crescent-shaped disk of the moon had just appeared. Esak cast his glance behind him now and then, and steadily advanced towards the house of Haider.

The door was shut from outside, and in the house there was no lamp. Esak stayed outside. Alas! the magic oil lost all efficacy, where was the girl gone to? On the shoal the fisherman had placed food to tempt the fish, but it did not turn up. The *kheda* was ready, but the wild elephant did not enter it. The bird *dahuk* escaped the trap laid for it. The monkey did not fall into the net spread for it,—the banana that was placed to tempt it failed to attract.

Esak walked all round the house the whole of the night, expecting the return of Amina. The gnats attacked him and drank his blood all the time. In the morning the disappointed youth returned home in a dejected spirit.

Now when the time for supper was up the parents returned home but found the house vacant. Near the door Amina had left her two ear-rings. She had also left her *satin* bodice and the nose-ornament that she used to wear.

"Oh my parrot! what pain, what grief seized you that you cut open the bars of the cage and to which land have you flown away in the darkness of the evening!"

We will here stop the narrative of Amina and resume the story of Nasir. (Ll. 1-30.)

(8)

Vicissitudes of Fortune: Nasir's New Life in a Strange Land.

In the port of Chittagong there was a fine sloop called '*Rome.*' Nasir had become the captain of this ship. The king Shekendar was making a chart of the sea for the passage of his ships over the deep. The chart was prepared by the king with the help of a bird called Hiramon which had a miraculous power—it could indicate where the sea was deep and where its water was shallow. The best sailors were engaged to steer the sloop aright. Nasir at first appointed as a Laskar gradually showed his singular merits and made a map to the full satisfaction of the king

Shekendar. He was raised to the post of captain and his fame spread far and near for expertness in steering the ships. He could observe the stars and study the weather. He was infallible in finding the right way through the deep. From the motion of the wind, he could presage a coming storm. From the position of a Laskar he became a captain and amassed large wealth. At this stage he went to the southern islands and built at a port called Angi a house on the sea-coast.

Here Nasir the captain became a dealer of various goods. This port was inhabited by a strange people. The women were devoid of all sense of modesty and did not observe the customs of zenana. The male members of the house cooked meals and did other duties of the kitchen, and the women went out for marketing. They would not relish fresh fish preferring Nappi—the rotten fish, in their dinners.

One gets nausea if one hears what these people eat. They fry 'কেয়ালিস আঁজিলা' in oil and eat them. The women wear rich *khami* cloth but only three and a half feet long which they wrap round their waists in a single fold. They crop their hair in the *babri* fashion used elsewhere by men and cover their breast with an *angi* (a sort of blouse). They keep betels in small boxes with them and offer these to strangers while they attract them with many a gesture. Generally they are handsome and their *babri* hair they bind into a fold in the manner of a *Kadamba* flower on their heads. Verily their breasts look like ripe *Narenga* fruits (oranges). Beautiful golden ear-rings called *Nadhang* move to and fro as they slowly walk in the public streets and they frequently cast their glances on passers by, winning them by their smile.

When Nasir came to this country where women were in power, he could not resist the charm of the young ladies of the place.

In this town of Angi there lived a person of great influence and wealth. His name was Mafo. He had a daughter whose beauty was the subject of talk everywhere; she was sixteen years old and her colour was bright as that of a *champak* flower. Youth gave her a sprightliness which made her gait attractive to everyone who saw her walking in the public street in gay steps.

Mafo had amassed wealth by selling dried fish. Nasar visited his house one day. He saw Akhim preparing betels in a corner of the big hall of her father. A charm played on her face like moon-beams and there was a sweet smile on her lips. As she glanced here and there her eyes moved playfully winning the minds of youngmen by the charm of her brows. Her colour bright as that of a *champak* flower fascinated Nasir's mind. The three letters পি-রী-তি (love) have a mysterious force. One who yields to their fascination becomes lost to all sense of shame and honour. Night and day Nasar visits now the house of Mafo. He thought not of his home which he had deserted, nor of his own beautiful Amina who pined there in his absence. He forgot all the little joys and sorrows shared by each in their childhood, he forgot that smiling face of Amina which was once his sole joy of life. He forgot his old playmates of home and all associations of the past. His mind was now filled with one image—it was that of Akhim who had maddened him with her beauty.

One evening Mafo was not at home and Nasar came to his house. Akhim was alone there and she offered him a betel with some significant gestures. Nasir felt a desire which he could hardly resist. In fact both felt that day that their love was mutual and that they had advanced too far to recede.

The jeweller knows the quality of stone, and the goldsmith knows his gold. When in love one can feel the other's mind fully. The tiller knows the soil he tills and the boatman the current of the canal through which he passes. An expert musician knows how to keep time with a song. A trader knows his business and a rich man knows the value of money. One who has tasted the joys of love knows full well the value of one's beloved who has won his heart. An expert captain can perceive the approaches to a shoal from a distance. Nasar in the same way, though he was a stranger, knew what metal fair Akhim was made of, and prized her.

Mafo the noble citizen watched the process of this love-affair with interest and then consented to his daughter's marriage with Nasar according to the rites and ceremonies prevalent in that country.

There is no trust in the cows near a hill (any moment they may be seized by a tiger) and there is no trust in the houses, however magnificent, on the banks of a large river,[1] no trust in the wife of a Mahomedan and in the beard of a Hindu.[2] In all these there is no trust, no security. I warn you my audience—do not believe in them.

Nasar was now steeped in joy getting this young lady for his wife. Alas! how could he forget Amina who was the life of his life—only a few days ago! (Ll. 1-78.)

(9)

Amina's Sorrows.

Oh, my boatman for what shore are you bound, plying your oar in the ebb-tide? On the banks of the river flowing near my father's home there are mango-trees in rows

[1] In Bengal especially, cities have often been swept away by the force of the current. The Padma has thus swept away many a flourishing city like Sripur, Rajnagar and others.

[2] This refers to the system of divorce and widow-marriage owing to which, according to popular notion, a husband's position is not as secure in the Mahomedan society as it is amongst the Hindus. It is curious that a Mahomedan writer passes a

which yield crops of fruits in profusion and the jacks are to be seen plentiful in their proper season. The long gourd I saw full-grown in the compound of our home; alas! I do not know what has become of it! There are pitchers in my home full of water and from them I quenched my thirst—how often my thirsty lips wish for a cup of water from them again! In that house of ours there is a Karai tree the leaves of which make a rustling sound, when the wind passes through them. My mind yearns for a sight of that old dear Karai tree! Oh brother boatman, tell my parents if you happen to meet them, that I am willing to go again to my home which I have left—so that I may dine with them as of old.

I have left my home alas! owing to the intrigues of that wicked man who has behaved as a foe. But my ill-luck has been mainly created by Nasar. He is alive but I pass my days like a widow—it is all for that cruel husband of mine.

Oh my parents! you reared me up from childhood with great affection—but at the end you have caused me great sorrow. What would you, alas, do with eight *kanis* of land on the fertile banks of the Sankha? There is a deep wound in my breast. How can the pain be assuaged by wearing golden ornaments? What shall I do with buffaloes, ploughs and acres of land? I could feed you by husking rice in the houses of neighbours and doing other jobs for them. You tried to pick up the spear that had pierced my breast, but in your attempt to do so, you have, oh my parents, made the sore more painful and the point of the spear has penetrated deeper into the region of my heart! I have already sold my heart to one and can it be possible for me to give it again to another? I have suffered greatly though I am

sneer on the marriage system of his own community. The wearing of the beard with a Mahomedan according to his religion is a compulsion, with a Hindu it is at best a fancy. He may do away with it at his sweet will.

yet quite a young girl. How can I preserve my youth for my husband from the inevitable decay to which it is doomed!

Youth with a woman is not like a fruit to be eaten and enjoyed by all ; it is not a commodity of the market to be sold ; neither is it a piece of fortune which may be distributed as presents amongst friends and relations. Oh my parents, you cannot understand what stuff my mind is made of.

(10)

Thus did beautiful Amina indulge in her grief. Sitting on the bank of a river and recollecting her father and mother she cried day and night. Two months passed since she had left her father's home and during this time her suffering was great.

Many a village, many a river and canal she passed through. Many wicked men, unscrupulous youths of loose morals, tempted her—but though her trouble was great for a time, none could touch a hair of her head. When a small river runs to the sea who can obstruct it? One cannot get the moon in his hand though he stretches his hand for it. The greatest wealth of a woman is her character ; if she is sincerely bent on keeping it unsoiled, there is no man, however wicked or powerful, who can do her any harm.

Amina in course of her wanderings found a shelter in the house of one Shek Gafur, an inhabitant of the village Ilshakhali. He was eighty years old. Farming was his profession. One could see him every evening returning from his fields with a plough on his shoulders. His brows and hair of the breast had grown white and a fine stuff of white beard 2 ft. 3 in. long gave a dignity to his look. His wife, an old hunch-back, had lost her sight. There was none to cook meals for the pair and they often felt the sharp pangs of hunger. Though he had a large stock of food-grains in his granaries and a good number of buffaloes and bulls in the sheds near his house, it was ill luck that made him miserable, for he had no issue. The old man, despite his plentiful resources, was a pitiable miser and he worked the whole day for earning money in this advanced age. He brought a child and adopted him but when Providence is against a man, vain is it for him to seek happiness in the world. The child died creating a rend in the heart of the unlucky pair which could not be easily repaired.

Gafur felt very miserable with the old hunch-back his wife. When they were thus spending their days in unhappiness Amina came to their house. She fell prostrate at the feet of Gafur and called him her foster-father. She told the whole story of her past life. The compassion of the old man was roused and he readily admitted her to his house, where after many a day of intense suffering she now found a refuge. The home of the old farmer, covered with darkness, seemed to be suddenly illuminated by a lamp. She cooked meals for Gafur and his wife and served them with tender affection. The old man thanked God with a sincere heart that at last the Lord had given him a daughter.

In the evening Amina took charge of the bullocks released from day's work and bound them with ropes in the shed. She gave them grains and grass and then came to her foster-father with a *hooka* ready with tobacco. She cooked meals twice a day. The old woman had no teeth, and Amina pounded betels and spice for her so that she could take them at ease. The hunch-back right glad at this attention from the girl often kissed her to show her great affection.

Amina spent her days in her new home in comfort and happiness but still she secretly shed tears at the recollection of her parents. (Ll. 1-66.)

(11)

In the south of the Bay there is an island called Paridia (isle of the fairies). It is said that fairies dwelt there in the olden times. They used to alight on the shores from the sky and often married men. And gradually a thick population grew in the island as people thronged there from many places. The fairies fled away in course of time and the island became a large habitation of men with market-places and roads. A large number of fishermen carried on their trade in the deep waters of the Bay and they dried the fish they caught in the sunny shores of Paridia. In course of time Paridia grew to be a flourishing centre of fish-trade and people from distant places came to carry on their business there.

Mafo had heard from his town of Angi about the growing importance of Paridia as a centre of fish-trade. He was told that fish from that island if brought to his native place would fetch double profits—especially the well-known '*laukha* fish'—which was to be found in Paridia alone and had a wide repute for its excellent quality. Mafo thought as to how he could go to that island for conducting fish-trade.

He called his son-in-law Nasar to him and related the tale he had heard about Paridia and asked his advice as to how the far-famed *laukha* fish of that place could be brought to his country. Nasar pondered over the matter for a little time and then said, "I will myself go to that island, father. If the sails can catch the southern wind it will take 12 days to reach that island. Anyhow I assure you that I shall return home within a month."

He went to Akhim to bid her farewell and said, "I shall be away from home for a month only. Do not grieve, my love, over this short separation. I will surely return within the time."

Akhim smiled and said, "Do not take another wife there in the meantime."

It was about the middle of February. The southern gale was blowing. Nasar was coming to the northern shores from Angi. His ship had twenty-two sails which made a great flapping sound as she proceeded onwards, and the rowers sitting near the prow merrily sang '*Sari* songs' as they rowed. They advanced towards north and on their right side lay the great shores of the sea. Nasar saw above his head pretty birds of different colour flying up, and on his left small isles of the sea, which displayed a rich variety of gorgeous flowers. It was a noble sight to see in these small islands the fine avenues of cocoanut trees. The cocoanuts fell on the sea by thousands and they looked like foams of the waves drifted by its current. There were besides small islands which had no tree, no plant, no grass, but presented a monotonous view of sands. There hundreds of crocodiles were seen resting on the land and enjoying sunshine. The crocodiles hatched large eggs which they covered with sands, and these huge animals could be seen in large numbers stretched out on the sands with eyes glimmering in silence. A little to the west were seen shoals of various sizes. There were to be seen enormous snakes, called Kalandar. In the jungles, which abound there, lived tigers, buffaloes, and other animals, which living for a time in one shoal easily swam across to another. Nasar saw many shoals and many isles inhabited by men as his ship flew like a bird in the mid-sea.

Helped by favourable wind Nasar reached Paridia in six days, ordinarily a journey of twelve days. Arriving there Nasar took care to purchase *laukha* fish of the best quality. When the ship was loaded he thought of the difficulty of his journey back. He would now have to go against the wind. He advised the captain to steer the ship northward, and after they had passed three days he ordered the ship to anchor in a place called the 'Majher gram.' (Ll. 1-54.)

(12)

Nasar came to the house of his former father-in-law, Haider. The old man had died and Nasar's mother-in-law, old and decrepit, now lived by begging from door to door. Nobody was there to enquire about her as to if she starved or was living at all. The house stood with broken walls. The roof leaked and the whole presented a look of utmost wretchedness. 'Where has Amina gone?' thought Nasar.

There was a brinjal plant in the compound which yielded crops all round the year. It had flowered. Nasar sat in the wretched hovel alone looking to these flowers. The day drew to a close but nobody came to that deserted house. Nasar thought, "Alas! what ghost had seized me! Why did I go abroad! Attracted by the joys of a foreign land I never cared to think what would occur to the immates of this house. Alas! how greatly they must have suffered for my sake!" When he thought of Amina his eyes began to shed incessant tears. The drops fell on his breast one by one, while he silently regretted his folly in leaving the house.

No one came there, alas none! The evening passed. Despairing Nasar came out of the house with grief piercing his heart like a spear.

He came to the market-place and became a guest in a house. There he talked with people, who told him strange stories in which truths, half-truths and lies mixed freely. "No justice in this world, friend, no equity, no trust in men," they said, "Amina was not chaste in her heart—the ruin of her parents was brought about by her wickedness. This bad woman left her old parents and absconded with some bad fellow. To what place she has gone we do not know. Old Haider died of broken heart and the old woman, his wife, shortly after fell down on the ground in grief never to rise again."

He heard these stories. That night he neither took his meals nor shut his eyes for a moment in sleep. (Ll. 1-28.)

(13)

The force of the wind increased and Nasar now wanted to start homewards. The captain and the sailors did not approve of his intention. But he did not listen to their counsel. Thus does a fly fall into fire—when its destiny calls it to death. When the ship came to the mid-sea fierce winds began to blow, threatening to upset it with goods and all. The flow-tide had set in and the gale was tremendously forceful. Hard was it for the captain to steer the ship southwards. The thunder roared and lightning flashed. The black clouds marched swiftly in the sky looking like demons. The sailors, the rowers, the captain and the *Tendal* all cried in despair. The force of the gale increased and nobody's head was steady at the menacing look of the sky. They thought that the presiding angel of the sea was showing all his destructive might, and there was no rescue. Nasar himself went to the helm and held it with his own hands. The waves of the Bay raised their heads as big as hill-tops. From both sides the big waves came rolling and dashing, and the sailors beat their breasts in despair. Some of them pledged offerings to Saint Badar, some began to cry aloud recollecting their little children left at home. Some loudly screamed indicating their agony of heart, saying, 'Hah! no more shall we meet our parents, our brothers and relations;' one lamented—'Alas! she who is dearer far than life will no more gladden my eyes. Alas! destiny had reserved my death in this mid-ocean. Why did I lose my senses and come here at the counsel of these drug-eaters? How sad it is that there is nobody to make even a grave or coffin for me at the hour of death. No Mollah will recite the usual sacred texts when I shall give up my breath.'

The ropes of the sails were torn to pieces and the mast broke. There were great uproar and consternation on board the ship. The ship could not be restrained and like one gone mad she marched heedlessly, drifted by the wind till she reached the island called 'Gobadhya.' (Ll. 1-30.)

(14)

The western sea in those days was the resort of Harmads who plundered all boats and ships that fell in their way. They would loot all they found and if the crew offered anything like resistance, they cut their throats and killed them without mercy. In the immense deep the Harmads were a terror. So the sloops in those days went in a body,—a good number of them together all compact, when they had to travel a long distance by sea. The sailors and the crew took with them guns and gunpowder, spears and other weapons. On the south of the Kaicha lay the port of Diang and from that port the ships all started on sea-voyage, forming a strong fleet ready to meet the foe when occasion arose.

Nasar's sloop came to Gobadhya and was stranded on the sand. This was a notorious resort of the Harmads. Many a sailor and owner of ships had here encountered great dangers. The storm ceased and ebb-tide commenced. The water subsided and the night looked grim in its impenetrable darkness.

The island of Gobadhya was a dreary tract, full of sand and nothing else. Not a grass, not a straw was to be seen there. There was no mark or sign to indicate the way to the traveller, and Nasar could not know his whereabouts, nor the direction he should follow. The sand filled the deck of the ship and she became fixed to a spot without any power to move.

In the morning the flow-tide would begin, releasing the the ship from her stranded condition. In expectation they all sat together wishing for the approach of the dawn. They guarded with care the wealth that lay in the ship and discussed the way they should take to cross the sea.

The night was nearly over and the first streaks of the east appeared in the horizon. The Harmads were lying in ambush in the western shoals. The sun's disk rose as it were from the sea and peered through the east. At the sight the birds of the sea began to cry wildly, and gradually the flow-tide set in, merging the island in water. The Harmads were seen at a distance busy observing their ship with the help of telescopes. Nasar felt a shudder at the sight of the miscreants.

Ten or twelve of them approached Nasar, dressed in black trousers. Some wore short red coats and turbans on their heads. In the belt of their waists they had scabbards bound tightly and they had guns in their hands. The blood flowing in the veins of Nasar became frozen in fear. The captain and the sailors found their limbs paralysed and could not move their hands and feet.

The first thing the robbers did was to hold Nasar tightly by the neck. They slapped his cheeks and the blows were so sudden and severe that Nasar fell down on the deck. His sailors and other men lay more like dead than living beings viewing with their timid eyes the action of the robbers.

The next thing the Harmads did was to bind them all by strong ropes and then enter the ship for plunder.

They discovered great riches by breaking open the chests. Right glad were they to find a large quantity of Burmese gold there. The flow in the sea attained its highest point and it was now an easy task for the robbers to drag down the ship from the sands and float her in the sea. The heaps of dried *Laukha* fish had become wet and now being exposed to the rays of the sun a bad odour emanated from them and hundreds of sea-birds came swooping down from the sky and seized large numbers of these goods. The vultures which flew above the sea, the sea-pigeon and other birds all assembled in huge numbers over this booty, and it became a problem to the robbers as to how to preserve the fish from the birds.

The great ship of Nasar with all its valuable goods was now in the possession of the Harmads and they swiftly marched homewards with their loot. (Ll. 1-54.)

(15)

Now let me resume the story of good Amina. She was quite in comfort in the house of Gafur. But his wife the hunch-back died and the home was now quite lonely. Gafur's great anxieties were now centered in Amina—"If I die what will befall the lot of this girl? How will my riches be preserved? "—He pondered over the problem for many a day and at last called Amina to his presence one day and said, " I am your foster-father and you have been a true daughter to me ever since you came here. Who will protect my lands and other properties? I have settled that I shall give you in marriage to a suitable youth. This world is a very wicked place. How can you think of living with the riches that I will leave you, all alone in the house? I will select for you a handsome and clever youth. Do please agree to marry again. There is no knowing where your husband has gone for these six years. How long will you wait for him? According to our scriptures practically a situation has been created for you when you may claim the privilege of a divorce from your husband. Oh my daughter,—I am hearing a call from the other world. Give your unhesitating consent to my request so that I may die in peace."

Amina when she heard Gafur's words fell at his feet with tears in her eyes and said, "Oh my revered father, pray, hear my word. I have no thirst for worldly pleasure. Do not tempt and try to create a desire in my mind that is long extinguished. My own parents had made a request like this and I fled from my home to avoid them. Oh my foster-father do not cause fresh pain to my lacerated heart. Pray, do not touch that delicate topic again."

Gafur became silent on hearing Amina's words. He was sorry but did not press his request. As usual he went to the field the next morning, attended to his daily duties with plough and other implements of cultivation. Thus did the old farmer go on ploughing his fields from day to day, and they continued to yield him various crops of the season all round the year. (Ll. 1-36.)

(16)

I shall now relate to you many things which are not known to all. Yet these are facts and not creations of my fancy.

There was a great war and the whole country was in a state of anarchy. The Burmese people took panic and burying their gold, silver and other riches underground, left Chittagong in precipitous haste marching towards south.

One night some of these Burmese men suddenly appeared in the house of Gafur. There was a mound in the north of the compound of his house. The Burmese all came to this dese'ed spot and surrounded it with great interest and v'.lance.

The farmer Gafur took his stick and weapons in hand and came out of the house. He said to Amina, "To-day is my last, Amina. These Burmese will kill me straight. There in the bamboo platform inside the house hide yourself as best as you can. If these Arakanese can get a clue they are sure to plunder you." Gafur was eighty years old. He could hardly walk erect. He reeled and staggered in his attempts. Amina got upon the platform as directed. The old man came up before the strangers supporting himself by his stick. The Burmese said, "Do not be afraid, old man. This homestead once belonged to us. How often we played here as children! We bear recollection of our dear mother whose lap was our first resting place. Then we got down to the play-ground and sported with our comrades. We buried twelve vessels full of gold coins underground here and went away to live with our uncle." As they were talking in this strain they dug open a spot and brought hoards of gold coins kept in twelve jars. "Now old man," they said, "you have guarded this great wealth of ours all this time and you deserve a reward at our hands. Take two jars out of these twelve." Saying this the Arakanese left the place in great speed and had gone far away before it was morn. The old man took possession of the two jars. He brought them before Amina and opening the contents found them to be all gold coins.

It was as if a childless man got a child all at once. He knows not how and where to keep the treasure secure, and timidly glances at the jars.

Old Gafur after consulting with Amina at last buried the wealth again underground.

They passed sometime more in the house in the usual manner but shortly after the summons from above came upon old Gafur who said to Amina a little before he expired:

"Stretch your hands towards me, dear daughter." And when she did so, he placed her hands on his bosom. Amina began to cry whereupon he said, "Wipe the tears away.

I cannot resist my tears seeing yours. Do not weep Amina, all my riches I hereby give you.''

His eyes became steady and his tongue grew speechless. The good neighbours assembled at his house and gave him a burial.

For two months tears incessantly fell from Amina's eyes. She cried and said, "Where hast thou gone, oh my father.—Your affection was so great that I had forgotten even my own parents all this time. Woe to me that wherever I go to find a shelter, there fate runs adverse and destroys my refuge. My own parents, alas! have been long separated from me but the grief caused by your death I cannot bear. It breaks my heart already heavy-laden as if by strokes of hammer.''

Thus passed two months. Providence alas, made Amina subject to all kinds of misfortunes. (Ll. 1-60.)

(17)

Esak of Majergaon had all this time kept full information about Amina. He one day paid a visit to her old mother who lived by begging. Esak told lots of stories to the old woman and brought her to his own house giving her all sorts of false hopes. When the old dame came to his house, a right royal reception he gave her and provided her with rich meals. Excellent curd, butter and other delicacies he served her, so that in a short time she felt quite hale and hearty.

Some days passed in this way and he once began to speak to her about Amina. He said many things and gave a lively account of her present fortunes. She said, "Well Esak, if it be all as you say, it is very good ; how glad shall I be if you go and fetch her here once more.''

Esak said with a sigh, '' I tried to swim across the sea but vain was my attempt ; she is, owing to my ill-luck, cruel to me. If I go she will not come, alas she will not come ! ''

By many a wily talk Esak settled everything favourably for him with the old woman.

She had just lighted her evening lamp and lo, she saw a palanquin come to her house. Who is it that has come to my house ? With this anxious query in her mind she came out to see. When the woman came out opening the door of the palanquin Amina began to shed tears on seeing her mother once more and clasped her to her bosom. The mother and daughter stood locked up in each other's arms and they shed incessant tears.

Tenderly did Amina give her a fine mat to sit on ; when she heard the report of her father's death and the misfortunes that the mother had passed through all this time it seemed as if her heart would break. For the whole night Amina wept as she heard further details of the sorrows that had befallen her parents.

In the morning the old woman awoke and was served with a good repast. During all this time Amina was all attention to her.

The mother said, "Come daughter, and let us return to our home at Majhergaon. Here you have no kith or kin and it does not look well that you should put up in this house all alone. Majhergaon is your own home. Thither let us go together."

Amina.

I entreat you with all meekness, listen to my words, mother. What is there at Majhergaon on which we would live? Here I have plenty of lands. There is no anxiety on the score of food-stuff. The paddy that I get from my lands not only provides me with food for the whole year but a considerable sum I get from the sale of what I do not require for home-consumption. What is there at Majhergaon on which we may depend for sustenance?

Besides paddy, there is my garden of trees yielding mangoes, jacks and other fruits of the season. Where shall I leave my goats and cows and implements of agricultural work? Look at my granary, it is full to the brim. If I go from here all these will be lost—none is here to take care of them. Stay with me, good mother, and do not return to Majhergaon. You will be the mistress of this home and of all I have. Whatever you will like to eat, you will get here to your heart's content. No anxiety you will feel on the score of your clothes or meals.

The old woman understood the force of her daughter's arguments and agreed to stay with her.

It chanced one day a guest came there from Majhergaon. He had a private talk with Amina's mother. Both whispered to one another for some time, and Amina did not know what all this was about. The guest was entertained in the house and in the evening he took leave. Then followed something which I am going to relate presently.

In the night Amina lay unconscious in deep sleep when her mother gently opened the door. Three persons entered the apartment of Amina. First of all they tied her mouth, then bound her hands and feet. They then took her on their shoulders and cleared off.

She could neither cry nor move her limbs. Once only did she glance at her mother, the root of all this mischief!

Alas the ways of the mother! Where is happiness in this world when even mother's heart becomes hard as stone!

Oh foolish hard-hearted mother, you know not what you have done! You have got a bead of glass in return of a gold coin.

The three knaves carried Amina to a boat that lay at anchor at the river-bank. There did they cut off the cords with which they had bound her. Amina began to cry aloud and throw her limbs in violent fits.

The boat passed through many a small canal till after a full day they reached Majhergaon.

They carried Amina to the house of Esak. (Ll. 1-78.)

(16)

Let us now turn to the events that followed when Nasar was made a captive.

His ship and all the goods it contained were sold by the robbers at an enormous price. In the west where the sea ends and land begins—there the custom prevailing is strange. Men there sell their fellow-men and there is a brisk trade going on. The captives were all sold there and Nasar the expert captain was sold at a high price. The Harmads thus completed this wicked transaction and returned to their own places.

The man who had bought Nasar gave him a small boat; with this he was sent to the market-place from where he brought the goods required by the master. From the market he carried loads for him and visited many places far and near with that boat, ordered by his master.

Nasar, otherwise prudent, lost his head one day. When making a trip in this way he passed through the small canals and reached the big sea. At the sight of the sea he felt a strange desire to cross it. He had no liking for his life and took his boat recklessly to the mid-sea.

For four days he continually rowed. The fatigue of the journey and want of food enfeebled him. His arms were swollen by continual rowing till they became devoid of strength. They became completely paralyzed, and the vast sea lay in the front without any sign of land in all the four directions. Waves rose above waves and the small boat passed through them. It was through the mercy of Providence alone that it did not yet sink. The sea-leviathans rose huge as mountains. They made strange sounds like the moanings of the wind. Nasar had lost his eye-sight owing to emaciation and fatigue and his head reeled. When thus disabled he fell prostrate in the boat relying on the mercy of Allah and praying to Him.

While reciting the name of God he became unconscious. Alas, what great miseries were in store for poor Nasar! It seemed that the presiding saint of the sea took pity on him.

Long boats passed by that part of the sea at this time, each with a sail on it, and these belonged to fishermen who sang *sari* songs as they rowed. They had nets with them for catching fish. Astonished were they that a small boat was floating in the sea like a toy-thing and they caught hold of it. They found Nasar lying there in an unconscious state and gently raising him had him removed to their boat. For some time they had doubts as to if he was dead or still had some spark of life left in him.

Cold water they applied on his head and slowly put into his mouth a few drops of cocoanut-milk till after a time his condition improved a little.

When Nasar could speak a few words it was found that the fishermen did not understand his language nor he—theirs.

Nasar, however, made his condition known to them by gestures and signs.

At this stage a rice-merchant was going with his ship. The fishermen gave charge of Nasar to the master of this ship. (Ll. 1-46.)

(17)

In the city of Angi, Mafo began to be uneasy on account of Nasar's long absence. He was to return within a month, but a year passed. There was no news about him all this time!

"'I sent him,' thought he, 'to Paridia' for purchasing *Laukha* fish. Surely the fellow has seized the opportunity and gone back to his own native country. These men of the north with dark skin are very unscrupulous, I placed hoards of money at his hands on implicit trust. I was not right in doing so."

Thinking in this strain he took possession of all the goods belonging to Nasar and sold them and what was more he got his daughter married to another man!

After one year Nasar came back to the town of Angi and hearing all that had transpired during his absence, did not return to the home of his father-in-law.

"No trust is to be placed on the dacoits of this place. They may stab one on some little plea," he thought. He tarried not but at once left the country not caring to see Akhim before he left. When he heard that she was happy in the arms of another husband it seemed that his heart was going to break.

"These women have no *parda*—no self-respect, no affection or sympathy in their soul. Strangers are welcome to their doors, unknown men are favoured by women here. They have no idea of devotion or love. If one gives them money they are his, and when money is scarce they quarrel or seek divorce."

Thus thought Nasar and made his heart hard as steel till it was devoid of all tender feelings. He at once left that land of dacoits, resolved never to come there again. He was painfully conscious of the curse of Providence that followed him everywhere and turned half-mad with harrowing thoughts and despair. No money had he,—a veritable beggar of the streets had he become. None was there whom he could call his own, not a spot in the whole earth was there which he could call his home. He wandered in the northern country for some time. For lack of a dwelling place many a night he passed under the shade of a tree.

One night he dreamt a strange dream. Amina, he saw, came and stood before him—her two eyes were sparkling like evening stars—her colour looked bright as the *champa* flower. Purity had given her a grace and dignity and she looked like the very jewel of her sex and community. Her youthful charm had not grown a whit less—it was full to the brim—she was faultless and immaculate. Her heart was full of tender compassion and sympathy for all, and a beautiful smile played on her lips. This flower was not a faded thing but fresh as if it had bloomed to-day.

When Nasar dreamt in this way his mind yearned for a sight of Amina. (Ll. 1-40.)

(18)

Esak the knave had brought Amina to his house by plunder. He tempted her by a hundred hopes every day but the wild tiger could not be made tame. As a cobra, hurt on the head, hisses and casts its angry look, so did Amina as often as the rogue approached her. All the charms and incantations of Buddhu, the mystic, became powerless. His magic art and spells all came to no use. His lockets, his incantations were all unavailing. It is fire that is the true test of gold—the sufferings that Amina passed through proved that she was a true woman.

Six months passed in this way and all attempts of Esak to win her failed.

One day when evening covered the fair face of earth like a veil, Esak came to the presence of Amina and said, "You are the daughter of a mean fellow and your heart is mean. In this house of mine there will be no place for you any more. You have given me all kind of trouble. I have suffered for your sake what few men suffer for a woman.

Get out of my house quickly. Do not stay here a moment. My wife Mema Bibi is very angry. If you tarry she will turn you out dragging you by the hair. Here in this house of mine there is no room for you any more."

When she heard Esak say this, Amina looked like a volume of smoke about to break into fire. A drop of tear glistened in her eye as she came out. She visited her father's house and found that the roof of her house was gone and the walls all broken. There on the floor of the deserted hut roamed foxes at night and the whole place abounded in unclean things. There was no door. How could she spend the night there.

Still she sat on a little spot of her old home. When it was mid-night the crescent moon glittered in the sky like a streak of gold. Esak had no sleep in his eyes, he was seized with a beastly passion and came there in quest of Amina. She lay in a corner of the broken hut, but all on a sudden in that dead of night perceived that Esak was coming towards her. She trembled like a poor antelope at the approach of a tiger. But suddenly the hut seemed to shake and there was a commotion. A moment after, it was seen that Nasar had struck Esak with a heavy bamboo-pole.

Southern wind was gently blowing and the moon-beams fell on the earth like showers of gold. They disclosed the beautiful pair Nasar and Amina bound in embrace.

No word they spoke while both shed tears. Nasar had only a piece of loin-cloth on his person. His face looked pale as he had been without any food. Amina's heart broke at the sight. With the hair of her head she wiped away the dust of his feet while she murmured in soft accents—"How could you, my darling, forget me and live far away?"

Nasar was silent; he gave no reply but followed the footsteps of Amina as she went out of the house. (Ll. 1-48.)

THE BALLAD OF BHARAI RAJA

PREFACE TO THE BALLAD OF BHARAI RAJA

The ballad of Bharai Raja was collected by Babu Chandrakumar De with the help of Babu Bijaynarain Acharya of Muktagacha in Mymensingh. A Mahomedan Fakir named Nazir supplied him with the earlier portions and the subsequent part was mainly obtained from another Fakir of Phulpur. A Vaishnav mendicant named Ishan—an inhabitant of Simulkanda—supplied Chandrakumar Babu with the concluding songs.

The stigma attached to our countrymen that we have no liking for historical studies is to some extent removed by ballads like these which give a connected narrative of events, though couched in a poetical style and often mixed with legends and mythical stories. However small their intrinsic value may be as contribution to historical material, they show that our rural people had an instinctive desire to listen to the tales of important events transpiring in their localities, particularly when their burden is some love-episode breathing the spirit of inspiring sacrifice and martyrdom.

The materials of the ballad no doubt came from that remote period when the *tantras* exerted a great influence in our country, and though the ballad is mostly sung by Moslem minstrels now, there is no Mahomedan element in the subject-matter to show that it was composed during the Mahomedan times.

This country of ours was at one time full of Rupkathas in which the superhuman feats of the Tantric masters played a considerable part. The wars described in this ballad are controlled and stamped by Tantric influences. In the description of the concluding episodes it bears a striking analogy to the legends of the Mainamati tales,—and reminds us of the stories of the thief Inda in the Dharmamangal poems, and of the feats of Mahi Ravana now incorporated with some of the Bengali recensions of the Ramayana. Such tales are to be found in the Gaelic legends of the West. The change of shapes which the two contending heroes of the ballad adopted are almost like those of Rani Mainamati and Goda Jam or of the three sons of Tuirenn and the princesses of Hesperides in the Gaelic tales. In hundreds of Rupkathas of Bengal we come across similar stories of wonderful powers of Siddhas. They belong to that dark period of our history which is stamped by the black deeds of the Yogis and Kapaliks who acquired their power by miraculous actions performed on funeral grounds where the yells of jackals and other beasts of prey, the ferocious dance of ghosts and even the dead starting to life, could not disturb their sombre meditations. Like the Druid priests they could by their incantations call to life a mutilated corpse and the disjointed limbs were made whole again. The marvels performed by the Masters of Black Art have found a place in the Arabian Nights tales and in many stories current in Persia, and scholars are of opinion that these tales were originally inspired by Indian fables.

It was the Vedic religion which fought hard against the black art of the Tantrics on the revival of Hinduism after the downfall of Buddhism in Bengal. In the 11th and 12th centuries the whole atmosphere of this country was rife with legends of Tantric deeds, and though it was the Sen dynasty that inaugurated the movement of simpler Vedic rituals, discarding Tantric modes of worship, the country could not make itself absolutely free from Tantric mysticism for a long time, and even Ballal Sen himself, one of the pioneers of Hindu revival, is said to have freely indulged in such practices, sanctioned by religion, with the co-operation of a low-caste woman. The age of this Black Tantricism may be traced back to the 5th century A.D. King Chandra Gupta (Bikramaditya) is said to have achieved superhuman powers, having obtained sway over two evil spirits—Tal and Betal—and having secured a miraculous throne presided over by thirty-two spirits who endowed him with a vision which no mortal is privileged to behold. Tantricism is not yet dead in India and occasionally we hear of some great *Siddha purushas* endowed with power of performing marvels.

But the period pre-eminently stamped with the spirit of Tantricism is 11th to 13th century, and tales like what is described in this ballad owed their origin to this dark age of Bengal.

This ballad is certainly not so old, it may not be even earlier than the 14th century, but the inspiration and echo of some of the incidents of the ballad have no doubt come from a remote age; the language has passed through changes from age to age till its transcription in its present shape.

As I have mentioned in my Introductions to the various parts of Eastern Bengal Ballads, there have been many stories in them of warfares, enterprising sea-voyages, sacrifices undergone for love or some other higher motive, of transformation of assassins and robbers into saintly characters. And if the more important of these are collected, they would contribute an interesting chapter to the future history of Bengal. But if this work of research is given up, the materials will be all hopelessly lost. The very nature of the work is such as hardly admits of any undue haste. It is patient and steady pursuit which is expected to yield the wished-for result, and any dictation as to finishing the whole thing within a specified time-limit is out of the question in this case.

The main seat of Tantricism from which Bengal had her inspiration was Kamakhya. The shrine is in Assam valley, and not only the Rupkathas and ballads are full of references to it, but even the Mahomedans of the countryside in many of their books written in a language called the *Musalmani Bangla*, show a great respect to this shrine of the Hindus and ascribe to it miracles and legends beyond the boundaries of ordinary belief. There is a reference to Kamakhya in this ballad also as the principal seat from which people learned witchcraft and black art. Tantricism of this type is still current in Bhutan, and I heard many marvellous stories about the black art that prevailed there from my friend late Lama Dausan Dup, a native of that country, and formerly a lecturer of the Calcutta University.

This ballad is written in a simple and beautiful style ; the difficulty which the reader may occasionally feel is due to the archaic words of local origin which though simple are obviously not quite understandable of the people of other parts of Bengal. There is a poetical grace in the stanzas, and the author seldom strays beyond the actual needs of the narrative. There is much animation in the accounts of war, and we find in them the names of many weapons and instruments of war-music, not familiar to us. It also gives us a vivid picture of the political condition of the country showing the ruthless manner in which the kings and the chiefs devastated the country while satisfying their caprices or trying to pursue a determined course of action prompted by a false idea of prestige. It also shows how far the question of blood and honour attached to families brings into play an unsparing spirit of vengeance. The sufferings of the innocent and their martyrdom for the sake of love and honour, specially in womankind, are brought into contrast with vindictive, unswerving and implacable hatred rendering the heroine an object of our admiration. The love of the pair, the young prince and princess, during the few hours of night in a prison, is the one redeeming feature of this cruel and tragical tale and shines as a streak of lightning in a sky filled with black clouds.

That the author has the gift of true poetical art will be apparent from his simple metaphors all original and culled from the countryside, from his not over-doing a poetic situation till the matter is made threadbare and monotonous and from his strict relevancy and restraint. The pathos created by the princess's forlornness and her lot claims a tear of the reader towards the end of the story. There were many that I shed over the original though in my weak translation the effect of such simple pathos can hardly be expected to be maintained.

Raja Bharai like all people of hill tribes is over-anxious to form an alliance with the Hindus of the lower valley. For a favour like that he made large concessions and trusted the enemy, too proud to wilfully entertain a proposal of the nature. This was Bharai's vulnerable point and he brought all subsequent calamities by placing implicit confidence on the pledge of his foe. The Kshatriya Raja is a type of arrogance and craft which are seen in the high-caste Hindus when a question of caste and social status arises. The depressed castes and the hill-tribes are treated in such a way as if they are worse than lower animals. Raja Birsingh easily takes his pledge as a manoeuvre which is not only expedient but even fair and just, for what moral law in his view should be observed in dealing with a hillman? His ethical sense is completely blunted by the thought of his own immense social superiority. He violates his sacred promise and he ruins the life of an innocent girl. Even his pride and craft may be excused as being natural in a Hindu possessing a high status in society, though it is condemned by the ethical codes of all countries, but his rude conduct towards the queen of his adversary shows that all humane element was dead in his character. Whatever his social position might be he appears to be the type of a true monster even compared with his savage adversary of the Hajan tribe.

But if even the ruthless father is forgiven, we can have no pity for his cowardly son, though in the field of battle he is so brave and valorous. He evidently accepted the bride pledged to him. He got his release by the martyrdom of one who was from all points of view, his wife and recognised as such by him. He called all the planets of the sky to be witness to his solemn promise that he would cling to her all his life. He was anxious to make his escape and in his eagerness to achieve that end he never cared to enquire under what conditions the girl got his release and if she incurred any risk or danger by doing so. Inspite of this omission we are prepared to take all his sweet words of love, his kisses and tears to be *bonafide*. But when the princess fell in distress, he did not care to say even a kind word to her ; he totally disappeared from the scene like a veritable coward. There is a suggestion that he was entertaining at the time a proposal of his marriage with a girl of the Dakhin-patan. Heroes of this nature are not altogether rare in our ballad literature. We have his parallel in the prince of the ballad 'Dhopar pat' or Kanchanmala. We consider the prince of this ballad as equally treacherous and a villain of the same type. We know that in orthodox Hindu society, the old men will applaud the conduct of this perfidious prince and praise him for his docile submission to the will of his father and even for his discarding a pledge for the sake of keeping his caste-prestige, than which no consideration weighs more with them. When a society loses all regard for the simple ethics which govern all human institutions, the time may be said to have come when the young men should openly revolt against their parents and completely upset their rotten social fabric.

But true poetry is not to be judged by an ethical test ; we have, however, discussed this question here as the prince is likely to be accepted as a model son inspite of his villainy, by the orthodox Hindu readers.

The patience and devotion of Champabati knows no bounds. The cruelest hit aimed at her by fate was this wicked conduct of the prince and she referred to it with her never-failing good will and love for him even at the last hour.

The poet closes the ballad with an artistic line which is matchless for its effect on the reader. Her grief was so great that her father's mute stone image shed drops of tears at her distress.

DINESHCHANDRA SEN

January 27, 1931.

The Ballad of Bharai Raja

(1)

Listen, oh my friends, to the tale of Bharai Raja of the city of Amgoshala. He was a powerful Raja—in fact matchless amongst the princes of that province.

The river Sundasuti flowed in that country and on its banks was the fair city of the Raja where he held the helm of the state.

His army and retinue were so vast that they were the objects of wonder of all people.

Now, my audience, comprising Hindus and Musalmans, you have assembled here to hear my song. My salam to you all. To-day my subject is the story of Bharai Raja. I sincerely apologise to you, for my capacity is limited, and little power have I to judge between good and bad.

The Raja had a large number of elephants and horses. Buffaloes and hybrid animals called *maials* (born of bulls and she-buffaloes) abounded in his pastures. They were countless. Guards and sentinels were plenty at the gate of the palace.

At a little distance from his city there were large pastoral areas where legions of his milch cows grazed. He was the lord of the country. In the southern regions none there was who could be called his equal.

He was a Koch by birth. (Ll. 1-18.)

(2)

One day he took a fancy to see the lands on the other side of the Sundasuti. He found there a large and impenetrable jungle. At the Raja's order a vast number of day-labourers were called there and they were engaged in cutting down the jungles. "What could be the object of his clearing this jungle of Bheur ?" asked the people of that locality to one another.

Twelve thousand Koch labourers assembled there at the command of the Raja, and when his officer beat a huge drum, all the Koches, men and women, started work. Some entered the deep shades of the forest and cut down the tall trees ; others levelled the ground with the help of spades ; some set fire where access was difficult. The tigers and bears inhabiting that wilderness were alarmed and began to fly in all directions, without knowing their place of safety. The birds left the nests they had made with care, and flew in the distant sky. The red tongue of the flames pursued them even there. Their scream and chatter were heard from a long distance. They surely cursed the men who destroyed their peaceful nests.

Now the days of April were hot, and May was in sight with prospects of the coming monsoon. Bharai Raja consulted his courtiers, as to the *modus operandi* of agricultural work to be carried on there.

He called the expert farmers and tillers and appointed them to carry on the work of cultivation. Ploughs were driven by bulls and buffaloes over the land thus acquired. (Ll. 18-44.)

(3)

The report of these operations reached King Birsingha in due course. The reporter said—"My humble respects to your Majesty. The base-born Raja of the Dhangar-tribe has usurped a part of your dominions."

On hearing the report, the Raja's soldiers brandished their *lathis* and other weapons and showed an impatient desire to fight. Some carried *lathis* ; others were equipped with bows and arrows. Amongst them were seen men wildly dancing with spears in their hands. Some wielded sharp and pointed tridents and others had barbed arrows in their hands and '*Jhuka*' on their heads. They set out with great speed towards the banks of the Sundasuti. The Koches who were working in that forest-region with their ploughs, all fled away, terror-struck at the sight of Birsingha's army.

They approached Bharai Raja and said—" Oh Raja, King Birsingha has arrived here with his army and driven us by force from the fields."

Bharai Raja was highly incensed at this report. He was red with anger and looked like a gunpowder-magazine that had caught fire. " Where are my men ?" he roared. " Come and be ready for war. Take up arms. Let me try my strength with that son of Singhi. I will destroy his capital and throw the relics into the sea. Let a brave man in my army come forward and claim a reward from me by producing in this court the decapitated head of Birsingha."

As he commanded, his army got fully ready wearing war-robes. He himself jumped upon the back of a fiery horse. His army was considerable and they followed him with the cry, " Strike the enemy."

When the two armies encountered one another in the field, their great uproar sounded like that of the turbulent waves of the sea under a storm. Some fell there, receiving wounds from spears that pierced their body; others vomited blood and some had their breasts torn by arrows.

Bir, the general of Bharai Raja, marched at the head of the army and though all pointed out the great risk, he was firm and undaunted.

On his head he wore a rich turban, in his hand was a mace of iron. Those whom he struck with it fell on the ground never to rise again to see their parents and relations. The head and limbs of soldiers, separated from the body, rolled in the mire. Some began to cry aloud despairing of seeing their beloved mothers again. The water of the Sundasuti was coloured deep-red with the blood of soldiers. The army of Bharai Raja seemed to be completely defeated.

With a bow in hand Raja Birsingha who was a master of martial tactics aimed his shaft at Bir—the general of the hostile camp. The shaft was of iron, it flew in the air and pierced the breast of the general,—its pointed head appearing from his back. The soldiers of Birsingha were jubilant and they set up a wild cry of victory. The enemies terror-struck and crest-fallen mourned their evil lot in plaintive laments.

Bharai Raja was initiated in black art. His *mantras* and incantations were infallible. He took a handful of dust from the earth and charmed it with some mystic words and having offered his respects to the memory of his preceptor he blew the charmed dust with his breath. It immediately had the desired effect. The soldiers of Birsingha lost their power of sight, as the particles of dust spread in the air. The men became totally blindfolded and could not see their way. They were then easily taken captives being rendered incapable of finding out their way of escape.

Raja Birsingha saw no way to save himself. He sat on the back of his horse in an attitude of despair. Bharai Raja made him a captive. He was made to wear handcuffs, and his feet were bound by ropes. Placed on an elephant he was carried to the palace of Bharai Raja. (Ll. 44-98.)

(4)

A few of his men had, however, escaped and they carried the news to the prince, his son. They said—'Your Royal father is now a captive in the prison of Bharai Raja.'

As soon as the prince heard the report of his father's disgrace, he immediately robed himself in war-mantle, and riding a red horse started at once for Amgoshala. The generals and soldiers of the palace followed the prince. Some showed their great enthusiasm by high jump and speed, looking like a dreaded meteor in the sky. Some carried on their shoulders spears with barbed iron points. They soon surrounded the city of Amgoshala.

Bharai Raja called all his people again to arms. The war music of *Kara*, *Nagra* and *Danka* rose high in the air. The generals had all assembled there. A tremendous uproar arose on all sides. Their thunder-sound deafened the ears of all. The young prince cut the heads of his enemies by strokes of his sword, and the jackals gathered to drink the blood. Though young he looked like the very lord of death and his horse marched in lightning speed ; and he flew like a star with his sword in hand, cutting people on right and left like banana plants.

The men of Bharai Raja were filled with dismay. Their royal insignia bearing the sacred name of Katyayani was thrown into the ground.

The carrier of the news submitted to the Raja :—"Your Majesty is idling your time in this palace, while your soldiers are being mowed down like long reeds and plants in the battlefield. Oh, what a havoc has the young prince done!"

The Raja with his bodyguards and retinue of the palace marched to the field.

Again he took recourse to his magic tactics, caught hold of a handful of dust and uttering some mystic words charmed it and threw it up in the air, blowing with his breath. Oh, what a mighty charm and what a marvellous effect of the training of the preceptor! By the power of the *mantras* and the grace of Kamakhya Debi the dead are restored to life and the limbs become sound and whole again ; the man that is killed returns home without a scar. But he who incurs the displeasure of the goddess falls dead though struck by a stalk of lotus, and he cannot save his life though he may strive to hide himself in the very depths of the sea.

The army of the prince was alarmed at the sight of the charmed dust. In their anxiety to beat a retreat, some broke their legs and some lost their arm. They all seemed to be struck with a thunderbolt. The horse which the prince rode lost a leg, and being drawn by the power of the charm he did not know which way he was led to. The effect of the charm was now complete and the prince soon found himself a captive in the cell where his royal father lay. (Ll. 98-144.)

(5)

The father and the son lamented bitterly their hard lot. A stone, twenty-two maunds in weight, was placed on the breast of each, crushing them to suffocation.

Their laments seemed to melt the very stone, and while they lay in this plight—the day passed and the night also drew to an end.

Raja Bharai consulted his ministers and came to a decision. One of his ministers was Digambar who enjoyed the Raja's great confidence. He was sent by the Raja with an embassy of truce to the prison.

Digambar to Raja Birsingha.

"Oh King, I have come with a message to you from my master. Bharai Hazra, the Raja of the Koches, is actuated by generous intentions in regard to you, and wants to treat you kindly. He has a fair daughter named Champabati. She has attained her youth and in this city she is known to all for her many noble qualities. Need I say anything about her beauty! The very lamp grows lustreless in her presence.

She looks like the moon in full splendour. Once seeing her it is difficult to forget. She has made the dark clouds of the sky a captive in her long unbraided hair. The moon is a captive in her beautiful face. Her eyes are two captive stars, and in her breast the two buds of flowers seem like captives with their permanant charm, and in her lips which have a deep red colour she seems to have made the very lightning of heaven a captive by the frequency of their transient smiles. Imprisoned in her loose *sari* are all the stars of the sky. See her but once and you will not forget her in life.

Now, oh king Birsingha, agree to marry your son to our princess. Half of his kingdom will the Raja offer as dowry to you, besides the bridegroom will get presents of many valuable things—horses, elephants, five hundred milch cows with calves, five hundred maid servants—each beautiful as a nymph of heaven—these and much more will be presented on the occassion, but the greatest of all is the gift of magicart which the Raja will teach you with all *mantras* and incantations. If you would consent to this proposal of the Raja, triumphantly may you return to your capital, loaded with the rich dowry.

King Birsingha did not apparently seem to relish the offer made by the minister Digambar. For a little time he sombrely meditated upon what seemed to him to be insulting to his dignity. Then after a time of hesitancy and unwillingness he at last yielded and consented to the proposal.

He had naturally a high notion of his family status, and he thought he was quite justified in taking recourse to a stratagem. Apparently everything was all right. There were music and glee in the palace when Raja Birsingha gave his consent. Everyone was glad that the beautiful princess was going to be married.

The two Rajas embraced each other as they were going

to be close relations ere long. Bharai Raja loaded the back of buffaloes with the precious things from his treasury to be presented to Birsingha who also seemed to be quite happy. He returned home with his son.

On coming back he could by no means forget the deep sense of insult which he secretly bore in his heart. He again ordered his people to be ready for war. (Ll. 144-192.)

(6)

The young prince bowed low before the Raja and said :—"Will your Majesty permit me to lead the army? I give you my word, oh king, that I will bring Bharai Raja here bound in fetters. If I fail to do so, I will throw myself into fire and avoid the disgrace of a defeat. I will never show myself to my people at Nehali, humiliated by the enemy."

The prince got permission. With a shield and sword in his hand he marched at the head of the army. He rode a red horse ; it was a fiery animal, its tongue was deep red like a living flame ; it had the speed of winds and when the army marched, it seemed to fly in the air. The prince arrived at the capital of Bharai Raja and threw out his challenge in this way : " Oh king, you are our sworn enemy. There is no time for you to lose, I have come here with your death-warrant."

Bharai Raja burnt in anger and came out to accept the challenge.

The two armies met. Their great generals were seen in their midst dressed in war-robes, but the army of Bharai Raja could not resist the prince who committed an indiscriminate havoc in the rank of his enemy. Bharai took recourse, at this stage of war, to his black art. He uttered mystic words and thereby charmed a handful of dust. The prince and his soldiers saw everything dark before their eyes blindfolded by magic. His people saw the day lost for them and raised an uproar of despair.

The prince was bound hand and foot and imprisoned in a cell. A slab of stone weighing twenty-two maunds was placed on his breast. His army was dispersed ; they fled away. (Ll. 192-222.)

(7)

From her pleasure-house princess Champabati heard the cruel news. Tears flowed from both her eyes. In the deep shades of the jungle at Bharua there were rows of trees from one of which bloomed two flowers on a single stalk. The princess mournfully looked at them and said to herself: " Men and women are like these two flowers made from dust by God's own hands. By the will of the same Providence that joins a man and a woman in this way, you, oh prince, came to our country. From the day my father pledged his word of honour, I have been, oh lord, thine in every way. In my life and at my death I am yours and can be of no others. You are the lord of my heart and I am your loyal servant for ever. The flower bloomed only yesterday. Was it for fading away to-day and so soon? I sat in this pleasure house of mine and wove this garland of flowers with great care and hoped that I would myself adorn your breast with it. Sandal, Chua and other scents are in readiness to be offered with my youth and all to your feet. I longed for the day when I would be able to wipe away the dust of your feet with my loose, flowing hair. I longed for the day when you would be seated on this couch of mine and I would offer you sweet Bangla betels. I waited with a thirsty soul for meeting you here. Delay was painful. My days passed anyhow, but my nights seemed wearisomely long. I had hoped that wearing a garland of Champa flowers, you my love, would come to my chamber to accept your bride.

How is it that you came as an enemy instead? How unexpected is it that in the place of bridal music you came with the war-drums! You sounded the shrill pipe of war when we expected the sweet flute of bridal music. In the place of great joy and glee of the auspicious festivities in which our citizens had expected to participate, there is a deep wail raised in their rank and file. Is this the way in which you wanted to fulfil the pledge of marriage?

Know prince that I will put an end to my life by swallowing poison or cutting my throat with a knife. My last prayer is that you should not for a moment doubt, whatever might be the circumstances, that you are the lord of my soul. In life and at death I shall always remain yours and yours only. I have not yet seen your fair, moon-like face but I dream it every night. Without any enquiry, before seeing you with my eyes, I have surrendered myself to you. Alas, is our life to end thus struggling between hope and despair? Is human life frail and vain like the dust which the wind raises to the sky for a moment and then throws down to cold forgetfulness and oblivious neglect! (Ll. 222-253.)

(8)

The Nurse.

"How are you faring, oh princess? Do you know that the bridegroom-elect is a prisoner in your father's jail? He has been bound in fetters, hand and foot, and a stone weighing twenty-two maunds has been placed on his breast. It is not known if he is still alive or is already dead. The Raja has now turned his enemy and seems bent on destroying his life."

When Champabati heard this report, she fell prostrate on the floor helplessly like a '*cowli*' creeper when it loses the support of the tree to which it had clung.

The Princes to her Nurse.

"Dear nurse, hear what I have resolved to do. Anyhow I must visit the prince now. Kindly lead me to him in the prison. Providence, it seems, is my enemy. I am doomed to wear widow's weeds even before I am married. My father is now my enemy. He has forced me to break my shell-bracelets of luck. Father and mother are both hostile to their daughter. Alas, whom shall I accuse! Who is it, I know not, that has cursed me, so that before my marriage I am widowed. Woe to the Providence which cut off the stalk before the bud bloomed into a flower. The river is rendered dry before the coming of the tide. The happy night was coming but the moon has disappeared from the sky all on a sudden. All my hopes, all my pride of youth are now gone. Oh dear nurse, do me this favour, lead me to the prison at once."

Leaning on the shoulders of the nurse, grief-stricken Champa hied to the prison-house like the mad stream of August flowing in an uncertain path in darkness. (Ll. 253-278.)

(9)

"Oh executioner, be my benefactor and release my husband from the prison."

From her head she took her crown of gold and gave it away to the executioner. Her diamond bracelets she offered him and began to cry bitterly. She offered him besides her beautiful armlet, her necklace studded with pearls and diamonds, and last of all her sweet-sounding anklets. "Take all these, oh executioner," she said, "and grant my prayer."

Her earrings were wonderfully nice. Her blue-coloured *sari* called 'the pride of spring' was a delight to the eyes. All these she presented to him and she clad herself in rags.

All her precious ornaments she thus offered and holding the executioner by the hand began to cry bitterly saying, "Release him, taking all these. Alas! What more can I offer? Though I am the daughter of a Raja, you see how miserable I am. In the place of my husband make *me* a captive. I will gladly court death by impalement to-morrow by the order of the king. Put that stone of twenty-two maunds on my breast. My bridegroom will not be able to bear the pain of this heavy stone. Women, though fragile and soft, are doomed to life-long sorrows. They are inured to suffer all freaks of fate, so their heart is hard. If any one is able to suffer this cruel punishment, it is *I* and not *he*."

The beautiful maiden wept and told her little tale in this way. The executioner's heart seemed to melt at her importunities. The cell was the veritable prison of the Lord of Death. It was a heavy iron construction. The portals of this abode of Death were opened. Inside there was nothing but darkness. The princess lighted a lamp. The chains and handcuffs of the prince were removed.

The Princess.

"Arise, oh prince. My father is now your enemy. He has put you in this dark cell. Accustomed are you, oh prince, to sleep in a golden couch. Your bed used to be strewn with flowers. How could you, alas, lie down on this hard ground! Even a golden couch and a bed of flowers might seem rough, and fain would I make my own breast a bed for you. You were used to sleep in the pleasure-house of your palace enjoying all comforts. Here are you doomed to suffer the pain of a life in a cell like this! How do I wish I could have an opportunity to wash your feet with cool scented water and fan you with a beautiful mica fan! How I wish that I could serve nicely prepared betels to you in small golden boxes! How I wish that when you would feel uneasy in the bed I would offer my own breast as a soft bed for you!

The Prince.

"Do not weep any more, oh daughter of the Raja. Your father is hard-hearted. I never saw you before this. Your colour is wonderfully fair. After having had the pleasure of seeing you to-day I shall not regret to lose my life to-morrow. I am to lose my life by impalement to-morrow at the order of your father. Thank God for the great fortune granted to me of seeing you even for this short time before my death. Sit by me, dearest, let me see your moon-like face with my insatiate eyes. Your father has pledged his words to marry you to me. I am pained at the thought of separation from you soon. Three-fourths of the night is past. Only the last part is left. Death stares me in the face and at this moment how precious do you seem to me! My heart is rendered hard. As soon as you will be away, this heart will lose its best happiness. How do I wish to embrace you once, my dearest, though it be only once in life! How delighted am I to look at that angelic face of yours even for a few moments, though it is certain that my death takes place to-morrow morning!

The Princess.

"Oh prince, oh my dearest, your chains are all removed. Now you may return to your home. If ever you be so kind, think of this poor girl as a servant devoted to your feet for ever. Hard has been your lot here—in this country of your enemies. I shall always feel pain at the thought of what you have suffered here. But more than all, my grief will be great if I am forgotten." (Ll. 278-350.)

(10)

She led him by the hand and showed the path through a forest. As the moon flies away—chased by the demon Rahu, so hastily did he flee away, and the poor maiden's eyes were flooded with tears ; when bidding adieu to him she said again "Oh my dearest, when shall we meet again? When will that fortunate hour come? Like a fish dragged from water, or a living being of the land deprived of air, how shall I be able to drag my existence separated from you?"

The Prince.

"Weep no more, oh fair Princess. Have patience and wait. You should not be allowed to be left behind for long, but your father is cruel and may take some drastic measure. To-night was fixed for our marriage. What an irony of fate is this! Control your mind, if we live, we shall meet again."

In the forest he had tied his horse to a tree. He jumped on its back and before bidding final adieu, the princess bowed down to the feet of her Lord, saying—"Oh the planets of heaven, the sun and the moon and the stars, oh trees and creepers, be witness. You have all heard what has fallen from the lips of the Prince." Saying so she could not say anything more, her voice was choked with tears. Controlling herself she said again—"To-night our meeting is in deep sorrow" and then again she dedicated herself to his lotus-feet. She said "In all the three worlds none is so disowned by all, none so helpless as I am. May you, oh Prince, reserve a little space for me at your feet." Thus saying her last words, she bowed down to the feet of the Prince once again.

He gently and tenderly touched her. He wiped away her tears with great affection. His own eyes were not dry.

He wiped them also and said, " Thou, oh Creator and Master, be witness, oh sun and moon, the beasts that roam in the forest and the trees and creepers that abound here, be witness ye all, and ye oh rivers and canals of this country, the wind which touches us, all be witness, this princess is mine, in my life and in death I will cling to her."

He embraced her after these word and rode fast. The bee flew away leaving the imprint of his last kiss on the flower. (Ll. 350-386.)

(11)

Now listen to what next befell Raja Birsingha. When he heard the news of the prince being made a captive he at once left his city and paid a visit to a place named Kamina (near Kamakhya) where lived an old woman named Maina. She was a mistress of the black art, and knew all the *mantras* and incantations—wherewith to perform marvels. The *mantras* were given to her by the spirit Tal. By their charm she could transform a human-being into a tree or a bird. The victim would at once lose his human form and fly up in the air if she wished it. An old man regained his youth and a man would turn a woman by the force of her *mantras*. Our Raja Birsingha on his arrival at Kamina approached this old woman.

The King.

" Look here, Maina, I have come to you from a long distance. Many places have I travelled in order to meet you. Kindly instruct me in the art of restoring life to the dead and of killing the living by magic; you will have all the wealth of my royal treasury as reward."

The old woman made a ball-shaped thing with the following ingredients collected from various places :—Blind gnats, malignant flies, the eyes of tigers and buffaloes and the legs of crabs. All this she mixed up and stored in a small box. On a Saturday night she secured the bones of an owl and the quills of porcupine. The liver of a vulture was added to these. She made charmed pills with these things; she also got a handful of dust from the cremation ground. Then she gathered a heap of fuels from different species of wood. A fire was made there and the Raja was asked to sit near her. In the deep hours of the night she gave him the *mantras* he had desired.

Thus crowned with success the Raja went back to his city. When he was on his way he perceived that the mystic words of the great god Shiva, together with some of his knotted hair, the evil spirits Dakini and Yogini, a whirlwind and the Mahavidyas accompanied him through the air unperceived by others. He also perceived that Bhagabati, presiding over all esotoric knowledge, had become his friend and ally. He propitiated the last named goddess by going through due rituals and sacrificing at her altar a pair of buffaloes. And after having taken all necessary action preliminary to war he now became ready for fighting Bharai Raja again. (Ll. 386-415.)

(12)

He arrived at the city gate and threw his challenge. The war drum was sounded in the city and Raja Bharai came out with his great bow in hand. Its terrible twang was heard from a distance resounding in the sky as he drew the string. In front of him stood Raja Birsingha in an attitude of firm determination, grim and terrible as a live coal.

For a time it was a drawn battle. No party seemed weak or inclined to yield, but in the meantime Raja Birsingha uttered the *mantras* given by Maina and spread a handful of charmed dust in the air. The army of his enemy became blind and he easily cut them with his axe. A sound of alarm rose on all sides while Raja Birsingh exclaimed to his army, "Strike, strike the enemy." Bharai Raja changed himself into a serpent, Raja Birsingh became a peacock and chased it. Bharai next became a pigeon ; his enemy, who was now more than his match, became a vulture and sprang upon the pigeon. The pigeon changed shape and became a fish. It fell into the sea. Its adversary followed it there becoming an otter.

Then the Kotch Raja changed himself into a hawk. Birsingh became a vulture and pursued the hawk. Thereupon Bharai finding no way of escape reduced himself to dust, the small particles mixed with sand and could not be discriminated. Bir Raja next became a whirlwind and scattered the dust in the air. Then he resolved to aim his last blow at the enemy. He recited some *mantras* praying that Bharai Raja might be reduced to a piece of stone. He conjured a Dakini to help him and blew three times with his mouth. He uttered some incantations and thus charmed a handful of dust. He threw this dust at Bharai Raja uttering the curse—"Turn into stone, oh wretch!" As soon as the dust touched the body of Raja Bharai he became a statue of stone. (Ll. 415-444.)

(13)

The people of the country filled the air with wild laments and the queen was mad with grief.

The treasury was seized and Raja Birsingh became the master of the land. The queen then threw away her eight valuable ornaments and wearing the rags of a beggar came out in the streets. Her daughter whose beauty dazzled the eyes of all who beheld her, followed her mother's steps with down-cast eyes. The citizens could not suppress their tears at the sight.

Her chignon was bound up with gold and silver threads.

She wore a matchless *sari* called 'the starry sky' but her profuse hair of black colour and her brilliant robes looked cheerless and faint. She looked like the moon covered by clouds. Like a gold image she shone in beauty and grace. This handsome princess was now a beggar in the streets of the city.

See, my friend, the unsteady nature of things and the wild freaks of fickle fortune,—to-day a monarch, to-morrow he turns a Fakir!

The queen approached the court of Raja Birsingh and submitted, "Oh Raja Birsingh, when I find my husband turned into stone I cannot see my way through tears; but let that pass. It is quite natural that I should feel my responsibility in respect of the young princess, my daughter. My husband pledged his word to marry her to your son. Your accomplished son is in every way fit for my handsome daughter. All my riches, my kingdom itself have I surrendered to your Majesty. I have nothing else to give you. I now hereby offer my daughter in fulfilment of my husband's pledge. She has suffered hard. She is dear as my life-blood, and precious like my eyes. If I do not see her for a moment I become restless and unhappy. Little do I care for myself. I am ready to die, indifferent to whatever might befall me. But my humble prayer to you is this: be pleased to accept my daughter as the bride of the prince, your son."

The cruel king abused the queen fallen in distress. He spat three times as a sign of great contempt. His words were ungracious and rough, and his eyes were reddened by anger, as he said,—"Do you dare, oh queen, to hope that I would marry my son to the daughter of a chief of the hill-tribe? What is the value of pledges in this case? How can a proposal of marriage be possible with the daughter of a Kotch? Did you ever hear that heaven made friends with earth on terms of equality? I am descended from Gods and hold a high lineage. What relationship may ever exist between a lion and a fox? It is sheer madness to hope that the noble *Aswatha* tree and the despised *Saora* plant (abode of witches) would be bound in friendship. I have already settled the marriage of the prince in a southern country—in the Dakkhin Patan. Go away from my presence, oh queen of Raja Bharai. I can have nothing to do with you or your daughter. You may select a groom for her from one of the hillmen of the Hajang tribe."

The queen cried aloud without any power of restraint and struck her head with her hand. She embraced her daughter and said crying, "Oh my poor daughter! oh miserable girl! Who knew that such things were in store for you?"

As she cried, the daughter cried also, and all the citizens were in deep mourning. The queen had secretly carried with her some pills of poison. She swallowed them straight, and before she expired, said:—"In this whole world there is no place for you, my sweet Champabati. I leave you alone and absolutely helpless making over my charge to One who cares for all."

Then her two eyes closed for ever. Alas! what became of Champabati? Hear, oh my audience, the end of my sad tale. (Ll. 444-502.)

(14)

Champabati.

"Oh mother dear, you have left me quite helpless and all alone. I have lost my father and the kingdom and last of all, *you* my dear mother. There is none in the world to give me shelter or even an encouraging word of hope. One whom I thought to be my own and to whom I resigned myself, takes, alas! no notice of me. He has not come even once to say a good word. The deep wound I bear in my heart is not to be told to any body. It is due to my ill luck. I wanted a little water from the sea and it has refused to give a drop. The entrance to my pleasure-house has been barred by a hedge of thorns. I saw the dark-blue clouds arrayed in the sky, and approached them for a drop of water to quench my thirst, but instead of cold drink got a thunder-bolt hurled on my head. How unfortunate am I. If I go to the sea it becomes dry. If I want to have a place in the land it slips away from my sight. When I wander in the forest wishing to be killed by a tiger or bear, the ferocious animals avoid my track. Even the monster-snake which devours goats and other animals seems to fly away from me in an instinctive dread, as I am unlucky.

"Oh Lord of my heart, my last prayer to you is this, enjoy your kingdom with your new bride. From this distance my *pranam* goes to you. May you live for a hundred years. Do not recollect poor Champa. The memory would cause you pain."

With folded hands she bowed to the memory of her husband and turned mad. As she wandered in the country-side she wept all the time.

Even the statue of Bharai Raja became instinct with life at this condition of Champabati, for it was seen that tears fell from the eyes of the stone image. (Ll. 502-528.)

BAGULA—THE MERCHANT'S DAUGHTER

PREFACE TO BAGULA—THE MERCHANT'S DAUGHTER

This ballad was collected by Babu Chandra Kumar De in April, 1930, from two persons—Nakul Bairagi and Kristaram Mal—both residents of the village Madhyabati in Pargana Khalijuri (Mymensingh). It is a small ballad complete in 427 lines.

Like Mahua, Chandrabati, Sham Rai and Dhoparpat this song is characterised by a terseness and a rapid succession of incidents knit together into an interesting plot. It is permeated by an exuberance of lyrical element and can be easily rendered into a melo-drama. Prosaic details are mostly omitted in this song and the author, far from elaborating the story in the manner of classic poets, has in many places given mere gestures and suggestive touches, leaving the blanks of the narrative to be filled up by the reader.

We are at first ushered into a chamber of the village-school, where the girl Bagula just at the dawn of her youth is attending her lessons. Here a class-fellow, a young merchant, is her sole companion. The evening is past and the sky with its crown of moon and stars has just made itself visible through a window of the room. She sits high up on the gallery and the youth's seat is on the ground-floor. She drops her pen below, as if through carelessness, and makes a request to our young hero to pick it up for her.

The youth is shrewed enough to understand her tricks and says that she has dropped her pen in this way, not once, not twice but this is the third time that she has done so. He seizes the opportunity and asks a favour. Should she agree, he would pick up the pen for her; otherwise he would no longer allow himself to be duped and worried in that way.

The girl, it seems, had dropped the pen this time with a purpose. She wanted to have an opportunity to open her mind to him. She says that the young prince of the country has taken a fancy for her and that her father tempted by the prospects of seeing his daughter made the consort of a prince, has given his acquiescence to the offer.

Here now she plainly tells the young lad what she would do. She would rather prefer to wander in forests and dales, living on forest-fruits and sleeping in a bed of leaves. She does not covet the luxuries of the palace; but in no case will she marry the prince. She frankly says, "I hate him," adding that she would marry the young merchant if he would care to have her and that she is resolved to speak to her father plainly all these things. "There will be no more any shilly-shally," she says, "over a vital question affecting the happiness of my life."

The first canto ends here. The author omits the events that immediately follow, *viz.*, her refusal to marry the prince, her father's consent to her marriage with the bride-groom-elect, and an account of the elysian days of nuptial happiness which follow, he at once introduces an episode which separates the pair. The husband is bent on a sea-voyage. With tears in her eyes she performs the usual religious rites preliminary to his departure and gives him many a sound advice as to how he should conduct himself in the sea under violent storm.

The third canto opens the picture of her disconsolate and lonely life separated from her husband. Here the conventional *Baramasi* or an account of each of the twelve months of the year associated with her sufferings is introduced. The monotony of *Baramasi* in the Bengali literature sometimes repels the reader; but yet to the Bengali, when the poet refers to the harvest in the field in *Āgrahayan*, to the golden sheaves bending low under the breeze and the festivities of the rural folk when paddy has been heaped in the granaries—the women with lamps in their hands receiving the peasants who return home with harvest,—the account of these cannot fail to be interesting though told a hundred times as it reminds him over again of his sweet home—his earthly paradise. The darkness of mist veiling the face of nature in *Paus*, the biting cold of *Magh*, the fresh-blown flowers and the gentle touch of the wind surcharged with their honeyed fragrance reminding one of Bengal in the months of *Falgun* and *Chaitra*, the sweet-smelling screw-plants [1] and the floods of *Āshar* and *Shraban* when the villages are resonant with the sounds of the bells and musical instruments for worshipping Manasa Debi,—down to *Aswin* when every little child and every young man and woman of the country-side put on their gay attire and enjoy the gala-day of Durga puja—the pleasant associations of festivities and religious observances during the different seasons have an indescribable attraction for the Bengali readers and they are not weary of hearing them once again, though they have heard the *Baramasi* repeatedly in many of the poems. The poet here while describing nature's picturesque scenes skillfully shows the background of a persistent and dogged pursuit of the prince to tempt and threaten Bagula during the course of the whole year. She finds herself in a bed of thorns and takes to devices to save her loving husband from danger. She is compelled to go on lying, and howsoever culpable she might be in the eyes of society as regards the ethics of her attitude towards the prince, her conduct will certainly command justification in consideration of her utter helplessness and of the designing ways of the wicked prince.

[1] Screw plants = Pandanus odoratissimus.

This ballad does not certainly rank high in our folk-lore; its poetic merits are moderate, though the lyrical resources of the poet occasionally reach a high level of excellence. But of all things in respect of transcription it is the hardest to reproduce the felicities of emotion described in a lyrical poem—particularly so in the rendering of a Bengali song into English. The two languages are poles asunder as vehicles of thought. There is nothing in Bengali of that manly and almost savage grandeur of a Teutonic language like English, whereas the tenderness of Bengali, specially when it deals with an emotional subject and its appeal to the heart make the reproduction of its original charm in English an almost hopeless task.

The character of Bagula presents a conception not very congenial to the Hindu mind as constituted in the present society. We have always noticed that the heroines of these ballads are generally shown from a background which is not at all orthodox and conventional. The woman is tempted by the prince—the messenger comes and goes and when the letter-bearer gets a rebuff and is prevented from visiting her, a trained pigeon takes her place as message-bearer. No Hindu woman unless she is absolutely perverse would write a letter to her seducter in the present society. She does not say anything of all that transpired to her mother-in-law or sister-in-law but she conducts a steady correspondence without their knowledge. All this no member of a Hindu society to-day would tolerate, nor would any one amongst us consider such a course as consistent with the chaste life of a woman.

The question of social condemnation apart, there is surely a justification of her conduct to those not prejudiced by the orthodox notions and conventions of the present day.

The mother-in-law and her daughter would certainly have

created a row endangering her husband's life at the hands of the prince, had she given out all that happened. She could not openly reject the prince though so cruelly tormented by him. She is not half so courageous as Malua, nor ferocious as Mahua. She tries to evade the danger-zone by a policy of continued tactics which are all of questionable ethics according to the present standard of Hindu society.

Here we have a woman who is as chaste and spotless as any described in this ballad literature, but she is a type quite different from many of the other heroines. It is the thought of her husband's safety above all that makes her adopt tactics from the beginning to the end, raising hopes in her lover, while she was always true to herself. Though the story is one of great tragic interest, the end is happy and we feel a breath of relief when the husband and wife meet at the end—the *bona fides* of the latter being made clear to the young merchant who had just grounds to suspect her fidelity.

The society described in this ballad seems to be a loose one not controlled by the rigid canons of to-day. The first part is closely analogous to the story of the Sakhi-sona rendered into classical verse by the poet Fakirram Kabibhusan in the 16th century. There also a prince's daughter drops her pen and requests her lover to pick it up which the latter does on certain conditions but the agreement in the two stories does not go beyond this episode. Fakirram Kabibhusan evidently took his inspiration from a ballad prevalent in the country before the 16th century and here again we find a similar type presented in the rustic language of the ballad-maker. Whatever changes might have been effected in the language we believe that the original ballad was composed in the 14th or 15th century.

From the style in which the song is composed I find that

it contains some characteristics of the period in which Chandidas flourished.

In my introduction to other parts I have mentioned some ballads which possess kindred ideas and an unmistakable phraseology which show that they are products of a common age. Kanchanmala or Dhoparpat, Mahua, Mahisal Bandhu, Sham Rai and a few others are characterised by a similarity of style and an analogous conception of poetic situations more or less of the nature of those described in Chandidas's poems.

I have also referred to the fact that in the 13th and 14th centuries Bengali language was already in a highly advanced condition. It had developed a subtle and fine stock of emotional expressions which is peculiarly Bengali. There is hardly any influence of Sanskrit or of Persian though the country at the time not only abounded with Pandits but also Maulavis. We not only find in these poems words current in particular localities of Bengal and a galaxy of phrases which the woman of Bengal still use in the remote moffusil, but the very subject-matter of the poems belongs to a period, when in sexual matters there was a distinctive Sahajia element. This school of the 13th and 14th centuries is permeated by a spirit of freedom specially in the conception of female characters which we miss in the subsequent literature of Renaissance. There is no rigour in caste rules. Women do many things not compatible with the scope of their recognised duties in the present society. In love matters they show a forwardness and lack of a sense of decency—a little too much in comparison with the present standard. How far the women exercised their liberty within the four walls of the zenana may be understood from the fact that the heroine not only expressed her willingness to marry the young merchant without any hasitancy or blush, but she kept up a steady and long correspondence with her lover though she was a married woman. In spite of all this the woman Bagula betrays some complications which show a considerable literary power on the part of the poet.

The latter part of this story bears a close analogy to another ballad which has been just received by me from Babu Chandra Kumar De. The ballad is of Prince Purandar. It appears from these similarities that the country had been full of old ballads which were partly forgotten in course of time and their parts dove-tailed to subsequent compositions.

DINESH CHANDRA SEN.

Bagula—the Merchant's Daughter

(1)

Bagula.

"All that I read or write, oh friend, scarcely makes any impression on my distracted mind. Here have I dropped my pen. Will you kindly pick it up for me? Vacant is my mind and my hands have lost all strength. The flow-tide has set in, and the river is all on a sudden flooded. The lamp gives a glimmering light. It scarcely dispels the darkness of the room. I entreat you, friend, pick up the pen that has dropped from my hand."

The Young Merchant.

"But this is not the first time that your pen has dropped from your hand—it is the third time. Yonder shine the moon and the stars and the wind comes from afar gently touching the waves of the river. In the deep forest the bird has retired to its nest—its wings dripping dews blown by the breeze. A shepherd is playing on his flute from a distance. At this tranquil hour of night will you make a promise to me? Oh maiden! Promise that you will do what I will bid you—the moon and the stars be the witnesses. If you make the promise I will gladly pick up the pen for you."

Bagula.

"What promise, what word shall I give you, youth? My father wishes that I should marry that wicked prince. But I tell you quite frankly I do not like to marry the prince.

I would not be the bird of a cage though it has golden bars. Free like a bird of the sky I want to live,—in forests and dales. What course I should take I do not know. That wicked prince shadows me everywhere and insists on a reciprocation of his passion from me, and to tell you frankly, my youth, my life itself, are being poisoned by his importunities. He has made my very existence unbearable to me. Please pick up the pen that has dropped on the ground this time and I call upon the moon and stars to witness my vow. I will marry you and none other. You will be the husband of my heart. In life and in death, dear, you will be my love. Neither do I wish for the treasure of a king, nor for his palace or kingdom. I will live happily with you under the shade of trees. Golden ornaments and jewellery do not tempt me. You will pluck the fair forest-flowers, and weave them into a garland for me, I will prize it the most. No desire have I for golden couches and cushions decked with jewells. If you will allow me to lie down at your feet, my life will be thrice blessed. Let this night be my witness, all that I have said is true and not one word of this is untrue. To-morrow I will plainly tell my mind to father. Oh my pretty bird, whose nest is in yonder banana plants, sing to-night a bridal song and go to-morrow wherever you will ; oh wind, your dance is playful on the river-bank and there you love to dwell. Be witness, I have opened my mind to my love to-day. Here is this garland of flowers which I have prepared with all the hopes of youth. I present this to you. Pray wear it on your neck as a bridal present. Neither my father nor my mother knows of it.

"The moon and the stars alone know of it ; the wind alone knows of it." (Ll. 1-46.)

(2)

The trumpet is sounding and the sweet sound of *shanai* is heard at intervals. To-day the beautiful girl of this tale is going to be married to the merchant's son. The young merchant is going on a sea voyage.

Bagula.

"Oh husband of my heart, remember a poor woman's entreaties. When there will be storm in the sea anchor your boat near the coast. When the southern wind will blow, do not venture a voyage in the sea. Do not go very far to the north. If you happen to pass by a river near the hills, you should not trust the turns and nooks; they are dangerous. In the east the sea is deep and illimitable and there are islets full of man-eating monsters. When any danger comes recite the name of Durga. And remember, my love, your promise to return within a year. If a storm overtakes your boat pray to Manasa Devi, and bear in mind that He, the lord of the universe, is our only stay—the help of the helpless."

As she said all this her tears began to flow incessantly. She took in her hand the lamp to bid him farewell. Like the rain of August her eyes dropped tears. She became maddened with grief like the snake on the point of losing the gem from its hood. She placed at the prow of the boat sacred grass, and rice and with her two soft hands folded together she prayed to Manasa Devi for her husband's welfare. With incense and flowers the boat was decked and purified, and as she said "Victory and success attend my husband's journey," she washed his feet and with her hair all loosened she wiped them again. There she bade adieu to her husband for a year. The tide was against but the wind puffed up the sail and carried the boat fast. She returned home from the bank with a pain in her heart which pierced it like a shaft. (Ll. 46-74.)

(3)

Alone she slept in her chamber, she lay down in her bed and then rose again, restless and unhappy. There was a rich cushion decked with flowers and sweet smelling buds close by, but she lay on the bare floor. She cast away her jewells and ornaments, and the night seemeed too long to her. Her love for flowers was gone. She cared not for garlands and wreaths. She lost all taste for food. Sometimes with a sigh she heard the cuckoo singing in the near forest—its sweet note making the leaves tremble. She saw the *malati* creepers bending low under their floral load. There on the small boughs of the plants, the *champa* flowers looked wonderfully beautiful, and as she saw all these she cursed her youth. "What is the love of these men! she said to herself, "Alas! he has left me in this pleasant season. How can I control my mind which has run mad after him? How can I resist the course of my youthful nature? Youth will decay. Had I been a bird, fain would I fly to the region through which the boat of my love is sailing. Oh my beautiful bee with a jet-black colour and eyes which sparkle like silver, you wander about all places. Hum unto my ears a message from my love. How pleasing would it be! Oh wind, your march is through unbounded space. Tell me on what sea you have met my love. Oh moon and stars, earth hides nothing from you, can you not tell me where my love is wandering in this pleasant night?" (Ll. 74-100.)

(4)

It is now dawn. The flowers are in full bloom in the bower. A maid-servant has come with a letter in her hand. She wiped away the dust from her body as she had laid herself down on the floor, and she pondered as to whose letter it might be. Was it one sent by her beloved? Her eyes sparkled with joy at the thought. She opened the letter and read the contents. It was a love-letter from the prince whom she had rejected. A thrill of fear passed through her as she read it. The prince wants a reciprocation of his love from her—this is the burden of the epistle. The maid-servant whispered to her ears, "Why should you lie down on the floor? There is a rich cushion for you in the right royal style. Come with me to the prince's abode. Your fair person has no ornaments—this does not look well. Your body will be decked with gold and gems. The garden of the palace abounds with *champa* plants and there are hundreds of flowers full-blown ; maid-servants will pluck and gather them for you. In a golden box betel with lime will be stored for you and presented by the servants. You will be in full enjoyment of all comforts of life like a queen. The maid-servants will be in readiness to serve you with scented oil of all sorts. They will arrange your hair and make fine braids, and you will look like a queen of beauty with them. Know it, dear girl, that the golden flowers that bloom to-day lose their charm to-morrow and are thrown away as faded things. The smile that adorns your lips to-day will fade to-morrow. The youth of a woman, her most valued treasure, is just-like tide. When it begins to ebb there is no force that can stop its course."

Bagula.

"Oh dear messenger, tell your prince all that I will say and also deliver this my letter to him. Tell him that my husband is away from home and I have taken a vow of which I will speak presently. Explain to him my situation. Like a good friend you should kindly acquaint him with my sorrows. My mother-in-law and sister-in-law treat me very cruelly in the house. Silently do I shed tears oppressed inhumanly by them. Ill can I suppress the desires natural to youth. Owing to the cruel treatment of mother-in-law in concert with her daughter it has become difficult for me to stay in this house. But yet my vow is a vow, and ask the prince to wait for one year, for my vow is for one year. During this time I will not lie in my bed but sleep on bare floor. I will not besides look at the face of any male person other than my husband. I have vowed to forego all enjoyments of life for one year. You see just the mat spread on the floor soiled with dust. That is my bed. I do not touch a couch or cushion. For one year in conformity with my vow I will not touch a flower or any scented oil, nor will I bathe. After one year my youth will still be a blooming thing. Explain, dear messenger, all these facts and ask him to feel compassion for me. After one year I shall visit him in his palace. Take this letter and when you will hand it over to him speak a word in my behalf so that he may feel pity for me and excuse me.'' (Ll. 100-150.)

(5)

The maid-servant took the letter and went away and the girl in her apartment all alone, wept bitterly saying, "Alas! alas! the prince is a wicked man. How can I dare live all alone in this house? He may do anything in a fit of rage out of disappointed pride. Oh God, who knows what harm may come to my husband through this man. Wild as a forest tiger is he—bent on his prey. I I do not know what harm he may do to my abode of peace. For a long period has my husband gone abroad for what unknown treasure he may get in strange countries. If God is kind He may vouchsafe the return of my husband in six months. But if He is unkind and it is so destined that we shall meet no more I will cut my throat with a knife."

The girl lamented in this way in her lonely room and passed a full month. (Ll. 150-164.)

(6)

Cold wind came with December (আগন মাস). Her elders prohibited the messenger from visiting the girl ; so her correspondence was kept up with the help of a trained pigeon. Her letters came flying through the air.

Bagula.

"The cold wind of December makes one shiver in his house. The new harvest is pleasant to see, as the ripe corn-stalks bend low when the wind blows over them. The housewives with their sacred presents to the harvest-goddess welcome her in their houses and worship her. Unfortunate as I am, my voice fails in my throat trying to join with theirs while reciting a hymn. Oh mother goddess, bless me, so that I may meet my dear husband when the day will dawn to-morrow."

Prince.

"Oh fair merchant's daughter, I send this pigeon unto you. If you have any message to deliver you may send it through this bird."

Bagula.

"Oh prince, listen to my prayer. Wait this month with patience!" (Ll. 164-180.)

(7)

Bagula (aside).

"January has come with its thick shade of mists. The touch of the cold wind makes one feel feverish. My husband alas, is not at home. A sigh comes from the recesses of my heart, oh what a pity! How fortunate I should be to behold the face of my husband to-morrow!"

Prince.

"Oh my fair one! will you tell me how long you will deceive me in this way!"

Bagula.

"Your pigeon, prince, comes and goes through the air. I solicit this favour from you that you may wait with patience for some months more.

"The mother-in-law and her daughter are cruel to me. Their evil tongue is ever busy abusing me." (Ll. 181-193.)

(8)

Bagula (aside).

"It is February now. I feel biting cold as I sleep on the bare floor. My flame-coloured *sari* is rotten, yet I do not wear a new one. My blanket is full of fresh cotton and my bed-stead fits the mansion of a rich man. But these I do not use. Alas, if my husband were here we would sleep together on the rich bed-stead there and his broad chest would be my most comfortable bed. The long winter night would pass away quickly when we two would remain together enjoying each other's company.

May my body be reduced to the dust that it is. When I have lost him who valued it most, what is the good of my existence? Once I was his pet, nay, his very life. When he has left me, there is none to look after me and hold me dear. What is the use of this life? It is now a burden to me."

Prince.

"Oh, merchant's daughter, three months have passed since I have been courting you. How long can I wait for you?"

Bagula.

"I assure you, prince, I will surely visit you in your house. I too am passing restless days. It is only for my vow that I am suffering in this way and depriving myself."

(Ll. 193-219.)

(9)

Bagula (aside).

"It is now March—the prince of months. All around me, I find beauty and fragrance of new-blown flowers. The plants and trees look gay with new attire, they are decked with new ornaments. Alas, how can I expect this gay nature to feel sympathy for a sad soul like mine! In this heyday of spring wherever I cast my glance, the vision of my husband seems to appear before me from all sides. I see him in the flowers, in the creepers and I seem to hear him in the hummings of bees. But when I try to touch him, the vision fades. I breathe him in the fragrance of flowers and I hear his voice in the note of birds. But alas, I find him not in actual life, and pass my days and nights weeping."

Prince.

"Oh fair merchant's daughter, it is four months now, I can no longer keep my patience."

Bagula.

"Oh king's son, oh prince, for one month more I want you to wait." (Ll. 211-225.)

(10)

Bagula (aside).

"It is April. Blooming Spring appears on all sides. My mind knows no rest. I sit in my bed for a time and then rise up restless. Sometimes when I close my eyes in sleep for a moment I dream that my hushand has returned home. I dream as if he has embraced me sitting on a couch and kissed me tenderly. When it is midnight I dream again that he has clasped me with his arms warmly, and when the night draws to a close I dream that we have fallen in deep sleep in each other's arms. But when the day dawns I awake to find that he is not by my side. The cuckoo awakens me from my sleep by its sweet note only to bring in a consciousness of the sad fact that my husband has gone away. He appears as a vision everywhere but not in reality. I seek him vainly in my flame-coloured *sari*, I seek him in my dishevelled hair, but alas, he can be found nowhere. He is in my heart and I perceive his presence there but the vision vanishes and he never becomes visible."

Prince.

"Listen to me, oh fair one, have mercy. Five months have passed away. How long will you beguile me in this way?"

Bagula.

"Half of the year is gone, oh prince, wait a little more. Let the new year come and I shall go to your palace." (Ll. 225-243.)

(11)

Bagula (aside).

"The new year has come with *Baisakh* (May.) I do not know what is in store for me. The soft wind blows but it does not cool my burning heart. Like the slow fire in a dry piece of dung, my heart burns incessantly without remission. I cannot control my mind which madly yearns for my dear love. Here I spread my purple-coloured *sari* on the floor and sigh for my absent husband. The vow that I say to the prince, I have taken, is a vain pretext. If the lord of my heart would come here now, fain would I sit to weave a floral wreath to garland him with the fresh flowers of my garden. In the pleasant bower there I would make the bee a captive for life and would not let him go again. But now I pine for him in the lonely chamber and pass wakeful nights."

Prince.

"Oh fair girl, how long will you play deception on me? Six months have already passed."

Bagula.

"But wait a little more and have patience. We shall surely meet after a short time." (Ll. 243-259.)

(12)

Bagula (aside).

"It is June now. The mangoe-groves abound with ripe fruits. My life, my youth are all gone for nothing. Empty is our pleasure house in the midst of yonder tank. If he were with me, fain would we enjoy each other's company in that pleasant but now deserted house."

Prince.

"Oh, my fair lady, this month has also come to an end. There is a limit to one's patience. How long shall I be beguiled in this way?"

Bagula.

"To be honest and frank with you, oh prince, there are five months more for the observance of my vow and you will have to wait till this time." (Ll. 259-269.)

(13)

Bagula (aside).

"It is July now. The rivers have overflown their banks. Dry streams are inundated. The clouds roar and they shed cooling showers, but my thirst is not allayed. The cloud and rain cannot soothe me. I look towards the sky and watch the planets, praying them to be favourable till my overstrained eyes close in fatigue. When Providence is inclement, the river dries even in July. Just hear the sound of thunder. Its deep-mouthed roar makes the earth tremble and quake. My youth will pass away in this way. Oh ye winds and thunder, tell my lord that his once dear wife is on the point of death."

Prince.

"Have mercy on me fair one, do not beguile me by false hopes in this way any further. A golden palanquin I will be sending to you and I have kept a diamond necklace for you."

Bagula (aside).

"Oh wicked prince, you talk of diamonds. Know that I value the dust of my husband's feet more than all your diamonds." (*Aloud*) "Be patient, prince. Long have you waited. A little more will you have to wait." (Ll. 269-289.)

(14)

August has come with its flood. Water has submerged lands. They all worship Manasa Devi in this month. Our fair damsel began preparations for worshipping the goddess in right earnest. When she dedicated the cup to her she was in tears. She wiped away the floor of the temple with her unbraided hair and decorated it with *alipana* paintings. Powdered rice mixed with water was her paint. She drew a picture of the goddess with a crown of five serpents in deep devotion. She bowed to the goddess with all humility and with folded hands prayed for granting her the boon of her husband's return.

Prince.

"Now listen to me fair one, I will not allow myself to be beguiled any more by your tricks. This time my soldiers will go to bring you to the palace by force."

Bagula.

"But wait, prince, only for a short while. The period of my vow and its conditions are almost over. There will now be no more delay in our meeting." (Ll. 289-303.)

(15)

Bagula (aside).

" The moon of September is so bright that it shows the very bottom of rivers. Alas, has my husband's ship stuck on some bank or has he grown so cruel as not to feel a desire to see me? But lo! the sail of a ship is seen yonder, pushed by the wind. Is it the ship of my husband? To be sure it is my lord who is coming home with his ship filled with cargo." She brought out from her chest her valuable flame-coloured *sari.* With sacred grass and rice she went to the landing ghat to escort her husband after observing the usual religious rites. At this time the trained pigeon of the prince came with a message. The letter it carried was to this effect—"Oh fair damsel, you have put on your choice attire all in vain. The merchant—your husband will not come to your house again. He has got himself drowned with all his men in the Abanga."

Bagula.

" Oh king's son, let my husband be drowned, let the treasure of the ship be all lost. I do not mind all this loss if I can get a right royal husband like you." (Ll. 305-321.)

(16)

Bagula (aside).

" In the month of October they all worship Durga. He will surely come home to worship the goddess. I have collected all the lotus flowers of the lake and their leaves for worship. The beautiful *singara* flowers are all abloom. But they are fading away. He has not returned even in this month. November will soon be over; alas! alas! Who will save me from death which is imminent? "

Prince.

"Oh my young beauty, do no more play your cruel tricks on me. One year is nearly over. There is only a month to complete the year. But I warn you, repose no trust in your husband. If he happens to return I will confine him in the prison and there kill him outright. In December I will marry you. You will have precious stones and pearls to decorate your person with. Your bracelet and necklace will all be of diamond."

Bagula.

"But the completion of the rites prior to the fulfilment of my vow is near at hand. Why should you be impatient? I shall not be sorry if you kill my husband for I will find in his place a royal mate by the grace of God"

She returned to her chamber and began to cry helplessly. She kept hidden within her braids a deadly poison. The prince in the meantime made grand preparations for worship as avowed by the girl. Hundreds of black and white goats were brought for sacrifice. Buffaloes and pigeons in large numbers were brought there for the same purpose.

Bagula.

"It is November. My mind is all at ease. My husband has died in a strange land. To-morrow in the midnight be pleased to send your palanquin. I will go to your chamber." (Ll. 321-349.)

(17)

The pigeon flew up with the letter but the sister-in-law was lying in wait. She caught the bird by a net and read the letter. "You, shameless unchaste woman!" she said, "It is proper that you should drown yourself to hide your shame or kill yourself by fire." She took the girl to a solitary room and kept her in the lockup. The pigeon she put into a cage.

Just at this time her husband arrived at the landing-ghat. The trumpet sounded and the report went through the town that the merchant had returned with his cargo.

He left his ship and at once came to the compartment of his wife. "Oh my Bagula!" he said, "Oh! my life, for a full year I have not seen your smiling face. We live in the land of a wicked prince, who under various pretexts sent me from place to place all this time. I shall no longer stay in this monster's country. Open the door, oh my love, after a long time have I come to see you."

Just then the sister-in-law came and said addressing her brother, "Scandal has spread in the country. No remedy do I find. Your wife has played a deception on you." She opened the cage of the bird and showed the letter of his wife. He read the contents and was fired with rage. He ordered her to be sent to exile on board one of his ships. (Ll. 349-375.)

(18)

Alas for Bagula, she cried and lamented in this way—"Oh forest tiger, eat me up. But do not let the report of my death reach the ear of my husband. Without any fault he has banished his true wife. It will surely give pain to his heart if he knows the facts of my death. My husband is not in fault—mine is the fault. I did not swallow the poison, I kept tied in my hair. I was afraid lest the wicked prince would kill my husband. Hence I beguiled him by telling him of a false vow. If I would die by poison I would certainly be out of his range and if my husband would have gone to a different country, he would certainly avoid all risk. Little would I mind if I were to die, but how glad would I be to know that he was out of danger. Oh trees and creepers, oh sun and moon, be witness of my sufferings but I entreat you to observe silence. Let my husband not know of my death which would cause him pain. The life of this unhappy woman Bagula is a song of woes."

In the forest she passed a few days sorrowing and lamenting, when another prince happened to find her there and forcibly carried her to his capital. (Ll. 375-394.)

(19)

Bagula (to this Second Prince).

"Hear me, oh prince, I took a vow of abstinence and worship for a full year. The time is nearly up and it is now required to fulfil the conditions."

Prince.

"But good girl, will you tell me what things would you require for the fulfilment of your vow?"

Bagula.

"Goats white and black, buffaloes and pigeons will be required for sacrifice and over and above a lakh of *champa* flowers made of gold will be required for making a garland for the deity. In order to complete the conditions of sacrifice a merchant's son handsome and accomplished in every way should be brought before the altar of the goddess."

The prince was so greatly enamoured of her that he did whatever she said. Any young merchant passing by the river was made captive and brought before Bagula to judge if he would do. Thus many a young merchant was brought but she nodded her head each time indicating her disapproval. Thus hundreds of young merchants were brought to the palace and made captives.

After a long time fortune smiled on her and they brought her own husband as captive. The merchant, her husband, remorseful after having banished her was seeking her in all directions and had steered his ship upstream and arrived there. Like a vulture that hovers over the sea when there is flood* the young merchant was travelling in the sea in quest of his consort. When the men appointed by the prince caught hold of him and brought him to the palace, Bagula saw him and said, "All right, this is the man, release the other youths and you need not seek any more."

The day of worship was near and one night she privately despatched a letter to her husband stating all the facts of her case.

It was the deep hour of midnight, and the young merchant, her husband, took her to his ship which lay anchored there. They set sail to it and marched northward in great speed.

When the day dawned, the people of the city came to know that the girl had fled away from their place. (Ll. 394-427.)

---

* The sea-vultures are attracted by flood where the fishes come up the surface of the sea. The vultures hover near them and swoop over their prey. This is a tradition, how far true, I cannot say.

THE BLIND LOVER

PREFACE TO THE BLIND LOVER.

This short ballad was collected on the 22nd March, 1930, by Babu Chandra Kumar De from two men. One of them is a Hajang named Buddhu, a native of Susang, and another is a Vaishnav mendicant of Khaliajuri, named Mangalnath. Another ballad of a similar nature is current amongst the Hajangs who live in the hills. The Hindus and Hajangs of the plains have probably adopted that ballad, changing it in some places, both in language and in spirit. The profuse Vaishnav element introduced into the frame-work of the story originally conceived by the hill-men, is the work of a later period. But from the language of the ballad it appears to me that the Bengali version was composed at a period not later than the 15th century. There is an allusion to Chandidas in this poem and to another princely lover who fell in love with a woman named Nilmani and turned an ascetic. The phrases and expressions to be found in the poems of Chandidas abound in this ballad and though we are bound to say that the ballad possesses evident signs of the influence of the great poet in the context, there is a kindred element and affinity in the linguistic forms of the two, suggesting the probability of the ballad being composed not much later than Chandidas.

In my General Introduction I shall point out the passages for which the author of the ballad is indebted to the Vaishnav poets. The poem has been constructed on the basis of very liberal sexual ideas which have the flavour of Sahajia. The flute and the marvellous effect of its sound have been the most engaging topic of the earlier Vaishnav poets, particularly of Chandidas. The flute-player here like the pastoral god Krishna or the Greek Orpheus is credited with the marvellous power of creating an extraordinary commotion in nature. The birds come down from the sky and sit mute listening to the flute, the course of the river suddenly changes, the leaves of the trees droop down, and men and women come out of their houses entranced by its charm. We have found similar accounts showing the wonderous effect of the sound of the flute not only in many of the Vaishnav lyrics but also in the ballad of Mahisal Bandhu (The herdsman-lover) and conspicuously in this song.

In Bengal which is pre-eminently an agricultural country the effect of the music of this simple instrument made of a reed or bamboo plant is still irresistible. The poets exaggerate, but whoever has listened to the song of a flute played by a cowherd in the hours of noon, spreading indescribable pathos and sweetness along the country-side, must testify to the wonderful power it exerts. Even now the cowherd plays on his flute to while away the time when the herds are at large in the pastoral ground. I remember to have heard a cowherd singing in chorus with a flute played by his comrades. The song ran thus—' Alas who is the fisherman from whom I purchased fish in some past life and refused to give him the price? Has his curse resulted in this dire calamity of mine? ' It is well known that the Hindu widows of upper classes even when they are mere babies are not allowed to taste fish or meat. The woman of the song who has been just widowed attributes her sad lot to her not having paid the price of fish, which, she thinks, has made her lose the privilege of eating fish in this life. But that is of course not the greatest of her misfortunes. Far greater sorrow looms behind this reference which is but a hint to her lifelong misery. In the still hour of the noon the plaintive but extremely sweet voice of the cowboy mixed with the thrilling sound of the flute spread a charm and an indescribable wail in the air making it resonant with a tender appeal, and as I passed by a boat in the river the sound seemed to create feelings which cannot be adequately expressed. If a lover calls his sweet-heart by the flute, the significance of the melodious sound being understood by her alone, it is easy to imagine how she struggles in her heart to suppress her passionate desire to meet him. To go out from the four walls of the zenana in the day-time, is of course out of the question. Bengal owed in the past a good deal of her happiness, power and poetic inspiration to the bamboo-grove with which the valley abounds. The bamboo-plants supplied her with the flute, its price being nothing. It is not sold in the market, generally speaking, but each cowboy and shepherd cuts a branch and makes a flute for himself. But compared to its sweetness of sound all the musical pipes—the Sanai, the Clarionet and other costly instruments fall into the background. The bamboo supplies the Bengalis with *lathis*. In the *lathi*-play Bengali soldiers were at one time invincible. There are still skilled *lathi*-players who, it is said, can successfully defend themselves from gunshots by a dexterous motion of *lathis*. The flute and the *lathi* were in olden times the craze and inspiration of the Bengalis. In the Vaishnav literature the flute is a suggestion reminding the reader ' Of that music in our eternal souls ' which has distinctly a spiritual meaning.

In the ballads, however, there is no spiritual association with the sound of flute. It is for this that though there is much in the phraseology of the songs which has the flavour of Vaishnav lyrics, the ballad literature is restricted to its characteristic zone which it seldom crosses. In its spirit and in the conception of its free course, the love followed by the sexes keeps its aloofness from the Hindu classical ideal. Here in this ballad the princess wants a boon—not of course of her own seeking. It is her husband who gives the suggestion which the wife takes up with some hesitancy at first. No doubt her royal consort shows his great renunciation by foregoing his claims on his wife because of his taking a vow. The Buddhist idea of renunciation (त्याग) is there, but the woman will never be praised in Hindu society for asking her husband to give her up. According to Hindu Jurisprudence she has no power to separate herself from her husband in that way. But the poet does not acknowledge any limitation of the sort. His business is to show that the princess is true to herself and though she is a married woman even that sacred tie is of no value to her. The fact is that in sexual love the ideal of these poets is very high. It is beyond all convention, beyond anything which stresses the inviolable sanctity of nuptial vow. The heroine once in love forgets absolutely that she is a member of the society. And in the princess even her worst critics will not detect anything like cravings of animal life. Though the love has not been spiritualised here as we find it in Vaishnav poetry, it is a pure and immaculate flame—an unmixed piece of gold—which establishes the superiority of the emotional felicities of that passion over every other consideration of the world.

The exuberance of lyrical element in the poem has made the translator's task very difficult. The beauty of the original cannot be preserved in the translation, as it is a piece full of subtle emotions, and no person can be more conscious of his limitations and inability than the translator himself.

There is no incident, no dramatic situation, except in the very last canto. There are repetitions which sometimes tax the patience of the reader. This defect will strike one more prominently while reading the translation. The inevitable *Baramasi* is here also though not in a pronounced form. The vow of the prince and the clever way in which the princess seeks a boon and gets a sanction from her lord to cut her off from the palace and become another man's, the pure love of the blind man full of self-denial, and the pathos of the tragic end—all this forms some of the interesting features of the ballad. The most notable element is its absolute freedom of tone from conventional beliefs and canons of the society.

DINESH CHANDRA SEN.

The Blind Lover

(1)

Though a blind beggar, the young man looked like a prince as he stood at the door, crying, 'Oh citizens, give me alms.'

The early dawn tinged the clouds of the horizon with the colour of catechu, and gradually the deep red of vermillion gently spread over them. Who is it that sounds his flute in the public street at such an hour standing under that tree whose leaves rustle pleasantly in the morning-breeze? How sweet is the music of the flute that comes floating in the air! The waves whisper to one another. 'It is ebb-tide, but such is the charm of the flute that the stream flows up and its swelling waters wash the banks.'

In the early dawn there see the boughs of the pomegranate tree,—they are aglow with red flowers. The earth and the sky look strange to-day. The moon and the stars are blotted out of the sky. But how strange the world looks to-day!

The flute of the blind youth plaintively sings:—'Give me alms, oh citizens, give me alms.' The sound fills the whole air's space. 'In the world I have none to call my own. I wander alone; no home, no house have I. I live under trees. If I approach a tree for cool shade to save me from the heat of the day, the tree itself becomes fire to burn me. Alas! my luck is my foe. When a-thirst I go to the river, it dries up at my approach. My luck, alas! is my foe.' This is the burden of the blind man's song. 'Give him alms, oh citizen.'

Maid Servant (Soliloquy).

" From what lovely land has he come,—so handsome, so bright he looks? His colour dazzles one's eyes like gold. I never saw a figure so handsome, one would easily like to make him one's pet like a *shama* or a *suka* bird. What a wicked providence was it which by its freak created such an angel without eyes?"

She comes to the princess and says, 'Listen to me, oh princess. A strange beggar is at your door. On his back hangs a wallet. He looks bright as gold. But cruel providence has given him no eyes. If you should like to see him, hasten to the door and take with you what alms you may be pleased to offer him. Like gold or fire or *gorochana* he charms by his very colour. One could hardly forget him if one saw him but once in life. A strange youth is he,—one of his eyes sheds tears and the other seems to smile.' (Ll. 1-38.)

Chorus.

' Oh my jolly boat, made of *manpaban* wood from what country hast thou come and whither art thou bound? '

The sound of the flute comes from upstream and goes afar flowing in the down. The weary breeze whispers a message to the ear but what it is, it is difficult to define. Perchance the flute sings of that beautiful land from where the charming youth has come !

Princess.

' Sing, oh flute, sing your sweet song again. My ears are a-thirst. Let me hear it over again. When the sweet song of the flute is heard, the wakeful hearer is gently lulled to sleep. His eyes are closed and he passes from the world of fact to the world of dreams. Oh what a mystic power is in the sound of this blind man's flute! Confined to the four walls of home, as I am, my mind is carried adrift beyond this narrow space.'

'Oh princess' cries the blind man, 'keep aside the string of flowers that you are weaving. Be gracious to accept this gift of song from a blind young man.'

Princess.

'Oh my maid, what can I offer to this youth? The music of his flute has maddened me. Go and tell the King —my father, to open the treasury-room with doors of gold and bars of silver, giving this beggar a free choice to take from it anything that he desires. But stop, there are some to whom the dust of earth and precious stones have the same value. First let us know what is it that he seeks. A suspicion lurks in my mind that he is not what he seems to be, but a prince who owing to some mishap has lost his eyes and wanders from door to door to hide the great pain of his heart. One's physical suffering is nothing as compared to ones mental pain. What treasure is in the earth which can make a blind man happy?'

The Maid.

'I will tell you princess what you can give to the blind man to remove the pain of his heart. Night and day are the same to the blind man. If you can somehow or other restore eyes to him it is then only that he may feel happy.'

The Princess.

'But the royal treasure cannot give him his eyes, oh maid. Tell me what can I do to help him?'

The shadow of a deep sorrow fell on her face, beautiful as a *champa* flower and from her hand dropped the wreath of flowers that she was weaving. Her eyes shed tears as she said, 'Take my two eyes and present them to him.'

The Maid.

'Alas, what purpose would your eyes serve? The blind man may be happy if you would give him your heart.'

(Ll. 1-46.)

(2)

Chorus.

'Oh, who is it that plays on the flute? what weary soul, what agonized mind—sings that melody? go pilgrim and let me know all about him.'

The King rose in the morning from his bed hearing the sound of the flute. 'Such a honeyed sound I never heard in life.' He cried, 'The sound has maddened the morning-breeze. It is difficult to remain at home when the attraction is so forcible outside. Go, ye messengers, and let me know who the player is. It seems that the pain of first love disappointed has inspired this music.'

The messengers came and said, 'A very handsome young man is playing on his flute.' 'Call him to my presence'—was the King's order.

With his flute in hand the young man stood before his Majesty. He seemed indifferent to everything; a heavenly light seemed to emanate from his face. That light illuminated the path. But eternal darkness lay before his blind eyes.

The King.

'Tell me, oh handsome lad, what pain of heart, what despair makes you wander from place to place in this way?

Where is your home and who are your parents? Have you any companion who travels along with you?'

The Blind Man.

'No, King, neither father nor mother have I, nor have I any brother. Like the bird of the weather I fly from sky to sky. My creator is surely stony-hearted; He has doomed me to eternal sorrow. So unfortunate am I that I had not the luck of seeing the face of my parents when I was born. Nor did I ever see the golden rays of the sun or the light of the fair moon. Night and day to me are alike, oh King. Vain it is for me to accuse God or my lot. For some wrong done in a previous birth have I been doomed to this punishment! I carry the load of my sorrows wherever I go, and when I stretch my limbs for rest in the shades of a forest I weep and weep till my eyes close to sleep. The forest, truly speaking, is my home. The young one of cuckoo begotten by its parents is left to the care of a crow,* but even such a refuge I have not got in life; no one is there to take care of me.'

The King.

'Lament not, my young lad! From to-day, throw up your wallet and give up the avocation of a beggar. Live in my palace happily. From to-day I shall occupy the place of your parents. The doors of my treasury will remain ever open to you. You will wear a necklace of diamonds and get fine dress and ornaments. A well-furnished room will be given to you and there you will lie on a soft milk-white bed. In the morning you will awaken me from sleep every day by the music of your flute. I have got a daughter who is the life of my life, you will teach her to play on flute. These are the two things that you will have to do here. Nothing more shall I expect from you. Here you will

* The tradition in India is that a cuckoo has no nest of its own, it leaves its young one in the nest of a crow to be taken care of by it.

have perfect happiness in all matters save in one where none can help you. No one can restore eyesight that you have lost.' (Ll. 1-57.)

(3)

The Blind Youth.

'Take from me, oh princess, your lesson in music. But I am afraid I am not a worthy teacher as I am blind. The world is dark to me, I have had never the privilege of seeing this fair creation of God. It seems that a cruel Providence played a childish prank with me by throwing dust in my eyes at my birth so that I was born blind. I see neither how the river wends her course nor how darkness comes to the world after light has faded away. I wonder how the sun and the moon look in the sky! What sort of thing is light? From what horizon do its streaks first burst forth? How does the bud develop itself slowly into a flower or how it looks when the air is still? I hear of trees and creepers but I have never seen them. God has made me miserable by depriving me of sight. What is the form of a human being? How does a smiling face look? I hear the words of men. How it pains me that I never saw the beauty of a moonlike face. I am not privileged to see all these though my mind imagines many incoherent things. Near about me stands an avenue of trees and creepers laden with a hundred flowers and above me are the sun, the moon and stars. But dearer than all sights is that of your face, and though I cannot see it I think I can imagine its beauty. You are not in my eyes but always in my mind.'

The Princess.

'Oh stranger, oh friend, what a deep sorrow moves you! Will you tell me, my blind friend, from what country you hail? Who are your parents? What bird sheltered the young one of a cockoo who had no nest of its own! Will you tell me, dear, by what name your countrymen call you?'

The Blind youth.

'I have no name, princess. They call me a "mad fellow" and mock me. There are some who take delight in throwing dust at my person and annoying me in other ways, while there are kind men who receive me well. Some serve me with refuse food and think that the mad man would be glad at such an act of charity. Some turn me out from their doors, crying aloud, "go home." But there are others who open their hospitable doors and say, "be pleased to come in." Whatever they do I bear patiently and hiding my tears take my stand at the gateway of people. I have now and then met excellent men who took paternal care of me. But others thought that I was an enemy to be pursued with hate and anger. This is the way of the world, princess, I do not accuse any one. I have no complaints to make. I am really a mad fellow and mad is this flute of mine that you see in my hand. With this flute I am absorbed in my own thought and wander about playing on it in the public street. Call me by the name which I have deservedly got from the people—"A mad fellow."'

The Princess.

'People fear you since you have the power to fascinate man and woman by the music of your flute. The sound of your flute cuts the heart like a sharp sword. One who hears this painful and melodious strain will never be able to forget it. Play on the flute, friend, and teach me the art. From to-day I count you as my dearest. I will not part with your company for a moment from to-day. Like the beautiful black paint that adorns the eyes I do prize you and hold you dear. If people spread scandal I will hide my feeling in the heart of my heart so that others may not know of it. I will hear your flute hiding my joy from others and even then if they would whisper a tale, your thought will be like a precious jewel put secretly within the casket of my heart. You will be verily like my *sari* with which I clothe myself—like a wreath of flowers, which I put on my breast, like the red powder of luck to paint my forehead—like the sweet-scented sandal wherewith to perfume my body, my joys and sorrows will spring from my love alone and manifest themselves in the tears of my eyes. If people would still charge me I will not mind it at all. You and myself will merge in one another and will be one body, one soul. You will see this world through my eyes and thus will I remove your pain of blindness. I will be one heart with you when you will play on your flute moved by the same emotion. And for life I will be your true and loving servant.'

The Blind Man.

'Oh love-sick foolish princess, think thrice before you settle your course, it will be sheer madness on your part, to take on your head the burden of life-long sorrow. Accustomed as you are to all the comforts of life and its smooth and rosy way, why should you choose the thorny path ? There is nectar in store for you but what insanity has seized you that you would prefer poison of which you are not aware the bitter effects ! Do not, oh princess, strike a blow to your fortune and indulge not, I pray, in thoughts which would lead to disaster. After what I have heard I would not like to stay here. Adieu to the comforts of life in a palace where I found shelter for a few days, adieu princess, permit me to depart.'

Chorus.

'No, it cannot be, dear, I cannot allow you to go. You will be like the paint of my eyes to adorn them for ever.'

The Princess.

'From the day I have heard your flute, I have given up all thought of my position, honour and status. I have resolved to be your devoted companion of life. I tried to dissuade my mind but like the wild Jamuna my mind has ever flowed against the tide, and all sober thought is of no avail. My mind has yielded to the irresistible sway of your flute. If I am separated from you for a moment I become like one mad. My mother has ordered me not to play on flute any more, but my mind is not to be lessoned. It would not listen to any counsel. Like fire that lies buried in wood-dust, this love of mine, hidden in my heart, slowly and steadily consumes me day and night. Where is real happiness in all these vanities of the palace ? Alas, who is there to fulfil the yearnings of my heart ? My love is like the white ant that eats up a young grove of bamboos. It has sapped the peace of my heart, alas! my eyes know no sleep. Your love to me is like nectar mixed with poison. I have drunk it deep. Without you I wish no other happiness in this world. I would turn an anchorite and go to the forest with you. I will apply sandal paste to my hair and make it knotted as the ascetics do. Let the palace remain here with all its happiness and pleasures. These are not for me. Let my father and mother live here in peace. I have nothing to do with them. We two will live on forest-fruits. My day will be spent in weaving flower-garlands for you—how happy! I will gather honey from the flowers like the bee and hold the cup to your lips for drink thrice every day—how happy! A bed of soft leaves I will prepare and there happily lie down.

I do not know, dear, if all these will make you happy. So long as life will exist I cannot think of parting with you. The hair of my head will be the chain by which I would bind your feet so that you may not go, leaving me. Inspite of all these if you would still persist in going away, kill me first and then go, or I would kill myself, and would not make you responsible for my death any way.'

The Blind Youth.

'Peace, oh princess. Restore peace to your heart which is unduly ruffled. I have taught you how to play on flute, your lessons are complete now. If any thought of mine has spotted your heart, remove it at once. Why should you suffer for a blind man and stranger like me? Go and occupy your chamber in the royal palace. You are the bird *Hiraman* or *Sari* nourished in a golden cage.

'Your place will be that of the queen consort of a great prince. A hundred maid-servants will be ready to serve you at call. A hundred ornaments will adorn your person. Why of your own accord, oh princess, will you court a life of woe prompted by foolish love? The course that you want to follow is full of misery at every step. This love is like a thorn, which, if it once pierces your foot, will come out through the heart. The whole system will bleed. Have you not heard that Chandidas fell in such mad love? His whole life was slowly consumed as if by fire in wood-dust. You have heard too of a prince who loved a woman named Nilmani and turned an ascetic. Wherever people fall in intense love, they bring, on themselves, the punishment of life-long misery. Just see the bee making love with flowers. The flower fades prematurely, loses all its honey and falls down on the earth, faded and neglected. The word love sounds very good but is like the *Makal** fruit

* Makal = *Cucumis colocynths*.

which has a dazzling exterior but black coal inside.' (Ll. 1-122.)

(4)

The flower bud of March blooms in April. Days pass away, and there comes ebb in the water of the river. The sweet April—the honeyed spring—also flies fast. Then comes the season of extreme heat. The old leaves drop down one by one, the note of cuckoo is no longer heard and the flute sounds no more. The hot wind blows and the mind feels ill-at-ease losing its interest in the environment.

Then comes the new-year rejuvenating the youth and filling it with new hopes. But the mind of the princess even at this season feels a strange thrill of pain. She sees the bees flying about the flowers of the garden. But the King has forbidden her to go there.

In early May the trees are adorned with new leaves. The match-maker comes to the city of the Raja with some news. Alas! the play-house is broken. The flowers of the garden are all faded. That smile of her face which was sweet as the *champa* flower no more plays on her lips. Her curling hair becomes like torn jute. The white ant of despair has eaten up all joys of the green heart.

The drummers beat their drums and players dance in the palace. The sound of music rises high. Who is this prince and from what strange country has he come to take our fair princess from her father's palace?

The Blind Youth.

'Oh monarch of this vast kingdom, respectfully do I approach you with a prayer. Be pleased to give me permission to depart. I will go hence to some other country.'

The King.

'But why should you be in such a hurry for it? Stay here in this palace of mine. Here will I provide for you all that is required for your happiness. My treasure will satisfy all that you need. I am like your father and the queen will take care of you as if you were her son. I will get for you a princess who will be your bride, and I will build a summer-house in the tank where you and your wife may live in comfort. A hundred maid-servants will be engaged to serve you. You will live like a prince in the palace in every way. One thing is indeed to be regretted. I shall not be able to give you your eyesight. But I assure you you shall have a good share of this kingdom.'

The Blind Youth.

'Oh great King, my debt to you is immense. There is none in this world who has befriended me in my distress as you have done. I enjoyed my life here beyond my remote expectations and this is all due to your gracious feeling towards me. In every respect I have been happy here. My only regret is that I could not have a sight of your smiling face. Your Majesty must have been my father and the good queen my mother in some past life or else how could you have so deep an affection for one poor as I am. I have no word to express my gratitude to you or praise you sufficiently. I have none to accuse. If I am miserable still, it is all due to my ill-luck. My evil destiny pursues me like an enemy and drives me from place to place allowing no rest. What shall I do with kingdom or riches? This flute in my hand never allows me to stay anywhere long. It impels me to go from place to place, singing my song. And in this the flute acts as my enemy, yet I cannot throw it away, for I like it as my life. Its sound brings tears to my eyes and its song gives me pain but still it is my dearest. Its music kills me and revives me at the same time. It is my religion—the main spring of my action. It is not in your power, oh great King, to make me happy nor can I be happy by my own efforts. My luck would not allow it. One's happiness is not like sandal that one would put it on the forehead and by its sweet scent remove the headache. It does not lie in rich robes that one would cover oneself with and make one happy. If the house has lost its main pillars inside, how will a support from outside keep it standing? Happiness is not in my luck. Alas! who can give it?'

He left the palace with all its treasure and comfort. In unknown lands and in out of the way parts people heard a strange music bursting forth from his flute. Even the birds and beasts of the forest were moved by the pathos of the melody. People whispered to each other, 'Cruel must be the lady who has turned out her young lover to wander about in despair with this sweet flute. It is a pity that the wretched woman did not know the art of binding her lover to her house by ties of affection.' Some took him to be a mad man and threw dust at him, others offered him meals. One said, 'Oh man with the divine flute, be pleased to take me with you. I will follow you anywhere.'

The flute ceased not; it sang and sang till he reached the kingdom of another Raja and here its pathos rose to a pitch beyond all bounds—bursting into a wild lament. (Ll. 1-63.)

(5)

Chorus.

'Decorate the bower with flowers and leaves. To-night Radha and Krishna, the divine pair, will meet.'

Let us now talk of another land. It was the dead hour of night. The residents were all asleep. Reclining on its bed of leaf the flower-bud lay silently asleep, and on the bosom of the flower the bee slept sweetly. On the breast of the king lay the queen like a loose garland of flowers unconscious in sleep. Everything around was mute. The adjacent hills, the banks of the hilly river all seemed to have fallen into deep sleep. The river alone was wakeful with its gentle murmur of waves. And at this dead hour of night one lady in the whole city had no sleep in her eyes, separated from her mate.

Just then the sound of the blind man's flute rose in the air, with its strange melody. The cuckoo and the lark were on the boughs of the tree with their eyes yielding to the attraction of night's rest. They awoke with a start at the sound. Then see, what a spell the stranger's flute cast on the city! The bud gently opened its eyes of tender petals and the whole garden became awake at the sound. The clouds wore a glow of red colour. The housewife rose from her sleep at the sound maddened by its charm, and the flute's wail penetrated the inner apartments of the king.

'Oh princess, awake, how long will you sleep? See the morning-flowers are blooming. The garland of the flowers you wore in the night has got faded. Throw it away. Listen and enquire, who is it that is playing on the flute, whose song is it that cries in pain in the street.'

The Princess.

'The flute, oh prince, sounds not outside but in the very recesses of my heart?'

She seemed to be lost in reveries at the sound of the flute. It seemed that the very problem of her life and death was being solved. The sound was as it were the elixir of her life and it was to her poison also. She sat mute while her two eyes shed incessant tears. She thought, 'the flute forgot me all this time. It now calls me again. I remember the days of childhood when sitting in the flower-garden of my father's palace, he used to play on the flute and I remember many other things besides. The sound brings all these reminiscences to my mind. To me the sound has nothing of outside interest. It has brought a message for my heart, oh how marvellous! I saw with my own eyes the bud blooming into flower at the bidding of the flute. I remember the day when he used to teach me the choicest songs of the flute full of melody and joy. At that time, this small musical instrument was dear to me as life. My youth and its dreams blossomed at its sound, yes it made the course of the Jamuna run upstream and my heart also became like that. This life of mine is passing away, but in my next life and in all my future lives I shall be thine and thine alone, oh flute. The pain and pleasure,—the nectar and poison of this music, I can never forget, what alas! shall I do with this palace, its prestige, honours and pleasures! I have cast away my honour, my religion and everything, charmed by your song, oh friend! Know it dear that I have not forgotten that smile on your lips which is to me like life-giving nectar. If I can go to the forest and meet you again I shall lay my heart open to you and show whose image is painted there. For a moment I cannot forget the sweetness of your songs. In everything that I see, in every thought of mine I see your sweet figure pictured. I do not covet riches or royal honour, what shall I do with these? Does the bird of the sky feel at ease in the golden cage? I was trying to fly away each day ever since I have been cruelly separated from you. I would have poisoned myself and put an end to my unbearable misery but the hope of seeing you again has prevented my taking that course.'

The Prince.

'What makes you sit still and inert like that,—absorbed in thought? Have you not strength enough to rise from bed? Shall I help you?'

The maid-servant came and said, 'The song that you have heard comes from the flute of a blind young man in the street. We never heard a flute so sweet. The citizens have run mad at the music. The birds in the sky as they hear the flute, come back charmed by it. The river flows against the tide and the beasts run to the spot where he plays on the flute.'

The Prince.

'The man is a beggar. He stands at the royal gate, what shall I give him as a reward?'

The princess says slowly (weeping all the while—aside) 'Why should you ask me that? You are a mighty prince. If you wish you may give him a part of your empire. What's the good of your asking me?'

'I have resolved in my mind that I will give him whatever you will ask for him. There will be no breach of my word. This is my vow.'

'I am a servant to you, my lord. What good will come by asking me on the point? Suppose I say that you should give him the whole of your kingdom, what will you do?'

The Prince.

'Thrice do I take the vow. Yes, the empire will be his, should you ask me to give it to him.'

The Princess.

'But if I say all the golden jewels of your treasury and those to be found in the city should be given to the blind man what will be your answer?'

The Prince.

'Dear to me as my eyes thou art, my lovely consort, my vow remains unaltered. I will open my treasury and give him all that you would say.'

The Princess.

'Then if you are in right earnest take the vow solemnly again, and say that you would give that blind man whatever I may wish you to give him.'

The Prince.

'Yes, here do I take the vow thrice solemnly.'

She rose slowly from bed and wiped away the tears of her eyes and said: 'Heaven be witness. Be true to your vow, oh Prince, I wish that you should offer me to the blind man.' (Ll. 1-94.)

(6)

On the banks of the wild river wending its mad course in full tide—banks adorned with plants of blooming *champa* flowers—he is going without a destination, singing a song on his flute.

The flute sounds languidly and sweetly. Its songs are heard off and on. The housewife loses herself in the pathos of the strain and cannot attend to her household duties.

On her chignon was fixed a gold butterfly which fluttered at the gale. A bird of the sky flew near her. Her dishevelled hair, the braids all loose, hung behind and touched her feet. The anklets made the sweet jingling sound '*runu jhunu.*'

This sound was familiar. He was accustomed to hear it long ago. The blind youth stood still with the flute in his hand listening to the sound. 'Who is it,—whose anklets make a sound like that?'—he thought within himself. 'It brings to my mind some message of joy and an old world charm. My joy and dream of past life are recalled by this sound. From whose tender feet does this charming message come? It refreshes the memory of long forgotten things. In the flower-garden the Princess used to listen to my flute, and my ears were charmed by the sound of her anklets. Yes it cannot be any other. Why is it that those forgotten days are recalled to my memory? If you are the Princess, my adored and beloved, tell me frankly.'

The Princess.

'Oh my love, your flute has maddened my soul. I have left my home, broken my honour and all home-ties. Here am I for you. The irresistible charm of your song has brought me up here. Play on your flute, come, for it is for hearing it that I have given up my all.'

The flute was near his lips but alarmed and wondering he held it down in his hand and said, 'Short-sighted girl, what is it that you have done? Go back—go back to your palace. Do not, I pray you, lose your kingdom and your great status of honour and happiness for nothing. Just see the difference. You take your meals in golden plates and wear silk *saries* of great value. I am but a poor bird of the forest; you are, good lady, a great princess used to wear gold ornaments studded with gems. How will you live in the forest wearing a bark dress? The daughter of a great monarch and mistress of a kingdom, why should you be so indiscreet and short-sighted? Just think for a moment what your royal father would say to this. I am a blind man and a mad fellow. You know I have not a farthing with me.'

The Princess.

'From the day I have first heard the song of your flute I have been yours for ever. From that day I have given up all thought of riches, wealth and honour. Ask the lark of the sky if it would prefer a cage of gold. Earthly comforts and enjoyments I do not seek. I am indifferent to all that people prize. If you are with me and play on the flute—that is all that is needed to make me happy. Kingdom and riches are nothing to me. The happiness that your company gives me can be had nowhere else. One can put fetters and chains and make another man a prisoner, but who is it that can sway his mind? Force is of no avail there. Plenty of fruits are in the forest and the bark of trees will not be difficult to secure. We would sleep together under the shade of a tree and my eyes will close in sleep listening to your sweet flute. When the morning comes it is the sound of your flute again that will awaken me from sleep. What happiness can be compared to such a life ? Empires seem valueless compared to the life I have pictured. Know for certain, I repeat, that earthly pleasures have no attraction for me. If I am taken away from you, my heart will cease to beat.'

The Blind Youth.

'But you are deceived. Your judgment is immature. You have fallen a dupe to an unsound imagination. It is for this that you want to prefer the fruits of forest to the delicious meals served on gold plates. Your couch is made of golden frames and there the bed is of flowers, and these you want to forego in preference to thorny grass which you propose to make your bed. The fruits of the forest are not all sweet. They are often bitter and of unsavoury taste. You will grow sick of them in no time and then you will have to repent and cry. A golden house Providence has built for you. Do not, oh dear Princess, burn it unwittingly with your own hands. Be well advised and give up this mad course and return home.'

The Princess.

'I tell you the plain truth. Your flute has a charm which allows me no rest at home. Your flute calls me and I cannot live in the palace. It maddens me like some drug and when my ears catch the sound I become insensible to everything else.'

The Blind Youth.

'Hear me, oh short-sighted girl, if my flute is the cause of all this trouble, here do I throw it away for good. (He throws his flute into the river.) Now all worry of your soul is removed. Return home in a peaceful spirit. No more will the sound of the flute be echoed in these forests. There see, it goes floating on the waves.'

The Princess.

'Let the flute go, but, dearest, you are here. If you would not take me with you, my mind will follow you wherever you may go. I shall not be able to live a moment in this world without you. Devoid of your presence the world would be like a bed of fire. I am sorry I cannot explain my case to you. If you are determined to be unkind, stand where you are, and see how I die.'

The Blind Youth.

'You; imprudent girl, return home. From to-day no one will find me in this world. Stand here and measure the waters of this river. See the course of events and extinguish the fire of your soul.'

Saying so the blind man jumped into the deep waters of the river. Wildly did the Princess cry : 'Take me, my dearest, take me with you.' But no response came. Swiftly as a shooting star she too fell into the waters of the river. She looked for a time like a *safla* flower floating in the flow-tide. They both floated in the waves for some time till they were carried into the illimitable sea.

From the next day the flute never sounded in that place. (Ll. 1-93.)

PREFACE TO RATAN THAKŪR

PREFACE TO RATAN THAKUR

The ballad of Ratan Thakur was collected by Babu Chandra Kumar De about a year ago from two men—Gachim Sekh of Katghar and Ramcharan Bairagi of another village in the same district (Mymensingh).

The ballad is interspersed occasionally with prose portions, but that is not considerable. It is complete in 262 lines.

The exhuberance of lyrical beauty of the ballad is its chief feature. There is a well-defined plot and the incidents are strung together with artistic skill; but the lyrical interest of the ballad predominates and is much greater than its dramatic quality.

We have found in many of these ballads specially in those which belong to the 14th and 15th century a recurrence of the Sahajiya element though not with any specific spiritual pretensions.

In some of the Tantras it is clearly stated that a spiritual devotee who wants to attain final beatitude through sexual love must court a handsome woman other than his wife from the rank and file of society. A barber-woman, a *chandal* girl, a courtesan, a washer-woman and a flower-girl are chiefly recommended for culturing a highly platonic form of love verging on worship. The Sahajiyas have got an extensive literature enuntiating the principles of spiritual culture based on sexual union And this creed is traced from the second century B.C. when *Samavippayis* (Samavipprayis), a Buddhist sect, held nocturnal meetings amongst their own Vikshus and Vikshunis and commenced a process of Sadhana which latterly proceeded through a hundred channels, sometimes aspiring to reach heaven by a practice of really noble spiritual principles and at others coming down to the lowest pit of moral depravities.

But it is not our look-out to trace the ethical development of the Sahajiya cult or its deterioration here. The ballad literature exclusively deals with the secular side of sexual love. Though often it soars in the higher atmosphere of selfless emotional felicities verging on final beatitude, it nowhere stresses the spiritual side. There is no mysticism in the ballads and the rustic poet never cares to grapple with spiritual problems. But the Sahajiya had certainly a historic background and this history may be gathered from the accounts given in the ballads. Chandidas says that the young men and women of the country were at his time mad after the Sahajiya creed, and hundreds of them attempted to attain spiritual culture through sexual emotion. But the poet gives a warning here. He says that it is doubtful whether one in a million has the power to fulfil the hard conditions of the Sahajiya creed. He further says that a man who can hang a mountain by means of a cob-web may attempt this impossible culture. His general tone is one of disparagement to the young aspirants.

We find in these ballads how men and women without any pretension to Sahajiya culture often fell in love in a way not sanctioned by the society and made great sacrifices. The present ballad is of the same type as the 'Dhopar Pat' (Vol. II, Parts I and II). There a prince falls in love with a washer-girl and betrays her. Here in this ballad a prince is enamoured of a flower-maiden and is responsible for causing her death by his treachery. The prince of the 'Dhopar Pat' plays the downright rogue in the last part of the ballad. Here the prince, though he fell a victim to the snares of a bad woman for a time, redeems his character by a real and sincere course of repentance which made him forego all the pleasures of life. The heroine is the same sweet fragile creature resigned to her mate in absolute trust and a living personification of innocence, simplicity and faith of which instances we have so often met in our rural literature. There is a great freedom in these women and though they are as tender as fresh-blown buds, they have the courage to do many daring things at the dictate of the blind deity which even the steel frame of a soldier would hardly venture to attempt. The Sahajiya cult and the incidents of ballads such as these show how the aristocratic youths of our country often played cruel sports with the lives of the innocent rustic girls by temptations and impulsive freaks of passion. Through all these trials and hard experiences the all-sacrificing womanhood of Bengal stands in bold relief against the treachery and perfidious conduct of their impulsive lovers.

The preliminary portion of the ballad, where the flower-girl just falls in love and uses all the manoeuvres of the sex in seeking opportunity to catch a sight of the prince, giving an outlet of her romantic feelings in a hundred fascinating tricks, is very beautifully sketched. The ballad discloses its emotional treasure of expressions in every turn making me almost feel repentant at moments as if I have sinned in attempting to translate it into English.

DINESH CHANDRA SEN.

Ratan Thakur

(1)

'From the garden of the moon I got my flowers, and the rays of the sun supplied me with thread, and with these I have prepared this garland of mine. The garden is now bereft of flowers. I have plucked them all. My garland is named "the Pride of Spring."

'Another garland I have prepared with a hundred *champa* flowers, it is interwoven with white and black flowers at intervals.

Oh my old papa, go with these garlands to the market of Tipperah which sits every morning. The price of each garland is one Kahan (one rupee). It is nicely done and I hope you will find customers for them. Come back with the money.'

The old gardener took the garlands and went to the market-place. The maiden lay on her couch and had a pleasant nap all alone in the house. (Ll. 1-14.)

(2)

'Now, will you, oh gardener, tell me the truth! Who is it that has woven these garlands? I know one and all of those whose profession it is to weave garlands, but in the whole country of Tipperah, there is none who can do a thing as nice as this. It seems the fragrance of a hundred screw-plants are spreading their spell in the air. Tell me, old man, who is this clever artist.'

'I have got an only daughter in the house—dear to me as my eyes. She it is who has plucked flowers from the garden and woven these garlands. You see the eastern gale has turned its course and is blowing westward, the waves of the river are high. I must go home quick. It is a poor house and the roof of it leaks. I am without means. If I can sell the garlands, I may expect to meet my daily expenses.'

'Will you tell me, old gardener, what is the age of your girl ? Is she married? One who is so accomplished, should be the bride of a worthy man of high status in society.'

'My daughter is still unmarried. She is fresh as a new-blown flower. Like a fairy she is the presiding angel of my house. She cooks for me and gives me drink when thirsty and looks to my comfort. How can I live in the house if she is given in marriage and leaves me? '

Ratan Thakur said smiling : 'What price would you charge for your garlands ? '

'*Boories* multiplied by *boories* make a *pan* and *pans* multiplied by *pans* make a *kahan*. If I get a *kahan* of cowries, I may part with the garlands.'

Ratan Thakur smiled at his words again, and paid one *kahan* of cowries. He took the garlands and wore them on his breast. (Ll. 1-26.)

(3)

'Alone are you on the banks of the river. The flower is full of honey but no report has gone to the bee. Alone do you live in your house. You yourself do not know that you have grown adult. Youth is in full bloom. You are unconscious of it yourself, neither is this known to others.'

The girl lifted her eyes and saw a handsome young man before her.

On the screw-plant the flower has bloomed and a solitary bee is flying over it.

'The light of the day is flickering. It is nearly dark. It were better if the light of the night would appear now, but the moon is not seen ;—the close of the day has rendered everything dark. This is not the time when I should be alone with you. Do not obstruct my path, young man. I must return home now.'

'Who are your parents, oh girl! kindly tell me all about you. You say you are all alone and there is hardly any light of the day, but do not be afraid, I will lead you myself through a well-known path of the village. So do not fear whether you know the path or not. I will lead you wherever you may wish to go. If your pitcher of water proves too heavy for you, I shall help you to carry it home.'

'My father is in charge of Your Lordship's garden. Here I stand in the midst of water and tell the truth which you should believe. This water, this land, are all instinct with life, and may hear and see and make a disclosure. I am not afraid of the river or anything else not even of darkness. I am frightened by the thought of scandal. Oh Lord! I do not fear a tiger nor a bear. I have a status in society and scandal is it that I fear most.

'The stars illuminate the sky but the earth is in darkness. Do not, oh young Lord, obstruct my path. I must go home now.'

'The trees and plants are rustling in the wind and the ripples of the river are gently whispering. No human being is here. You may speak to me the secrets of your mind here.'

'Excuse me, my young Lord, for this evening. In yonder garden of flowers we shall meet to-morrow in morning hours.' (Ll. 1-33.)

(1)

'Now forsooth I have at last found you out, my charming thief. You break the branches of my plants and take away all the flowers—the small plants are thus robbed of their treasure every day.

'To-day I have kept watch over the garden and have caught you red-handed. You must take the punishment of a thief, fair damsel.

'I will cut off your fine stuff of hair and thereby make a rope to hang you with. I will make a garland of your youth, which has bloomed like flowers. Your eyes are like two blue *aparajita* flowers and your face has the colour of *champa*. These are the flowers with which I will make a garland to adorn my neck. You are a thief. It will not be a sin to commit theft on the goods of a thief.'

'It pains me to hear your words, oh young Lord. In this country there is no justice—how can I expect fair treatment here? The police is the master of the land, the Prince does the work of the police and acts as a guard! How strange it is that he for whom I have stolen charges me as a thief. I will leave this land and go elsewhere.

'Release my hand from your grasp. I have no need of flowers.'

'No,—that cannot be. I shall not allow you to go. Pledge your youth to me, fair maiden.'

'The flowers have bloomed in the morning breeze. I shall have to do marketing. It will be too late hereafter. Release me from your hold, young Lord.'

'Then give me word that you will see me in private at your convenience.'

'Call at my house to-night. Yonder see my house surrounded by banana and Beur trees. I will meet you in the shade of those banana plants.' (Ll. 1-27.)

(5)

'Come in slow paces near my bed to the direction of my feet, and when you will depart go by the side of the pillow. In a small box there are betels. Take care that you do not mix excessive lime with them. I am a frail girl and this is my first love and first meeting. You see I am trembling with emotion and my face is perspiring. I am afraid of scandal which my bad neighbours are sure to spread around.'

When my lover touched me gently with his hand a throb passed through my body and I shook in all my limbs like a banana leaf. When my lover gave me his first kiss my body became inert and motionless, and my heart began to throb.

Be witness, oh sun and moon, and the planets of heaven, here do I offer my body and soul, and my youth to the young lord.

I have offered my heart and soul. What else can there be for me to offer?

When I awoke in the morning I found that he had gone away leaving me alone.''

She awoke in the morning and found that the flower-basket was near her, but sleep was still lingering in her eyes. How could she weave garlands?

'I cannot go to the market place,' she said to herself. 'What shall I do with scales and weights. I do not relish any meal, nor my daily bath affords me any pleasure. I care not for my life. What shall I do with baths and meals? Neither do I care for sleep. Nothing, nothing do I want. I keep gazing on the path with all the ardour of my soul wishing for a sight of him and for nothing else.

'My father and mother have turned hostile. They have prohibited me to go to the bathing ghat. I am not allowed to go to the river.

'' Yes, they are hostile to me. They have also prohibited me to go to the garden for plucking flowers.

"I cannot cook the meals nor serve them to the inmates of the house. It seems that my body is being burnt by poison. Mad is my heart. It becomes restless in the house and wants to find rest outside. A feeling of unrest makes me move about here and there like a bird that has cut its chain and goes flying from house to house seeking rest.

'The neighbours are wicked, they are making me unhappy in the house. Come, dear lord, let us go away from here and live in some foreign land.'

With a towel thrown carelessly on his shoulders Ratan Thakur goes to the landing ghat of the river for taking his mid-day bath. Through a broken fence of her house does the flower-maiden cast her longing look at him. Sometimes she sits on the bank of the river and there weeps all alone.

When Ratan Thakur wanders in the streets with a flute in his hand, the flower-maiden comes out of the house with a pitcher on the pretext of going to the river for water. On the bank of the river Ratan Thakur is seen loitering. The flower-maiden empties the water of the pitcher to fill it again. And there she is seen weeping again.

Ratan Thakur attires himself in a fashionable dress. The flower-maiden sees him ; she arranges her own dishevelled hair to make a chignon and after doing that she beholds her face reflected in the mirror and weeps again.

Morning and evening Ratan Thakur takes his usual rambles on the river bank. The flower-maiden takes the basket in her hand and goes to the garden on the riverside for plucking flowers and there again she weeps as she sees her own flowers.

Ratan Thakur goes to the market place towards the close of the day. The flower-maiden whispers her request that he should bring for her a bottle of scented oil. (Ll. 1-54.)

(6)

The Flight.

Lo the clouds are roaring in the sky and there is no ferry-boat in the river. The shadow of *Jhau*[1] and *Hijal*[2] trees shakes and fades away on the surface of the water at every dashing wave.

The flower-maiden sits at the landing ghat and weeps for Ratan Thakur.

The lightning flashes quickly with its dazzling light and the wind moans and the thunder roars. The ferry boat of Sadhu, the boat-man, waits at the landing ghat.

'For you,' says Ratan Thakur, 'I have abandoned home never to return there. With you, sweet love, I have cast my lot in the wide, wide sea—of which I see no coast. I have abandoned my kingdom, my wealth, my doting parents and all. Alone with you I have left my home, resigning myself to fate.

'This land of trees and creepers—of crows and cuckoos — this my beautiful city and a hundred home-ties I give up for ever. The land of my birth—my dear native land—will now be a foreign land to me and the foreign land will be mine from now. Oh the pain of parting from one's own parents, dear friends and sweet home! What will the people say of me to-morrow when they will miss me. Such is the course of life. The house built with labour of months and days crumbles to dust in a moment.'

They are now in the country called Sajinta. It is a beautiful place. Disguised as a gardener and flower-maiden respectively they build here a small cottage; with thin pieces of wood they make the walls. The roof is made of dry *khagra* plants, and hedges are constructed by reeds. They get the permission of the Raja for preparing a plot for gardening.

[1] Jhau=*Tamarix Indica.* [2] Hijal=*Barrengtonia acutangula*

Their only work is to take care of flower plants, to pluck flowers and make garlands.

The gardener's reputation as a maker of fine garlands has now spread in the harem of the Raja. (Ll. 1-21.)

Prose—[In the meantime a vigilant search was made in the city. The informers at last reported that disguised as a gardener and flower-maiden, the prince and his consort were living in the country of Sajinta.]

(7)

The villagers and the citizens assembled and discussed with the king as to the course they should adopt for rescuing the prince from that degraded life. There was a courtesan named Rangila. They sent her to the country of Sajinta.

The old Raja said to Rangila : " My son has turned mad and gone to a foreign country. If you can help me to get him back I will give you a part of my kingdom—I will besides give you golden bracelets and a necklace studded with jewels."

Her lips were of a coral hue, and the red colour of betels she chewed added grace to those lips. She was at the dawn of youth and she was adept in sorcery. She knew how to charm betels by *mantras.* One taking them, though an enemy, would turn to be a fast friend. She could beguile away the husband from a darling and chaste wife, and a true wife would, if Rangila sprinkled a charmed drop of water, leave her husband and turn mad for another man.

Now the courtesan Rangila went to Sajinta and there in the heart of the city made a house and proclaimed her arrival to the public by a beat of drums. Many a nobleman of the court she entrapped by her fascinating qualities.

The Raja of the place got a report of her beauty and paid her a visit one day. She had a face whose charm was irresistible and the Raja's head turned giddy with love. When already fascinated in this way he took a betel served by the beautiful enchantress.

The Raja as a sign of his royal pleasure gave to Rangila the garland which the gardener had woven for him that day. Rangila was pleased with the gift and admired the skill of the weaver.

'How nice is this garland; how beatifully has he woven it!' she said, 'I wonder what a nice fellow is this gardener who did this fine artistic work.'

The Raja said 'It is my gardener who has woven this garland.'

'What sort of man is he,' said Rangila. 'The next time you come here, bring the gardener with you, bidding him weave another garland like this for me.' (Ll. 1-29.)

(8)

The Flower Maiden.

'Oh prince, I have dreamt a bad dream this night. What is in store for my unfortunate self I cannot say. I dreamt that from a dead tree a crow was croaking, and an owl was disturbing the house by its sullen hooting. What this omen means I do not know, but my heart is sick, and ever since the thought of my parents whom I have left is causing me pain—I wish that you remain near me, so that I may see you every moment. Do not, oh darling, go anywhere to-day leaving me alone. I will myself pluck the flowers. You need not bestir yourself. Remain close to me, so that every moment I may feel your touch and do not, oh dear, leave me alone—if you part from me for a moment the separation will be unbearable, so dear you seem to me to-day! My eyelids are trembling. It is an ominous sign and I feel a tremor of heart as I speak. Some unknown and strange fear has come upon me ; there is a misgiving in my heart lest I lose you—my greatest treasure. We have been here for these six months but I dreamt last night that you left me and I was all alone.'

Ratan Thakur.

'Do not weep, oh dear maiden, do not shed tears in this way—know that I shall ever be near you ; my heart is knit to your heart and I feel a throb of love each time your breast touches mine. If you die, I shall die also. Living or dead we are united for ever.' (Ll. 1-20.)

[*Prose*—The day when Ratan Thakur went to the house of the courtesan Rangila, to offer her a garland at the Raja's bidding he did not return home. On enquiry it was found that both Ratan Thakur and Rangila had absconded. The Raja was greatly incensed at the report and ordered that immediately the house of the gardener with all its goods should be burnt down. The people of the Raja informed him that a very beautiful damsel was staying at Ratan Thakur's house. The Raja ordered her to be brought to his palace.]

(9)

The Flower-Maidan (soliloquy)

'Not a moment there is to lose. Oh my love, come and let me have a sight of your face but once. The poison I have swallowed has already made my whole body pale and dark. Here come near me so that I may bid adieu to you for the last time.

'You used to pluck flowers and I wove them into garlands—Happy were we in this way. Your treatment has not been fair. Why did you leave me destitute and helpless, alas ! for what fault?

'I left my parents, my hearth and home—leaving my own country for your sake. I chose a foreign place leaving mine own. Those who were near and dear to me are now nobody to me.

'Alas, alas! we two would no more keep wakeful nights watching the moon in the sky, while talking gaily reclining on one another!

'Oh, far dearer than life you were to me! You have played foul with me—a poor helpless woman who lost her all, loving you.

'At this last hour I do not feel any wish to accuse others —who, alas! gets a treasure as I did in you? Who, alas, loses such a treasure after having acquired it as I have done?

'My action in some past life is responsible for all these happenings—whom shall I accuse?

'At this hour my main sorrow is that before parting with the world I could not have a sight of you!

'Oh my neighbours, if any of you would feel sympathy for all that I have suffered, do not report to him that I have died in this way.

'No more—I have no time—the call has come, adieu.'

[*Prose*—When at last released from the snare of Rangila's charms Ratan Thakur returned to the country of Sajinta he no more found his true love in this world. No one told him of her death but the wind moaned and the birds with their plaintive warble indicated her sad and tragic end.]

When at last he knew for certain that his true love had left the world for ever he turned mad; he forgot his parents and abandoned once more his joyous home.

The mother looked mournfully towards the path by which he had departed and shed many a tear.

He never came back nor did he visit his palace again—He journeyed from land to land like a mad man and his poor mother mournfully looked towards the path by which he had departed shedding tears all her remaining life. (Ll. 1-38.)

BALLAD OF SANNAMALA

PREFACE TO SANNAMALA

The ballad of Sannamala was collected by Babu Chandra Kumar De from Mymensingh about two years ago. It is composed in brisk measures not exactly in the style of the usual '*Payar chhanda.*' Each of the couplets of the first three or four cantos contain seven or eight letters. It does not conform either to the *Tripadi* metre which in old Bengali classics is called the '*Lachari chhanda.*' The metre used in a considerable part of this ballad reminds us of that used in the aphorisms of Dak and Khana and in some of the old Bengali Ghatak Karikas. From the archaic words used in the ballad as also from this peculiarity of metre I conclude that the original ballad was composed in the beginning of the 17th century. Of course no one can say with any degree of certainty that a particular ballad belongs to a fixed literary epoch as the material used in it may generally be traced to still older times than when a poet actually put it down in writing. He generally collects old popular traditions and the remnants of lost ballads, giving them a place in his new composition.

It is an incomplete ballad. There is a promise in this preliminary part that the character of Sannamala would be developed in the latter cantos in such a manner as to make it a match for the other heroines of our ballad-literature. But unfortunately we have got only the first part and there is no hope at the present moment of recovering the portion that is now lost. As it stands this ballad contains 278 lines only. The main portion being lost, the development of the chief characters cannot be traced. So we cannot give any credit to the poet for his power of characterization at this stage. But there can be no denying the fact that there is considerable lyrical beauty in the poem which cannot but strike the readers. Wherever a woodland scene is introduced the description becomes vivid and life-like. For instance the picturesque scenery of the forest where princess Sannamala is exiled is full of poetical charm (p. 267). There is another such account of the garden attached to the palace of the young princess—the friend of our exiled Sannamala. The whole ballad is fresh and delightful and its reading leaves an impression of the beautiful landscape of rural Bengal with all her tender domestic associations.

In this ballad-literature we come over again in contact with a heroism akin to Behula's sacrifice. There are so many songs in old Bengali containing accounts of a hero being bitten by a snake and the sacrifices made by his consort for restoration of his life that we are often reminded of this marshy Gangetic valley of ours full of reptiles, snakes and poisonous worms and of the annual havoc made by them on human lives. The story of Behula being associated with a religious cult has survived many tales of a similar nature and found a field for being enriched by the poets of many successive generations, and in this ballad as also in that of Malua and Pirbatashi we find a poetic imagination in a budding stage, which attained its flowering point in the conception of Behula. There is no doubt that at one time the puja of Manasa Devi was the greatest national festivity of Bengal. The abundance of poisonous worms in this country accounts for the great popularity achieved by the songs of this class.

There are occasional stanzas in this poem which would remind one of Chandidas's lyrical poem. For instance on page 271 where the heroine complains of her wretched luck destroying the very trees, the cool shade of which she seeks for refuge, and utters similar sentiments, the passage seems to us to re-echo the ideas of our great lyrical poet.

We enjoyed the ballad as a small poetical piece full of charming lyrical beauty. Beyond this we cannot give any higher credit to the poet. As I have apologised in regard to my poor English translation of many a ballad I also do so very particularly here. The lyrical beauty of a Bengali song is very hard to reproduce in English translation specially in the translation of indigenous poems which scarcely bears any sign of alien influence. The Gitanjali is a production of this age and the poet is profoundly conversant with the poetry of the West. Hence his translation enjoys a peculiar and decided advantage over the classical Bengali lyrics—an unmixed product of the poetic imagination of the children of the soil. My own limitations—as regards English composition—is also a great drawback of which I am painfully aware.

One thing more before I conclude. The prophecy of astrologers was at one time held as inviolable as the country's law. In the ballad-literature we have often got instances of inhuman cruelty shown to a child on account of astrologer's prophecy. We have an anecdote similar to that described in this ballad in the story of Kajal Rekha (Vol. II, Parts I and II). One might suppose that these stories are pure fiction but we have instances of such barbarous superstition even in our own days. Referring to the old history of Bengal we find that Maharaja Pratapaditya of Jessore who had the courage to fight with the Moghuls was about to be slaughtered in his childhood because of a similar prophecy. The astrologers at his birth assembled in his father's court and prophesied that great misfortune would overtake the family and the country if the child was allowed to live. The father was about to kill him but intercession of his uncle Basanta Ray saved his life. This anecdote is related in all the biographies of Raja Pratapaditya.

DINESHCHANDRA SEN

Sannamala.

(1)

'Ujal Manik' (*lit.* the Bright Jewel) was born in the royal house and gradually attained her puberty.

Bright she was as the sun, moon and the stars—she was her mother's darling and occupied her whole heart.

The palace was brightened by her presence and the doors and gateways glimmered with the light emanating from her person.

The parents gave her the name of Swarnamala—a garland of gold.

Plenty of elephants and horses the Raja had in his stalls. Throughout the eastern districts his name and fame were supreme.

He was so rich that his coins used to be measured in scales. But master of immense wealth, the Raja had no male issue. Who, alas, after his demise, would light the evening lamp in the palace?

Lacking in this much-coveted fortune, the whole house seemed to be enveloped in gloom. The Raja and his queen were sad but their tears were all in vain.

By trade one can obtain wealth, but without the grace of the presiding deity of children—mother Sasthi—how could one get a son?

In the gateway of temples and in the shrines of *pirs* they were often seen to fall prostrate avowing the offering of valuable gifts, but the unlucky Raja got no son, no daughter.

[*Prose*—After a long time, passed between hope and despair, at last a daughter was born to the Royal pair. They endearingly called her by the name of Sannamala.]

She had the lustre of gold, hence they called her Sannamala—the garland of gold.

The parents prided in her—' There is the moon in the sky and numberless stars are there,—but who can match our Sannamala ? ' They said—' Is not our Sannamala more glorious than the moon? She is like a large diamond, which is worth all the wealth of seven emperors.'

She gradually grew—at first a baby of a few days and then, when she became a child of six months her growth under special care was so rapid that she soon after looked like a grown-up girl. She sat on her mother's lap and smiled; the smile like a fountain of light scattered its glimmer on the flowing edge of her mother's *sari*, and the mother in pride and affection used to imprint a hundred kisses on her darling's sweet lips.

Large and beautiful were her eyes—they looked like stars. Her long hair, whether they were bound in braids or lay dishevelled, fell below her knee-joints.

The queen often said to her attending maids, ' What do you see? I have got this little treasure after avowing great offerings to the temple of gods.'

The Raja called all the famous astrologers of the province to his court.

' Oh learned men,' said the Raja, ' tell me how will my daughter fare and all about her future—I will reward you with gold weighed in baskets. How long will she live? Will her married life be happy or unhappy?'

The astrologers—' Are we to tell the plain truth? Will you take offence if we do so?'

The Raja—' Tell the plain truth. Do not fear.'

The astrologers said :—

' Hear us, oh mighty prince. This daughter of thine is born under the influence of the angel of unhappiness and misfortune. For this daughter you will lose all that you have. No evening lamp will be lighted in your house.

'Your elephants and horses will die mysteriously of some epidemic disease and suddenly in the hour of noon when all eyes would be wide awake your palace will catch fire and be reduced to ashes.

'Your great wealth will disappear all on a sudden. Slowly but surely will your condition be reduced to that of a street beggar.

'You will have to wander about like a mad man from city to city and forest to forest and in great sympathy for your sad lot the milch cows will abstain from taking grass. Even the stone will melt at the sight of your distress. All your hopes will vanish like mist. In your great city scarcely will be a lamp lighted. If you want to escape the dire misfortune in store for you, banish the young princess at once.' (Ll. 1-73.)

(2)

The oracle created lamentations all over the vast city. The king, the queen and the attending maids in particular shed incessant tears in great grief.

The daughter enquired, 'Why should you, dear parents, cry in this manner? In order to assuage your pain if it be required to cut off a portion of my heart, gladly shall I do so.'

The king and the queen sat on the same couch, they spoke not a word but shed tears. A secret fire was burning in the mother's heart, which could get no outlet.

The Queen.

'I have nourished you all these years bearing the throes of child-birth when you came to the world first, and other pain too many to enumerate ever since, the intensity of which a mother alone knows.

'One who has nourished his pet bird with all the affection of one's own heart may partially feel when parting with it what I am feeling in a far greater degree now.'—Saying this she embraced her dear daughter and cried like one helpless.

'Oh my darling—after you have been exiled, what pleasure will there be to bind me to this palace? If one's priceless jewel is lost, why should one keep the knot which one had tied in one's *sari* for it? When you will be gone what shall I do with this kingdom? I will court the life of exile with you.'

The daughter consoled her weeping mother thus :—

'Do not, oh mother, feel sad on my account. Permit me to go to the forest. You have brought me to the world but it is not in the power of parents to alter the decree of fate.—It is written in the luck of your unfortunate daughter that she should be sent to exile. It is not in your power to alter that inexorable decree.'

For seven days and nights there was great sorrow in the palace, and on the eighth day the Raja accompanied his daughter to a distant forest.

In the depth of the forest the tiger growled and the lion roared. The king employed day-labourers to build a cottage there for the princess. The cottage was made of plants and creepers in the shape of a bower and the king said while bidding his daughter adieu :—

'Oh, what a woe was reserved for you, my darling! In the best room of the palace were you born. On a golden couch strewn over with blooming flowers would you lie down in the palace. You have now to live in this wretched cottage, poor soul!'

Crying like a helpless man, the father parted with the daughter who lived in that cottage for full one month. (Ll. 1-40.)

(3)

A merchant was passing by the river. He was ordered to carry out the wishes of the king of his country within a fixed time. The Raja had provided him with seven ships full of gold. There were seven sails attached to each of the ships. He had already travelled seven countries and had a provision for seven months. He was ordered to bring to the king things that he wished. If he failed to do so capital punishment was to be inflicted on him.

The sea was deep and the water was playing in restless dance. But what evil chance overtook the ships! They became stranded in a shoal when approaching the forest.

The merchant said to his captain and sailors—'Go to the forest and see what god or god-like saint is there in it who requires to be propitiated. I will give due offerings. How strange that a shoal has formed in the midst of the deep sea! If within seven months I cannot return with the things I have been ordered to collect I shall be executed by the king's order.'

The captain and the sailors landed there for inspection. They saw lions and tigers roaming for prey. They found peacocks dancing with their mates spreading their lovely tails. The deer and antelopes were seen running in great speed. They saw besides the forest-nymphs, birds of *Hiramon* species and on the boughs of Daruk trees, they saw gold-coloured pigeons which looked bright as the sun. In a corner of this wilderness they saw a damsel of bright colour. She was beautiful as an angel.

They came and reported to the merchant all they saw and said in conclusion. 'The maiden whom we saw possesses superhuman beauty. We could not ascertain if she was the presiding angel of the forest or a wood-nymph. We never saw a woman so beautiful as this girl.'

The merchant came to the spot where the girl was, accompanied by his people.

The damsel was sleeping on the ground spreading the flowing end of her *sari* over it. The merchant awakened her from her sleep by addressing her, 'Oh dear mother.'

'From where have you come, oh lovely girl? Evidently you are a princess. Why have you come to live in this wilderness? Why should the moon come down from the sky and lie on the hard ground of this earth? If your parents are alive, dear girl, their hearts must be hard as stone to bear the pangs of separation, subjecting you to a life of exile in this dreary forest.'

The Princess.

'It is true, I was once a princess. My people turned cruel and doomed me to this forest life. I pass my life in great unhappiness in this forest.'

She told every detail about her to the merchant who on hearing the sad story determined to take the girl away from that forest. 'Whatever my fate may reserve for me I am determined to take her with me,' he said.

It is a wonderful tale. As soon as the maiden touched the ship she floated and went on in a swift course. The beauty of the girl spread a halo of light round the ships. Like a star the beauty glimmered on the surface of the waters. The seven ships became bright with the glow of that beauty. After seven months the merchant returned to his own country.

This time wherever he landed on the way he derived double profits by his trade ; by selling goods worth a *pan* he earned one *kahan*, selling ordinary spices he got diamonds as price. The mind of the merchant was filled with joy. In full speed he came back to his country seven days before the specified time of seven months. When the ships laid anchor at the landing ghat the seven wives of the merchant came up for giving a fitting reception. They made an offering of sacred grass, holy oil and vermilion to the prows of the ships and carried home the cargo and the wealth contained in them.

They carried the great riches and valuable goods home. What else did they take with them? They seized besides the greatest treasure of the ship, *viz.*, the beautiful damsel whom they discovered there to their wonder.

The merchant had an only son prized by him as the one eye of a blind man, which had still a power of sight. The youth was very handsome. The merchant had given him some literary education and he had besides some training in trade. He was now twenty years old and at this stage he met the girl whom his father had brought there. (Ll. 1-36.)

(4)

The girl and the youth read and wrote sitting on the same floor. The merchant's son had taught the princess how to read and write. Their meeting at this early stage was happy as that of the sun and the moon at the dawn. The eyes of the passer-by heavy-laden with sleep became wide open if he saw the beautiful pair. The hungry man forgot the pangs of hunger at the happy sight. Every one who saw them exclaimed: 'Lo how beautiful the pair is! They look like a golden bird and its mate!'

She carried a basket for plucking flowers every day and her flowing hair touched her feet when she walked. She used to weave a garland every day with the flowers she plucked. It was to be presented to the merchant's son and she wove it into a garland with the utmost skill.

I will now tell what happened one day. When she was writing her pen dropped on the ground. Youth had just dawned on her and her mind was looking for something she did not know. She felt indolent and inactive and said to the merchant's son : " I do not feel quite at ease. I cannot rise from my seat. Will you kindly pick up that pen from the ground for me. Please comply with this my earnest request. I have no mind in my studies. I am indifferent to duty. If you do me this favour I will not again make a similar request to you. I will not sit here. I will go elsewhere and find a seat for me apart, next time.'

The Youth.

'I will pick up the pen for you but before I do so promise to me that you will marry me.'

The Princess.

'Such promises and vows are needless. I live here at the mercy of others. I feel sad at the thought of my own hard lot. My father drove me from his house as the astrologers said that I was unlucky. He banished me and left me in a deep jungle. Such was my cruel fate ordained by the providence that I had no companion to whom I could open my mind and unburden myself. I embraced the trees aud told them the tale of my woes crying. True, I saw the very leaves of the Daruk trees fall down on the ground in sympathy. I slept on the hard ground. Alas! where were my couches then ? The ground became wet with my tears which I shed incessantly.

'If you will marry me you will fall into danger. The goddess of fortune will frown at you. Who is there, friend, who would court misfortune in this way? Driven away as I am by parents and relations as a personification of evil luck what would you do with me, my friend! Abstain from this foolish course. If you want to marry, your parents will get you a handsome princess. There will be plenty such ready to offer themselves as brides.

'So unlucky am I that if I seek the shadow of a tree for taking rest under it, it catches fire from some mysterious source and is burnt down. If I go to drink a drop of water to allay my thirst the river dries up as it catches my breath. In your beautiful palace do not, I pray you, make place for one so unlucky as my poor self.'

The Youth.

'But you prattle in vain. I have decided my course. I want to marry you. If my whole goods and cargo are lost in trade I will not alter my vow. I must marry you and would not care what misfortune it may bring on me. I have turned mad at your beauty. Whether it be good or evil it is myself who is responsible for the result of my action You are not at all liable to any blame. Touch me, dear one, and promise that you will marry me.'

The Princess.

'Here do I sit on the ground and take the vow that from to-day I am a servant at thy feet.'

The merchant's son now picked up the pen and handed it to the princess. (Ll. 1-50.)

(5)

The report of the princess's beauty spread far and wide. Every citizen, every villager heard of it. The king of the country came to know of it and all his subjects had this for their topic. Her beauty had the glow of the moon and the light of the lamp. The merchant had brought her from the jungle. The king's daughter on hearing this report from her people sent two of the female attendants of the palace named Chamar and Dhamar with an offer of her friendship to the beautiful girl. They come to the merchant's house and said, 'The report of the princess found in the jungle has spread far and wide and the king's daughter Rupavati desires that she should make friendship exchanging flower-garlands with her. She has already engaged drummers and musicians and invited all people of the neighbourhood for celebrating the occasion. To-day the princess will formally make the girl of the jungle her friend.'

At the front of the palace is a beautiful garden of flowers. There in the spring season, seated on the boughs of flower plants, the cuckoo sang all day long. The *champa* and other flowers of the garden were of a superior quality and did not fade or lose their lustre for a long time. There one could see rows of *gandharaja* plants with blooming flowers. *Atashis* were seen in abundance fringing the borders of the garden with their yellow line. The two friends—the princess and the girl of the jungle—were bound in fast embrace and they wandered about the garden while the cuckoos sent their gay notes to the sky.

Both of them were young and both of them were beautiful. Their presence added grace to the garden and both of them plucked flowers and wove garlands with them.

One day by chance the hair of the girl was caught in the thorns of an Akra[1] plant; some of this luxurious black treasure were torn off. The princess said, 'Do your hair again, friend. They are in a dishevelled state.'

The Princess.

'Dear sister of my heart, will you tell me who is it that came to our garden yesterday?'

1 *Akra=Alangium hexapetalum.*

The Princess.

She is my friend, the girl who puts up with the merchant. She and I had a pleasant ramble in the garden yesterday.

The Prince.

What sort of woman is your friend? May I have a look at her?

The Princess.

She is a paragon of beauty. There is none in the world to match her. Her long flowing hair seem to kiss her feet. They are so beautiful that one could stake a lakh of rupees for that hair alone. She was found by the merchant in a jungle. I saught her friendship on account of her extraordinary beauty. I tell you, brother, she is a fairy, the glowing light that imanates from her body spreads a halo round it as she walks. She seems to scatter her beauty like golden rays all around.

The Prince.

Will you, sister, show me your paragon of beauty on some pretext or other?

There was an invitation for the girl from the palace the next day. The two friends met and embraced each other and they were full of glee.

The prince who lay hidden behind a tree saw the girl from a distance and became maddened by the sight.

The Prince.

Oh sister of my heart, know that I have taken a vow.

The Princess.

What vow have you taken, brother?

The Prince.

One who has such a fine stuff of hair must be mine. I will marry her. If I fail to do so, I shall starve myself to death in this parlour of mine.

The princess one day got her friend into confidence in order to sound her mind. She related her whole story to the princess from her early life in the palace of her father down to that of her exile in the forest. She did not omit to tell her of the vow she had taken to marry the son of the merchant. She concluded by saying, "Our marriage has been finally settled though no body knows of it."

"Listen to me, my fair friend, do not disclose the story of our love and marriage to any one. I tell you all in confidence. One day my pen dropped from my hand. The son of the merchant picked it up for me and I promised to him touching the pen that I would marry him. There were plenty of tagar, atashi and *champa* flowers there which witnessed my vow as I said to him: 'From this day I am a servant at your feet.'"

The princess told the whole story to her brother, who felt a wrong impulse and waited for an opportunity to carry out his wicked plan. (Ll. 1-35.)

(6)

He shut himself up in his parlour. He would not touch any meal, nor sleep at night. There was great consternation in the whole city and the queen became maddened at this condition of her son. Enquiries were made as to what he wanted and the informers told that he wanted a certain valuable thing.

'What is it?' was the query from all sides.

'It is the jewel from a serpent's hood.'

The king called the merchant to him and said :—"you are to bring a jewel from a serpent's hood within six months. If you fail, you will be killed with all the members of your family." The merchant pondered for a while thinking thus :—

"I have spent my whole life in trade. Now my hair is grey and my gums are toothless. I visited many principal cities of the world, capitals of kings and famous ports. I never came across a jewel from a serpent's hood. Nobody has seen it. It is a pure myth, though I have heard many people speak of it."

The merchant in a sad tone said to his son, "After all these years, I am doomed to death—probably I shall be devoured by one of the big tigers of the jungle. The king has ordered me to bring a jewel from a serpent's hood. But where that jewel is nobody knows."

The Merchant's Son.

"But father, why should you go on such an errand in this old age? I am quite ready for it being in the full vigour of youth. You have grown very old; enjoy the fruits of your well-earned rest at home. Order the ships to be ready. I shall go on a sea-voyage."

He did not listen to the opposition offered by his parents. He settled his course and undertook the voyage.

The Merchant's Son to the Girl.

"I have come to bid you farewell at this hour of leaving my country. I am bound for distant lands in search of a jewel from a serpent's hood. My old father was about to go, but this cannot be, so I have resolved to go myself. Wait here with patience and we shall meet again."

The beautiful girl said nothing but wept, and with her tears washed the youth's feet and wiped them again with her flowing hair. She said, " Your feet I know to be my sole stay—I do not know what is good and what is bad for me relying on your love alone. I pray to god that He may protect you in foreign lands." (Ll. 1-18.)

(7)

He started with his ships which displayed red and blue flags. Seven hundred drums beat as the ship proceeded through the waves ; the citizens everywhere were startled and made enquiries—"Who is it that sails so pompously ? " The answer was—" It is the son of a great merchant."

Everywhere he got a splendid reception. He returned home after six months. There was no jewel from a serpent's hood. It was all a myth. He had brought with him hundreds of serpents from the seas and hills and mountains—He had with him a large number of snake-charmers. The snakes were innumerable. Amongst them were *Sankharaja*, *Maniraj*, *Machua*, *Chilbaka*, *Khaia* and *Gokhura*, but none of these had any jewel on their hoods.

The Raja was told by his men that there were jewels on the hoods of these reptiles, but the merchant's son has secured them himself and deceived the king. The king said, 'The merchant's son should be doomed to be stung by those serpents. Provided this is done my son's life will be saved.' By the command of the king the merchant's son was bound hand and foot and thrown near the serpents.

The poison instantly entered the body of the young man and he was straightway killed.

The merchant's son lay dead, with his body blackened by poison. There was nothing of that golden lustre of his handsome person left. The merchant's wife placed the corpse in her lap and began to cry loudly. The merchant sat near by and wept.

The citizens in great sympathy and grief assembled there and expressed their sorrow.

The custom of the country was that the body of a person killed by snake-bite should not be burnt. A large raft was made of banana stems and the corpse was floated on it.

The girl all the while shed silent tears sitting close to the corpse.

The Girl,

"Oh, great king, you are the lord of justice. The sea is dry to-day. The impossible has taken place because of my ill luck. The tree under whose shade I had taken refuge has been burnt down and reduced to ashes. You are the lord of the country. Permit me to go with the corpse; know that he was my husband."

"Oh great merchant," she said again, "you do not know it. But you are my father-in-law. We two were married and the whole thing was kept a secret. He has left me wretched as I am in the dawn of my youth. Permit me, father-in-law, to accompany the corpse."

Addressing the corpse she said, "Who is it whose ready dinner I had seized depriving a hungry man of his food,—so that he cursed me in some past life? I do not know what calf was deprived by me of its mother's milk when sucking and throttled to death. Or in some past life I as a tiger devoured the darling son of a doting mother or as a serpent ate the young ones of a bird laid in its nest. Some such great crime must I have committed in a past life or why should my young husband leave me at this early youth of mine?"

As the corpse floated on the waves of the river she shed incessant tears adding to the volume of the river's water. She like one maddened by grief followed the course of the raft as it proceeded onwards. With the edge of her *sari* she wiped away her tears. The beautiful girl thus pursued her dead husband through the banks of the river. (Ll. 1-36.)

End of the first Canto. (Incomplete.)

BALLAD OF PRINCE BIRNARAYAN

PREFACE TO THE BALLAD OF BIRNARAYAN

The ballad of Birnarayan was collected by Nagendranath Dey from three different sources in 1929. Firstly, he got a few lines from one Kalachand Mal, a native of the village Salida near Muktagacha in Mymensingh. This man gave information that one Panaulla of the village Sankiura in the same district knew the full ballad. Nagendra Babu accordingly saw Sheik Panaulla who supplied him with a considerable portion of the song, and the rest, he collected from a person who goes by the name of 'Kalār Bap' ('father of Kala') of the village Jentulia in Mymensingh. But the ballad, though collected from these three sources after a dogged pursuit is still incomplete. It has been noticed by me several times that these ballads, as a rule, rise to sublime pathos towards their last portion. Unfortunately in this ballad we find an abrupt and incomplete conclusion, keeping us in suspense as regards the fate of the hero and the heroine. The heroine probably did some daring act of martyrdom or self-sacrifice to vindicate her character, but it is useless to give a catalogue of our imaginations on the point. The incomplete ballad contains 547 lines, and I have divided the whole into seven cantos.

From the language of the ballad it appears that it belonged to the 17th century, but one cannot be too sure of dates, as the ballads composed in a very early age are so recast by succeeding generations of minstrels that their language cannot always be accepted as a test of the time of the composition of the original.

There are romantic situations in this ballad which often remind us of the wanderings of Don Juan and Haddee of Lord Bryon or of Hewlett's Prosper and Isoult in "The Forest Lovers."

In some passages we have a distinct re-echo of the sentiments to be found in the ballad of Mahua. This ballad-literature of ours with its lively and felicitous accounts of poetic situations brings us every now and then in contact with the painful details in the life of our women. Subjected to cruelties of all sorts and severe treatment of a blind and orthodox society, our women display wonderful courage, angelic patience and a power of endurance which cannot but evoke the admiration of the reader. It is a pity that a girl like Sona, whose beauty and intellectual gifts were such that she could "lie by an emperor and command him tasks" was subjected to an extremely unkind and cruel verdict of the society ruining the prospects of her life for ever. Again and again we come across this hard-hearted treatment of the orthodox Hindu society towards the fair sex in our rural literature. We have it in Malua, in Khullana and many other women whose noble qualities challenge our admiration. Sona pays the penalty of being born in this society of ours where we find " destiny unshunnable as death," pursuing the fair creatures through life inspite of their high accomplishments and beauty.

The hero in this ballad, unlike the general run of male characters in our rural literature, shows a valour, steadiness and integrity which make him a worthy match of his consort. In this respect he bears a comparison with Naderchand of Mahua and one or two other heroes described in the ballads. The rest are generally found to be a set of cowards like Chand Binode.

One thing that strikes us in this ballad is the courage with which the subjects of the king came forward to criticise his action. We find here the people organising themselves against the will of a capricious prince and even daring to contemplate plans for his murder in case he touched the honour of their harems. The copper-plate inscriptions bear a testimony to the Bengali people rising in a body during a period of anarchy and selecting from amongst themselves their monarch. Gopal, the founder of Pal dynasty was elected king by the people, when the country was rent by what the scholars have designated "Mātsyanyāya."[1] The people living in the dominions of prince Birnarayan show a spirit akin to that evinced by the people of Bengal in the 8th century.

As the ballad is incomplete, we cannot give it its true value. Nevertheless the tradition in the localities from which it was collected is that Birnarayan met with his death in a truly heroic manner, scornfully rejecting all offers of amity and pardon from his royal father on condition of his giving up Sona. It is also said that the last part of the tragedy concerning the fate of this girl is full of pathos showing her character in its towering height. I am sorry that I have not been able to collect the ballad in full.

DINESHCHANDRA SEN.

[1] Matsyanyāya. It is said that the big fishes eat up the small fishes. Here it means the anarchical condition of a country in which those in power oppress the weak.

RAJA BIRNARAYAN

(1)

It was a terribly dark night,—but even such a night had its end. It dawned. Prince Birnarayan awoke from his sleep. When stepping out of the room the lizard made its ominous '*tik-tik*' and some one sneezed from behind, but the prince was a dashing young man and little cared for signs or auguries. He went out of the house without caring much for the inauspicious signs.

But stop. Though he was a daring fellow, yet in his heart of hearts he could not help feeling a hesitancy in starting the work of the day. "Will my day pass in peace?" was the thought that lurked in his mind. Inspite of his seeming sprightliness and courage the traditional superstition he could not resist. He advanced a few steps and then retraced them. He came back to his room and tried to go, but there was again a doubt that the day might not be favourable. These cogitations kept him indoors the whole day. But when evening set in he could no longer stay at home. He went towards the river-side all alone and without any weapon in his hand. He strolled by the bank of the river enjoying the sight of the waves which were playfully dancing. A merchant's boat was passing by laden with goods. The tide was favourable and the boat ran so swiftly that one might think it was running a race with the winds, but that was not the only boat. There was any number of them of various sizes and colours. The sight was pleasing. The prince sat for a time under the shade of a tree, gazing at these. Gradually he felt a sense of repose and his eyes shut in sleep. The sight of the setting sun was splendid, it made the whole western sky aglow.

At this hour a beautiful damsel came to the river bank with her pitcher to fetch water. She was the darling of her parents. She had her pitcher full but she emptied it in order to fill it again from the river. Before the evening was over she had come there for water. As she walked, she looked on all sides with eager curiosity. She too was attracted by the sight of the beautiful boats. Her face had the charm and light of the morning sun. When she came down to the river, the water caught the rays of the setting sun and as the waves touched her beautiful person, they sparkled like gold. Then did she rise again and essayed to return. Here by the river-side she happened to see the handsome prince enjoying sleep under a tree. The more she saw him she felt the attraction the greater and there was no satiety of it. She glanced a hundred times and yet she cast her glance again to satisfy her eyes. She was transfixed to the spot by the sight of the prince and was not conscious that the evening had passed and night had already veiled the fair face of earth.

She had just stepped into youth. The sight of the prince enkindled in her the first desire of a woman's heart. The secret of her heart she revealed to none. It was treasured up in her heart. As she saw the prince again and again a strange sorrow overcame her and she began to shed tears. She thought—"This handsome youth is a prince and I am the daughter of an ordinary village-man. Like a dwarf aspiring to touch the sky is my foolish desire to love him. Like a fly that wishes to reach the starry regions it is vain for me to indulge in such a hope. But though I have analysed all the reasons and perceived the foolishness of my course, my mind obstinately clings to the thought and does not listen to good counsel." As she went on thinking in this strain her tears began to flow again.

At last she felt a relief at the thought that though it might not be possible for her to expect a return of love, she might offer herself to him, without a thought of getting any return of love. "Oh my jewel," she said to herself, "who is it that has plunged you in the depth of ocean making you inaccessible to me." She brooded over her bad luck and again and again wept. In the meantime as she glanced around she perceived that the whole earth was enveloped in darkness. There was no glimmer of the evening rays. The night was dark and terrible. She began to realise her position—"What will my parents say as I have tarried so long in the river-side? What explanation shall I give?" Alarmed at this thought she hastened her paces and made herself ready to proceed homeward. (Ll. 1-72.)

(2)

As darkness now prevailed on all sides, the merchant whose boat with its cargo was going onward by favourable tide asked his captain to lay anchor at the landing ghat and there he espied the beautiful girl. The sight of the youthful maiden inflamed his mind. "I will risk my life for her" he said, and as the girl was busy in filling the pitcher in all haste, he seized her from behind her back and led her onward by force. In the meantime he called his men who immediately thronged there like an army of ants. There was none near, so no one came to respond to the appeal for help which she made, loudly crying. In that lonely region of the river-side she could expect no man to come to her rescue at night. The cruel merchant caught hold of her and tried to throttle her voice by force. The cry of agony that she sent to the sky in that condition roused the prince from his sleep. He saw that the merchant was carrying away the girl by force and that she was already brought to the boat. The prince was very sorry at what he saw. There was no one in the locality who could come to the prince if he called for help. "What is the good of my ruling the country when a foreigner is allowed to do such acts of atrocity on my subjects?" This was his first thought. At the same time he perceived that any attempt to rescue the girl would be fruitless as he was all alone. But he was full of sympathy for the girl and without losing heart managed to creep into the boat all unperceived in the darkness. (Ll. 1-48.)

(3)

Carrying the girl to his boat the merchant ordered his men to raise the anchor and start the boat in full speed. The boat rowed by many hands flew like a bird on the waves.

The boat was passing along the stream and the merchant said many a sweet and seductive word to win the heart of the maiden. "Your youth, dear maiden, is manifest in all parts of your handsome person. But when this youth will decline, all will be over with you. Make a gift of your youth to me when you have this treasure, I confess I am so greatly attracted by your charms that I am prepared to stake my life for you. Just look at my goods in this boat. They possess the value of a lakh of rupees. Everything I have got here is choice and rare. Ready am I to present them all to you. My aspiration is to carry out your wishes as your slave. Hundreds of maid-servants will be near you to serve your least wishes. They will be obedient slaves to your feet. I will adorn your beautiful body with gems and stones. Your bed will be on a couch of gold. Your beautiful feet will not have to tread the hard earth. Your order will be the law of my country, and my subjects will offer their tribute of worship to you even before the gods of the temple have received it from them."

But all these proved fruitless. She would not glance at him once nor say a word in reply to all his fine speech. She shut her eyes in contempt and sat at a distance from him. If he sat facing her she bent her head low with her back turned against him. The more the merchant expressed his ardour, the more she became icy cold and shed incessant tears.

The prince saw all these from a distance and began to consider the step he should take at this stage.

Slowly did the prince proceed to carry out his plan. Availing himself of the darkness that pervaded the place, slowly did he lay his hands on the weapons stored in the boat and dropped them all into water except one sharp sword named Ramdao which he selected and kept by himself. He stealthily sat behind the captain and cut off his head which fell into the water without noise. He next sat at the helm and steered the boat till it reached a shoal where it got stranded. The boat could not be moved an inch and lay hopelessly fixed, inert and motionless. The boatmen and the rowers all got down and tried their utmost to pull the boat into the water. But the boat lay stranded in the sand and would not move. The merchant himself got down from the boat in order to see what had happened. Availing himself of the merchant's absence the prince came near the maiden who at once recognised him. She clasped his feet and began to weep. The prince asked her not to lose her hope. He would help her to get out of the difficult situation, he said. He at once untied a jolly boat which lay attached to the big boat and floated it in the river. Carrying the woman thither he sat by her side taking with him some oars and the great weapon—Ramdao.

The merchant now saw this and pursued them with loud cries. Boatmen all joined him in his pursuit and set up an uproar. They were resolved to catch the boat. The prince brandished his sword sitting in the front while Sona sat at the helm directing the course of the boat. The merchant entered his boat in search of his weapons. Alas! where would he find them! They had all been thrown into the river by the prince. The boatmen were all killed one by one as they approached the prince. Horror-struck at the sight of this dreadful slaughter, the merchant did not venture to proceed further but beat a retreat. In the meantime three quarters of the night passed away and the boat with the pair reached their own landing ghat at that dead hour of night. (Ll. 1-66.)

(4)

She had gone to fetch water in the evening and the night was so greatly advanced now. Her father Radharaman could not make out the cause of this delay and he silently searched her in all the known parts of the locality. Both the parents were struck dumb, afraid of the scandal and silently and diligently made a scrutinising search talking in whispers between themselves and did not disclose it to anybody at first. But when after a careful search they failed to trace her they were obliged to take their good neighbours into confidence and tell them that the jewel of their house—their only child—was missing. She was their pet and there was none else in the house who could fill her place. Saying so Radharaman cried like a child. The neighbours took pity on him and ran in all directions to search for her again with a good number of people. Radharaman went to the banks of the river and looked around closely watching all possible clues. They saw after a time the empty pitcher lying near the landing ghat but found no other trace of the girl. They suspected that she might have been drowned. Some said that she might possibly have been devoured by a crocodile. Some of the more energetic amongst them went into the water and searched there. Others searched in the land. They spent a considerable part of the night in this way till it was past midnight. At this time the moon was up in the sky illuminating the river, when they perceived that the girl Sona with the prince were in a boat. The pair came to the landing ghat and got down from the small boat. The people assembled there like ants making enquiries. The prince related all facts in a straightforward manner and Radharaman believed the story saying that the prince had saved his family from a great dishonour but the neighbours said it was all a fabricated tale. The girl had been dishonoured. The couple now tried to hide their guilt by false pretexts. She could not be given a place again in her house. The wicked woman must be banished from the village. Some one said the woman should be cut to pieces and thrown into the river. The more merciful ones recommended that she should be driven away to some foreign land. One of them arrogantly stopped others and insisted on their putting her inside a gunny bag and throwing her into the river at once. With these threats he valiantly approached the girl. The prince brandished his sword at him. With one hand he caght hold of the girl and with the other he was about to strike the assailants. The crowd dispersed in fear. (Ll. 1-39.)

(5)

Sona, the girl, fell at his feet and said 'Now tell me what course I should adopt ; a weak woman as I am, I am still proud of my purity. I do not know what is in store for me for I find that Providence is against me. You are the son of a Raja ; you will have no cause of sorrow. No evil can touch you. I regret that without doing any wrong I have been made a victim to a great scandal ; it breaks my heart when I think of my condition.'

The Prince.

"I risked my life to save you, dear girl, I cannot bear to see you distressed in this way. I will tell you a bit of my mind. Your face like a full-blown lotus has charmed my soul. Your hair has the dark hue of scattered clouds. Your eyes are like two beautiful stars and your limbs are tender as stalks of lotus plants. I never saw a woman as beautiful as you are. For the sake of your beauty I have turned a beggar at your door. Many proposals of marriage are before me in the palace but none of the girls proposed have I liked. I solicit your hands. Will you not, dear girl, kindly accept my humble proposal."

Sona.

"You are a big Zemindar and I am the daughter of an ordinary householder. Love between you and me will be unsteady as a drop of water on a lotus leaf. You are the master of the land and after your first infatuation you will busy yourself with State-affairs and would hardly think of me. Why should you bring scandal on yourself for a fleeting impulse which would last for a day or two. Forgive me, dear prince; go to your palace and be happy. As for myself, I tell you, it will be my lot to turn a wretched wanderer in the forest but I would prefer to throw myself into fire before you and thus end myself. Why should you run great risks for my poor self. You will earn nothing but scandal by paying attention to me. Your parents, though you are their darling, will not bear it. They may even ask you to leave the palace. Why should you, oh prince, court all these ills when you have such a promising career before you. Be well advised, go back to your home and look to the interest of your State, which as a prince you should do. I have been already made a victim to great scandal and my place will soon be in the depths of yonder river."

Saying this she proceeded onwards in order to plunge herself in the river when the prince stopped her by force and said, "You have not understood, oh girl, the deep-seated sorrow of my heart. Without you my life would be dreary like a wilderness. Separated from you I do not covet to live. If really you would drown yourself, I would do so first. Heaven itself would be hell to me without you. What do you say of the pleasures of the palace! If you refuse me you would just see I am going to drown myself in the river."

He not only said this but advanced some steps to get down into the river. She clasped his feet and said: "You have saved my life and you have been a victim to scandal for my sake. How can I bear to see you distressed; if really you covet my wretched self, here am I at your feet. I offer my life and soul unto you. Let the moon and the stars behold it; from to-day I offer myself to you and I shall be yours in weal or woe. My father and mother have given me up. The good neighbours have been unkind to me. I do not know what sin I have committed, yet Providence seems to be against me. Fallen into great disrtess as I am, you have protected me as a god would have done."

When the prince heard these words he raised the girl from the ground and in great happiness embraced her. He thought that heaven itself had come from its high place down to this earth yielding him an easy access. There in the still hour of the night they pledged themselves to one another and were secretly married. They thought not of the world or what the people would say. They became one in life and spirit in the holy union of mutual choice. They forgot the rest of the world and as they glanced at one another they thought that their bliss of life was complete.

After a time they began to think how could they live in that Raja's town. Subject to a great scandal their name will be for ever infamous in the country. Parents even would not excuse them and might pass the sentence of death for their rash act.

"But if we both leave this country all our dangers will be over."

They resolved to do this. As soon as they decided their course in this way they got upon a small boat and their great love lent force to the winds which carried the boat like a bird over the waters.

It was a woeful night that the parents passed. The night seemed too long for them and they bewailed their lot in utter helplessness. (Ll. 1-92.)

(6)

The people of the locality accused the Raja and said that in his palace a dog was born in the wicked prince. Everywhere the king protected the people but here that dog of a prince was allowed to do whatever he liked. "He is destroying our caste, honour and ruining us. To-day the victim is Radharaman ; it will be some one else to-morrow. In the jurisdiction of such a Raja we are all unsafe. We must find out that dog and cut him to pieces and throw him into water."

"We need not fear for consequences. We will face all dangers. But this conduct cannot be tolerated." They all assembled and took spears and *sarkis* in their hands and marched in quest of the pair. They made a search by the banks of the river. They made their way through the jungles rooting out the shrubs and wild plants to make a path. But their vigilant search proved vain. The pair could not be traced.

They waxed in sullen wrath not being able to find out the prince. In great disappointment they began to indulge in all kinds of wild thought. Some one said, " the Raja has secretly kept the prince hidden in some place—after all he could not resist the natural affection of a parent." But others suggested that it would be well if they openly asked the Raja as to the whereabouts of his son.

Deciding on the last course, they approached the Raja and acquainted him with the wicked acts of his son. Vehement was their language when they said that such a wicked son should be killed and his corpse should be floated in the river.

They concluded by saying, "Be pleased, oh Lord, to do justice. Your Excellency should not do otherwise because your son is implicated."

The Raja was greatly incensed. He called the Police Prefect to his presence and ordered him to bring prince Birnarayan to his presence. 'If the charge is true,' said the indignant Raja, 'he will have due punishment—not a whit less because he is my son. It is better not to have a child at all than one so wicked. Such a wicked child only brings infamy to the family.'

The Police Prefect made investigations and informed the Raja that from the day before prince Birnarayan was missing; he could not be traced anywhere.

The Raja gave further orders—" Wherever he would be found he was to be brought there bound hand and foot."

The Raja thought that the charge was real, otherwise the prince would not have fled away. Everyone said that for the last two days no one knew where he went. He again ordered the police to bring the prince to the court bound in fetters. "If such a wicked son is allowed to live he will be a permanent scandal to the family. I shall not feel a sense of relief until and unless this villain is sacrificed at the altar of our family deity. All my State will be in utter confusion and fall into anarchical condition if such a man is placed at its helm. I will not like to see his face again."

Passing the above order upon the police the Raja called his principal subjects to his court and gave a general mandate that all of them should try to find out the prince—" Whether in my own State or in the neighbouring ones, wherever he was to be found he should be forthwith arrested and brought here. But if any person out of a false sense of regard or affection tried to hide him he would be very severely punished. Such a man would be driven away from the land—from his hearth and home."

The subjects as they heard this order were filled with alarm and began a searching enquiry to find out the prince Birnarayan. (Ll. 1-78.)

(7)

Meantime the prince and Sona proceeded onward till they passed through the capitals of three kingdoms. Here the weakened arm of the prince could no longer row the boat. They were both upset by an acute hunger and a feeling of exhaustion. Here they landed ashore leaving the boat behind. They found a deep impenetrable jungle. There were delicious ripe fruits of various sorts hanging from boughs of trees and they ate them to their heart's content and appeased their hunger.

" Here shall we live amongst birds and beasts far away from human habitation—so that none will be able to discover us," they said to one another.

They did not think of their condition, as to where they would find a place to live in—they lay steeped in the joys of mutual company in the embrace of love.

But the day passed and the night came in. With the approach of night the whole place was covered with an impenetrable darkness. The tigers and other beasts were observed here and there. Where would they find a hiding place? The tigers and bears growled ferociously all around. After a search they found a cave. They entered it but, lo, they found some beast inside. They were alarmed, but the prince with his usual pluck took up his sword and with mighty force gave three strokes to the beast and cut it to pieces. They discovered that the animal the prince had killed, was a lion.

But they were afraid lest there were snakes or reptiles in the cave but there was no help. They had already entered it.

In the daytime they plucked fruits of which there was an abundance and they appeased their hunger with them. Like an antelope and her mate they found their life happy still in that wilderness. They occupied themselves night and day with sweet talks and their love was their only source of joy. It was a romantic place where love alone reigned supreme. They thought of nothing else. In the morning prince Birnarayan went in quest of fruits, and when he had gathered a sufficient number he brought them to Sona and they had a delightful repast. The fruits gave them a strength which rice could not. They lived in terms of amity with tigers and bears and were not at all afraid of the beasts. The beasts would pass away avoiding the track of the pair. Such was the condition in which Birnarayan passed his days—a prince once, and now a woodman—his change of fortune being brought about by love. (Ll. 1-36.)

(8)

Meantime the informers and other men belonging to the Raja's staff made a most vigorous search for the prince. They traversed the countries of different Rajas, and left no river-side, forest or village unnoticed, but every bit of earth through that vast tract of country was scrutinisingly searched. Nowhere they obtained a clue to the fugitives.

They were filled with dismay as the order was to find out the prince anyhow. If they failed in their mission they were to lose their lives with the women and children of their house. Greatly alarmed they again took up the search and investigated all possible localities. All places within the range of their sight were examined but alas! where was the prince gone with the girl ? No trace, no clue, no information could anybody give them.

" How can we return home now ! " They discussed the matter amongst themselves. One man said, ' Perhaps the king has killed our women and children incensed at the delay, taking us to be traitors. What good would come out of our going back as we also would share the same fate? Here is a deep jungly land, let us settle here and live in peace. Fruitless would it be to return to our deserted home under the shadow of the king's displeasure. Let us build houses here and start life anew in this jungle. There is no tax to be levied by any Raja here—nor shall we have any risk of being victims to his whims and caprices, of losing life at his sweet will. The jungle is a large tract and we shall be able to lead a peaceful life here.'

An old man said—" This is not a sound decision, my friends! How can we cut off the sweet ties of affection which bind us to the homes of our fathers? We shall be subject to great repentance if we pursue the course suggested of cutting off all association with our motherland. We have not investigated this part of the country. Who knows the prince might be hidden in this jungle? If we fail to find him here we will have another discussion on the point and settle our future course. But return we must to our dear motherland and see what step the Raja takes in respect of us. (Ll. 1-32.)

(9)

Here Birnarayan and his consort were leading a romantic life. They were passing their days in a dreamy sort of joy indifferent to every thing else. They talked with each other day and night yet those unmeaning talks would have no end. They decorated their body with field-flowers, fresh and fragrant. There was no enemy, none to envy their uninterrupted happiness. They wandered in the jungle in full contentment undisturbed by any gloomy thought.

The Raja's men searched the jungle but did not meet the prince for some time. One morning as they rose from sleep they felt greatly dismayed and were discussing as to whether they should now return home or not. At this stage the prince happened to pass by their side. They looked with anxious eagerness at the figure and were convinced that it was that of their prince. They encircled him and catching hold of his *dhuti* they seized his person. They were right glad to have now Prince Birnarayan for whom they had passed so many anxious days and nights. The prince appealed to their compassion saying that he had one in the forest who helplessly depended on him. They heeded not his request but caught hold of him saying. " A compliance with your request, oh prince, would lead to our death. Excuse us."

They brought him home leaving the girl alone in the forest. (Ll. 1-30.)

(10)

Sona in the meantime was anxiously awaiting the return of the prince. He had gone in quest of food but it was too late now—" Where is he tarrying to-day ? The delay made her anxious and she sometimes sat in her lonely cot brooding over her lot and at others came out in the lonely path of the forest. The whole day she passed in this manner, her anxiety rising to the highest pitch in the evening when darkness covered the land. With the advance of the night she despaired of his return ; she took the prince's sword in her hand and wildly wandered about the forest seeking him. Her thoughts were wild. At one time she thought that he might have been devoured by a tiger. But in that case some remains of his corpse or a few bits of bones would have been there. "Besides my husband is strong enough even for a strong tiger. It may be that some fairy or courtesan might have taken fancy for him and carried him away. But can it be that he has really been tired of me and left me alone wishing for the pleasures of life in the city. Wherever you may have gone, oh my friend, whatever may be your object, may you be happy and may I not live to hear any unpleasant news about you. For me I shall seek heaven and earth for you and try my utmost to have once more a sight of your sweet face." These were some of her musings.

Baramashi

"This is April, oh friend, the breeze of the spring is blowing sweetly. In vain quest after you my days pass, but unbearable are my sufferings in the night which seems to me too long. In May the air in the evening is cool and sweet, but this does not assuage the pain of my heart. In June the cuckoo's sweet notes seem to me dire as thunder. Oh! where can I hear his sweet voice once more? July comes with its unbearable heat but still more unbearable is my separation from him. August brings its showers which drench my body but it cannot put out the fire that is in my heart. In September the *jhils* are full of full-blown lotuses. If you were here you would have plucked some of these for me to adorn my ears."

The girl ran mad seeking the prince in that wild tract. Whomsoever she met she asked—"Have you seen my young friend?" The big trees of the forest she approached and addressed them saying—" Hoary are ye with age and know what have transpired during all these ages. Can you give me any news of my friend?" To the birds she said—"You wander in the sky and observe all that passes in this earth. Did you see him anywhere? I will follow him wherever he is if I simply get a clue from you. Oh ye stars—you twinkle wickedly but this is no time for joke. You certainly see with your far-reaching ken where my friend is staying now. Tell me something about him.

" He left his father and mother for my sake and I cannot reconcile it with my mind that my beloved would give me up at the last hour in this way. Had I known that you would desert me so cruelly I would have drowned myself in the river to avert the mishap that has befallen me. (Ll. 1-64.)

(*Incomplete.*)

CHANDRABATI'S RAMAYANA

PREFACE TO CHANDRABATI'S RAMAYANA

This poem written in the form of a ballad has a unique interest for those who are studying the literature on Rama-Saga, and though from the point of poetic merit it may not stand on the level of the other exquisitely beautiful ballads such as Malua and Kenaram composed by the gifted poetess Chandrabati, its bearing on some of the intricate questions relating to the origin of the Ramayanic legend is considerable, offering suggestive points for reaching a solution.

It appears that not only in India but in a large part of the south-east of Asia people were conversant with the Rama-story during the palmy days of Hinduism. Some of the old versions were probably older than Valmiki's Epic. Amongst these the Pali Dasaratha Jataka might be reckoned as one. I have given my reasons for this view in my book "The Bengali Ramayanas." Valmiki had some crude materials before him which he touched with his powerful pen investing them with an unsurpassed poetic grace. The story of the 'Andha Muni' in the Ramayana is a reproduction of the tale described in the 'Sama Jataka.' The words that fell from the demon in the 'Sambula Jataka' have a distinct ring of Ravana's threat to Sita in the Asoka garden, and the speeches of Vessantara and Maddi in the Vessantara Jataka are so alike those of Rama and Sita on the eve of their exile that the conclusion seems inevitable that one is the original and the other its copy. These are not all. There are other analogous passages in the Jataka-stories which lead us to the supposition that the Ramayanic legend had existed in a crude form before Valmiki and the great poet touched all available resources that lay in the country at his time with his inspired pen, so that all that was inelegant and lacking in polish became exquisitely beautiful and refined in the noble edifice that he constructed, as if by a touch of his magic wand.

Amongst the old materials the Jain Ramayanas are certainly noteworthy. Paum Chariam or life of Rama written in the first century A. D. by Bimalacharya in Prakrit deviates in many points from Valmiki and even the most modern of them compiled by Hemachandra—a Jain poet in the 11th century—record traditions and poetic situations which are at variance with the accounts of Valmiki whose fame must have spread far into the country in that century. That the Jain poet at such a late period dared to deviate from Valmiki in some vital points of the Rama-legends proves that the Jain community had deep-seated beliefs and old traditions which their poet could not help recording, even knowing it fully well that the popularity of Valmiki's epic had grown so extensive at the time that any version of the story which materially differed from it would not be read or appreciated beyond the Jain community.

Rama was certainly a historical figure and the story of his exile is founded on facts. All the versions whether Jain, Buddhistic or Hindu have this common ground of the story but the matter becomes complicated when the story of Sita is introduced. It is a historical fact that the custom of marrying their own sisters was prevalent amongst the Sakya people of old. It was a custom which existed in many parts of the world in olden times. The ancient Egyptians and Babylonians had this custom, and in the Jataka-stories we find frequent references to princes marrying their uterine sisters in particular clans. The kings of Java followed this custom. The other tribes and communities naturally looked upon this custom with derision and contempt (*vide* Kunal Jataka, No. 535, pp. 219, translated by H. T. Francis).

Nothing could be more abhorrent and shocking to the

orthodox Hindu community than the custom of marrying one's own sister. The 'Dasaratha Jataka' says that Sita was Rama's own sister and in all probability this was a historical fact. The poet Valmiki, who it is now unanimously believed by scholars, wrote the Ramayana from the Book II to Book VI did not stress the point of Sita's birth, but the later poets who hated the custom prevalent amongst the Sakyas but thought that the story would be incomplete without a reference to the birth of the heroine, employed their imagination to fill up the blank by tracing her pedigree.

One might say that they could have easily linked her with some ancient royal line in order to avoid the difficulty. Those who have read Mr. Pargiter's latest work on the genealogy of the Kshatriya princes will easily understand why Sita's parentage could not be associated with any Kshatriya Raj family. The genealogy of noted princes of India was known so widely in the country and Sita was such a distinguished woman that all attempts to link her with any of the principal royal dynasties of India would not meet with popular acceptance as the fraud would be immediately detected. Easier far it was to hide the fact under some legend, which, however monstrous or extraordinary it might bc, would readily appeal to the credulity of the populace.

The orthodox Hindu community under the circumstances created stories of a wild nature and thus patched up what in their eyes appeared to be a defect in the Ramayanic legend. The stories thus fabricated might be as old as Valmiki or even earlier. We have a series of such wild and extraordinary tales relating to the birth of Sita, though we do not find any trace of them in the epic of Valmiki.

But the most interesting point to us is that such legends existed even in Bengal side by side with Valmiki's epic. The writers of Sanskrit except in a few stray cases have ignored these legends. The question is why did Chandrabati, the writer of the present ballad, and herself a great Sanskrit scholar, prefer the indigenous legends to the epic-version while writing the story of Ramayana? She wrote her Ramayana about the year 1575. Krittibas's recension was composed long before this time,—it was at least a century earlier. I cannot exactly say whether in the course of a century the fame of Krittibas had already penetrated the backwoods of Eastern Bengal and found appreciation in the district of Mymensingh. No version of Krittibas's Ramayana has been recovered from Eastern Bengal earlier than the 17th century but that does not undoubtedly establish the point that Chandrabati did not read Krittibas. We cannot arrive at any definite conclusion in this matter. But it is certain that she had read Valmiki. Her father Dwija Bansi was a profound Sanskrit scholar and he ordered her to compile a Ramayana in Bengali. Chandrabati was, as already stated by me, herself a good Sanskrit scholar.

Even so late as 1575 East Bengal, specially Mymensingh, was not free from Buddhistic and Jain influences. About this time the poet Ramananda, a Buddhist, wrote his Ramayana in the *Rarh*-country, declaring himself as an incarnation of Buddha commissioned to re-establish Buddhism in India. The *Shaiva* religion that prevailed in Mymensingh during Chandravati's time had elements of Buddhism and Jainism in them, and the Hindu public had not altogether forgotten the Rama legends according to the version given by the scholars of these two creeds. Chandrabati wanted to make her recension of the Ramayana acceptable to her countrymen in a way which would accord with their traditional beliefs. In those days poets never cared to give a literal translation of Sanskrit epics. Neither Krittibas nor Kasidas did it. They based their recensions on the Sanskrit originals up to a certain limit, but wrote for their own people pandering to their tastes and established traditions.

Chandrabati did neither follow Valmiki nor Krittibas but introduced matters in conformity with the traditions current in her country. She, however, fabricated nothing. One not knowing the Ramayanic tales prevalent in provincial dialects outside Bengal, might be wrongly led to suppose that she invented many portions of the story, but taking a bird's eye view of the extensive Ramayanic literature of indigenous origin prevalent outside Bengal, we find that what had appeared to us at first to be her coinage is to a great extent based on an earlier authority.

For instance the story of Kukua, the daughter of Kaikeyi, is to be found in the Kashmiri, Malayan, Javanese, Cambodian and Tibetan versions of the Ramayana,—not exactly in each case as Chandrabati gives it, but the story in all these sources is substantially the same.

In the Kashmiri version written by the poet Dibakar Prakash Bhatta who lived during the reign of Sukhajiban Singh, Raja of Kashmir (1786 A.D.), we find an account of Kukua. She is not named so in this version, but the account given of her tallies with that of Chandrabati in its main points. Sir George Grierson writes in the series 'Bibliotheca Indica,' published by the Asiatic Society of Bengal in 1930 :—

"Sita now (pregnant) had a sister-in-law (husband's sister) who hates her with jealous treachery. She asks Sita to draw for her a portrait of Ravana."

In the Malay Ramayana this sister-in-law of Sita is called Kikawi and in the Javanese version she is Kikevi Devi. In the Javanese Ramayana it is not Kukua but her mother Kaikeyi herself who draws a picture of Ravana on Sita's fan and lays it on her bed where Rama finds it.

That Rama exiled Sita owing to the intrigue of a third party is a common factor in the various recensions of the

Rama-story written in provincial dialects of many countries. In the Khemir versions from Cambodia "A Yakshini of the demon race determines to separate Sita from Rama and persuades her to draw a portrait of Ravana on a slate. She then incarnates herself in the portrait which she is consequently unable to rub out. Sita in a fright hides it under the bed on which Rama subsequently lies down and is seized with violent fever. The room is searched for the cause. Sita confesses that she was the artist and Rama orders Lakshmana to take her away." The above is taken from Miss S. Karpete's 'The Influence of Indian Civilization in Further India" in Indian Art & Letters, Vol. I, No. 1 (1927), pp. 33ff. Sir George Grierson refers to it in his work on the Kashmiri Ramayana (p. xlii).

Mr. W. F. Stutterhen, Honorary Secretary, Holland-India Society, and an authority on the Ramayana amongst the modern Orientalists addressed me a long letter in which he asked me if I could find similarities in Indian sources with the accounts of the Javanese and Malayan versions of the Ramayana. He referred to 19 points in which the versions deviated from the Sanskrit epic of Valmiki. These points are as follow :—

"1. The story commences with a full description of Ravana's exploits. He is the son of Chitrabahu, has 3 sons : Indrajit, Patala, Maharayan (= Mahi Ravana of page 252 of the book Bengali Ramayanas) and Ganga Mahasura.

"2. His wife is a copy of the wife of Daçaratha (Dasaratha's wife called Mandodari, was summoned by Ravana, but she made a copy of herself by means of the secretions of her skin).

"3. Ravana's wife gives birth to a daughter who is cast into the sea (in an iron coffin) and picked up by the ṛishi Kala. She is called Sita.

"4. Dasaratha's first wife (Mandodari) gives birth to two sons Rama and Lakshmana, his second wife Balyadari also to two sons : Bardan (Baradan) and Citradan and a daughter Kikevi Debi.

" 5. Ṛishi·Kala hides Sita in a temple, among 100 idols (after the victory of Rama on the occasion of the Svayambara). Rama discovers her.

" 6. Rama fights (after his wedding) against four princes on his return to his father's town.

" 7. Rama decides not to return as he hears that the kingdom is promised to Baradan.

" 8. Hanuman is the son of Rama and Sita. They are changed into monkeys. They cohabit and are once more changed into human form. Sita vomits the embryo which is wrapped in a leaf and dropped in the mouth of Devi Anjani ; or in another story, Rama sees Devi Anjani performing her austerities in the midst of the sea. His semen virile appears and is dropped in the mouth of Anjani by the wind god (here Hanuman is only a son of Rama).

" 9. Anjani, the daughter of Gutama and sister of Sigriva and Subali gives birth to Hanuman.

" 10. The story of the apes is told quite amply.

" 11. Rama meets with Sugriva by accident. Sugriva sits weeping on a tree; his tears fall on Rama's breast as he sleeps under this tree; or in another story, Sugriva is sitting on a hill of the secretions of his weeping eyes, a brook of his tears flows. The water drank by Rama is saltish. Thus he is discovered.

" 12. Hanuman after visiting Sita in Lanka and after fighting some Rakshasa takes a bath in a sea or lake. Thus refreshed he fights again, etc.

" 13. The story of Mahi Ravana and Bhasmalochana occurs also in the Malayan Ramayana.

" 14. Ravana's son Ganga Mahasura destroys the causeway.

" 15. Story about Kings Jayasingh and Suranala with whom Rama fought before his attack on Lanka.

"16. Hanuman meets with his son Hanuman Tugunga (this story is told in the episode of Mahiravan. Hanuman's son is the door-keeper of Mahiravan's palace. He is the son of Hanuman and a fish queen.

"17. Ravana's adopted son (Mulamatani) with 500 heads fights Rama.[1]

"18. Ravana does not die.

"19. The story of Kukua is told. Kukua is called Kikevi Devi."

One of the peculiarities of the Jain Ramayana and those prevalent in Southern India and in the islands of Indian Archipelago generally is that a far greater stress is laid on Ravana than on Rama. In the Northern legends Rama's character stands prominently out and Ravana occupies the next place in the success of his arms and in his valour. But in the former versions Ravana occupies a far greater place of importance and is the most conspicuous figure,—a point which I have elaborately discussed in my "Bengali Ramayanas." In the epic of Valmiki itself there are passages which show Ravana's outstanding personality and greatness. We need not take into account the legendary accounts of Ravana's expeditions narrated in the seventh book which certainly was not Valmiki's composition. When Hanuman disguised as a monkey of a very small size entered the harem of Ravana and saw the Rakshasa king for the first time sleeping in his bed, the impression on his mind was one of great admiration for the adversary of his master.

In the Ramayana by the Jain poet Hemachandra, the accounts given of Ravana's *Tapasya* (religious austerities) and of the superhuman powers that he acquired, throw into shade all the achievements of his adversary—the glorious

[1] There are some poems in old Bengali in which Sita fights with and kills hydra-headed Ravana.

incarnnation of Vishnu. Numerous temples in Southern India are said to have been founded by Ravana (see Bombay Gazetteer, 1, 7, 190, 454, No. XVII, 76, 290ff.,·341). He performed his austerities at Gokarna in Canara (Bombay Presidency). This district is full of legends about him. Ravana was held as a great and saintly king by the Mahajan Buddhists. He had a world-wide celebrity for his wisdom. In the Lankavatar Sutra, composed in the second century A. D. Ravana argues with the Buddha on various ethical and religious points, and after holding his own for a long time at last acknowledges the superiority of the Buddha and accepts him as his Guru. The Buddhists of the Mahajan school hold Ravana as a saintly king of spotless character, and Dharmakirti who flourished in the sixth century A.D is indignant against Brahmanic writers for staining the fair name of Ravana by attributing to him deeds which were not true (see Bengali Ramayanas, pp. 33-34).

Curiously, amongst the masses of Bengal there seem to have existed in older days a tradition of Ravana's great wisdom. The epic and the literature that grew on it have pictured him as a wicked king who committed all kinds of atrocities on gods and men—particularly on the fair sex. The seventh book attached to the Ramayana of Krittibas records some of his foul deeds, the most atrocious of which was his rape of Rambhabati and Satyabati. The orthodox Hindus in Bengal have nothing but a deep-rooted hatred for him. But the Buddhists believed him, as already stated, to be a just and wise monarch and the Jains have magnified his *tapasya* and religious practices.

In the lower stratum of our society he was honoured as a wise man in the past. There is quite a store-house of Bengali aphorisms still current in the country-side like those of Dak and Khana which are attributed to Ravana; and his sayings are quoted by the people as authoritative in regard to agriculture, astrology and other subjects.

As the names of Mahiravana and Bhasmalochana could not be traced by me in the earlier days of my research to any Sanskrit sources within my knowledge I thought they were coined by poets like Krittibas and Kabichandra. But now I find that these stories are also described in the Tibetan, Javanese and Malay Ramayanas.

But far more widely known was Bhasmalochana in the world's mythology. We not only find him mentioned in the versions referred to above but in the Oriya Ramayana which is a mere copy of Bengali he is described exactly as in Bengali. Curiously we have found him too in the Gaelic legends. There he appears as the god Balor. This god had two eyes, one of which was always kept closed, for "it was so venomous that it killed any one in whom its look fell." On days of battle he was placed opposite to the enemy, the lid of the destroying eye was lifted up with a hook and its gaze withered all who stood before him (Celtic Myth and Legend by Charles Squire, p. 49). The Hindu poets inspired by a spirit of deep-seated anger against the Rakshasas made both of his eyes venomous so that the wretch was deprived of seeing his own kith and kin, in fact everything of this fair world. Is it not curious that the old Bengali literature has preserved some traditions prevailing in remote parts of the world and which are evidently not derived from Sanskritic sources?

Now to refer to Chandrabati's Ramayana.—The birth of Sita described in this ballad is embodied in a legend which, differing in certain minor points, agrees in the main with the accounts given by the people of widely distant lands particularly with those of Southern India and Indian Archipelego.

In the Javanese version she is the daughter of Ravana and Mandodari. The queen believing in an oracle which said that the child would be ill-fated, puts the infant into a box and casts it into the sea. The box is washed ashore and is found by Janaka. In the Malay Ramayanas Sita is a daughter of Mandodari, and in the Tibetan Ramayana she is the daughter of Ravana,—at whose birth the astrologers declare that she will ruin her father and all the demons. She is put in a vessel made of copper and committed to the waters, being ultimately found and adopted by Indian peasants (Rama-legenden and Rama-beliefs in "Der Indische Kulturkrei's," Munchen 1925, pp. 75ff., by W. Stutterhein —referred to by Sir George Grierson in his edition of the Kashmiri Ramayana, p. XX). In the Kashmiri Ramayana the poet Dibakar Prakash says that Sita was the daughter of Ravana. Queen Mandodari heard that the astrologers had said from a study of her horoscope that she would kill her father and that if she were allowed to marry, she would become a dweller in the forest and would come from there to destroy Lanka. Mandodari tied a stone round the neck of the child and threw her into a river. The baby was washed ashore and found by Janaka.

It is a noteworthy fact that even in small details Chandrabati follows some precedent or says something agreeing with the other poets. She carefully seeks all available traditions while writing her story and conforms to many of them.

In the Javanese Ramayana the child Sita is picked up from waters by Risi Kala who delivers her to Janaka but in the Tibetan version she is found by "Indian peasants." Chandrabati's statement that she was found by a fisherman accords with the Tibetan account for a fisherman may be taken to belong to the peasant class. Our poetess shows considerable power in delineating the picture of this fisherman and his wife Sata. The sketch is original—a product of her own poetic fancy. In the Malay Ramayana the baby is put in an iron coffin. The Tibetan poet makes it a copper-vessel and Chandrabati says that it was a golden casket on which the divine egg was placed and floated in the sea at the desire of Queen Mandodari.

A careful study of the Bengali literature would provide us with a clue to many facts of history which neither Sanskrit nor that part of vernacular literature which is purely derived from Sanskritic sources would supply. The purely indigenous literature of Bengal of the past serves to establish our relationship and connection with the vast Hindu world which in the remote past was certainly not as narrow as it is now, but comprised a far greater geographical area—beyond the limits of modern India.

We should be wrong in stating that nothing of these indigenous tales which were current in the country in ancient times has been accepted by our Sanskrit scholars, and that the tales on the Ramsaga outside Valmiki's epic with all its appendages of latter-day interpolations have been totally ignored by them. The Advut Ramayana says that Sita was a daughter of Mandodari. The word Advut which means here 'outlandish' suggests that the tales described in this book were collected from other than strictly Hindu sources.

Chandrabati follows the traditions spread in the country not through the medium of Sanskrit but through earlier songs stored in the memory of the people and sung by women and the peasantry. Whether Bengal got this store-house of ancient traditions from the Tamil or other Dravidian countries or from the North-West is a problem which has not yet been solved. But it is interesting that the Ramayanic legends which abounded in India not incorporated in Valmiki and existed probably in an earlier period, have survived in a country like Bengal—ridden and domineered over by Valmiki and an army of Sanskritic poets who had the utmost veneration for our great epic master.

Chandrabati's ballad along with other classical works of Bengal which are true to indigenous traditions in a far greater degree than purely Sanskritic works, gives us glimpses of a culture which owned a kinship with many distant countries the Hindus had colonised or had constant communications with in the hey-day of their glory.

The Ramayanic tale composed by Chandrabati is, as I have stated already, a ballad, though the subject is a *Pauranic* one and differs from the contemporary classical poems in many respects. The lines and stanzas have the distinct sound and music characteristic of a ballad and the usual phrase so common in our ballad literature when introducing a new development in the plot " *Ki Kam Karila* " is also met with in this poem in several places. The frequency of the monosyllabic word 'গো' with a prolonged sound proves that the whole poem is a song. The word gives a poetic ring to almost each line and at times invests the song with exquisite pathos.

I have already stated that this ballad of Ramayana by Chandrabati is sung all over the district of Mymensingh by women on bridal occasions. It is really to be regretted that a ballad so popular has not yet seen the light though there is no lack of enterprising publishers in Mymensingh. I have given only an incomplete version of it. I am sorry I could not secure the whole but I am in correspondence with some gentlemen who have promised to collect the remaining portion. As the ballad has not yet been published, there are very few singers who can reproduce it as a whole. These ballads as a rule are sung on festive occasions. The whole song is often sung by many persons in a chorus. Even the memory of a professional minstrel fails at times and he is then helped by some one from amongst the chorus. Individually the singers can seldom recite the whole song without such aid. It is therefore so difficult to collect a complete ballad without consulting many singers. On festive days one can of course meet a full party of the minstrel and his chorus ; but it requires the help of a short-hand writer to take down a song when it is sung, and that is not possible so far as Bengali is concerned. This explains the reason why even such a popular song as this ballad of Chandravati could not be recovered in its entirety. But I am hopeful of securing it in the near future.

It is interesting to note that in her attempts to follow the traditions current in her country from olden times, Chandrabati has described some incidents of Rama-story in a way different from the accounts of Book I of the epic. This book is not the composition of Valmiki according to scholars. Dasaratha, according to that Book of the Ramayana, got four sons as the result of a sacrifice performed by him. The account is an attempt to establish the divinity of Ramachandra and his step-brothers. Chandrabati did not accept this story but gave one which is in accord with the other ballads of the country. A Sannyasi came when all the sacrifices performed by the Rishis at the request of Dasaratha had failed in their object of getting for the king the boon of a son, and this Sannyasi gave the Raja a fruit which had to be taken by his Ranis ; this produced the desired effect. Mymensingh was not in Chandrabati's time yet so thoroughly under the control of priestly revival, hence Chandrabati could venture to declare the failure of the religious sacrifices performed by the Rishis. In those parts of Bengal which are ridden over by priestly influence the failure of a sacrifice performed by Rishis would not be believed and if anybody would say something so sacrilegious he would be condemned. The advent of the Sannyasi in critical situations is in perfect accord with what we so often meet in the Ballad literature. (See Kajal-Rekha, Vol. I, Parts I and II, Kanchanmala, Vol. II, Parts I and II, E.B. Ballads and Malanchamala, pp. 267-344, Folk Literature of Bengal, Calcutta University.)

There are many passages in this poem which establish its kinship with the contemporary ballads of Mymensingh.

The practice of measuring gold in baskets (p. 325), the mention of shell-bracelets called ' Ram Lakshman ' (Mainamati songs) are to be found in this song along with other things of the sort so common in Ballads,

It should, however, be remembered that though the Ramayanic legend has been couched by Chandrabati in the form of a ballad she was not illiterate like many of the other ballad-makers. On the other hand she had not only mastered the rhythmical Bengali expressions but had a respectable knowledge of Sanskrit. This knowledge is in evidence in many passages of the song. The line 'সূর্য্য হতে কাড়ি নিল সহস্র কিরণ ' (L. 8, Canto VI, Book I, Vol. IV, Part II) is an echo of "সমস্তরোমকূপেষু স্বীয়রশ্মিন্ দিবাকরঃ" of the famous Sanskrit work মার্কণ্ডেয় চণ্ডী. After the Vaishnava poets who gave a hundred endearing names to Krishna, she calls Ramachandra by various names given with affection by his kith and kin and the passage beginning with 'কৌশল্যা রাখিল নাম কাঙ্গালের ধন (p. 26, Canto VII) has borrowed the very expressions of Vaishnav poetry. Besides this Ramayanic ballad Chandrabati wrote many other poems amongst which the contribution she made to her father's celebrated Manasamangal is important. Incorporated in it is the famous ballad of Chandrabati on Kenaram the robber. We find her signature (ভনিতা) in the colophon of these poems, but in her most celebrated ballad, Malua, we find her name in the colophon of the preliminary hymn only and not in the body of the texts. The reason is not difficult to guess out. The oppressions of the Kazi and the arbitrary deeds of Dewan Jahangir are exposed in this ballad in the most outspoken manner, so our poetess preferred to appear *incognito* as a safe course. She was evidently a contemporary of the Dewan Jahangir. The Kazi's oppression and the anarchical condition of the country that she describes so vividly in Malua are borne out by the account she gives of her times in Kenaram :—" The dacoits are the real rulers of the country and the Badshah is so only in name. The country is going to rack and ruin under the rule of the Kazis''—(Kenaram, Vol. I, Parts I and II). That both Malua and this Ramayanic ballad came from the same pen is proved by the use of many words and phrases showing the mannerism of the poetess. We find in this Rama-ballad জয়াদিজোকার, পঞ্চগাছি, উবাসে কাবাসে and other similar expressions which occur both in Malua and in the song. In the locality in which Chandrabati lived, the deities Manasa Debi and Bana Durga were worshipped by the people ; there were other evil spirits such as Darai aud Dakini who had to be propitiated on particular occasions. We find offerings being sent to these from the palace of Dasaratha after the birth of Rama ! All these show that the poem had not any pronounced connection with Valmiki's epic but was inspired by the vast folk-literature which existed in Mymensingh about this time. Ram and Sita here play at dice—a fashion which was in vogue amongst men and women of the aristocratic classes during Mahomedan rule. The line উপকথা সীতারে শুনায় আলাপিণী (L. 9, Canto II) is significant and distinctly proves that there was a class of female story-tellers who were appointed in palaces for giving amusement by means of Gitikathas and ballads with ethical lessons to the princesses. The audience of the Gitikathas and Rupakathas consisted of wives and daughters in aristocratic families. (The Folk Literature of Bengal, p. 261.)

That the Ramayana of Chandrabati derived its chief inspiration from the southern versions of the story and not from Valmiki is evidenced by the fact that the poetess, like Jain authors and the recensionists of Tamil countries and of Malaya, Siam and the islands of Indian Archipelago, began the story of Ram with a description of Ravana and his Lanka, the account of Ram being introduced later on.

This poem of Chandrabati which may not rank in poetical merit with Malua is nevertheless a fine creation of poetic fancy. The conception of the story shows great artistic power on the part of the poetess. She traverses the field of the whole Ramayanic legend in the shortest possible space, but the book does not, owing to this brevity, look like a summary or catechism. It is enlivened everywhere with sparkling passages and exquisite touches of poetry and nowhere is this brevity combined with wit and pathos so much in evidence as in Book II where the story of Sita's past life is related by herself. The description of her life in Dandakaranya will remind one of the Meghnadhbadh Kabya where Sita describes the same episode of her life to Sarama. There is some striking affinity between the two accounts and I have some suspicion that Michael might have heard this Ramayanic ballad in Mymensingh on some bridal occasion and got his inspiration from there. The pathos of Michael's poetry as far as this part of his great poem is concerned is justly admired. But an unprejudiced and impartial critic will surely admit Chandrabati's description to be more refined and exquisite—though lacking in the splendour of Madhusudan's word-painting, whilst her simplicity gives an undoubted grace to this picture of forest-life. Compare Madhusudan's account "ছিনু মোরা সুলোচনা গোদাবরী তীরে, কপোত কপোতী যথা উচ্চ বৃক্ষ চূড়ে—বাঁধি নীড় থাকে সুখে" with "গোদাবরী নদীকূলে গো পঞ্চবটী বন। ঘুরিতে ঘুরিতে আইলাম আমরা তিন জন॥ কি করিব রাজ্য সুখে গো রাজসিংহাসনে। শত রাজ্যপাট গো আমার প্রভুর চরণে॥" etc.

I have already referred to the fact that Chandrabati like a true artist has given a polish by her poetic touch to this short episode of the Ramayana which in the hands of an inferior poet would have sunk into a prosaic summary only. In this short space she shows us lively scenes and beautiful poetic situations as in a panorama. Her great power superbly manifests itself in the description of Sita's past life where scenes follow scenes in quick cinema-like succession reminding one of Byron's famous poem, 'The Dream'.

I have given an account of the life of Chandrabati in my preface to Kenaram and elsewhere; so a repetition here is unnecessary, but I should say here that the pathos of Sita's misery has been so vividly described by her that one would not be wrong in supposing that she could do so because she herself suffered from her disappointed love which brought on her premature death—full of tragic interest.

The incomplete ballad contains 776 lines.

DINESH CHANDRA SEN

Chandrabati's Ramayana

(1)

On the sea-coast there was a golden city called Lanka and there ruled Ravana—the king of Rakshasas.

The golden city was built by the divine architect Biswakarma ; its grandeur was beyond all description. The breadth of the city was a *yojana* (eight miles). The huge mansions in it looked like hills and mounts.

The waves of the sea incessantly dashed against the city of Lanka and the diamonds and pearls that adorned its palaces shone brilliantly from afar. There were large tanks there with landing steps made of solid gold and silver. They were wonderful to behold.

We have heard of Nandan—the garden of Indra's heaven. The famous Asoka garden of Lanka was a match for it. Night and day flowers bloomed in the Asoka garden and when a flower bloomed there its fragrance was carried to all the three worlds by the wind. The bloom of a flower of Asoka lasted for a full year. With such flowers of the Asoka garden did the Rakshasa girls decorate their hair. During all the seasons of the year one could see fruits,—ripe and luscious,—hanging from the boughs of trees. They were so abundant that the boughs seemed to break under their load.

The lights kindled in the night were not allowed to be put out in the day, for dance and music went on unceasingly and nobody cared to notice that the night was over. Such was the dread in which the city of Rakshasas was held, that the very birds,—while flying above, divided themselves into two rows as they flew beyond the city without daring to cross it so as to cast their shadow on the fair city, and thereby irritate the monarch, and the angels of heaven in their march through heaven paid salutes to the palace from afar.

In the houses of Lanka the towering height of which exceeded that of great mountains, dwelt the Rakshasas. The walls of these mansions were plated with silver and the roofs were supported by golden beams and rafters. Those houses, though they rested on the earth, touched the very sky by their towers.

Surrounded by these noble mansions stood the pleasure-house of Ravana, as the stars are seen to surround the moon. This pleasure-house had a thousand door-ways and their glass-panes sparkled in the rays of the sun. The doors and lattices had the decoration of pearls and diamonds—and one seeing it must confess that such a house was not to be found elsewhere in the world.

The Rakshasa women were of peerless beauty. They used to decorate their braids with the garlands of Parijat flowers. Some of them decked their hair by an artistic setting of diamonds and other precious stones. The perfumes they used in their person scented the air, and these women were so hand some by nature that the precious stones they wore grew lustreless before the dazzling beauty of their person. They changed their fashion and taste so frequently that one would see them wearing new apparels and costumes every day. They stretched their tender limbs on couches of gold and slept at ease, taking nectar which the gods alone are privileged to enjoy for their daily refreshment.

Surely the heavenly architect Biswakarma had built this city of Lanka as a unique thing of beauty and joy and of which a parallel was not to be found in the world.

Mighty was the Rakshasa chief whose will was hard to resist. He cared not the gods of heaven, and was immortal by the boon of Brahma.

Even the great Indra—the Lord of gods—and all his mighty comrades dreaded the Rakshasa monarch. His sworn enemies were men and monkeys [1] alone. The wealth of the great king was measured in big baskets and not in ordinary scales. No one in the world was as rich as Ravana and it is impossible to give a description of his untold wealth. The diamonds and pearls were spread in the compound of the house for drying up in the sun.

One day Ravana sat in his court and began to discuss his future programme of work with his ministers and courtiers.

It was settled that he would lead an expedition against the gods. As soon as the idea struck him, he marched heavenward with his vast Rakshasa army. This army, invincible in war, who struck terror everywhere they went, at once came up to the gate of the abode of gods and attacked them.

The informers approached Indra, the king of gods, and gave him the tidings of this attack of Ravana. Indra and other gods fell into a dilemma and their city trembled at the great noise raised by the Rakshasas.

Ravana was grim as the Lord of Death himself. There was no warrior anywhere who was his equal in arms. His heads if severed from the body grew anew upon the trunk instantly. Fire could not burn him. The wicked monarch of Rakshasas had thus grown invincible by the boon of Brahma.

The gods in a body fled from heaven. Amongst them Indra, the king of heaven and Yama, the Lord of Death, were bound in chains by Ravana and carried away. The Parijat, the wonderful tree of plenty, which adorned the garden of

[1] Brahma's boon was that no God or angel or any other spirit or animal of the creation would be able to do any harm to Ravana, his only objects of dread were to be men and monkeys, but the latter were utterly slighted by the monarch who told Brahma that he cared not if such despicable creatures as men and monkeys were his enemies.

Indra was uprooted, with its leaves and branches, and taken to Lanka. The redoubtable elephant Airabat and the peerless horse Uchchaisraba which Indra had got by churning the ocean were also carried by Ravana who besides took possession of the great aeroplane, the Pushpaka of heaven's lord, and seated on it, he marched through the sky. Of all the valuable things in the treasury of Indra nothing was left. Every article of value he looted. The beautiful wives of the gods he did not spare but forcibly carried them in the aerial chariot. There crowned with laurels of victory and seated on the Pushpaka, the great Rakshasa king with his noble captives marched homewards through the airy path. Chandrabati says that the whole heavenly region looked dreary and desolate as cremation ground. (Ll. 1-76.)

(2)

After this conquest of heaven, Ravana next planned to carry an expedition against the principal monarchs of the earth. These kings as they heard the rattle of the weapons of the Rakshasas, did not venture to defend themselves but all of them beat a retreat acknowledging the victory of their terrible assailant.

Heaven and earth thus subjugated, the next move of the Rakshasa king was towards the nether-land. There his great war cry struck terror into the heart of Basuki—the hydra-headed snake and other noteworthies. They acknowledged their defeat in humiliating terms without daring to offer any resistance at all.

Ravana, after this, went to the famous hermitages of the world where the Rishis and saints practised religious austerities. With his eyes rolling in anger the great Rakshasa wanted his due royal tributes from those ascetics. He caught hold of their knotted locks and binding them with one another committed cruel atrocities on them. A strip of bark round their loins was all the wealth they possessed and they lived on roots and fruits of trees. There they lay prostrate near the feet of Ravana rolling in the mire. He had no feeling of compassion and played cruel pranks on these innocent spiritual men.

With the sharp ends of the *kusha* grass the Rishis pierced a little of their breasts and extracted some drops of blood. This tribute from the Rishis Ravana realised and put the blood in a casket. Glad at heart owing to his unbroken victories everywhere Ravana returned to his capital and visited his queen Mandodari, presenting her with the casket tinged with the blood of the ascetics. She asked him—"What treasure, oh lord, have you brought in this casket?" Ravana replied, "The Gods are my enemies. They drink nectar which has rendered them immortal. I have brought their chiefs, Indra and Yama, as captives here. Here is poison in this casket. I will kill the gods by means of this poison. Do keep it carefully. I will call for it when the proper time will come." Saying so the king left the harem.

The great Ravana thus ruled his vast kingdom advised by his ministers and courtiers. I will next relate to you the birth of Sita.

Ravana took the beams from the moon-god and adorned his crown with them. From the sun-god he took a thousand rays which now added brilliance to his person. From the fire-god he took the burning flames which now emanated from his twenty eyes. The thirty-three millions of gods were brought to the city of Lanka and there they stood with joint palms singing the praise of the great Rakshasa king—some of them acted as sweepers in his city, others as gardeners busy with the flower-plants of his garden. The Rakshasa generals lorded over them and supervised their works. Kuber, the lord of heaven's treasury, became his treasurer. Eleven Rudras were appointed to serve as his body-guards at night. The twelve Adityas held the royal umbrella over his head. The god of winds waved the *chamara* when he sat on his throne. Baruna, the god of the seas, washed his feet and Yama, the Lord of Death, became his police-prefect, responsible for the safety of the capital. Indra himself, the lord of the gods, had the charge of Ravana's stable and he was frequently seen to cut grass for his horses. The moon-god and the sun-god ministered light to the city of Lanka, day and night,—without cessation throughout the year.

From the city of the Gandharvas, Ravana had secured Gandharva-maidens by force. They were now captives in his harem. Seven hundred beautiful damsels he had brought from heaven. Some of these women were made to accept him as their Lord by force or temptation ; others during their travel to Lanka fell down from the aerial chariot and got themselves drowned in the sea.

In that beautiful garden of Asoka, Ravana indulged in all sorts of pleasures in the company of these handsome women and there Madan, the god of love and Rati, his consort, themselves decorated the person of Ravana with pearls, diamonds and other precious stones.

One of the female attendants of Queen Mandodari approached her and said : "You were so long the king's pet, oh queen, but now he is mad after the heavenly maidens. Day and night he remains steeped in the pleasures of the Asoka garden."

The queen Mandodari, as she heard these words, shed incessant tears in secret in wounded pride. When she was convinced that Ravana was no longer true to her but was addicted to many, she remembered the poison in the casket—"The poison which can kill the immortals will be my last resource. Why should I not end myself by taking this poisonous drug?

Thinking in this strain, she swallowed the blood in the casket, but who can oppose the decree of providence?

The result of taking this blood was that she became *enceinte.*

Time rolled on, and on the tenth day after the expiry of ten months[1] she felt a great pain and fell unconscious on the floor. The whole day passed and night approached. At the approach of the evening of one Saturday she curiously delivered an egg. (Ll. 1-74.)

(3)

The messengers acquainted the monarch with the news. He at once called the court-astrologers to his presence. They came with their mystic books and began a long course of calculations and passed a unanimous verdict—"Oh great lord, listen to our prophecy. A thunderbolt has been hurled by Providence on the loftiest pinnacle of your palace at Lanka. From this egg, a girl will come out for whom the whole kingdom of Lanka will be destroyed. All the Rakshasas will meet with destruction and what more should we say? none will survive to light the evening lamp in the great city. Another thing which we must say to our great grief is that even your life, oh great monarch, will not be spared. For this girl your majesty will fall a prey to untimely death. This ill-fated girl will bring ruin and devastation on this golden city—famous throughout the world."

When Ravana heard this report, flames of fire emanated from his fierce twenty eyes, and he sat quiet for a time brooding over the course to be adopted.

Some said, "Cut the egg to pieces." One Rakshasa said, "Break it instantly," others advised that it should be at once thrown into fire.

[1] This is the settled convention of the Bengalis; they believe without much accuracy in their calculation that it is exactly after 10 months and 10 days that a child is delivered from the mother's womb.

When the queen Mandodari heard all these discussions going on in the court, she felt a great grief. After all she was a mother. Incessant tears dropped from her eyes. "Even the beasts of the forest feel intense and acute pain if they lose their children ; whatever may be the issue, the mother's heart is the same in every case." She plaintively said to her royal lord, "Do not destroy the egg, do not break it nor put it into fire. If you would not keep it in the palace, float it in the sea."

On this prayer of the queen Ravana took immediate action. He employed five skilful artists and made a beautiful casket of gold with a silver-padlock. The egg was carefully put in it and the king with the name of the Goddess Bhavani on his lips floated it in the sea.

It was evening ; the rays of the setting sun illuminated the western horizon, when the casket stopped at the landing ghat of the river on which the city of king Janaka stood. (Ll. 1-38.)

(4)

In the city of Mithila there was a fisherman named Madhab. He used to catch fish by means of his net and had besides the charge of the ferry boat in that river. In that large city there was none so poor as Madhab. He had no field to grow rice but purchased it from the market, he had no pond of his own but had to draw water from the public landing ghat. He was clad in rags for want of cloth and his hunger was not appeased as he could not afford to have proper meals. His wife Sata was smitten with anxieties day and night as to how to secure food for the day.

There was one piece of good luck in which Madhab prided. Providence had given him a very chaste and devoted wife in Sata. She was miserable all her life but to her own sorrows and wants she was perfectly indifferent, caring for those of her husband only. If she saw him happy she felt happy herself inspite of her own ill luck.

After having drawn his net in the water the whole afternoon, Madhab returned home with dust and mud in his feet. She came up with a cup of water, washed her lord's feet with utmost care, wiped away the water, and brought him home hand in hand.

When poor Madhab in the burning heat of the sun felt agonising pain after the day's labour there she used to stand with a fan in her hand removing the drops of sweat on his person by waving the fan of *tal* leaf. In the biting cold of January, she covered him with the flowing end of her *sari*, when their poor beddings proved insufficient to protect him. Whatever meals she cooked,—rice-dust or other poor edibles—she served him with great care and the leavings she took herself, relishing it as something sacred and delicious.

Their cottage was made with leaves of trees and creepers. The fences around were all broken. But with her husband near her she felt the joy of a truly happy life and never grumbled against her fate though it was so untoward. Rejoicing in nuptial felicities she considered herself lucky.

Owing to fasts her body was reduced to a skeleton. With her torn *sari* of jute round her waist, she visited the houses of her good neighbours, carrying a basket of fish on her head seeking customers. Her face looked weary and haggard. Excessive sweat, result of walking long distances under the sun, made her long hair wet and knotted, but in spite of all these a beautiful smile adorned her face as she spoke to her customers.

One day with a fish-basket bound to his waist, Madhab went to the river-side in order to draw the net. It was dusk but no fish he could catch in spite of his utmost efforts. But though he toiled till night was advanced in the silent banks of the river his attempts proved all futile, and he naturally felt sad and worried owing to his failures. Then for the last time he recited in his mind the name of Manasa Devi and threw his net. He felt that something had stuck in his net and as he drew it, he perceived that he had got a casket in the tangles of his net.

Says Chandravati—" Oh fisherman! Do not waste your time any further. Take with you what you have got. The night of your misfortune is over, the dawn of your happiness is in sight."

Madhab returning home, called his wife loudly three times. She came up in all haste. " Surely my husband has got a double quantity of fish to-day," she thought, and she immediately lighted her evening lamp.

" How unlucky am I! Not a fish worth a cowri I have been able to catch by my net drawn through these long hours. But stop," here he whispered to the ears of his wife something lest the neighbours had any inkling of the matter. He gave the golden casket to his wife. She took it in her hand, and bowing to it with her forehead bent low, she spread a seat and placed the casket on it.

She slowly cried ' victory ' as a sign of something auspicious that had happened, and with tufts of grass and a few grains of rice she placed a cup near the casket. On it she kept the branch of a mango plant. Five candles were lighted and after burning incense in front of the casket she prostrated her body and made obeisance according to the current rites. From that time forward Lakshmi, the Goddess of Fortune favoured the house making it her abode for future.

The night of sorrow passed away and it was now the dawn of happy days. From that day all the sorrows of Sata's heart were removed. In the cowshed the cow which had been barren, yielded plenty of milk. All kinds of paddy and corn were now abundant in her fields. If he carelessly threw a handful of seed there, they yielded double harvest. Madhab never went to the river-side from that day with his net, nor his good wife Sata went hawking in the village with a basket of fish on her head. She wore a pair of shell-bracelets of the famous pattern 'Ram Lakshmana.' Her *sari* was transparently white woven with very fine threads and called ' Gangajali ' (*lit.* the stream of the Ganges). An outer robe made of valuable jute she wore round her waist and she carried a small box of gold containing betels and betelnuts. Her couch was now strewn over with flowers and there she slept at ease in night-time. The neighbours began to whisper, " How has Sata come by such good fortune?—we knew her to be wretched all her life." Sata said to them, " My good friends, wait with patience, if it be in your luck to have the favour of fortune, that must come one day sooner or later. (Ll. 1-74.)

(5)

Then one night a strange thing happened to the couple. It was past midnight and Sata slept soundly in her bed while the compound of the house was all flooded with moonbeams.

Just then a little baby came out of the casket and warmly did the sweet thing embrace Sata addresssing her ' Mother, oh mother.' The child was surprisingly beautiful and she looked like a little Kamala, the Goddess of Fortune. Fresh and handsome she was like a bouquet of flowers and the whole house seemed lit up with her smile.

The little child placed her small arms round Sata's neck and said with affection and tenderness, " To-morrow when it is dawn take me to the court of Janaka, the king of the city. He is my father and the queen consort is my mother. Hand me over to the queen."

A few moments before the dawn she rose up from her bed and she tied the casket in the flowing end of her *sari*. Straight did she come up to the presence of the queen and related to her the strange dream that she had dreamt. She put the sacred trust in her hands after narrating her short story.

Right glad was the queen at the gift and said to Sata, "What can I give you in return for this valuable gift?" She presented her with a string of large pearls and with her own hands placed it round the neck of Sata. She ordered besides gold and silver to be awarded to her in a basket. But Sata said, "I am a poor woman in your city used to the hardships of life. These valuable presents are too good for me. I have however a boon to seek of you which I hope you will confer on me.

"If my dream is fulfilled and really a child comes out of the casket call her by a name which will remind one of my name Sata—give her the name of Sita, this is my humble prayer, oh esteemed queen."

Saying so, the fisherwoman departed from the palace. With a heart palpitating with hope and doubt, did the queen keep the casket in a secure place with care.

The auspicious moment came at last, and a child appeared there bursting the shell of the egg. She was simply faultless in all her limbs and her signs were declared auspicious in every way. She looked like Lakshmi, the Goddess of Fortune herself, and the whole city of Mithila resounded with gleesome voices according her a warm reception. The women in the streets and lanes of that vast city sounded conchshells and cried, '*jai*' (victory). Music, vocal and instrumental, was heard in the temples at short intervals. The gods mingled their voices with those of men while they sang the praises of Janaka the king for having Lakshmi herself for his daughter.

After the name of Sata, the child was called Sita. Chandravati says that the little child was a thing to be adored in the whole world. (Ll. 1-36.)

(6)

Now my readers hear the sacred tale of the birth of Rama—an incarnation of Vishnu.

He is one, but divided himself into four, and these four incarnations were born in the city of Ayodhya.

King Dasaratha ruled in Ayodhya. With justice and mercy he governed his people and considered them as his own children.

The Raja had no child. In order to have one he took three wives one by one. Kausalya, Kaikeyi, and Sumitra were his three queens. Advised by Vasistha—the court-priest and councillor, the Raja at last began to perform a Jajna (sacrificial ceremony) with a view to propitiate the gods and move them to grant a son.

Sages and rishis were called from the different provinces of India, and the Raja consulted them on each point during the ceremony wishing a fulfilment of the desire for getting a son. But all the pains he took and the sacrifice he performed proved fruitless. He was not blessed with a child. His ill-luck stood in the way.

Then was the Raja sad at heart : within a curvilinearly shaped house called Jormandir, he slept in his bed. He closed the doors and took the vow of fast. He resolved to give his life up in despair and three days passed, but he neither opened the doors of the room nor touched a morsel of food.

It was by the will of Providence that a sage came at this stage and knocked at his gate. His knotted hair in many a curl fell down to his ankles and rolled in the dust,

On his forehead, there was a *tilak* mark which shone like a star. His right hand held a staff made of *tal* wood and over his shoulders hung a tiger-skin. The guards of the king greatly feared him and allowed him entrance. Before the door of the room in which the king lay, the sage stood and called him thrice in a loud voice. The king opened the doors in response and gave him a cordial reception. With Kusha grass and water did the king receive him as befitted a sage and then spread a valuable carpet asking him to sit thereon. The sage declined to sit there but spread his own seat of Kusha grass and sitting there he asked the king why he had taken the vow of starvation. The king related to him the sad story of his repeated disappointments and submitted his case to the Sannyasi for consideration. The latter spoke tender words which served to assuage the pain of his heart, and then from his wallet took a mango which had grown out of season. He gave it to the king saying "Receive this fruit, oh monarch, and give it to your chief queen Kausalya. If she eats it, she will have a son by the grace of the gods."

Dasaratha with the fruit in hand went to the apartments of his chief queen Kausalya. She rose up from her couch and received the king with due respect. He related to her all about the Sannyasi and his gift.

Kausalya was right glad and kept the fruit in a golden cup. The queen who was generous and loving in nature cut the fruit in three parts and took one of these herself and sent the remaining portions to the other two queens to be taken by each.

The three queens became *enceinte* simultaneously. The news reached the people of Ayodhya and they all set up a cry of joy wishing happiness to the king. The people were astonished at what they heard of the sage. The drummers beat drums and musicians played on their instruments, the sound of trumpets rose to the sky. The subjects distributed charities to the poor as a token of their great happiness.

The king gave a large number of milch cows with cowherds to the Brahmans. When five months passed, the elderly women of the royal harem, the aunts and grandmothers entertained the queens with *sad* as was usual on such occasions. The whole city resounded with joy.

The queens grew feeble as time advanced and preferred the bare floor to golden couches and cushions. They relished broken pieces of burnt clay and always felt sleepy. Chandravati says that the birth of a child was not distant.

Ten months and ten days were now complete. A very handsome son with all the auspicious signs of greatness in his body was born to Kausalya. The nurse cut the umbilical cord by means of a golden knife. In the apartments of queen Kausalya every one rejoiced and immediately a report was sent to the king. The king took a handful of the best of the diamonds out of his treasury and other valuable jewels and presented them to the baby as he saw it for the first time.

Sandal and other perfumes were sprinkled over public places as the king drove his chariot through the road leading to the apartments of his chief queen. Flags were raised over the houses of the citizens of Ayodhya, and sacrifices of goats at the altar of gods took place in the temples of the city accompanied with loud beating of drums. The women filled pitchers with water brought from the famous shrines, and as an auspicious sign branches of mangoes with new leaves were placed on them at the gateway of each house—the dancers danced and the singers sang and the whole city looked like an abode of joy. The Goddess Mangalchandi and Subachani —the presiding deities of the household—the goddess Bana Durga and the spirits Darai and Dakuni, the family deities Sitala and Shashthi and Manasha Devi with her attendant Neta were all worshipped in the royal palace.

On the sixth day they gave name to the child. The citizens with the help of the astrologers found various names for him.

Kausalya, the queen-mother, gave the baby the name 'Kangaler Dhan' (the wealth of the poor). The king called him 'Ayodhyabhusan' (the ornament of Ayodhya), the citizens gave him the name 'Rama Raghubir' (Rama—the chief of the Raghu dynasty) and the women of Ayodhya called him 'Shyamal sundar' (the beautiful one with *shyam* colour), Vashishtha—the sage and family priest of the Ayodhya-Raj—after a deep meditation found out a fitting name for the prince. It was Ramachandra Kamalalochan (the lotus-eyed Ramachandra).

The royal astrologer came to foretell the fortune of the new-comer from examination of his palm. With his books and old manuscripts he approached the king and ocnsulting all the authorities gave his verdict thus :—"His eyebrows are joined together and eyes are bright as the sun. On the forehead there is a brilliant mark indicating royalty. Fire will not burn him nor water drown his sacred person. He will be a skilled archer and have great physical powers. Mighty will he be as the god Indra and would lord over a vast empire. The great enemy of the three worlds will be killed by his arrows. In the seventh place of the baby was a zero indicating unhappiness in domestic life. But the astrologer did not refer to it too definitely and tried to keep an unpleasant thing secret.

That Rama would be exiled from the palace and be unhappy—this fact the astrologer found from his calculations but kept it secret. He further saw that owing to the curse of a Brahmin, King Dasaratha would have to die parted from his son. These were the unpleasant things that the royal astrologer concealed.

Chandrabati relates the birth of Ramachandra and

dedicates her poem to the memory of the queen, Kausalya. (Ll. 1-112.)

(7)

Five or seven maidens attended Sita in her beautiful room of the Jormandir palace and asked her to relate to them the story of her life in the Dandaka forest. "What were your great sufferings during the twelve months of the year," they asked.

Sita.

"It burns my heart like a fire when I recollect my misfortunes and what I suffered in the past. Miserable have I been all my life though I got such a husband as Ramachandra.

"I will begin with the story of the days when I lived in my father's palace at Mithila. We were four sisters and passed our time merrily; sometimes with joyous heart we sat on our mother's lap and at others played on the floor of our compound. My father took a vow which was strange: 'He, who would be able to break the great bow of Siva, preserved in my household would get my Sita.' Many a prince came and went but none could break the bow of the Great God.

"One night I dreamt as if my lord Ramachandra came to me and said, 'How long will you sleep, oh Sita—I am Ramachandra and you are to be my bride. From a long distance I have come to your city of Mithila. I have resolved that I would break the great bow.'

"The day dawned and the dream faded away, but in my eyes was the image of the beautiful youth—dark-blue like the new grown grass-blades which I had beheld in my dream - the impression which the sight of the two young heroes Rama and Lakshmana had created remained in my memory.

"My dream seemed to be fulfilled soon, for with Vishwamitra the sage Rama actually came to Mithila on that day. The prince hastened to the place of sacrifice.

"The citizens of Mithila admired the princes and they all said, 'Here are these princes worthy of Sita and her sisters. They have come to fulfil the vow of our good king Janaka.'

"His arms reached his knee joint and it was an easy thing for him to break the great bow of Siva. There arose an uproar of joy through the whole city of Mithila when the great bow was actually broken. The women sang and danced. The ladies of the royal apartments who were struck with the wonderful power of the prince cut jokes and said humorously: 'In spite of his heroism his colour is dark.' Some said seeing me with him—'Look here is a streak of lightning in the clouds.' Thus with gay laughter and jokes, they made the night pleasant.

"Soon after my lord started for Ayodhya taking me with him.

"I was happy in the house of my lord and one night I dreamt when sleeping by his side that my lotus-eyed lord was seated on the throne of Ayodhya. I saw also his brothers standing behind him. One of them held the royal umbrella over his head and others waved the *chamara*. They were near his feet ready to carry out his orders.

"This dream I dreamt again—and lo! my dream actually came to pass. I heard a report which was circulated in the city that Rama was going to be installed as king on the throne of Ayodhya; my dream was fulfilled—the day of installation actually came, but destruction came to our hopes and happiness through the intriguing wicked counsel of Manthara—the maid-servant. When Ramachandra would sit on the throne with *tilak* mark of royalty on his forehead, it was Kaikeyi the queen who made him wear bark-dress and go to exile. The clear autumnal moon-beams became covered with clouds. The smiling city of Ayodhya with its dazzling splendour of gold was enshrouded in darkness.

"It was in the month of April that my lord Rama wore the knotted hair and took the vow of *sannyas*. In May the scorching rays of the sun burnt us and the face of my lord looked pale and weary. Once when my feet slipped over a stone and bled profusely, my loving husband sat by my side in deep sorrow and fanned me. My brother-in-law Lakshmana brought some water in a lotus leaf. I do not remember how long I was unconscious in the arms of my lord. But time passed away and we three wandered about in the forest-path till we reached a place called Panchabati on the river Godavari. Here my husband ordered Lakshmana to build a cottage. With creepers, leaves and branches of trees he built a nice cottage in that wilderness. We two remained inside the cot. But my brother-in-law Lakshmana guarded the place with his bow and arrows standing under the shade of a near tree. How can I adequately praise my brother-in-law! He secured for us the most luscious of fruits in large numbers seeking through the forest regions. These fruits were all of good flavour and taste. In this bower-like cot of plants and leaves we felt so happy that we forgot the pleasures of our palace at Ayodhya. Lakshmana brought fruits from the forest and with cups made of lotus leaves I brought water from the river Tamasha. I washed the feet of my lord with water and spread a bed of leaves for him. Even this life of exile in the forest appeared so sweet and pleasant that we regretted not the loss of our kingdom.

"What should I do with the throne of an empire and pleasures of the palace, when such joys I found in the forest-life? A hundred thrones with their joys and powers I could forego if I could be in the company of my loving husband. His feet were dearer to me than a hundred empires. In the morning I rose every day and with forest flowers I used to weave garlands, and how glad was I to put the garland round the neck of my lord Ramachandra!

"I remember how happy I felt when I made a pillow of his manly and handsome arm. Each night to me was the record of the joys of paradise. The deer, the antelope and the birds of the forest were my companions all day long and they were full of sympathy for me.

"A *suka* and *sari*—the happy pair—were my pets. They were my neighbours in that wild life of ours—sometimes they sweetly sang and we were their delighted audience, and at others hand in hand I walked in the forest with my lord. Just as a thing is inseparable with its shadow so was I with him. We three wandered through hills and dales and passed our time in perfect happiness.

"One day—the story is painful to relate—came down all on a sudden a great sorrow as ill-luck would have it.

"The night of joy passed like a sweet dream in the company of my loving husband. The evil day dawned. It was about three *dandas* or half-a-quarter of the day. I cannot describe to you the sorrows that began on that day. I and my husband sat outside our cottage; under the shade of a near tree sat Lakshmana with his bow in hand. I felt sleepy and with half-closed eyes I saw the dear face of my lord as though in a dream. Perceiving my inclination he placed my head on his lap and spreading a part of my *sari* over it, I was about to close my eyes for sleep. Just then at an evil moment an antelope came in my view. It had the colour of gold and so fleet was its motion that like lightning it brightened quickly the places it passed through. My sleepy mood was gone in a moment and with joined hands I made a request to my husband. I knew not beforehand the dire effect of what this would lead to

"I said, 'I never saw an antelope so beautiful. Would you, my lord, secure it for me? How glad would I be to possess a thing like that. So long as it did not grow absolutely tame, I would keep it tied to a post of my cottage binding it with a cord made of dry creepers ; when we shall return to Ayodhya we will carry it home and keep it with us as a token of this forest.

"With his bow in hand my lotus-eyed husband marched forward to catch the animal. He addressed Lakshmana and said, 'Guard Sita with care so long as I do not return.' With this brief order he passed out of sight.

" Lo, shortly after I heard his voice as if crying in agony. The voice called for help saying—' Where are you, dear Lakshmana? My life is at stake, I am in the hands of a Rakshasa. Come quickly and help me.'

" I had laid myself down but as I heard his voice I rose up in all hurry. Again the voice cried for help addressing Lakshmana.

" I said, 'By my life, dear brother-in-law, quickly leave this place and go to his rescue.'

" With his bow and arrows in hand Lakshmana immediately started in the direction from which the voice came. He too seemed distressed with anxieties and went swiftly like the wind.

" I was left alone in that forest ; my husband had left me there verily in that frame of mind in which the snake leaves its gem and goes in quest of food. Had I known, oh maidens, what a great woe lay in wait for me would I ever send my husband in quest of the antelope?

"Just then a Sannyasi stood near my cot and said, ' Victory be to Siva—the great God.' His body was besmeared with ashes and he had an iron stick in his right hand and the beggar's bowl in the left. Coming still nearer to the very gate of my cot he said, ' Alms, good lady, I want alms.' I said, ' Holy Father, what alms can I give you at this moment. My husband is away. If we had lived in our good city of Ayodhya I could have given you gold measured in baskets.'

The Sannyasi said, ' Little do I care for wealth. In your cottage there are fruits gathered from the forest; give me some of those. I am very hungry and I am your guest. If you do not give me anything to eat I will go away disappointed.'

" I took a fruit out of our small collection of the day and came out of the cottage with it. How could I know that the Rakshasa like a poisonous snake had come in disguise. I bowed to the seeming saint prostrating myself on the ground. Just like the eagle that swoops on and seizes the snake the wicked king of Lanka took me to his chariot by force. I addressed the gods of heaven and acquainted them with my sad tale. I took away ornaments from my body and hit the Rakshasa with them. But what hurt could clods of earth do to a giant like him ? After a little time did I lose my consciousness. It was such an awful hour of distress that recollection of it even now at this distance of time makes me lose my sense. When I regained my sense I found myself in the city of Lanka placed in the Asoka garden of Ravana. From that day I gave up all pleasures of youth and turned an ascetic though so young.

" I threw away all my costly garments and ornaments. I could not sleep and began to fast. In the house of the Rakshasa I would not agree to eat anything. Constant weeping gave my eyes a pale hue. Night and day I thought of my husband who had turned a *sannyasi* and I wished for nothing else than to have a sight of his face. Indeed I lived only with that object in view—once more to see his moon-like face. I did not wish death, as by death I would lose the chance of seeing his feet once again. In the Asoka garden my tears flowed freely.

" In the month of Ashar there was outpouring of rain in incessant streams. The clouds came roaring like angry demons in the blue sky but these clouds hardly had such plenty of showers as were shed by my eyes. The Asoka garden will attest to my tears which fell night and day. Sometimes I resolved to drink poison or drown myself. My friend Sarama consoled me by sweet words in those days of despair.

"In the month of Phalgun I dreamt that my husband had an ally and friend in Sugrib the monkey-chief.

"In the month ot Bhadra I dreamt as if I saw a bird seated on the bough of a tree near me. But it was no bird—a monkey it was, who had come with a message from Rama. Hanuman, the great monkey, took his seat on the bough of a tree and said many pleasing things to soothe me. My heart hardly felt any relief at his words. Then did he produce a ring that he had brought from Rama. As I saw that dear token of my lord, tears flowed from both my eyes without check.

"Ramachandra now received a message from me and came to know all about my miserable lot. Now listen to the story of my delivery from the garden of the Rakshasas.

"In the month of Aswin I heard the report that Rama was worshipping the goddess Chandika in his camp though it was not the proper season for worshipping the goddess. I heard that the object of his worship was to secure her help in killing the Rakshasa chief. My days passed thus in hope and fear.

"In the month of Kartik the days were short. But all day long I sat alone and wept. Sarama gave me some information which raised hopes in me. Though I was reduced to a skeleton I took heart at her words and felt that the days of my sorrow would be over ere long.

"In the month of Agrahayana I heard that my husband had built a bridge over the sea with the help of his monkey-allies.

"In Paush my husband came to the city of Lanka and with a vast army of monkeys laid siege to it.

"In a dream I seemed to behold in the month of Magh the death of the mighty son of Ravana—Indrajit—in a hard contested fight. Now all the good things I had dreamt seemed to be fulfilled. The news of the destruction of the Rakshasa army reached me from all sides, and from this garden of Asoka did I hear the great uproar of Rakshasas lamenting their lot in a wild strain.

"Then came the month of Phalgoon with the tidings that Ravana was destroyed with his mighty kith and kin. I heard the songs sung by the monkeys in praise of my husband from the sea-coast.

"The month of Chaitra was marked with the end of all my misfortunes. The night of sorrow was over and the dark veil of evil fate was drawn up disclosing the joy of a glorious morning of good fortune, when I and my loving husband were once more united. When a blind man gets his eyes restored his happiness cannot be described, even so it is impossible to describe my happiness on getting back my dear husband long parted from me."

The tale of the twelve months of Sita's life is a record of unspeakable sorrow, and Chandrabati describes them with a feeling of great sympathy for the unhappy queen.

(3)

Now listen to the story of how Rama and Sita passed once the happy spring season. There was a canopy overhead and below it was a striped mat of many colours. Rama sat with Sita there and played at dice. Beautiful mica fans were waved by attending maids of the palace, and Rama and Sita talked gaily as they held dice in their hands.

"Like stars around the moon the attending maidens were gay as they stood near the royal couple. Some of them laughed and others participated in the pleasantries that passed between Rama and Sita. The figures of dice were all made of gold and right earnestly Rama now challenged Sita in the play. While playing at dice they looked like the god Vishnu and goddess Lakshmi or like Indra and Sachi or like Madan, the god of love, and Rati or like Siva and Parbati.

The maidens intervened at this stage. They insisted on some condition as there must be success and failure in the play and said : " Now tell us, oh lord, what would be the reward for success and what the penalty for failure. Rama said, " If I lose the game I will stake my precious ring as penalty. But what will Sita give me if she loses, let her say."

The queen felt shame and was overpowered by a sense of delicacy. She looked like a bud of Champaka flower half hid by leaves. Now they threw dice while indulging in humorous conversation in this way. Sita won the play and Ramachandra lost at the first attempt. The maidens smiled but they feared not the king. Fearlessly did they get the precious ring out from the finger of Rama by force and then in the midst of laughter and merry-making they put the ring on the finger of Sita. " Being a male you could not succeed in play with a female! Fie upon you, oh lord," they cried from all sides. Sweet were the words of this censure which Ramachandra himself enjoyed.

'Six and three' was the cry against Sita this time and she lost the next play. Then did Rama appeal to the maids—" Now friends get the penalty from Sita," he said smiling.

The maidens were relentless. They forcibly carried Sita and threw her in the arms of her husband for a close embrace.

Rama kissed his loving wife and said, " Now, my darling, ask of me any boon that you may desire."

Chandrabati says—" Your night of happiness is over, oh Sita. Be careful when asking the boon."

Slowly did Sita say to her lord, " From a long time I have cherished the desire of visiting those old *ashrams* of which I have a pleasant recollection. I have often thought how glad would I be to walk in those sacred hermitages once more. I always think of the river Tamasha where the swans used to play shaking the lotus plants. On the banks there was the avenue of Tamal trees. Peacocks played there with their mates displaying their gorgeous plumes. The golden-coloured antelopes were my companions there every night. I dream as if I am once more in the company of the girls of the Rishis and that I wander in the forests with my lord as my companion."

Rama kissed her once more and said, " Sleep in the golden couch in your apartments to-night, to-morrow I shall fulfil your desire and send you to those hermitages with Lakshmana.

Chandrabati says " What boon, oh unfortunate one, have you asked of your husband? But the decree of fate is unavoidable."

In her apartments was Sita on a couch of gold in a bed of flowers.

Lotuses were strewn on all sides diffusing fragrance around. In a corner of the room was a golden pot filled with water from the Saraju. Fragrant and delicious fruits were kept in a plate. The maid-attendants were all there ready to carry out her least wishes. She felt idle and sleepy and was weak as she was *enceinte*.

The story-teller was telling a story to amuse her when her sister-in-law Kukua came to her room. She said, " I am curious to know, good queen, how you spent your time in the palace of Ravana. I have not seen the Rakshasa king.

" He had ten heads and twenty hands they say. Oh how terrible ! Will you kindly draw a picture of Ravana so that I may form an idea of him?"

When Sita heard the name of Ravana she fainted as the old recollection came to her mind. The maids came up instantly to her aid and some sprinkled cold water on her face, others fanned her. They told Kukua not to refer to those unpleasant things—"Our good king has ordered that nothing unpleasant or exciting should be told here as the queen is weak. Why do you, oh madam, touch a topic which is painful to her." But Kukua was not to be stopped. She again and again referred to that topic and as soon as Sita came round, made the same request.

Slowly did Sita reply. "I never saw King Ravana face to face. How can I draw the picture of that wicked Rakshasa ?" The more she tried to convince Kukua the greater did she persist in her request. With a smiling face she requested Sita again and again.

She was verily the poisonous fruit of a poison-tree. Her mind was full of poison and her very smile was poison. She had planned a wicked scheme.

Sita said, "I saw the shadow of the monster when I was being carried over the sea,—reflected in the vast waters. Oh! what a figure it was, the shadow was of a terrible figure with twenty arms and ten heads."

Kukua was seated on the golden couch of Sita. Now she stretched her limbs there and lay by the side of the queen. Again she made the request—" Draw a picture of the Rakshasa king, dear sister ; " she said this again and again.

Unable to avoid her by any means she drew a picture of Ravana on her fan as she had seen him in his shadow. The monster was drawn with his ten heads. She was naturally weak and exhausted by the effort yielded to the attractions of sleep. Kukua finding she was asleep put the fan made of *tal* leaf on her breast.

Kukua was like a snake—with its fangs full of deadly poison. She did not like to see Sita happy. She was wicked; ugly to behold and cruel and virulent in her tongue; she was trained by Manthara from her childhood up.

She was the younger sister of Bharat and a daughter of the queen Kaikeyi. She was married in a princely house where she quarelled both with her father-in-law and mother-in-law. The good neighbours knew her to be a slanderer, quarrelsome and full of envy.

Even if there was not the least shadow of a cause she could create a quarrel amongst friends and relations. She administered a drug to her husband with a view to bring him under her full control but the result was that he turned mad. When abusing others and finding fault with them her one mouth became loud as ten mouths. Only for the sake of seeing the fun of it she sowed the seeds of deadly quarrel between a husband and wife.

Such was this Kukua who, though her husband lived, led the life of a widow—the result of her own wickedness. For the last ten years she was living in the palace of Ayodhya in her father's home cutting off all connection with her husband's family.

She could not bear to see the sight of the happiness of Rama and Sita, though she smiled as she talked with them; in her heart of hearts there was that poison, which she concealed from others.

On a golden throne sat King Rama when Kukua approached him like a vicious reptile diffusing its poisonous breath. Kukua stood for a time before the king with her foul motive. Fire emanated from her eyes and short and rapid was her breath. She used storming words and strutted and fretted as she said, " My tongue disdains to tell the vile thing, but yet the truth must be spoken. You are full of affection, oh cousin, for Sita. She it is whom you adore in your mind. You think of nothing else. She is the only valued treasure of your life, you love her more than you love your own self.

"You would not, I am afraid, believe me, but take my word, she is a shameless unchaste woman. She is still devoted to Ravana, the Rakshasa king. I have not the courage to speak the truth. For I may lose my life for telling the plain fact. You have ruined your own life infatuated by the charm of a beautiful face, but more, you have brought scandal to our great family by taking this bad woman for your wife.

"Not a month nor two but full ten months she was in the palace of Ravana. If anyone refers to Ravana before her, tears come to her eyes and she weeps turning her face away lest she be detected. This is the state of the mind of your darling wife.

"You are a sincere and open-hearted man. You do not know the ways of this world. What you have taken considering it nectar is really poison. The garland of flowers on your breast is really a snake. It will at an opportune moment bite and kill you. A flower, though divine it be, loses its sanctity and becomes unfit for being offered to the gods when it is touched by a *pariah*. No one would eat the rice from a plate from which a dog has taken a mouthful. If you would not believe in my words, come with me, cousin, I will show you that she is sleeping with the picture of Ravana on her bosom."

Like a tigress running in great speed to take the life of an innocent deer did Kukua enter the apartments of Sita dragging her royal cousin by his hands. There she lay heavy with child in her womb these five months, and Kukua pointed towards her breast with her finger.

Rama saw the picture—he was struck as if with a thunderbolt. No words came from his mouth. He returned to his own chamber. It seemed that a poisoned arrow had entered deep into his heart. But poor innocent Sita, she was quite unaware of the great calamity in store for her. Rama looked grim with anger. He seemed terrible like the sea in flood or a great forest on fire. Like a stark mad man, who had lost all his senses sat Rama without power to control himself. His eyes reddened and blood was up in his veins. His breath was hot like living flame.

Oh Kukua! The fire that you have kindled to-day will burn Sita with her husband. Not only that but the whole kingdom of Ayodhya will suffer from this dire calamity. The empire will be shattered to pieces losing the favour of the goddess of fortune.

He that listens to the counsel of others without using his own judgment is doomed to destruction.

Says Chandrabati, Rama lost his good sense.

(*Incomplete.*)

THE BALLAD OF RAJA MAHIPAL

PREFACE TO THE BALLAD OF RAJA MAHIPAL

When my student Mr. Munsuruddin, B.A., then studying in the Fifth-year class, of Indian Vernaculars, Calcutta University, some time ago, informed me that he had collected a small ballad of Mahipal, I was beside myself with joy. That was, if I remember aright, in the year 1928. My enthusiasm, however, abated to some extent when I got the ballad actually in my hands; and there can be no reason to hide the cause of the disappointment that I experienced on the occasion. The ballad consists of 26 lines only. Long had I been expecting a ballad of Mahipal.[1] I had heard from my esteemed friend late Mr. Pransankar Roy of Teota Raj family that in his extensive zemindary lying in the district of Rangpur there were some minstrels who could sing the whole ballad of Mahipal. Mr. Roy said that he had himself heard a ballad of Mahipal sung by one of these men and that it was so lengthy that it took the singer and his party three successive nights to sing the whole. He promised to secure for me the entire song within a short time. Unfortunately however he died immediately after, so that I could not secure the song through his assistance as I had expected. Next I approached my relation, Mr. Priyaranjan Sen, M.A.,

[1] Mr. J. C. French, I.C.S., writes on pp. 15-16 of his work on the Art of the Pala Empire of Bengal—"Late in the tenth century came Mahipala famous in Bengal song and story. He recovered the kingdom of his ancestors by driving out the Tibetans. Tradition ascribes to him great public works, but all that remains of them now-a-days are tanks so vast as to resemble lakes and mounds and ruins. A saying is still current in Bengal which preserves his name: 'Dhan bhante Mahipaler git,' 'songs of Mahipal while husking rice.' Mahipal repulsed Rajendra Chola an invader from Southern India. In A.D. 1026 he did extensive repairs to the temples and shrines in Benares.

then a professor of Carmichael College, Rangpur, and tried to interest him in the matter ; he made some efforts to recover the ballad but eventually informed me that he was convinced that there were still some minstrels who knew the ballad but he could not trace them. One woman, a courtesan, knew the ballad and could reproduce the whole of it from memory ; but owing to the professor's moral scruples he did not like to approach her. Then my friend Mr. Donald Fraser, I.C.S., came to Rangpur as Magistrate in 1921 and I wrote to him seeking his aid in recovering the ballad. I quote from one of his letters dated the 30th October, 1921, which will show that he had right earnestly taken up the task. He says, "As regards the Mahipal songs, a cartman I asked, said he had heard them but did not know them. An old priest I spoke to yesterday, a man of Kotalipara in Faridpur settled in this neighbourhood, said he heard old songs but could not understand them as he was of another country. He thought that Mahipal songs were more likely to be sung in Dacca or Faridpur. I will do my best to find out where they are sung and then will get some one to try and record them as sung. I quite agree with you that a Bhadralog will probably spoil the transliteration."

The Swadeshi movement reached Rangpur in the meantime and its activities were at full swing there engaging the serious attention of the District Officer, and before his hands were a little released from that engrossing task, Mr. Fraser found himself transferred elsewhere. In 1928 I sent my own ballad-collector Mr. Jasimuddin, B.A., to Rangpur with distinct instructions to make a vigorous search for this ballad but though he said that he had heard people speak of it and he believed that the ballad still existed in that district he could not, for some reason or other, lay his hands on it during his tour. Next I sought the help of my friend Babu Purnachandra Sen who was then Manager of an estate in Rangpur but he sent me some scraps of Mainamati songs promising to give me Mahipal songs later on, but this he did not do.

As I was thus disappointed times without number in securing a ballad which was full of historical importance yet believing all the while that it was still remembered and sung in various parts of North Bengal, I naturally felt a great enthusiasm when Mr. Mansuruddin at last informed me that he had got a small ballad on the celebrated monarch of the Pal Dynasty who ruled in Bengal about the 10th century A.D. One of the finest species of rice in our country is still called after him and his great *dighi* still exists in Rangpur which is one of the biggest if not the biggest in the whole province of Bengal. It takes one more than an hour to travel the four sides of this *dighi* on foot.

These songs were very popular even six centuries later. Brindaban Das wrote in his Chaitanya Bhagabat (1572 A.D.) that the people of Bengal in the early part of the 16th century were very fond of thes ongs of Mahipal. In fact the popularity of the song has become proverbial in this country, for even in our childhood we heard a saying extensively known in the villages of Bengal which runs thus "Dhan bhante Mahipaler git."

There was another king of the same name (Mahipal II) in Bengal (about 1070 A.D.) whose maladministration produced disastrous results on the Pal Dynasty. It was owing to his misgovernment that Bhim, a Kaivartha, got to the top of the ladder and assumed sovereign power in Bengal upsetting the Pals for the time being. The misdeeds of this Mahipal II have been indicated in some of the copper-plate inscriptions of the Pal Rajas themselves and in other documents. Is the monarch of this small ballad 'Mahipal II'? The ballad clearly attributes the construction of the well-known Mahipal Dighi to its hero. But that *dighi* was certainly constructed by the first Mahipal (1026 A. D.). There may be instances of moral weakness and misdeeds in the career of a great man and though history sometimes brushes over them recording their glories only, the traditions and the ballads of a country record them faithfully or with some exaggerations natural to rural fancy. If the account of the ballad is to be at all credited as giving a historical sidelight to a point in the character of its hero we shall not feel any undue hesitancy in associating the great Mahipal with the events of the small narrative.

We have got another ballad connected with Mahipal but that is all about a love-episode ascribed to his son. The name of the prince is not given—he is simply mentioned in the ballad as the son of Mahipal. Beyond a mere reference to his name in connection with the prince nothing is to be found in the ballad about Mahipal. This ballad which was collected by Mr. Jasimuddin does not possess any poetical value. Mr. Jasimuddin noted it down simply because it referred to the name of Mahipal in two or three places as the father of the prince—the hero. I do not think it necessary to write anything more on that ballad.

We have already referred to the authentic sources from which I had come to know of the existence of this ballad even in our own times. Pandit Kokileswar Sastri, M.A., President of the Sanskrit Board, and Lecturer, Calcutta University, told me that in his childhood he had heard the song of Mahipal many a time, sung by an old minstrel who lived near his home at Kakina in the district of Rangpur. "My father," he added, "was particularly fond of this ballad." Unfortunately that minstrel is dead now, and Mr. Sastri lives far away from his native place, so that beyond giving me the above information he could not offer any further clue.

A ballad of so much importance on a well-known

monarch of India even with all its exaggerations and legendary accretions natural to folklore—cannot but be of unique interest to students of history as well as to the lay public.

When I got the small ballad I found that it was too little a thing to quench the thirst of curiosity that was raised in me. It sheds no light on the life of the great monarch so much praised in the inscriptions. On the other hand it refers to a small incident in his life, true or false, which may lower him somewhat in the estimation of people. It is not after all the great ballad which took three successive nights to be sung and of which Brindaban Das wrote in the 16th century. At best it is but a scrap from a love-episode described in that ballad ; or there might have been some small songs along with the more lengthy ballads current in the country on the same topic, and this song may be one of those little things. It may seem curious that I have had to write so much on a ballad consisting of 26 lines only but the subject is of more than a passing interest and my elaborate notice may awaken in some readers a spirit of search for the ballad which, I doubt not, still exists in North Bengal. Hence my readers should excuse this long preface. There would have been a greater chance of recovering the ballad if I could undertake a tour myself but it is not possible for me to do so in the present condition of my health. Conscious of this limitation I must look for a chance to have the ballad recovered by other agencies. But ballads as a class are fast disappearing and after a few years the ballad of Mahipal may be totally lost. The historical allusion in the Chaitanya Bhagavat refers to the ballads of two other monarchs of the Pala dynasty (Jogipal and Bhogipal) which according to Brindaban Das were very popular in the countryside early in the 16th century.

The few lines of the present ballad show a side in the

character of king Mahipal which is an unexpected revelation, but though I feel hesitant in accepting the story I cannot wholly discredit it as false. Great men are sometimes liable to flaws and foibles of ordinary human nature and the populace take a peculiar delight in poking their noses into the private life of great men, particularly in matters concerning the sexes, whenever they find an opportunity to do so.

The metre used in the ballad is a very irregular type of *Payar*—the doggerels are halting and the lines do not always rhyme. It seems that the ballad is an old one as there are many archaic expressions in it ; yet the words গোলাম, নফর, বাঁদি and বাপজান show that the song was recast in Mahomedan times. A little ruggedness of language and imperfect rhyming make the impression that the framework of the ballad belongs to older times though it is clear that the short ballad has been retouched from time to time till its transcription in the present form.

The ballad though small has the heart of true folk-lore and ballad poetry in it. In 26 lines we have refrains no less than eight times producing that singular effect for which rural songs are notable as vehicles of pathos and tender appeal. The lines in a short compass are also full of suggestive references. The word বাসর (bridal) in the first line and the waywardness of the girl to follow a course blamed by her parents indicate that a desire lurked in her mind to allow herself to be caught in the trap laid by the king. The words of the informer show that the king had suffered a great deal for the love of the girl and was ever trying to cage the bird. The parents were persistent in their objections to her going to the Dighi probably because there already existed a scandal in respect of the king and Nila. The king under the circumstances could not be blamed for catching a bird which came so near the snare itself,—perhaps intentionally.

Song of Mahipal

With sandal and *chua* paste did Nila fill her bridal cup and then did she sit to make a paste with powdered pearl and myrobalan. This she again placed in a mica cup.

"Oh my father," she said, "daily do I bathe at home; knotted are my locks, unwashed as they are by copious flow of water. The servants fetch water for me here. I want to go to-day to bathe in the great pond which King Mahipal has dug."

"Do not go there Nila" said her father. "Do not go to that pond Nila—already a subject of scandal as you are." But Nila heeded not her father's word of caution. The mother objected too, but Nila heeded not her mother's word of caution.

Deaf to all objections did Nila start for the great pond. With her went a train of maid-servants, some going in front and others in the rear. With her went a train of male servants too, some going in front and others in the rear.

Down she came to the pond till she reached its knee-deep point. There she stopped to cleanse her fair limbs awhile. She went further down till the waves gently touched her waist and there she stopped to cleanse her fair limbs awhile. Next did the waters reach the level of her breast and there also she stopped to cleanse her fair limbs awhile.

The informer gave the report to King Mahipal saying " That Nila for whom, oh monarch, six months have you roamed in icy frost,—that Nila for whom, oh monarch, you have roamed six months more in the burning sands, —Nila, the fair one, herself has come to your pond to bathe. Oh what a wilderness, what a treasure of hair is on her head! The curling hair have spread over the surface of the pond far and near. The small and big fishes cannot go ahead through the tangle of her long tresses.

The monarch himself at once hied to the pond and swam till after some vain efforts he succeeded in catching hold of a handful of Nila's hair. He would not allow her to go.

"Who is it that has caught my hair in this way causing me pain? My father objected but I lent deaf ears to his words and came to this pond. My mother objected but I heeded not and came to this pond. Henceforth will Nila's life be a tale of scandal and all her honour will go for nothing." (Ll. 1-26.)

TILAK BASANTA

PREFACE TO TILAK BASANTA

'Raja Tilak Basanta' was supplied me by Babu Chandra Kumar De on the 7th of September, 1930. He got it from one of the rural villages of Mymensingh. The story is in the form of a *Gitikatha* with occasional prose-passages. But such passages are not many. The main portion consists of metrical verse. The poetical portion is not always composed in *Payar chhanda* as is the case with a large number of ballads. Though a considerable portion of this ballad is written in a somewhat crude form of that classical and well known metre, there are stanzas which have the rhythm of sound of Ghatak Karikas or of irregular Tripadi metre. A number of stanzas have only eight letters in a line followed by lines of 11 or 12 letters. A regular system is wanting but the abrupt rise and fall of this irregular *chhanda*, which is a capricious departure from the well known classical metres, have a poetic rhythm and wealth of sound which please the ear. I give examples from a variety of such irregular metres, which, though they do not follow a fixed or stereotyped standard, peculiarly suit songs sung in chorus.—In the same stanza we come across lines of diverse metres.

"বনে থাকে কাঠুরিয়া
বুক ভরা দয়ামায়া
গাছ কাটে বিরক্ষ কাটে
বিকায় নিয়া দূরের হাটে।"

Each line consists here of eight letters only. This is followed immediately by another metre containing eleven letters in the first line and twelve in the next.

"মুখ ভরা হাসি চাঁদের ধারা।
না জানে ছল—না জানে চাতুরী তারা॥"

The poetical idea and the pleasing metre in which it is couched, are picturesque and interesting.

It is also noteworthy that though this ballad evidently belongs to the latter part of the 17th century when the rules of Payar and Tripadi became stereotyped in our classical poetry, the writer does not care to follow any canon of Bengali poetics but adapts his metre, which is partially his own coinage, to the requirements of a party singing in chorus.

Unlike the *Gitikathas* and other ballads which I have collected up till now, this story promulgates a distinctly Brahmanic idea. Though written in the indigenous dialect of the lower Gangetic valley and conforming to the characteristics of our ballad-literature in other ways, this *Gitikatha* bears the seal and stamp of Brahmanic influence on it in an unmistakable manner. We all know the story of Sribatsa and Chinta given in the Bengali recensions of the Mahabharata to which Pandit Ramgati Nyayaratna found no clue in Sanskrit literature. I have stated elsewhere how strenuously did the Pandit try to trace the story to some Sanskrit sources. It was evidently a purely Bengali story, showing all the characteristics of our ballad-literature though it must be admitted that the Brahmanical influence is clearly perceptible in the recension of the tale as given in the Bengali Epic.

This ballad of Tilak Basanta tallies with the story of Sribatsa and Chinta in all its main features. Queen Sula like Queen Chinta wilfully courts the ban of leprosy.

King Tilak Basanta like King Sribatsa lives in the homes of wood-cutters for a time. King Tilak Basanta and Queen Sula suffer from great calamities in life in consequence of the ire of *Karampurush* as Sribatsa and Chinta do from that of the planet Saturn. I need not point out other coincidences. They are too many, and the reader will be reminded at every stage, of the other story while reading this ballad. But in spite of this striking analogy one must admit that the story of the Bengali Epic is certainly less interesting and inferior as a production of art from a poetical point of view. The form adopted in the *Gitikatha* is less rigid and the descriptions far more fresh and natural than what we find in the story of Sribatsa and Chinta.

As regards the Brahmanical influence in the conception of this ballad we may note the following points.

The curse of a Brahman or a god is at the root of all the evils that befell the lot of King Tilak Basanta. In the purely indigenous *Gitikathas* such as Kajal-rekha, and Kanchanmala, the Brahman, his curse or blessing, seldom plays any part, though the heroes and heroines there are subjected to similar freaks of fortune, in no way less dire than what Tilak Basanta and his queen Sula suffered. This element of Brahmanic curse and blessing as leading the destinies of men is in striking evidence throughout the whole literature of our Renaissance. It appears in this ballad also showing how the new spirit of the age not only permeated the Bengali recensions of Sanskrit epics and eventually reached the huts of rustics—through Kathakatas, Jatras, commentaries and explanations of Puranas,—but also found a direct access to the ballad-literature which had little to do with the Brahmanic ideal and was solely the monopoly of the rural population of Bengal not at all influenced by scholarship or academic canons.

The idea of chastity of women appears in a greatly exaggerated form in this story. I wish to be very explicit on this point. I do not mean to say that in the characters of Sula or Pavankumari, extremely lovable, accomplished and immaculate as they are, there is anything that jars against our æsthetic sense; what I want to say is that the ballad stresses *chastity* whereas those which had not come within the range of Brahmanic influence stressed *love*. The heroines of the genuine Bengali ballads suffer all that a human being is capable of suffering inspired by that pure flame which does not take into account any thought of marriage, social rules or bondage of custom. But in this ballad the sufferings are all for the sake of *husband* illustrating the sanctity of wedded life. Happily the wedded wives here are not lacking in love, but that is a mere matter of coincidence; the writer does not, like other classical poets, give us a discourse on the duties of a wedded woman, so that nothing there is in this ballad of the nature of a propaganda to call for adverse criticism from a poetical point of view. But all the same, the Brahmanic stamp is clear and unmistakable.

Thirdly, following evidently the rules of Sanskrit poetics the ballad ends in happiness inspite of all the tragic situations created in it. The tragic ends of the greatest of our ballad heroines as Mahua, Malua, Chandrabati, Rani Kamala, Madina, Kanchanmala, and others are striking facts showing how the rural folks boldly deviated from the rules laid down by the Sanskritists. The rural poets had no doubt heard of this poetical law. For the singers of the Puranas proclaimed it every day before their ears by a beat of drums accompanying their musical performances that tragic end was not allowable in decent literature. But the rural poets followed their own traditions and did not care to surrender their own ideal to the Sanskritists.

The story of the heroine turning a leper at her own will reminds one of the tale of Nala and Damayanti, which no doubt formed the basis of the story of Sribatsa and Chinta as also of this *Gitikatha*.

The fourth point illustrating the Brahmanical influence on this ballad, is the anxiety of the father to offer her in marriage when she had attained her puberty. He was so much overpowered by traditional fear lest he was guilty in the eyes of god and men for not marrying her in her childhood as ordained by the Brahmanical canons of the priestly age, that he took a vow to get her married to whomsoever he might behold in the early dawn, the next day.

The washing of the feet of a Brahman guest as an imperative point of duty on the part of a householder is another instance of Brahmanical influence (p. 389).

The sketches often reach the level of high literary excellence. I particularly refer to the description of the woodcutters on pages 374-75, which gives a lively picture of these simple men of the woodland and their women. The scene of their first meeting with the king and her wife and their grief at parting with the king fallen in great distress is very affecting and full of pathos.

The great ideals of renunciation and sacrifice held before our rural folk in these stories disseminated a superior spiritual and ethical culture in the country-side of which any people might be proud.

DINESH CHANDRA SEN

Raja Tilak Basanta

(1)

From distance the course of the river might be seen by the passer-by; sometimes the boats went with the tide and at others against it. On the banks of this river lived King Tilak Basanta. Hear, oh audience, the story of this prince.

The assembly I see before me comprises Hindus and Moslems. To both of these people do I bow down. First of all I should pay respects to my preceptor, next to my parents. Six modes of music known as 'Ragas' and thirty-six Raginis (their consorts) should be saluted by me. Mother Saraswati, the goddess of music whose hand carries the pleasing musical instrument, the Vina—should receive my homage as it is through her grace alone that I expect to sing my song. I have no idea of time in music. Whatever little I have learnt of the science is due to my teacher. Now be gracious to come down to this house, oh divine mother Saraswati, and inspire me with song. If you forsake me as I am unworthy, I will not go away but like jingling anklets cling to your feet. You will be, oh mother, like a tree and I a creeper to cling to your feet. How will it be possible for you to shake off one so intensely devoted to you ? (Ll.-1-18.)

(2)

Now, oh lands and waters and ye plants, all listen to my song—to this tale of Raja Tilak.

There is no reckoning of the number of elephants and horses in his royal stables. Each compartment of his palace looks like the ward of a big town, and the pinnacles of the royal chamber smile when the sun or moon touches them.

Who was it that gave the king all this wealth ? It is Providence who confer on men the fruits of Karma.

But an idea of conceit and pride came to the mind of the monarch. In the depth of night—the *Karam-purush*, the dispenser of human fortune, came to the city of the king disguised as a guest. "Oh citizen, I am hungry, I want from you something to eat" cried this disguised god—but the citizens were all asleep and no one heard his words. "Hungry am I, thirsty am I" he cried over again but nobody heeded his appealing tone. The god was offended and turning his face in anger left the city.

The guards and sentinels of the palace had heard that cry but sleepy and idle, dozing and nodding in their seats they did not care to give any response. Thus was the ire of the god roused to destroy the happiness of the king and the queen.

The king knew nothing of this. With the queen he was sleeping in perfect peace of mind. The midnight had already passed and there remained a little more than the third part of the night yet, when the king dreamt a strange dream. "Happy are you, oh king, in your Jore-Mandir palace. A guest came to your city and went away frustrated. No one cared to give him alms. Your palace will be smitten by fire. These fine couches and cushions of your room will vanish. Those whom you know as your well-wishers will behave as strangers and will be apathetic towards you. Elephants and horses, and with them, your gilt-robed ministers and courtiers will forsake you in your distress and I will put you to all kinds of further losses and crosses. Your great pride which is aloft to-day like your golden tower, will crumble down to dust. No more, oh king, no more should you be privileged to enjoy sweet sleep; your store will be void of the grace of the goddess of fortune and to-morrow will you have to depart from this city—as a mean beggar. Those whom you count to-day as your best friends and well-wishers will turn hostile. They will plunder your treasure and you will not have a *cowri* with you to meet the expenses of your journey.

The Raja awoke in great horror. He saw no one though he remembered that he had heard some one's voice distinctly. In that golden compartment of the king a lamp spread its golden light. The light slowly passed away and the room was covered with darkness.

The king called his sleeping queen and said, "Awake, oh queen, open your eyes and behold. A dire calamity has befallen us. We were totally unaware of the danger, enjoying sleep, and the house caught fire in the meantime destroying all that we had. The honoured guest came here at midnight and went away displeased with us. Our great wealth and fortune are now lost in the deep. Know again, that all our prosperity, our wealth, power and children are the outcome of the boon granted by the *Karampurush*—the dispenser of fortune. All these I got on one condition. I swore to the god that I should be always on the alert, so that no guest might return from this city disappointed. If ever it so happened that I failed to give fitting reception to a guest, on that very day and hour all my fortune would vanish. When I received the god's favours, I agreed to this condition and now in the morning to-morrow I shall have to forego all I have and march off from here with the wallet of a beggar on my back. Suddenly had I risen to this eminence by the grace of the *Karampurush* and suddenly are all this to vanish as one comes to possess a gold mine in a dream and loses it in a dream. In a dream I got my wealth and power and in a dream too I am going to lose them. Fortune, my queen, is fleeting and unsteady as a drop of dew on the lotus leaf. Now before we are doomed to the great misfortune that awaits us, let us depart from here this very night to avoid exposure. I see that odd-shaped (with three legs) deity [1] before my eyes vividly.

[1] *Karampurush* or the god of luck is represented as having three legs.

For a slight fault of mine I have been responsible for the great misfortune and breach of condition.

"I am just leaving this city but I am sorry on your account. Even the birds and beasts will feel compassion when they will witness your great misery. You are the daughter of a king. Alas, how will you travel in the thorny forest! The thorns will pierce your tender feet. The scorching rays of the sun will burn your beautiful body far more valued to me than gold. Scarcely will you find a drop of water when thirsty, or even a scanty meal when suffering from hunger. There in the gloomy forest sleep will be denied to your eyes. If in agony of heart you will cry to the utmost pitch of your voice, no one will come to give response. To-day you are surrounded by maid-servants who wait upon you and carry out your least wishes but in the forest there will be none to help you in the least. For want of a drop of oil you will not be able to light the evening lamp."

As the king said all this his tears began to flow without check—"No remedy do I see," he added. "Go to your father's home."

Saying this he gave a discourse on what he considered the right course for his consort under such circumstances.

The Queen.

"People know you to be a virtuous king. Then how is it that you fear to take with you one whom you have married? You are like the body and I am your shadow inseparably connected with you. I am like the dust that you tread, glorying on the touch of your feet. You are like the sea, and, I a Karayat fish dwelling in it. I cannot live for a moment separated from you. You are like the brightest gem of my necklace and dearer to me far than my eyes. If I follow your advice and live in my father's house when you, my lord, will be wandering in the forest, what happiness can I expect to derive from my own riches, the gift of my parents? I do not covet at all for the affection of my parents. I desire for your company alone, and I beseech you most earnestly to take me with you. A woman does not care for golden cushions and gilt houses or a share of her brother's kingdom. Rather should I like to sleep on the ground, under the shade of a tree and build a small cottage with leaves and branches of forest trees to live in. Your unfortunate Sula will be fortunate to be allowed a corner there. I do not covet the delicious food, the thickened milk and butter of my father's palace. The forest will yield abundant fruits to satisfy our hunger.

"Both of us will wander in the forest, gathering fruits and in that forest-bower we will live in happiness. The beasts of the forests will be like our kinsmen. Living with them we shall enjoy their confidence and they will know us to be their own. Listen, oh king, the cuckoo is singing from yonder tree. There is not much of night left. If you should leave this city it is just the time for it." (Ll. 1-100).

(3)

The wood-cutters live in forests. Their heart is full of compassion and tenderness. They cut down the big and small trees and sell them in the distant market-places. How many trees shall I name! there are the *sal* trees, the sandal, the palm and the leafy *tamal* trees which the wood-cutters cut all day long. Six months they live in a particular locality and live in comparative affluence and the next six months they go away to another king's region. The wives of the wood-cutters are verily the queens of the forest. They wear their *saris* in the fashion of *Pachchara* and tower-like bind their hair over the head. They live mainly upon forest-fruits and enjoy the sweets of sleep all undisfurbed in their cottages of leaves. Their face is always adorned with smiles, pleasant as moon-beams. They are innocent and pure, and their sincere heart does not know the wicked ways of the world. In the forest-path they walk heedless of danger. There are tigers and other ferocious beasts all around. But they do not fear them. On the way they pick up here a fruit and there a plume of a peacock and walk merrily along.

These women suddenly saw our virtuous king and queen on their way. " Who are you two, dear people ? It seems you are a royal pair ; why have you left your throne and kingdom to share the lot of the wood-cutters? You are perspiring profusely. Bears and tigers dwell in the forest. It is haunted by demons and witches. Is it becoming that people of your rank should visit this wild region ? Sir (addressing the king), you have a lady with you. It seems that though you have fallen in distress the goddess of fortune still follows your footsteps unwilling to part with you ; suffering so much she is still devoted to you and follows you like a shadow. (They address the Queen) Renowned are you are for your beauty and accomplishment, oh lady, tell us all about yourself. Whose daughter, are you? Your tender body seems scarcely able to bear the hardships of forest-life. You should not have come here. Long are your hair and you have worn a silk *saṛi*. Surely you are the daughter of a king and the queen of another. Your beauty has spread a halo of light all around. What cruel god has put you into such dire distress ! His heart is relentless and hard. On a flower he has hurled a thunder-holt. He has deprived your lips of that sweet smile which once adorned them and sent you to exile from your throne to the wilderness."

When she heard the women garrulously express their sympathy in this way, the tears of the queen flowed without check and she told all about herself to her sympathisers. She concluded thus " You, girls of this forest, it is all true even as you have guessed. I was once the queen of a great king. I had a large body of servants—male and female, and an army of soldiers always followed us wherever we went. As ill luck would have it, I am now a dweller of the forest. I have grown callous by misfortune so that even if someone cuts off a portion of my limb, I would not feel pain. My senses have been benumbed by grief, but one thing causes unbearable pain to me, and this I cannot shake off. He who had once innumerable retinues, hundreds of slaves and servant-girls attending him wherever he went—one who lorded it over a vast kingdom from his royal throne—the great king Tilak Basanta is to-day reduced to extreme misery! Alas! Why has merciful God in what justice given him such a dire punishment? Unused to walk, the thorns of the forest pierce his feet as he proceeds through the jungly way. Alas, the flow-tide of good fortune has passed and the ebb-tide of misfortune has set in. In the place of golden cushion and couches, he sleeps in a bed of leaves. Where is his golden palace gone? The trees afford him a shelter to-day by their shadow. In his treasury-room a golden lamp diffused its brilliant light, now he has not a trinket with him (she weeps). For three days my hushand has had no food. He wanders like a mad man in great sorrow. Where is that golden umbrella gone which the servants used to spread over his head! Its place is now taken by the leafy branches of forest trees! His royal robes are all gone, a strip of waist cloth scarcely hides his shame to-day. His colour which was bright as gold has grown pale and darkish owing to bitter thoughts that afflict him day and night."

(Ll. 1-66.)

(4)

They carry fruits tied in the corners of their *saris*. Some fetch water from the distant river. Some break the branches of a tree full of leaves, and with them fan the good king and the queen. Some bring down from a tree a honey-comb and serve them with fresh honey.

The king and the queen shed tears as they saw their eagerness to please and help them in their distress. Even a mother could not show them a more warm affection than these forest-girls did. They knew not insincerity or the cunning ways of the world. They consoled the royal pair as best as they could, and took them to the forest and themselves cut off the trees with which they built a house with its gateway in the east. It was better than a five-storied palace though, made of wild plants and wood. No fuss they made. Each man silently did his best. The Raja and his queen were safely lodged in that house; with the plumes of peacocks they made nice fans. An old woman of that woodland lived there in that house and helped the king to kindle fire when it went out. Early in the morning rose the king from his bed and went with the wood-cutters deep into the forest carrying an axe with him as the others did. He knew the quality of wood better than they and secured the sandal wood only. He gathered the wood and bound them with strong creepers. The smell issuing from his bundle filled the whole air with fragrance. Some nights he passed in that dense woodland and in this way he spent forty nights in that strange forest.

One day the Raja went to sell his goods to a distant market-place. His load consisted of the valuable sandal wood and he got a *kahan* of *cowris* by its sale. The queen expressed the wish that she herself should cook and feed the foresters. Raja Tilak at once went to their houses and invited them one and all. The Rani cooked with great pains 36 different kinds of curries. The Raja had gone to the forest for cutting wood. She in the meantime prepared cakes and other sweets and placed them in cups of *sal* leaves. The rice she cooked was of a specially fine quality. She made a plate of leaves and kept this nice rice thereon. It spread a fragrance inviting appetite. When she had finished her cooking, the good queen went to the river for taking a bath. The women of the wood accompanied their beloved queen. Some of them danced and sang, others made themselves merry in other ways. Each one of them had a pitcher with her to carry water. (Ll. 1-36.)

(5)

Listen to me, my friend, what happened at this time. A great merchant was returning home by that river with a fleet of fourteen ships, full of valuable goods. The cargo was so heavy that the ships could scarcely bear their burden. An old Brahman beggar was going along the riverside. He cried in a loud voice, "Oh merchant, I have had no food for seven days, will you kindly give me a rupee? If you do not show any mercy I shall die. I wandered about the villages on the banks of this river seeking charity, but no one paid any heed to my request." The oarsmen and sailors laughed at him and went on plying the ships without caring to give any reply. The Brahman beggar cursed the merchant and went away. It so happened that the ships got stranded there. This sudden misfortune was verily like a bolt from the blue—when there was no sign of cloud in the sky. The merchant was quite unprepared and he struck his head with his hands and began to cry. The voice of the God of Luck was heard by him at this stage. It said from above "Vain are your laments, oh merchant. You must suffer for your sins. For full twelve years you will remain here with your ships stranded, and during this time all the money that you have got by trade will be spent. But that is not all; your city will be burnt and nothing of your riches will be left at home." The merchant struck his head against the prow of his ship and filled the air with wild lamentations. There was a deep cut on his forehead which profusely bled. The God of Luck felt compassion for the man and again his voice was heard from above. It said " Find out a truly chaste woman. If she touches your ships with her finger, they will float again on the river."

At this time the good wives of the woodmen arrived there with the queen. Her face was beaming with beauty and looked like the moon. The crew of the ships were filled with wonder. Some of them said in a whispering tone and others loudly, " What a wonderfully handsome lady is this! She must be the queen of a Raja sent to exile for some fault." The merchant heard this and alighted from his ship. He placed his towel round his neck (as a sign of humility) and fell prostrate at the feet of the queen saying, " Providence has for some fault of mine doomed me to a dire punishment. All my fourteen ships are stranded on the shore by divine curse. It has been ordained that if a chaste woman would place her feet on my ships they will be released. You are a chaste woman, good mother, oh my saviour—if you would not have any compassion for me, know that I will kill myself here striking my head against a stone."

She who had herself suffered great sorrows in her life was deeply affected by the tale of this merchant's distress. She touched each one of the ships with her hands and instantly they floated once more on the waters. The wives of the wood-cutters were all astounded at the sight, and the captain advised the merchant to take the lady with him in one of the ships saying, " If you want security you should do so. Her action is wonderful. You yourself, sir, know well the dangers of the deep. If we come to face similar circumstances again, who will save us? Verily she is our saviour and by God's grace we have got her all unexpected. It would not be prudent to lose what we have got as a special blessing from God."

The evil counsel prevailed and the merchant forcibly carried the queen bound as a captive.

The Queen.

" Oh good women of the woods, tell my husband the whole story—tell him that the merchant is a monster who has repaid my action with such inhuman cruelty. He carries me by force. Oh dear girls—the meals are cooked and ready lying in the straw hut. The mad Raja knows not how to put the meals in the plate of leaves. Alas! who will be there to serve him? Who will hand the pitcher of water to him for wash. I am not at all sorry for our lost kingdom but to-day I am truly a beggar. My real wealth is gone! When my Raja will turn frantic in grief, console him to the best of your power. Give him food when he will be hungry and water to appease his thirst. My prayer to you is Bless me so that the red powder of luck on my head may not fade.[1] Alas, my bed of leaves—that abode of heavenly bliss is left behind for ever. From to-day my life is doomed to eternal misery! Behold the fourteen ships have now started again and will be soon out of sight. I will never see you any more. The night will pass away and the dawn will, oh my lord, appear as usual but from to-morrow I will not awake to see your sweet face. To-morrow I will not see that face dear as life which I have been accustomed to behold on opening my eyes every day! I have perhaps done many things wrong to you all. Excuse me for those knowing me to be an unfortunate woman."

[1] When a Hindu woman becomes a widow she loses the privilege of putting on the red sign on her forehead. This mark she would never allow to be effaced so long as her husband lives. Here her prayer is that she might not turn a widow.

Her tears added to the volume of the flood in the river. The ships advanced in a row against the tide breaking down the high waves.

Queen Sula at her crisis remembered the God of Luck and crying all the while said, "Oh Lord, strangers have touched my body. I have lost by their touch that purity which is a woman's pride. This body touched by them I hate. Give unto me the boon that it may be destroyed by leprosy and become rotten. Grant this prayer and save my honour. If I am a chaste woman who has been devoted all her life to her lord and unflinchingly adhered to his feet, oh my lord, let my prayer be fulfilled. Verily I believe that it cannot but be so. If I am a chaste woman, let these fourteen ships be overtaken by some dire calamity!"

The words of the chaste woman were infallible and the fourteen ships were once more stranded on the shore. Her golden colour at once faded away and her body became rotten by leprosy. The crew of the ships, the sailors and rowers, were frightened by what they saw. They asked the merchant to leave her on the bank. "She is not a human being," they said, "it is now fit that we should have nothing to do with her." As she was left in that jungly land on the bank ; the ships once more floated and started ahead against the tide. (Ll. 1-100).

(6)

It was evening and the king came home in excellent spirit with a smiling countenance. Entering the hut he cried, "Oh Sula, where are you ? The day, dear queen, was specially lucky for me. I got some very valuable wood which is worth their weight in gold if I can only arrange their sale in a distant town.

"Is your cooking finished or how much time it will take? I shall presently go to take my bath. Meantime keep ready our meals. The wood-cutters must be very hungry by this time and have surely gone to the river for taking their baths."

The Raja said all these in a low tone, and called his wife again and again but no response came. Then he asked the good women there, " Where is my wife? It seems she has finished her cooking. Where could she go now? Perhaps she has gone to the river." Saying this like a mad man he ran towards the river, when the wives of the wood-cutters related the whole story.

Behold the tears that flowed from the eyes of the Raja like streams as he heard the woeful tale.

The simple-minded women wept as they told the story. Some of them cried aloud, others lamented wildly while describing how the merchant had carried away the queen by force.

The good king fell on the ground like a banana plant when cut down. On regaining his senses he lamented thus—" Though I lost all my riches and kingdom, yet happy was I in your company, oh queen. Though often did we live on the fruits of forest trees, I did not feel any want but felt blessed that you were near me. You were to me like a diamond worth all the riches of seven kings. Alas! who has robbed me of it? Who is it that has taken away the light from my eyes? To-day I actually feel that I am out of the grace of Providence. To-day I feel anew the grief of losing my kingdom and all. Behold the bed of leaves there. It was a heaven unto me. Who is it that has strewn a handful of ashes on my meals which were ready. This cottage which I valued so much, is not worth anything to me now. My best course would be to drown myself in the river. She for whom I delighted in cutting the woods and whose presence amply made amends for the loss of my empire, she—my sweet co-partner—my only source of joy has gone away, and what attraction is there for me to live in this wilderness ?

"Oh wood-cutters, who have been like my brothers, I bid adieu to you. I must leave this place full of painful association." When the Raja lamented thus, a confused voice of wild grief was raised by the wood-cutters. These simple-minded wood-men became overpowered by grief and cried bitterly. The night passed away and they consoled the king saying that they would go to places far and near seeking the queen to the utmost of their power. The Raja who had nearly lost his wits did not draw any consolation from the sympathy shewn by the wood-cutters. With his own hands he set fire to his cottage and burnt it. Before any person there could have a sight of him he had left that place in the last hours of the night. (Ll. 1-46.)

(7)

He entered another country—the jurisdiction of another king. The sky and the land there were full of splendour. The treasury of the king had untold wealth. The glory of the king knew no waning. In the stable there were innumerable horses and there were guards at each of the thousand gates of the city.

The palace was seven-storied, it had glass doors and windows. Here lived the king and the queen in great affluence. They knew no want. The nurses and the attending maid-servants could be counted by legions. The Raja had an only daughter. She was verily like the lamp in a dark chamber. It seemed that she showered gold by her smile and pearls by her tears. In the whole world there was not another girl who was her equal. Her hair, long and profuse, fell to her ankles. With perfumed oil and vermilion she bedecked herself in her toilet room. She was unmarried and many a prince came seeking her hands, but went away disappointed as the king did not entertain their offer for some reason or other.

One day, the princess entered her father's chamber. There was a pitcher with cold water in that room, and the queen who was thirsty asked her daughter to get it from there. The princess did not order any of her numerous maid-servants to do this but herself entered her royal father's compartment. The king was in deep slumber. All on a sudden he awoke and thought that he saw the queen filling a pitcher with cold water. Covered with her flowing hair which profusely fell round it, her face could not be seen. The moon as it were lay hid under the clouds. The Raja cut some jokes thinking her to be the queen but he perceived later that the princess, his daughter, was going away from the room in haste. "It is not the Queen then but my daughter and I cut jokes at her!" He was completely overwhelmed with a sense of shame at this thought and said to himself, "Woe to me that I have cut jokes at my own daughter! Where shall I go to hide my shame—oh sky! let there be a rend in thy bosom so that I may enter there, to conceal myself, oh what a fool I am. It is a pity that I have such a grown-up girl in the house and have not yet given her in marriage!"

After a good deal of thinking the king resolved that whomsoever he would see first in the morning on waking from sleep, the next day, to him will he offer the hands of the princess.

No one of the city knew of this resolution of the king. In the morning the flowers bloomed in the royal garden. The sun rose illuminating the eastern horizon. At this time came there a new gardener. He was perfectly a stranger in the city. Nobody knew whence he came or where his home was. No one knew him. He was working for some time in the place of the old gardener. He had a fair cemplexion and his limbs were symmetrically graceful and faultless. Some said that he belonged to the family of the gardeners, but others said he must be a prince in disguise, and a few suspected him to be possessed of some divine power.

The king had no sleep in his eyes that night. At the dawn as he rose from his bed, he saw the face of the gardener. The king's eyes floated in a stream of tears. Alas ! after all our diligent search for a suitable bridegroom all these years, the princess is doomed to be married to a gardener! Who can fight against his lot. I must offer her to this man whatever may be the result of this union! Who can violate the will of God ? He has ordained it that she should suffer. Who can alter the decree written in her luck ?

Thus was Pavankumari, the princess, married to the gardener. The citizens were smitten with grief and cried 'Alas!' 'Alas!'

Even such a night of sorrow had its end. The people of the city had expected feasts and presents of clothes on the occasion. They had expected to participate in the programme of many amusements and functions of joy, but what happened on the bridal night! Not a drum was heard, no conch sounded. Throughout the vast city, in the place of a general illumination as suited the occasion, not a lamp was lighted to dispel a little darkness. The poor gardener became the husband of the princess. It was the order of the king. In the house of the old gardener there was a wretched hut and here the gardener and the princess slept on a mat made of the material with which broomsticks are made. But the princess was not at all sorry. On the other hand, she was perfectly happy with her husband. The king gave an order to give to the gardener an abundant supply of rice and paddy. "Let not my daughter feel the sharp pangs of want in respect of her daily necessaries," he said. "Alas! she has been from her birth my pet. Even when she was in her golden couch I was afraid lest she was unhappy and not quite at case. If she was left on the floor I felt she might be tormented by the ants. I brought her up with the utmost care and affection." In this way lamented the king, and it seemed that even stone would melt at his piteous laments and the river swell by his tears.

In this way time went on.— (Ll. 1-35.)

(8)

Oh, what a cruel providence created you, my girl? One beautiful as the moon is doomed to everlasting sorrow. The mother brought her up with tender affection worthy of a child of a royal pair. But it was written in her luck that she should have a gardener for her husband. Now the despised gardener is her mate. Oh what a sorrow! If any one would strike her with the petals of a flower, it would hurt her as if it were a bolt from the blue, so tender, so soft is her body! How can that tender body of her be at ease on the hard ground which is to be her bed from now? Where are now the golden couches and bedsteads of her father's house? On a bed of mat made of reeds and grass she is now to take her rest. Alas! Who would listen to these painful details of her lowly life! In her father's house the mosquito nets are bright and transparent, dazzling the eyes. But here her tender body is exposed to the bite of mosquitoes. No ornament has she—the jewels and precious stones, alas! where are they? She passes her days in extreme misery. Famished without proper food, she has grown emaciated and pale.

The Princess.

"Oh my husband, take heart. Do not be sorry on my account. God has ordained for us a lot which we must bear with courage. For myself I do not care a bit. Believe me what can be my want when I have such a husband as you. When your arms are around my neck, happy do I feel as if I have worn a necklace of seven-stringed pearls. When you call me by tender names, the sweet voice seems to my ears as my best ear-rings. The dust of your feet will be the ornament of my body. Your company to me makes up for all the diamonds, pearls and precious stones which one may covet. You cannot realise but I tell you the truth that if I have the privilege of washing your feet with my tears and wipe them with my long hair it would afford me the highest pleasure. I consider this happiness to be far greater than what I might enjoy in the royal palace of my father. The thought that I am of some service to your feet supplies me inspiration for my work more than all that my high status in society could give. These feet of thine give me all the security of a royal bed and are holy as religion to me.''

The money she had with her she distributed among the poor. In fact the beggars of the whole country gathered at her new house. They would not go to the king's palace but went every day for alms to the 'gardener king's house.'

The seven sons of the king became jealous of him. What, the fellow is in charge of our garden, see how audacious he has become! His title is 'the gardener king.' All the poor people and beggars throng there every day. They sing his glory. If the old king, our father, were not here we would have ordered the executioner to cut off his head. Now listen to our order, oh treasurer, do not give even a blind *cowri* to that silly fellow. Put up three locks at the treasury rooms, let us see how that rogue can manage to live. The fool gets a supply of every thing from our palace. Ours are the elephants, ours are the horses and the funds he gets from our treasury, with these he makes a pageant.

By the order of the seven princes the doors of the treasury were locked up. The beggars, the blind, decrepit and the poor who used to get alms from the gardener king were thus deprived of their share. The queen-mother heard that her daughter had fallen into extreme distress. She privately told her maid-servants—"You are to give my daughter the rice dusts and the refuse of corn of this house. This you should secretly do." —They obeyed the order with a heavy heart and with great fear, and the princess and her husband lived on this wretched food. Their hunger was not appeased but yet the face of the princess had a smile which pleased all. There was no sign of sorrow in her countenance. The poor people of the locality did not know all that had transpired. As usual they came also now and stood near the hut of the gardener king expecting alms.

Then did the princess take her ear-rings and necklace and other ornaments which she had kept in reserve and with these she satisfied those who had appealed for help.

(Ll. 1-38.)

(9)

When everything was thus spent out, it so happened that a blind Brahman beggar with a staff in his hand came to the hut one day and cried aloud—"On mistress of the house, oh mother, will you kindly give alms to me !"

All that she had were exhausted. Not even a part of her refuse grains was there. The princess was in a dilemma and began to think as to what she could give to the poor Brahman. Then it struck her that she had a *sari* that she wore and she resolved that she would cut half of it ; she retained half for herself and gave the other half to the beggar. At this time the Brahman said aloud addressing the princess : "Oh Princess, oh Goddess of Luck personified—for twelve years I have lived a wanderer's life, travelling far and near countries—the kingdoms of many a Raja. No one has during all these years given me what I have really wanted. Some have given me money, great or small sums—from precious stones to *cowris*. I have received many a gift whilst there were people who often drove me from their house abusing me as much as they could. A blindman's lot is hard. I have passed through varied experiences when seeking for alms."

The princess said—"What is it that you want, oh Brahman. But first let me wash your feet with the water I have brought."

The Brahman.

"No need of all that. If you give me what I am seeking I shall return home perfectly satisfied. I had gone to the yonder palace of the Raja of this country. They did not give me anything but pointed out this hut, saying that I should apply here."

"What is it that you seek, tell me ?" said the princess.

The beggar said "Give me a pair of eyes."

The Princess was struck with fear at his words. How could she comply with this wish of the beggar! "Oh God! oh Lord! you have come to destroy what little happiness I am still enjoying now. I do not know who this beggar Brahman is! He may be a disguised god who has come to place me in a new trial."

While thinking in this strain she at last said in mild accents—"Be pleased, oh Brahman, to take your seat here. My husband is not here just now but he will come very soon. Know that he will not deny you anything. He will give what you may wish."

She thought: "If the beggar goes away disappointed the results of all my virtuous acts will be destroyed. Also what am I to do in the present crisis!"

At this time the "gardener king" with a sweeping broom in his hands returned to his hut.

The princess approached him and said—"See my husband, there is great danger ahead. All unexpectedly a Brahman beggar has come to this house begging alms. He does not want any rupee or *cowri* –but wants one's eyes —this is the beggar's prayer. I do not know what god has again come to try us. What happiness is yet left in our life possibly we shall be going to lose also."

When the gardener heard this, he thought within himself: "What should we do now? Who is this beggar? Is he some god in disguise?" Thinking thus he approached the Brahman and asked him some questions.

The Brahman beggar said, "I have come here afflicted with a great sorrow. I have heard that you are a magnanimous soul. So I have approached you, hoping to get redress, for my misfortune is very great.

"For twelve years I have been leading the life of a blind man. My dark night, it seems, will never come to an end! But if you are gracious and grant me the boon that I have asked, *viz.*, that of a pair of eyes, my misery may come to an end."

On hearing this the gardener contemplated for a while and then prayed thrice to the Lord of Luck. He said, "Hear me, oh Brahman! It is not in the power of man to restore sight to eyes that have been totally lost. But the grace of God can help a man in all matters and make possible what is impossible."

Then did he cruelly cut off his own eyes with a sickle and presented them to the Brahman.

Receiving the alms he had wanted the Brahman went away from the place. In utter distress the princess began to cry aloud.

She washed the face of her husband with cool water and wiped away the blood and said, "Oh! what a misery was reserved for me!"

The gardener said, "Do not weep, oh queen, let us

bear our lot with a smiling face. The God of Luck has given us the punishment. We must endure it with patience. If a person has given a gift and then he repents or feels pain for it, the virtue of such a gift he loses and God turns away his face from him." The princess replied : " God is so cruel to you, my lord, yet you have not lost faith in him. You are surely a wonderful man." The gardener said, " Do not weep, oh princess, one who wants happiness must first court misery. As the hard rind of a fruit is the first thing to get over before one is allowed to taste its kernel, so sorrow is the gateway through which one should pass before one can enjoy true happiness. One wishing to enter the mansion of joy, must have his passport from sorrow. If you want real happiness do not be afraid of sorrow at the outset. It is the way to Sadhana—an austere course which entitles one to the grace of God." (Ll. 1-84.)

(10)

The husband was now rendered unfit. The princess herself does the work of a sweeper in the inner apartments of the king—her father. All the year round she suffers her hard lot with patience. The wives of her seven brothers laugh at her in derision. She suffers in this way, it seems there is no end to her suffering. Her clothes are now tattered rags and she has not a drop of oil to do her hair. In one hand she carries a basket to keep the sweepings and with the other she wipes away her tears. When the maid-servants give her rice-dusts and refuse corn, she accepts them and ties them in a corner of her torn *sari*. This is the food with which the pair any how appease their hunger.

The mother does not dare speak to her for fear of the wives of her sons and she secretly bears the pain which pierces her heart like a spear. When the mother sees the dear girl—her pet—dressed in a tattered cloth she is maddened with grief and the word "Alas" comes almost unconsciously out of her lips. For fear of her sons she cannot give even a blind *cowri* to her daughter from the treasury. Even the inanimate trees express their sympathy by throwing off their leaves as she passes by. A mother's heart alone knows the pain, caused by a daughter's sorrows. Who, alas, can know it more?

Thus passed their days. The princess daily performed the duties of a sweeper in the Raja's palace. Even the cats, dogs and other domestic animals of her father's house are living happily,—all except the dear daughter of the house.

One day the music of the palace sounded indicating a hunting excursion. The sound of the trumpet, tabor, *Kara* and *Nagra* rose high in the air and there was confusion and tumult everywhere. The gardener asked, "Tell me, wife, why is this music in the palace?" The blind man thought, "Many a day I have not gone for hunting which was once my passion." He said, "Will you, wife, do one thing? Ask of your father an arrow of the *Sabda-bhedi* [1] class."

The Princess.

"Hear me, husband, abandon that idea of hunting. Swear by me that you would not go. You are a blind man and the paths of the forest are very intricate and difficult to pass. Danger is sure to overtake us if you persist. None in the world have I save yourself. My parents and brothers have given me up unkindly and like a weed floating in the stream, I am carried away by fate. While abandoned by my kith and kin I have taken refuge

1 *Lit.*,—That which pierces the aim following the sound. Where the aim cannot be seen the *Sabda-bhedi* follows the direction of the sound and hits the aim.

in you. None else there is to take compassion on me. I have given up the idea of enjoyment in life. A sorrowful lot have I courted. The sorrows of my wedded life give me an impetus for work but even if this be lost I shall sink into utter despair. A pitcher though empty is a hundred times better than one broken. Without you it will be impossible for me to stay alone in the hut. If you go away leaving me I will not care to bear this life. Before going, take a sickle in hand and cut my throat."

The princess began to lament in this way. Her blind husband consoled her by these words : "I have not long tasted the flesh of a deer. If I can secure one, it will afford me a great pleasure. So do not prevent me from going."

"Many a deer will be brought by my brothers. I will get a little meat for you from my mother. So give up the idea of going for hunting."

But her blind husband still persisted. So she went to her father and said, "Your blind son-in-law is bent on going for hunting. Give him a bow and an arrow of the *Sabda-bhedi* class.

The king began to cry like a child when he saw his pet daughter reduced to that plight. He gave the bow and the arrow wanted by her. The blind Raja took these with him and started. He followed the sound of music and proceeded on in the forest. He tried to find out his way by feeling things by stretching his hands on all sides. He would sometimes sit down exhausted and then rise again to pursue his course. Thus after some days he entered the reserved forest. (Ll. 1-55.)

(11)

For seven days and seven nights the seven princes sought game in that dense forest but not a tiger nor a dear came across their way. Not even a bird of the air could they find there to shoot. "What a disappointment! How shall we return to our city—Alas, with what face?" they thought.

Meantime the blind Raja wandered in that wilderness. He had walked a great deal and entered the very depths of that jungly region. He had no eyes to see whether a tiger or a dear passed by. No sound he heard anywhere, so he did not shoot the *Sabda-bhedi* arrow. He shot other arrows one after another. They flew into the air. So sharp were they that they penetrated stones and trees. The tiger and the bear fled away. At this time all on a sudden what is it that struck his feet? Is it a man or a beast? As soon as he had touched the object with his feet he regained the sight that he had lost. The Raja wonderingly opened his eyes and found the person lying prostrate before him, no other than his queen Sula dearer than life. When she had touched his feet the leprosy which afflicted her was at once cured. Her colour became once more bright as a living flame. Like a molten piece of gold, her colour looked bright and dazzling. It was a meeting after twelve years.

Sula threw her arm round the neck of her beloved husband and began to weep. The sorrows of twelve long years she narrated one by one to him. She told him all about the merchant and the story of her taking upon herself the ban of leprosy as a protection in an hour of crisis and how she was abandoned in that forest.

The king heard all that she said and thought the God of Luck was at last propitiated. He would do no more harm.

The King.

"Oh my Sula! oh my life, weep no more. When I have got you back little do I care for the loss of my empire. We will henceforth live on the forest fruits and dwell here. Where is the man so fortunate as I am who gets back his lost treasure in this way ? The wood-cutters and their women who were like our mothers, are dear to me. I do not know how they are ; I long to see them again. Now our happiness is unbounded as we have met again ! I am now convinced that our evil days will soon be over." (Ll. 1-16.)

(12)

The seven princes were now completely exhausted by their tiresome search but they got no game. Their face grew pale, " What shall we take with us home ?"—that was their cause of anxiety. As they proceeded, they saw a large *Daruk* tree. The roots of the tree seemed to have entered the very depths of the netherworld and its branches and leaves covered the sky. At the foot of the tree they saw a god and goddess sitting together. Before them lay the body of seven stags. The brothers asked—" Who are you two, men or angels ? "

The Raja said, " You do not recognise me ! strange ! Look at me and behold closely."

Then they recognised him to be the gardener. How wonderful ! How could he get back the two eyes he had lost. How could he possess such a golden colour. Surely the presiding deity of the forest has granted him a boon, out of kindness.

They talked among themselves for a time and then they asked the gardener, " We could not get a single deer. How is it that you got seven ? "

The princes were inspired by a wicked impulse. They thought, " How can we return home without any game ? We must wreak our vengeance on this wicked fellow. Let us kill him and take away the game by force."

Resolving in this way the seven brothers aimed their arrows at the king. The great hero Tilak Basanta took up his bow and by shooting seven arrows disabled the hands of his opponents and their bows fell down. He had them all bound by the string of their bows but did not take their life because of his love for their sister. He took the ring from his finger containing his royal seal and impressed it on their foreheads. The ring was called *Sri Angti* or the Ring of Luck.

"Take these stags. Why should you remain in this forest exposing yourself to such hardships. I give you my '*Sri Angti.*' Please deliver it to my wife. It is a token by which I will know if the princess still recollects me. One day she had asked me to tell her who I was, but I did not say anything in reply simply asking her to wait till she would know everything in the fullness of time. This Ring of Luck—the *Sri Angti*—will give a full introduction. Now for you there is no more any cause for alarm. Go to your palace from this wilderness."

Burning in insult and greatly humiliated did the princes return to their city and did not say anything to their people. The '*Sri Angti*' they gave to the princess and with tears in their eyes related to her how her husband was eaten up by a tiger. "At the time of death he handed this ring to us for being delivered to you. Who can alter the decree of fate? Our father turned your enemy and threw you into the depths of misery. So many princes came as suitors of your hands but they were turned out. This is Fate. Whom shall you accuse? Look at the moon-beams—how beautiful, how cool,—but Fate reserves these moon-beams to be devoured by vampires. Look at the golden lotus with all its honeyed treasure. The worms of the dung eat up the beautiful petals in the end. At the time of his death the blind man gave this message to be conveyed to you saying that should you wish to know who he was, this *Sri Angti* would acquaint you with all particulars about him." The princess took the ring in her hand. She neither cried aloud, nor shed silent tears. She looked sombre like the hailstorm of summer before it moves in the sky. She told the ring, "Oh my dear *Sri Angti*, will you tell me the truth? Have my brothers deceived me by a false report ? Tell me, oh Ring of Luck, all that happened in the forest without hiding anything."

The ring got power of expression at her bidding and said everything about the king. How he and his queen left their palace, stating all particulars of the country of which he was the ruler. The whole story was told to the princess. Upon which Pavankumari the princess with the speed of Pavana (wind) ran away from her father's city. Rivers she crossed and countries far and near she travelled, suffering all kinds of hardships in her journey. (Ll. 1-54.)

(13)

In the country of her lord there was a washerman in whose house she became a guest. Pavana said to the wife of the washerman that she knew how to wash clothes. "I will wash the clothes of the Raja for you, good mother, kindly carry them to the palace." She washed the clothes of the queen Sula as well, and within their folds secretly placed that Ring of Luck.

Sula Rani asked the old washerman—"Will you tell me who washed the clothes to-day? How nicely the task has been done!" Then as she opened the folds, she found the *Sri Angti* and showed it to the king.

The Raja wonderingly said—"Where is it, dear queen, that you have got this ring?"

The queen said that she found it in the folds of the clothes washed by the washer-woman.

A maid-servant was instantly sent and the washer-woman was brought forthwith to his presence.

She trembled in fear and said, "It belongs to one damsel, who is beautiful as Lakshmi and accomplished as Saraswati. I do not know who she is or where lies her home. She is staying with us and calls me mother. She speaks so sweetly that her words cool one's heart."

Raja Tilak at once sent the palanquin of the palace to fetch the girl. She entered the house of the king and the citizens said that in beauty she was a match for queen Sula.

When the king got a report of her arrival he forthwith came before her. She saw her husband and fell at his feet fainting.

The king said to queen Sula, "This lady has suffered for my sake more than what you have done."

Queen Sula embraced Pavankumari. They called each other by the sweet term 'sister.' They suited each other as do the diamonds suit a golden necklace in which they are set. They both adorned the palace—as if the two moons appeared from the same sky and dispelled the gloom of that royal house.

When the old king—the father of Pavankumari—got a true account of these developments, he bestowed half of his kingdom on Raja Tilak.

Here ends my story. Forgive me, oh president of the assembly, and accept my good wishes. (Ll. 1-38.)

PIR BATASI

PREFACE TO PIR BATASI

The ballad of Pir Batasi was collected in the beginning of this year by Babu Chandra Kumar De from three minstrels, (1) Brindaban Bairagi of Ajmiri Bajar, (2) Sridam Patani of Khala Lakshmiganja, (3) Jagabandhu Gayen of another village in the district of Mymensing. This ballad was composed by one Rajani Gopal who calls himself a native of Bhati (Eastern Mymensing). His father was Jagannath and mother Sonamani. He does not say to which caste he belonged but mentions his *gotra* as Madhukulya. The hymn given in the preliminary portion is evidently a composition of the Mahomedan minstrel. The usual practice is that the hymnic portion of the ballads is more often composed by the minstrel who sings the song than by the poet himself. The liberal ideas which prevail amongst these Mahomedans and the catholicity of their views are illustrated by the recognition of the Hindu shrines along with his own in the hymn of this Mahomedan minstrel. That the Hindus and the Mahomedans lived in perfect amity and were far from being influenced by bigoted notions which have created difficulties in the solution of present communal questions is clearly in evidence in these hymns which as a rule are characterized by large-hearted and sympathetic appreciation of each other's religious ideals. The Makka and Madina in the eyes of the Moslem minstrel possess here the same sanctity as Benares and Gaya.

The ballad contains 542 lines and I have divided it into 17 cantos. I cannot say that this ballad is of a type of excellence claimed by the very best ones from a poetical point of view. Its literary merits are mediocre though the lyrical element, as in most of the ballads, is here also a striking feature of the song. We have found numerous ballads of this type in which the mortal bites of serpents and their cure are prominently mentioned. We have got it in Sannamala, Malua, Manjurma and in some unpublished ballads such as Ruper Manohar. All these, as I have said elsewhere, are precursors of the great song of Behula which has given us the most striking ideal of womanly virtues, as conceived by the Hindus, and overshadowed a hundred tales of this nature by its unique excellence. The Puja of Manasa Devi was at one time the greatest of our National festivities and even now in the remote villages of East Bengal it continues to be so amongst the rural people. The Durga Puja within the last four centuries has grown in importance in this country and supplanted the festivities of the Manasa cult.

By far the greater number of the best ballads contains accounts which are realistic though blended with romantic elements. Mahua, Malua, Chandrabati and many such are composed in the fashion of modern fiction and there is nothing in them which overrides the range of ordinary belief. In the Giti Kathas of course we find a gallaxy of extraordinaxy incidents and the fullest scope given to imagination. The ballad of Mainamati or Gopichandra, as it is called, is a distinct type which claims little affinity with the "Eastern Bengal ballads." In this type the dominating feature we find to be the feats of Tantric saints. In the present ballad also we find such feats along with the incidents of simpler narratives. The extraordinary powers achieved by Sumai Ojha reminds us of the feats of Hādi Siddha. Like Hādi Siddha, Sumai could cross a river with sandals on his feet, and perform other miracles like the Druid priests of Gaelic mythology. The social laws that govern our country are set at nought by the ballad-maker. The most striking element in a large number of ballads is this freedom from the canons of the orthodox society. It is curious to find that our peasantry boldly stepped over all social restraints and proved themselves to be true children of nature untrammelled by bondage of any sort. Binath's wife goes astray and intrigues against him, and Batasi who loves him with all the ardour of a woman's soul is untrue to her husband. The poet does not comment on their action or promulgate any doctrine of social ethics but stresses the feelings of a lover throughout his poem, as the only point to be cared for, and it is love alone that supplies his pen with inspiration and poetry. He cares little what the society might say or do, but goes on analysing the tender feelings of a woman in love irrespective of all other considerations. The chief interest of the ballad lies in this nice and subtle delineation of female characters yielding to the call of the blind deity of love. When Binath sings a song through his flute its effect is irresistible on those who hear it. The women on the river-side with pitchers of water in their arms stand entranced by the music and when his own Batasi listens to it she is simply maddened. Such music is still to be heard by the side of the great rivers of Eastern Bengal. It sweeps over the vast waters with its tremulous melody full of pathos and fills the whole air's space. No one who has not heard the sound of a sweet flute by the banks of a large river in Eastern Bengal, which comes floating in the air from large pastoral grounds where the cow-herds tend their cattle, will be able to appreciate to the fullest extent these descriptions of the ballads. It is this flute which the happier Vaisnava poets have put in the hands of Krishna spiritualising the whole atmosphere and lending a permanent charm to the Mahajan Padavali. The study of these ballads will show how the great and far-reaching developments in popular thought have taken place in our country associated with situations which are observed daily in our village homes. In order to understand the Vaishnava poetry of Bengal and appreciate its value as a contribution by the whole nation to the spiritual message conveyed by the saints and apostles, it is essentially necessary that one should go through the whole of this ballad literature which in the words of Lord Ronaldshay (Marquis of Zetland) is "the seed" from which grew the harvest of our classical poetry, rich not only in its rhythmical beauty but also in its appeal to the masses by reason of its drawing largely from indigenous sources.

DINESH CHANDRA SEN.

Pir Batasi

(1)

I bow to the great Pir-Saheb Gazi. Now play on the flute, oh musicians! To the great Pir Saheb Gazi do I offer my salutes with all humility. First do I make my obeisance to Allah and then I bow to the feet of my parents. My preceptor do I salute next. I bow to earth with its four corners and stand firm on the solid basis of my devotion. Oh! Hindus and Musalmans who have assembled here, I salute you all. All the great religious places, Makka and Madina, Kasi and Gaya should also receive my homage. To seas and lakes do I bow, and prostrate myself in reverent humility before the holy tomb of Saheb Ali. My obeisance goes to this house which I am just going to address and now my purpose is settled. Let the great Jinda Gazi bless me from his place in heaven. I do not know the modes of music, nor how to keep time. Conscious of this limitation I tremble with fear. Once more do I bow to this assembly and crave your permission to begin my song. (Ll. 1-26.)

(2)

Now attend to the story as I am going to recite it from the beginning.

From his birth Binath was doomed to misery. His first six months he passed in his mother's arms but lost his father in the seventh month. While removing the weeds from the fields of Sali rice his father was bitten by a snake and died then and there. No friend had the poor widow with her orphan and she wept in despair, not knowing how to bring up her infant son. She had no means of livelihood and had nothing in store to appease hunger. Her clothes were all rags. The mother's heart melted in tears as she covered her son by a tattered piece of cloth.

After much hesitancy and doubt she decided upon a course and went to the house of Chand, the chief man of the village. Rich and powerful in the village was Chand and the mother was admitted to his home and brought up her son by serving as a cook in his house. And thus did Binath attain his sixth year. But branded by his evil stars he was not destined to be happy at any stage of life. He lost his mother in his seventh year. The boy was benumbed with grief and lay prostrate on the ground in utter helplessness. He loudly lamented his lot ; " How could you leave me, oh mother," he said ; "so tenderly attached were you to me ! You would not suffer even a little dust to soil my body but wiped it away with gentle hands before taking me in your arms. There is none here whom I may call my own as I cast my bewildered eyes on all sides. Where am I to go now ? Who is there to befriend me ? "

Binath served in Chand's household as a cowherd and in course of time the sore of his heart was gradually healed. By and by he grew up to manhood attaining his twentieth year. From a bamboo plant he made a flute and learned to play on it with the help of an expert. Tenderly did he address Chand's wife as ' mother.'

Chand had a daughter named Sujanti who was beautiful as the moon. It was hard to find her equal in the whole world. She looked pretty as a delicate flower-plant moving to and fro in the wind. She passed her twelve summers laughing and dancing. Her face was lovely and delicate, and sweet was the smile that played on it disclosing her pearl-like teeth. She it was who inspired the tunes in Binath's flute. (Ll. 1-40.)

(3)

Now hear, ye friends, what happened next. Chand the merchant decided to embark on a voyage for trade and took

Binath with him. Twelve ships and thirteen *pansis* loaded with paddy formed his fleet and with these he proceeded northward on his journey.

Beautiful was the sight that met Binath's eyes as the ships moved onwards. Groves of blooming screw plants welcomed them at every turn of the great river. Village-girls were seen bathing in the river-ghats, and many a boat passed them bound for unknown shores. The picturesque sight stirred Binath's heart and he took his flute in his hands and played his magic tune. Enchanted by that sweet melody the river seemed to change its course—an unexpected flow-tide overflowing it. The girls forgot to carry their pitchers which floated on the waves, while they stood enraptured by that delicious music, forgetting that the *saris* they wore were all wet.

They seemed to question with mute appeal in their eyes—"Who are you, sweet friend, playing on that celestial flute of yours? Tarry a little for our sake and do not go away so soon."

The sails fluttered in the wind that flew from the north, and the ships of Chand rushed through the waters with intense speed so that they seemed to cover a journey which would take six months on foot in a single day. Their movement was like the flight of the hawk in the sky. After passing thirteen turns the ships arrived at the confluence of the Kansa river and there they were moored. The Gaḍari region was Chand's destination. It was now only seven days' journey from this place.

At this stage a great disaster befell Chand's ships. Suddenly in the middle of the night the sky became overcast with clouds; thunders rolled and a great storm broke out. The boats were violently torn from the shore, and in the confusion that followed, Binath was washed away by the waves of the Kansa river like a twig in a stream. (Ll. 1-32.)

(4)

Now leaving Binath here, let us begin the story of Sumai Ojha.

The banks of the Kansa river were covered with an impenetrable forest. In that dreadful jungle bereft of human habitation lived Sumai Ojha the healer. Only from dire necessity men sought him in that dreadful jungle. Wise as the god Brihaspati himself Sumai was the possessor of many secret charms. Protected by those charms he could manage to defy the dangers of the forest. Five cowries had he endowed with supernatural properties. Through incantations he endowed them with the power of capturing the dangerous reptiles of the forests. All the poisonous species of snakes,—King Cobras, Kraits and Brahmajals lowered their hoods before him. Even the trees of the forest seemed to revere him and protected him from sun and rain. With wooden sandals on his feet the Ojha used to promenade on the banks of the Kansa, and so great was his power that even kings were afraid to offend him. He could direct his cowries at will and send them to capture all kinds of snakes. With his medicine he could resuscitate the dead even when the corpse lay rotten for six months.

He had a daughter named Batasi. Brought up under his care she grew in years and adorned his forest-home. A true forest-girl she was, brisk and beautiful as the wild deer, radiant as the precious gem that crowns the hood of a serpent; with her crimson lips and dark eyes she looked so charming that it would be hard to find her match in the whole world. (Ll. 1-20.)

(5)

Now hear, oh friends, how Fate interweaves the destinies of poor mortals bringing on perilous complications.

Binath was washed ashore on the banks of the Kansa river and there the girl found him. There was hardly any sign of life in Binath's body and, greatly agitated, the girl ran to her father and reported the case in breathless haste. "The handsome young man," she said "has scarcely any. sign of life. The Kansa river seems to have engulfed the moon itself in its whirlpool, so beautiful is he! Who knows where his bereaved mother is deploring the loss of her child in some distant country!"

Her dishevelled hair touched her very ankle as she followed the Ojha. The girl seemed to lose her senses, so overwhelmed was she with the thought of the stranger. Then Sumai Ojha with the help of his daughter, carried the stiff body of Binath to their jungle-home with great difficulty. The beautiful girl was all along shedding tears. Strange that one could be so moved for a stranger!

The Ojha laid the body of Binath on a bed and then entered the deep forest. He ordered his daughter to remain at the bedside and watch over the body till his return. Seated beside Binath's body the girl looked at him with fixed gaze, but could not ascertain whether he was still living.—"Who are the parents of this handsome young-man?" she wondered and wiped away her tears with the end of her *sari*. "How can his mother bear to live after losing such a son? Her home will now turn a dreary and dark abyss after this." Her whole heart longed to call him by his name but how could she know it?

At this time Sumai returned with his medicine and handing it to his daughter asked her to ground it quickly in a stone mortar. Carefully did she wash the stone and the muller and as instructed she ground the medicine and made a paste with it. Sumai administered the medicine with his incantations and the body of Binath seemed to manifest slight signs of life. Then the Ojha made a further effort to bring him round and Binath opened his eyes to find himself amongst strangers. It seemed to him that he was in a world of dreams. He looked at Batasi, and the girl blushing crimson before his gaze lowered her head. Unaccustomed as she was to ceremonies of all sort, whence did this shyness came on her! (Ll. 1-42.)

(6)

Three months passed and Binath gradually recovered. He remembered his parents and the home he had left before he came to this jungle-house. No mother had he, no brother nor any friend to feel sympathy for him. He recollected the facts of his past life. The girl Sujanti he remembered too, but gradually Batasi occupied his mind till he forgot everything of his former life.

Often do we find a wilderness preferable to the city. Strangers are sometimes more sympathetic than kinsmen—this was his experience and he was reconciled with himself in that forest-home.

He remembered his father's death through snake-bite and determined to learn the *mantras* that could cure it. With this object in view he accepted Sumai as his master. (Ll. 1-16.)

(7)

Binath.

"Who is it that created you, oh my lovely flower, and for what strange purpose did he put you in the jungle? Sweet is your smile, oh sylvan blossom! What god destined you for a forest-life? When you roam freely along this jungle, verily do you look like a wild antelope. The bee has missed thee, oh my lovely flower, till now, and does not know of thy rich promise of honey. Do please tarry and listen to me awhile.

"Who are your parents, I wonder! May I ask what home you do adorn living thus in the forest?

"The wind playfully moves your *sari* to and fro. Please stand before me and let me hear the sweet melody of your voice."

Batasi.

"No mother no father have I, oh stranger. From my childhood have I been brought up in this forest by a stranger. Under his care have I grown up to womanhood and I look upon him as my father and mother both."

Binath.

"I too am an orphan like you, oh sweet girl, I do not remember to have seen my father. He died when I was an infant, a snake had bitten him. My mother too left me when I was a mere child; and cruel is the Providence that has thrown me into the world which is like a sea to me. I am drifted here and there in the current of life like a weed. I have owed my life to you, sweet girl, this time."

The two were drawn by love and sympathy, and so deep was their attachment for each other that they could not bear separation even for a single moment. They were like two wild pigeons just mated. (Ll. 1-30.)

(8)

Binath in the meantime acquired the healing art and all mystic rites from Sumai. First of all he learned a *mantra* which gave him power over snakes—it was called Phulkari. Next he mastered the art by which poison lost its property and became harmless as water. He slapped the affected part a number of times and the effect was instantaneous. Then did he acquire the art known as *Brahmajal* by which a pot was made so potent that though full of water it leaked not a drop with hundreds of holes at the bottom. The power that the fourth art gave him enabled him to eradicate the poison by stopping its onward course and making it climb down. The fifth on the list was the *mantra*, named

Uttarpatar at the recitation of which even the most powerful snakes bent their hoods and retired into their holes. The sixth *mantra* he learned was called *Khaia.* The most dangerous snakes fled in precipitous speed as he uttered it. He could make the dust potent with magic powers and so overpowered the snakes as a class that even the deadly Krait, trampled under his feet, had not the power to raise its hood aloft. The Gadura *mantra* he acquired last—the glory of all healing art which made him great as Dhanvantari, the first and the wisest of all physicians of the world, who could restore the dead to life. He sat at the feet of his *guru* and gradually acquired the Jiban *mantra* which empowered him to restore a man to life though he had died of snake-bite six months before.

But jealousy slowly worked in the mind of Sumai at this stage, as his pupil seemed to surpass him in magic tricks.

The fame of Binath spread far and wide; and tortured with the pangs of jealousy Sumai resolved to put an end to his pupil's life. Binath was, however, kept informed of Sumai's plans by his daughter Batasi. The girl wept bitterly as she reported the matter to Binath. Binath after deliberating silently for some time said secretly to her—"Here me, oh dear girl. Is it not fit that I should now go elsewhere from this place? How can I stay here when my master whom I revere as my father has turned hostile to me? Settle, oh dear girl, your future course. I am sorry that I am not in a position to take you with me now. If you were, oh girl, like one of those flowers that has bloomed on yonder branch, or were like that pretty bird in the sky, the case would have been different. Fain would I take you with me to my heart's delight. But Pir Sumai is a dangerous enemy whom I dare not offend to that extent. The prudent course for me would be to leave this country alone. (Ll. 1-44.)

(9)

Evening had set in and the playful wind was breaking the waves of the river into a thousand ripples which gently touched the shore. It was extremely painful for the girl to part with her beloved, and Batasi wiped away her incessant tears while proceeding to the banks of the river.

" Be thou stationed in the midst of the jungle like one of those trees, oh my love, and let me remain near you like the shade of the tree. In the guise of a bee remain hidden under the leaves of trees, oh friend, and drink the honey of the forest flowers. Live in the moors as a crane, oh friend, and let us meet secretly under the cover of the night."

The boat was moored at the landing ghat. Binath loosened its ropes and stepped hastily into it. He struck the waters with the oar swiftly ; and the boat flew away from the place with the quickness of wind. From distance Binath's voice she heard—" Return home, dear girl, and wipe my memory away from your mind. This is our last meeting, but this parting scene will be ever fresh in my memory. May I meet a watery grave if I should ever forget one, who once saved my life ! "

The evening gradually faded away. Darkness stole over the forest and the girl had hardly strength to return home alone. Binath had left her and gone to his own country. With her eyes fixed vacantly on the darkness the girl stood there all alone—lost in her thoughts. (Ll. 1-22.)

(10)

Binath reached his country and went straight to the house of Chand Moral. The great power he had acquired became soon known all over the country and men poured in from all places asking for magic lockets and waters made potent by his touch. Fear of snakes was a thing of the past in the country where Binath lived. He restored men who had died of snake-bite, to life and Chand's own son Kusai was brought back from the very doors of death having once been bitten by a venomous snake, so wonderful was the medicine that Binath had given him. Chand Moral married his daughter Sujanti to Binath and the latter passed one year more at Chand's house.

But painful was the sequel of this union, for Binath and Sujanti never had a real liking for one another. Sujanti loved not Binath but another youngman of the village, and their secret meetings came to be known to her husband ere long.

Often did he brood on the past while Batasi's face flashed before his mind. The wind seemed to moan the tale of her sorrow at parting with him. He dreamt of the girl standing beside the banks of a river with her dress all torn and her dishevelled hair hanging in curls, matted for want of care. (Ll. 1-20.)

(11)

Now hear, oh my audience, what happened next. Sumai Ojha suddenly appeared in that land and so wonderful was his magic that the people, male and female, gathered near him from all around. Sumai took the help of Sujanti in his intrigue against Binath and secretly laid a plan for his ruin. Binath knew nothing about it. One day Sujanti approached Binath and charmed him by her wily ways and smile; she then asked him to teach her the *mantra* by which one could restore the dead to life. "I will keep it secret and no one else will know of it." She said in an imploring tone. But Binath said that his master had ordered him not to divulge the *mantra* to one of the fair sex; how could he violate his solemn oath? But Sujanti persisted in her request and at last Binath had to yield. It was a short thing of two and a half letters, and he imparted this *mantra* to Sujanti, but by doing so he lost his own power as he violated the condition of the gift. With his mission fulfilled Sumai returned to his place and Binath deprived of his main power lost the fame he had acquired. Like a serpent bereft of poison was he now powerless, and becoming now an object of public ridicule Binath left that country.

Doomed to misery from childhood there was no peace for Binath in the wide world. In his hour of gloomy despair, it was the image of the forest-girl that appeared before his mind, and he thought constantly of the dear one whom he had lost. (Ll. 1-27.)

(12)

"The Champaka flower has blossomed beside the banks of the river. Who are you, oh girl, sitting alone and drying your wet hair in the wind? The tree with its leaves shining in the sun stands yonder bv. Would you listen to a word of mine? "

Startled in the midst of her revery the girl looked back but saw nobody near. Did the voice of her beloved come from within herself? Her beautiful *sari* fluttered in the wind and tears trickled down her cheeks as she gazed far into the horizon. "From what distant shore have you come, oh boatmen, under the favourable tide? Did you see my beloved anywhere in course of your wanderings? If you ever meet him will you tell him that I am still his—waiting and weeping for his return on the riverside where he left me many long days ago? I wait for him to come here by a small boat. He lives in the land of flow-tide and here he is to come by the ebb-tide—to take me away.

"No more are we to exchange those sweet looks and smiles. Behold how the river shrinks when the tide flows down, but the flow-tide will come and she will swell again washing the banks. But, for a woman once her youth gone no more will she regain her charm. I cannot express my thoughts, oh my beloved, in fit words. Why should you be so cruel as not to feel for my sufferings?

"Parted from you my senses are lost and I am like the serpent who has lost the jewel from its hood.

"My father has arranged my marriage in a rich family but how can I think of living without you? Little do I care for rich bedsteads and cushions. Happy would I be if I could cover you with a part of my *sari* under the shade of a tree and live there thrice blessed in your company. I have no word to describe my misery. Know my beloved that parted from you all my happiness is gone,—my youth, my life are now like spoils of fortune. This curly hair of mine I would cut off and float away on the river. Why should I decorate my eyes with *kajal* when they cannot get a glimpse of your sweet face during the whole day? Rather I would tear them off as they are of no use. Death would have been welcome a hundred times if Providence had granted it before you left me here.

"But death does not come to one who seeks it. Fain would I fly away from this miserable spot had I the wings of a bird! Deathless have I grown merging in the stream of love. Love is like the fabled tree of plenty that has offered me shade, and its fruits like ambrosia have given me the boon of immortality. Rivers shrink away if I go there to drown myself and fire becomes cool if I wish for death in its burning flames. Behold, the creepers hanging down like cords from the trees. How often did I tie them round my neck wishing to die but the creepers became garlands on my breast. On a dark night did I take a pitcher and a rope and go to the river to end my life but there I heard the sweet melody of your flute so familiar to me. It appealed to me tenderly asking me to desist from destroying life. The very pitcher seemed to whisper to me—'Do not, oh maiden, drown yourself,—you will live to meet your beloved once again on this very bank.' The rope repeated the promise of my meeting with you in future and the knife I took to end my life said, 'Have faith in me, oh girl, you have no cause yet to be helpless and die.'' 'Do not seek my aid too eagerly, oh girl,' said the poison. 'You are sure to meet him some day if you live.' My pet bird tenderly asked me to give up the design of self-destruction. It seemed to say, 'Go maiden, I heard his flute only the day before. Surely is he coming to meet you.' The wild bird counselled patience, 'Fortune is cross with you to-day,' it said, 'but she may smile on you to-morrow. And think what will happen if your beloved comes here and does not find you. He will die for you—not being able to bear the pain of separation.' (Ll. 1-72.)

(13)

''How long am I to live thus struggling between hope and despair ? I cannot bear such a lot any longer. Verily did I make a garden planting a creeper there but its buds have not flowered and my life is on the way to ruin. Hedges I raised round my tree and watered it with the tears of my eyes but the tree withered away without yielding fruits. The blossoms of youth slowly revealed themselves like flower through long sunny days but now they are about to fade. I built a hut on the river-bank and decorated it for giving you a reception but my expectations have proved vain and I do pass my days weeping all the day. This life of mine is poison and wormwood to me. I can no more bear the pain of this existence.

"Where art thou listlessly going, oh beautiful damsel, carrying a pitcher in thy arms? May I ask you who is the fortunate one of whom you are thinking all the while? for evidently you look love-worn and sad."

"I have not come to the river-side to fetch water. I heard the flute of my beloved last night and I am distracted. Ill at ease am I at my home. My heart yearns for coming out. A wild bird am I, fain would I break the bars of my cage to set myself free." (She recognises Binath) "Your love has become a noose round my neck and I care not if I lose my honour to become your slave.

"Acute has been the pain of this love. It is like poison to me. Yet it is so sweet that I would court all pain and value it as if it were a garland of gems. I feel at other times that had I known this love to be like smouldering fire which wrecks one's life, it would have been perhaps safer to avoid you at the outset. Alas, my eyes have been deluded. Safer it would have been if I would have shut my eyes to avoid a sight of you."

Rajani Gopal the poet says—"Oh damsel, love does not deserve such a comment from you. When you will get him back all the pain of separation will be gone and once more will you be blessed in his company. Love is no punishment. Be devoted to your love and make your love another name for worship. Recite the sacred word 'love' night and day as a saint does the holy name counting his beads of rosary. Then you will see that love will adorn your breast like a garland of flowers.

"The seers have extolled separation more than the union of lovers, and you will come to know later on that hunger is preferable to satiety. Better if the dear one is parted rather than united. For if there is true love between the pair, mutual attractions are better felt in separation. Union is sweet after a long separation as is the drink after prolonged thirst. The pleasure of union will be doubly sweet after long partings, and for this reason God has created the flower with thorns. Sorrow heightens happiness—placed side by side." (Ll. 1-42.)

(14)

"Following the call of your flute have I come to the banks of the river. I was afraid lest somebody should see you near my house. My father has married me to another man of his choice, and my heart alone knows what I suffer in my husband's home. A wild bird I was, but they have caged me and bound my feet with chain. My mind is ill at ease at home. In the kitchen when near my cooking pot I shed incessant tears, I say they are caused by smoke. I do not sleep on the bedsteads but lie on the bare floor. Some one has set a seal on my lips and I seldom speak. My heart was once like iron-gates, but they are rusty and cannot hold my secrets. Scarcely have I the power to hide my feelings from others. I even declare it openly on being questioned that my mind is on fire. Days and nights I seem to see your face vividly before my eyes.

"It is not safe for us to remain here any longer. Delay will lead to exposure. But even now I find it hard to tear myself from you. My legs seem to be benumbed in my attempts to depart. Hide yourself, my love, in me as a bee hides itself in a flower. In the still hour of night we shall again meet on the bank of this river."

At the dead of night the melody of the flute was heard in the forest. The girl who was awake all the time sat up and after arranging her dishevelled hair and carefully adjusting her *sari* went out with the water-pitcher in her arm. She then went to the door on the west side of the house and paused for a moment. Once more the flute sounded as the girl sat with her head drooping low in agitation of mind ; darkness prevailed on all sides. She was now resolved and opened the door quickly and stepped out. The water-pitcher she left on the ground and threw away her necklace of jewels. One by one she took off all her ornaments and left them there. Then slowly did she cross the yard.

The night was terribly dark. One could hardly see the palm of one's hand in that darkness but the girl went on without fear. The woman of the house left the house for good, all alone. Not for a moment was she swayed by worldly considerations. Her house she abandoned for forest ; for a stranger she left her own kith and kin. The black scandal she prized as the dear black paint of her eyes. For social status she cared not a bit. See friend, who is there to control one on whom love has set its seal and whom love has claimed as its own ?

It was the deep hour of night, even a bird did not flutter its wings or give a shrill cry—so still was the air around. At such an hour did the girl step out of her house impelled by the sound of a strange flute from a region which was unknown to her—leading her perhaps to unfathomable depths of future ills. A deep forest they entered reaching in a single day what in ordinary course it would take three days to travel. In that dense forest hitherto untrodden by human feet, Binath built a cottage with creepers and leaves of trees. Verily they lived there like a pair of doves, happy beyond measure in each other's company.

What is it that one would do with a wig if one has no head ? What will a woman do with her social honour if she loses her beloved ? (Ll. 1-44.)

(15)

Sumai Ojha in the meantime guessed that Binath was at the root of all mischief. He became furious in anger. He called the great snake Padmanal to his aid and by his incantations directed it to go as the messenger of Mother Manasa in all haste impelled by its poison and bite the villain. The serpent hurried on its winged course till it reached the forest where Binath lived.

Happily was Binath sleeping in the bridal hut he had made, and Batasi's head lay tenderly on his breast. Sudenly he was awakened. The deadly pain caused by the bite of the serpent took away sleep from his eyelids and he woke, up crying "Awake, oh my love, see I am mortally bitten. It is a pity that I have lost the power to restore life. To-day my life ends with all the happiness that I had pictured to myself."

His body grew dark as the poison spread itself and his breath became scarce and life was about to be extinct in a short time. The girl struck her head with her hands and thus lamented: "Leaving me alone in this lonely forest whither dost thou go, my love? The morning is coming but that sweet smile which adorned your face like moon-beams, it will not be for me to behold again. There is no one in this dreaded jungle of Behur to counsel me as to what I should do." For a little time she thought of the course she should adopt and then made a rope with her long hair and tightly bound his foot with it in order to stop the course of poison. But the poison had already rushed onward to the brain and its course could not be arrested. Unconscious Binath lay, his head resting on the lap of his sweetheart.

At this stage Sumai Ojha following the course of the serpent had entered that forest. When the girl saw him she fell prostrate at his feet and with her wild laments melted the heart of the healer. He recited his incantations but even that infallible *mantra* by which the dead revived had lost its potency, as out of greed he had been taking money from people. His infallible cure failed this time and the last spark of life was extinct in Binath. The lamentations of the girl filled the whole air with a spirit of tender compassion. Even the birds and beasts of the forest seemed to feel for her and their eyes shed tears. She cried all the while, saying—"Oh my love, how is it that in this first youth of mine have you forsaken me? People will accuse me that I induced you to come to this forest to be killed by a serpent. Oh cruel Providence, be merciful; take my life, if you will, but grant life to my dear husband." (Ll. 1-44.)

(16)

The river near by ran in its mad course. It was so large that its other bank could not be seen. There she went with the corpse of Binath. She invoked the sun and the moon and prayed them to behold her sorrows. Then with her lover's remains she flung herself into the wide bosom of the vast waters. The mad stream was bent on some uncertain destination—without any bank, without any sign of land on the other side. It was like the illimitable sea where the breakers rose and fell in their wild dance. She, the object of scandal and contempt of all, left her house and her community, and surrendered herself to her fate as unsteady and changeful as the waves of river. There she floated like something carried by the current.

Love, my friend, is the greatest *mantra* of the *yoga*—the *ajapa*. Take your refuge in love—it is like the ferry boat to cross the river of life. By dint of love, men can aspire to win the favour of immortals. Rajani Gopal knows the secret of this holy passion and believes in what he says. He is the son of Jagannath, an inhabitant of Bhati (Eastern districts of Mymensingh). His mother's name is Sonamoni and the family belongs to the Madhukulya Gotra. I have now introduced myself by the above lines and my salutes to you. I have now finished this ballad. (Ll. 1-20.)

INDEX

A

B

C

54

T

U

V

Y

OPINIONS

ON

THE EASTERN BENGAL BALLADS

Times Literary Supplement (London).—His journeyings should become a legend and the Bengali imagination centuries hence, should see one figure eternally traversing the Gangetic plain, now beaten upon by the fierce sun as he makes his way across the red, deeply fissured fields of Vishnupur now floating on the rain-swept rivers of East Bengal. He has coaxed a cautious peasantry into opening their store of traditions.

... ...

And Dr. Sen throughout his long and successful career as discoverer, has never done his country greater service than by saving these stories that would have so soon faded out from the world.

The Oriental List (London).—Great as Dr. Sen's other services to the cause of Bengali Literature have been, it is doubtful whether any of his previous work is a more valuable contribution to our knowledge of Bengali life and thought than this collection of Ballads which but for his enterprise and the praiseworthy efforts of his collaborator, would, in all probability in the course of the next few years, have been lost beyond recovery.

The following letter has been written to Dr. Dinesh Chandra Sen by Andree Karpetes Högman.

FEUILLES DE L'INDE
C. A. Högman Editeur
' Chitra

20, Rue Mahias
Boulogne S/Seine
Pres Paris

Dear Dinesh Chandra Sen Babu,

My friend Mademoiselle Madeline Rolland, sister of Romain Rolland, lent me during our stay in Switzerland your Eastern Bengal Ballads. I was then for nearly an year resting in a sanatorium and in the peace and rest of that nursing home, I enjoyed so fully and deeply your wonderful book that I often thought myself transported in some Bengali village amongst the people I love and in the midst of a landscape that appeals to me more than any other.

These Ballads were a revelation to me. Though since 20 years I study as much as I can anything that concerns India, I never suspected such treasures were still in store for me. Those characters of Bengali heroines ought to be familiar to everybody and my dream is that they should be translated in French. I thanked Mlle. Rolland for the joy she gave me in lending me that book and I want to thank you for the wonderful thing you did in publishing it. Perhaps my name is not quite unknown to you as I have many friends in Calcutta. I have painted much in India and have translated most of Rabindranath Tagore's booklets. My husband who shares my veneration for India has become a publisher, devoted solely to Indian subjects. The first book he has edited 'L'Inde et sen āmi'. has helped much to the knowledge of India amongst the French public. Now we are launching into the world Rabindranath's 'Fireflies' translated by me. Could you grant us the permission to translate and publish some of your ballads. Oh! all those wonderful plucky women! They ought to be known like the women in Shakespeare and Racine! and the charm and setting of all these little dramas, those inimitable touches of nature!! I simply adore your ballads. Mlle. Rolland is ready and willing to translate them. It is not a business my husband is making as publisher, so he could not pay you the rights of translation at once; would you accept simply a royalty on the sale of each book? Or perhaps give us the permission without any condition? I am writing to you on behalf of Mlle. Rolland and of my husband Dal Högman.

With our best congratulations for the work you have done in adding new beauty unto this world of ours. All my personal thanks for the enchanting hours I have passed, thanks to you, and our best wishes for you and the welfare of India.

With my *namashkars*

ANDRES KARPETES HÖGMAN.

From a review by Mr. F. E. Pargiter (I.C.S., Retired) in the Royal Asiatic Society's Journal, October, 1924—"The stories are charming, both happy and tragic and are told generally in simple language fresh with country scenes and feeling and illustrated with pretty sketches by a Bengali Artist.

Romain Rolland—" I was specially delighted with the touching story of Madina which although only two centuries old is an antique beauty and a purity of sentiment which art has rendered faithfully without changing it. Chandravati is a very noble story and Mahua, Kanka and Lila are charming (to mention only those ones)."

Dr. Sylvain Levi—What shall I say of Dinesh Chandra Sen's Eastern Bengal Ballads. I must confess that I have a peculiar fondness for the man and for all his publications. He carries all his work, however technical it may be, in such a rapt of enthusiasms; he has such a love for whatever is Bengali, and his mystical love is not afraid of the most minute technicalities. No living man has probably contributed more to make Bengal understood, realised, felt, enjoyed by the western mind.

Sir George Grierson—I may say that they have been long waited for and that they entirely fulfil the expectations aroused by the publication of the first volume. They throw important light on the history of Bengali Language and Literature and contain much charming poetry that revives memories of my own happy days spent in India. Mr. Dinesh Chandra Sen's enthusiasm and scholarly treatment compel me to offer to him and to the Calcutta University my congratulation on the successful production of the valuable work.

William Rothenstein—I plunged into your book and finished it only too quickly. It is of the greatest possible interest and full of beauty and drama. Through every ballad moves that marvellous being, exalted, grave, shy and passionate, reserved and bold—and how nobly beautiful—the Indian woman. She has remained unchanged through all the phases of Indian culture, religious and social. Her lovers carved her in stone and marble at Barhut, Sanchi and Amaravati, painted her sinuous, radiant, and bejewelled at Ajanta and Bagh and delighted to honour her in thousands of humble studios in Jammu, Jaipur, Delhi and Agra, Muslim as well as Hindu, well into the 19th century. I am interested to find some among your Bengali Ballads date from the middle of the last century. Indian Art is unique in having preserved a robust, primitive spirit throughout what in Europe were late and sophisticated periods; I notice the same quality in the late literary examples you gave. No revival seems able to preserve the strength and directness of the true Indian tradition which is still alive in your last Ballads.

Francis H. Skrine—The Professor has rendered immense service to his country in rescuing the charming ballads of Eastern Bengal from oblivion. His labours, indeed, may well be compared with those of Sir Walter Scott and Joseph Ritson who who did the same thing for the melodious songs of the Scottish Border.

E. F. Oaten—" To the Western critic stumbling by good fortune upon Dr. Sen's book, these ballads straight from the unsophisticated people's heart, come fresh and stimulant as the breeze that revives the jaded traveller from Calcutta, as he sits in steamer and ploughs across the monsoon gusts of Eastern Bengal."

Lord Ronaldshay in his introduction emphasises their importance " as the seed from which Modern Bengali has sprung. They will also prove valuable as a source of historical information. But one cannot but dwell here on their intrinsic value as literature since it is hoped that Bengal will eventually value them most as such."

Jules Bloch—" My opinion of the work may be guessed beforehand from the eagerness with which I have long followed Rai D. C. Sen's admirable labours, happily supported by the help of the Calcutta University. He has revealed a great part of Bengal to itself and to the world."

L. D. Barnett (London University) says—" The book is a remarkably valuable and attractive work which throws real light on a very important department of literature and culture."

Mr. F. H. Brown of the editorial staff of ' The London Times ' writes—" It is in the spirit of true scholarship that you carry out your heavy labours in the field of ballads. I am taking immediate steps to lay one of the two copies before the editor of the ' Times ' with a strong recommendation that it should receive the attention it deserves in ' The Literary Supplement.' Your work has been noted there in detail again and again and I hope that the editor will concur in the view that this volume merits much more than a mere short notice in Book Notes."

Dr. Abanindranath Tagore, C.I.E. (Translated from Bengali)— " These very precious treasures of Bengali literature would have run into oblivion had not Dr. Sen through help received from the Calcutta University compiled and brought them out. The Calcutta University should lend their further co-operation to Dr. Sen for recovering these priceless gems of our old literature. There is no question as regards the great ability and enthusiasm for work which distinguishes Dr. Sen's valuable researches.

An appriciation by **William. D. Allen** (Columbia University, New York)—from the " Liberty," 24th November, 1929:—

" To an American after three years in ' old ' worlds it was like home-coming to read Dineschandra Sen's translation of East Bengal Ballads. I was greatly surprised to find literary fruits of this ancient nation containing a freshness and boldness usually found only in regions where the age of pioneers is not too far in the past and where the creators of nations linger still in the folk's memory as in its blood.

In these Mymensingh ballads I found an instinct for original thinking, countless instances of individual "swaraj" and a high value attached to deeds in contrast to passiveness......all of which confirmed my conviction on reading history that India could never have reached such age unless bearing within it the roots of unweakening youth.

For an occidental to doubt the essential unity of East and West is impossible, if he has the pictures and emotions awakened by these ballads in his mind. The same love of nature, the same desire for freedom, the same exaltation of the individual's right to live happily which we are proud to discover in our literatures we find in these songs by and for the simple peasants of Bengal.

Mahua and Kamala.

From Mahua the gypsy to Kamala the heiress this strong individuality persists. I felt that the contact with nature needed to develop normal humans (and Bengal surely got an abundant share of it) was at the base of Mahua's capacity to cope with any crisis even with that of avenging the apparent murder of her husband. In her fight with her husband in her back, one suspects a symbol of dormant deep heroism in the Bengali folk.

And just as Mahua represents the normalcy of the Bengali growth within nature so Kamala demonstrates the normalcy of a child's growth within the Hindu village. Often strolling in Bengal it has struck me to see children, boys and girls abandoning their games to sit awhile by their father in his shop or office and listen hungrily to his discussions with cronies or clients. This is how Kamala the wealthy official's daughter, a gay child in love with bracelets, flowers and mischief came to be prepared to fight like a full-fledged lawyer for her family threatened with destruction by a false accuser. She gathers her evidence and pleads her case before imposing strangers with a legal logic which shows her mute share in the solving of problems brought before her father to have been an admirable method of education.

Longing for Personal Life.

Sometimes the hero or heroine of a Mymensingh ballad seems a fatalist in clinging to a course of action which persistently causes pain.

But at bottom the reason for this is truly not resignation but a longing for personal life. For instance Malua, whose husband is crushed by a ruler who desires her, Malua might by accepting her parent's prayer escape from the cruel ruler's land thereby avoiding danger to herself and freeing her husband of responsibility for her. But she prefers to remain in the danger zone in abject poverty without even the joy of her husband's presence. Is this a lack of will ? Is it fidelity and passive love? Is it not rather a great love coupled with a longing to follow the intense full life of the ego and instinctive insistence on the individual's swaraj ?

In others of these ballads so rich in surprises and in lessons for the understanding of the true India, I am struck by the exclamation of men, " I will go to strange lands " and of women, " I will fly with you to distant lands." For people rooted in the soil to include geographic space among the possible solutions of their problems may show a sub-conscious remembrance of ancient migrations and in any case shows an imagination and flexibility unexpected perhaps in a peasantry possessively in love with its birth place.

Strength of Personality.

A striking impression gathered throughout the ballads is recalled to me by this capacity of the young to think of themselves as separate from their childhood environment. It is that love of village and elders and devotion to duties to society and parents are all strong factors but stronger yet is love of one's chosen mate and devotion to one's personal freedom. Much of the greatness of the chief characters in these ballads lies in their deciding their problems for themselves with a firm base of conventions and love of their childhood-home to work up from towards a solution perhaps not bringing a maximum of peace or temporary pleasures into their lives but manifesting very fully their love of liberty. Even in 'Chandravati' whose theme is an exception to the above viewpoint in some respects, the poet has expressed regret and even resentment that religion and tradition should have succeeded in separating the maiden from her repentant Jaychandra.

The Bengali Girls.

But resourcefulness and strength of personality are not the only characteristics of the Bengali girls in the Mymensingh ballads. The beauty of maidens and young wives is sung enthusiastically and with a sense of good taste rooted in nature. One girl-child 'shines like a bright stone in a dark house.' Kamala when angry is a 'flower garden on fire.' A girl goes to the pond to bathe and when at the water's edge the wind blew the veil from before her face 'the bees left the water-lily for the lily of the shore;' another maiden's cheeks 'have the glow of a hundred champak flowers.'

More subtle and even more firmly true to reality than such praises are the songs telling the effect of young women's beauty on others. When a child enters her youth and becomes beautiful the neighbours with whom she has passed her life suddenly discover her and exclaim: "From what place has this beautiful one come to our village?" Most delightful of all is the tale of how Kamala brought joy into the life of the aged cowherd who gave her shelter in her flight. The good old man firmly believes it is the goddess of good fortune in person who has come to his hut. For the cows have suddenly begun giving more milk and, miracle of miracles, a buffalo long thought barren has given birth...Modern psychology and the herdman's piety are strikingly in harmony; who in the twentieth century would say that a beautiful and helpful woman is not a goddess of good fortune!

Dinesh Chandra Sen's note on the dates, environments and circumstances of the composing of these East Bengal Ballads were indispensable to full appreciation of them as well as affording delightful reading for their own sake. Yet they served to convince me that such works of art in which art shines through an utter lack of affectation and through a tenacious hold on the natural and the true works sung joyfully by the unlettered to give joy to the unlettered—are above questions of date, environment and circumstances."

Elaborate and appreciative reviews of this work appeared in many of the leading Continental journals such as—

Mitteilungen Des Seminars
für orientalische sprachen

Zu Berlin
Jahrgang XXXII
Abteilung II
Westasiatische Studien
Sonderabdruck
Berlin 1929.

Revue Critique
Histoire et de Littêrature
Recueil Mensuel
Soixante-troisiene année
Novembre 1929 etc.

There is a very appreciative foreword to the first volume of these ballads by Lord Ronaldshay (now Marquis of Zetland) our late Governor. Further on he says on receipt of the second volume "I congratulate you most heartily on the industry, ability and perseverance that have enabled you to bring your task to a successful issue in the face of the formidable difficulty of which you tell me."

His Excellency Lord Hardinge of Penshurst in his Convocation Address, dated the 16th March, 1912, as Chancellor of the Calcutta University: " During the last four years also the University has from time to time appointed Readers on special subjects to foster investigations of important branches of learning amongst our advanced students. One of these Readers, Mr. Sen, has embodied his lectures on History of Bengali Language and Literature from the earliest times to the middle of the 19th Century in a volume of considerable merit, which he is about to supplement by another original contribution to the history of one of the important vernaculars of this country. May I express the hope that this example will be followed elsewhere and that critical schools may be established for the vernacular languages of India which have not as yet received the attention they deserve."

His Excellency Lord Carmichael, Governor of Bengal, in his address on the occasion of his laying the foundation stone of the Rameshchandra Saraswat Bhavan, dated the 20th November, 1916: "For long Rameshchandra Dutt's History of the Literature of Bengal was the only work of its kind available to the general reader. The results of further study, in this field, have been made available to us by the publication of the learned and luminous lectures of Rai Sahib Dineshchandra Sen. In the direction of the history of the language and literature Rai Sahib Dineshchandra Sen has created the necessary interest by his Typical Selections. It remains for the members of the Parishad to follow this lead and to carry on the work in the spirit of patient, accurate research."

His Excellency Lord Ronaldshay, Government House, Calcutta 25th June, 1924—

"I need hardly say that I have read, 'Chaitanya and his Age' with the utmost pleasure. It seems to me to give a vivid account of the time when there was a great flowering of the emotional temperament of Bengal due in a large measure no doubt to a reaction against the frigid intellectualism of the monastic school of Vedanta Philosophers or as you call them Pantheists.

Your chapter on Sahajiya is extremely interesting and recalled with great vividness the talk which we had at Barrackpur on that subject. But until I read your recent volume, I had not realised that there were so many sects of Sahajiyas, or that the cult was so widespread.

The Bengali language in its present form is a thing of recent growth. It has been fashioned gradually during the past one hundred years. Less than a century ago the Committee of public instruction with Macaulay at its head declared that the vernacular language contained neither the literary nor the scientific information necessary for a liberal education. Nor was this all. For not only was the Bengali language of that day considered inadequate to the needs of the times but it was looked down upon by cultured Bengalis themselves, and it is on record that a suggestion made by an Englishman, Mr. Adam, that some at least of the lectures to be delivered in the educational institutions which were then being established might be given in Bengali was vetoed by the Indian members of his Committee on the ground that anything said or written in the vernacular would be despised in consequence of the medium through which it was conveyed.

With these estimates of the Vernacular language of Bengal less than a hundred years ago contrast the description of it given recently by Mr. J. D. Anderson as one of the great expressive language of the world capable of being the vehicle of as great things as of any speech of men.

A language capable of undergoing so great a transformation in so short a time must surely have been sound at the roots. What of the seed which was garnered and cultivated by those gardeners in the philological field—Rajendralal Mitra, K. M. Banerji, Ramkamal Sen, Isvarchandra Gupta, Bankimchandra Chatterji, Dinabandhu Mitra, Askhoykumar Datta to mention but a few ? It is a matter of common knowledge that such vernacular literature as flourished at the beginning of the 19th century was in verse rather than in prose and was in possession of the masses rather than of the classes. A peculiar interest attaches therefore to any specimen of the literature which can now be collected. I have just read Rai Bahadur Dineshchandra Sen's translations of a ballad of Eastern Bengal entitled Mahua. Here is a delightful specimen of the seed from which modern Bengali has sprung, It is charming in English; but from the point of view from which I have written above it is the language in which the ballad is sung that is of paramount interest and importance.

Mahua is but one of a large number of ballads now being translated and commented on with the untiring interest of the enthusiast and the skill of the expert scholar by Rai Bahadnr Dineshchandra Sen. And it is obvious that in addition to the philological interest attaching to such a collection it must possess also a special interest in respect of its subject-matter. And here the Englishman unacquainted with the technique of the Bengali language can appreciate the ballads to the full in their English translation. For it is in such compositions that one finds sketched with an unconscious and for that reason perhaps an all the truer pen, intimate pictures of the life of a people. And since these ballads are believed to cover a period of roughly three hundred years from the 16th century onwards, they should throw much light surely upon the political history of Bengal. For it was during this period that Moslem influence was pushed eastwards, the Moslem capital transferred by Nawab Islamkhan from Rajmahal to Dacca and colonies of Moslem feudal barons planted out in the eastern districts. In short these ballads should prove a mine of wealth alike to the philologist and the historian and last but not least to the administrator who seek to penetrate the inner thought and feeling of the people.

Extract from a letter by His Excellency Lord Lytton Governor of Bengal to Maharaja Sir Pradyotkumar Tagore— " It is clear from those publications (Eastern Eengal Ballads) that the line of research now being pursued by Dr. Sen is of great interest and importance. If as Dr. Sen states these poems range in date from the

16th to the 19th centuries, they must obviously possess great literary and historical significance. A glance at the poems so far published, shows that they throw much light on the social history of that part of Bengal, where they took their rise. Their importance as additional material for the history of the rise and development of modern Bengali needs no emphasis.

Dr. Sen asserts that he has evidence that a considerable volume of ballad poetry still remain to be collected from the singers and other sources not only in Mymensingh but also in other districts of Bengal. The financial difficulties of the University however make it impossible for Dr. Sen to arrange for a systematic research for these ballads on a reasonable scale. It is obvious that with one solitary worker in the field collecting the ballads progress must be slow. Dr. Sen has therefore appealed to me for financial assistance to enable him to prosecute these researches with additional agents and on a systematic plan. For this purpose a sum of rupees five thousand is required immediately while a larger amount still will be required to meet the cost of printing the ballads subsequently. A total sum of rupees fifteen thousand would place the work on a sound footing for some time enabling Dr. Sen to carry out systematic researches on a wider scale, and subsequently to edit and publish the poems in a worthy manner.

After a lifetime of devotion to his mother-tongue Dr. Sen assures us that nothing but the limited financial resources available to him prevents him from enriching the Bengali language by a large volume of hitherto unknown poems of a remarkable and important character. I am sure that the wealth and culture of Bengal will regard it as pious and patriotic duty to assist Dr. Sen to complete what may prove to be the most remarkable of his many services to his mother-tongue and they will regard it as a point of honour that the proposed extension of his work would be financed not from official sources but from the private generosity of those whose literature his researches are enriching. As the sum is a comparatively small one I do not think that general appeal to the public is necessary or desirable. If the facts are brought to the notice of a limited number of gentlemen interested in the language, literature and history of Bengal I am sure they will readily provide the amount that is necessary for the prosecution of Dr. Sen's researches. I know that an interest in literature and the Arts is traditional in your family and that you personally appreciate the value and importance of

Dr. Sen's work. I therefore feel that I can confidently appeal to you to undertake the duty of collecting the Rupees fifteen thousand required."

History of the Bengali Language and Literature (in English) By Dr. Dinesh Chandra Sen, D. Litt., Rai Bahadur, Published by the Calcutta University. Demy 8vo., pp. 1,067 with illustrations. Price Rs. 16.

Extract from a long review in the Times Literary Supplement, London, June 10, 1912—" In his narration as becomes one who is the soul of scholarly candour, he tells those who can read him with sympathy and imagination, more about the Hindu mind and its attitude towards life than we can gather from 50 volumes of impressions of travel by Europeans. Loti's picturesque accounts of the rites practised by the Travancore temples and even M. Chevrillon's synthesis of much browsing in Hindu scriptures seem faint records by the side of this unassuming tale of Hindu Literature. Mr. Sen may well be proud of the lasting monument he has erected to the literature of the native Bengal."

From a long review in the Athenæum, March 16, 1922—" Mr. Sen may justly congratulate himself on the fact that in the middle age he has done more for the history of his national language than any other writer of his own or indeed any time."

From a long review in Spectator, June 12, 1912—" In its kind his book is a masterpiece—modest, learned, thorough and sympathetic. Perhaps no other living has the learning and happy industry for the task he has so successfully accomplished."

From a review by Dr. Oldenburg in the Frankfurtur Zeitung, December 3, 1911 (translated by the late Dr. Thibaut)—" The account of Chaitanya's influence on the poetical literature of Bengal contributes one of the most brilliant sections of the work."

From a review in the Revue Critique, January, 1915 (Translated for 'the Bengali.') " One cannot praise too highly the work of Mr. Sen. A profound and original erudition has been associated with a vivid imagination. The works which he analyses are brought back to life with the consciousness of the original authors, with the movement of the multitudes who patronised them and with the landscape which encircled them. The historian though relying on his document has the temperament of an epic poet. He has likewise inherited the lyrical genius of his race. His enthusiastic sympathy vibrates through all his descriptions......

The appreciation of life so rare in our book knowledge, runs throughout the work; one reads these thousand pages with a sustained interest ; and one loses sight of the enormous labour which it presupposes ; one easily slips into the treasure of information which it presents."

From a review in the Pioneer, May 5, 1912—'Mr. Sen is a typical student as was common in Mediaeval Europe—a lover of learning for learning's sake. He must be a poor judge of characters who can rise from a perusal of Mr. Sen's pages without a real respect and liking for the writer, for his sincerity, his industry, his enthusiasm in the cause of learning.'

Sylvain Levi—" I cannot give you praises enough—your work is a *Chintamani*, a *Ratnakar*. No book about India would I compare with yours. Never did I find such realistic sense of literature. Pandit and Peasant, Yogi and Raja mix together in a Sakespearian way on the stage you have built up.

Barth (Paris)—" I can approach your book as a learner, not as a judge."

Vincent Smith—"A work of profound learning and high value."

F. H. Skrine—" Monumental work—I have been revelling in the book which taught me much of which I was ignorant."

E. V. Havell—" Most valuable book which every Anglo-Indian should read. I congratulate you most heartily on your very admirable English and perfect lucidity of style."

Emile Senart (Paris)—" I have gone through your book with lively interest and it appears to me to do the highest credit to your learning and method of working."

VANGA SAHITYA-PARICHAYA OR TYPICAL SELECTIONS FROM OLD BENGALI LITERATURE

By Prof. Dinesh Chandra Sen, Rai Bahadur, B.A., D. Litt., 2 Vols, Royal 8vo., pp. 1914 ; with an introduction in English running over 99 pages.

Published by the University of Calcutta with 10 coloured illustrations. Price Rs. 18.

From a review in the Athenaeum—" Here are the materials carefully arranged and annotated with a skill and learning such as probably no one else living can command."

Sir George Grierson—" Invaluable work......that I have yet read through its 1,900 pages I do not pretend, but what I have read has filled me with admiration for the industry and learning displayed. It is a worthy sequel to your monumental History of Bengali Literature, and of it we may safely say, 'finis coronat opus.' How I wish that a similar work could be compiled for other Indian Language specially for Hindi."

THE VAISNAVA LITERATURE OF MEDIAEVAL BENGAL

(Being lectures delivered as Reader to the University of Calcutta).

By

DR. DINESHCHANDRA SEN, D.LITT., RAI BAHADUR.

Demy 8vo., 257 pages, with a preface

By

J. D. ANDERSON, Esq., I.C.S. (RETIRED). PRICE Rs 2.

Times Literary Supplement—" The Rai Sahib is filled with a most patriotic love of his nation and its literature and has done more than any contemporary Countryman to widen our knowledge of them.

It is an authentic record of the religious emotion and thought of that wonderful land of Bengal which few of its western rulers, we suspect have rightly comprehended, not from any lack of friendly sympathy but simply from want of precisely what Mr. Sen better than any one living better than Sir Rabindranath Tagore himself can supply.

When all is said there remains the old indefinable charm which attaches to all that Dineshchandra Sen writes, whether in English or his native Bengali. In his book breathe a native candour and piety which somehow remind us of the classical writers familiar to our boyhood. In truth he is a belated contemporary of say, Plutarch, and attacks his biographical task in much the same spirit."

J. D. Anderson, Esq., retired I.C.S., Professor, Cambridge University—

" I propose to send with it, if circumstances leave me the courage to write it, a short preface (which I hope you will read with pleasure even if you do not think it worth publication) explaining why in the judgment of a very old student of all your works, your book should be read not only in Calcutta, but in London and Paris, and Oxford and Cambridge. I have read it and am reading it with great delight and profit and very real sympathy.

Think how great must be the charm of your topic and your treatment when in this awful year of anxiety and sorrow, the reading of your delightful MS. has given me rest and refreshment in a time when every post, every knock at the door, may bring us sorrow."

THE FOLK LITERATURE OF BENGAL

By

Dr. Dineshchandra Sen, D.Litt., Rai Bahadur,

Calcutta University Press.

Times Literary Supplement, May, 13th, 1923—" What makes Mr. Sen's books so delightful to us in Europe is precisely this indefinable Hindu quality, specifically Bengali rather than Indian something that fits itself with exquisite aptness to what he knows of the scenery and climate of the Gangetic Delta where Mr. Sen was born and where he has spent the whole time of his busy life as a student of native literature."

From the *Revista Trimestrale di Studi Filosofici e Religiosi* (translated from the original Italian). " This volume devoted to the popular tales of Bengal also constitutes a contribution of the first rank to such a subject. The tracing of the history of the Bengali Language and Literature in this University is one of the most well-deserved studies of Bengal. To it is due in fact the monumental and now classical History of the Bengali Language and Literature (1912) in which, so far as our studies go, we value most the accurate estimate of the influence of Chaitanya on that literature—accompanied by the grand Bengali Anthology—Vanga Sahitya Parichaya, 1914, and then above all the pleasing and erudite researches on Vaishnab Literature and the connected religious reforms of Chaitanya.

A world wholly legendary is depicted with the homely tenderness in the most secluded locality of Bengal and half conceived in the Buddhistic epoch with delicate phantasy and fondness; the world in which Rabindranath Tagore ultimately attained his full growth is revived with every seduction of art in the luminous pages of this beautiful book. The author came in touch with this in his first days of youth when he was a village teacher in East Bengal and he now wishes to reveal it by gathering together the most secluded spirit and also the legends collected in four delicious volumes of D. R. Mozumdar yet to be translated."

Bengali Ramayan—D. C. Sen. From a review by Sir George Grierson in the *Journal of Royal Asiatic Society*—"This is the most valuable contribution to the literature on the Rama-Saga which has appeared since Professor Jacobi's work on the Ramayana was published in 1893."

Chaitanya and his Age—D. C. Sen. F. W. Thomas (Literary India Office, London)—"You have gone on to finer developments and made your prose-writing a real art, capable of reflecting not only the general level of thinking but also the subtleties of the idiosyncracy of particular writers.

I have taken note of some eloquent passages in which your personal sentiment is in fact distinctly helpful to the reader by enabling him to realize the matter from the inside. And your book seems to me indispensable both for those who approach Chaitanya from the scholarly side and for those who wish to understand the mind and history of Bengal."

Times Educational Supplement (13th March, 1932) in connection with the injury Dr. Sen received from a bullet aimed at H. E. the Governor of Bengal on the 6th of March, 1932.

"It is significant ef the reckless folly of perverted Nationalism that the narrowest escape on Saturday was not of the Governor whose end was sought but of Dr. Dinesh Chandra Sen, the aged Professor of Bengali Literature, for one shot cut through the cloth of his shoulder. Probably no other scholar in India to-day has such a record in any field as the aged Doctor for patient, enthusiastic pioneer research into old Bengali Literature and History, and none is more deserving of honour and affection from the ardent Bengali Nationalist."